OHIO RULES OF CIVIL PF

As Revised Through July 1, 2019

This 2020 edition of the Ohio Rules of Civil Procedure provides the practitioner with a convenient copy to bring to court or the office. Look for other titles such as the Ohio Rules of Evidence 2020.

ISBN: 9781652293491

Peter Edwards, Esq.
Ohio Legal Publishing, LLC

OHIO RULES OF CIVIL PROCEDURE

Title I SCOPE OF RULES-ONE FORM OF ACTION

Title II COMMENCEMENT OF ACTION AND VENUE; SERVICE OF PROCESS; SERVICE AND FILING OF PLEADINGS AND OTHER PAPERS SUBSEQUENT TO THE ORIGINAL COMPLAINT; TIME

Title III PLEADINGS AND MOTIONS

Title IV PARTIES

Title VII JUDGMENT

Title VIII PROVISIONAL AND FINAL REMEDIES

Title IX PROBATE, JUVENILE, AND DOMESTIC RELATIONS PROCEEDINGS

Title X GENERAL PROVISIONS

APPENDIX OF FORMS

TITLE I. SCOPE OF RULES--ONE FORM OF ACTION

RULE 1.   Scope of Rules: Applicability; Construction; Exceptions

(A)   Applicability. These rules prescribe the procedure to be followed in all courts of this state in the exercise of civil jurisdiction at law or in equity, with the exceptions stated in division (C) of this rule.

(B)   Construction. These rules shall be construed and applied to effect just results by eliminating delay, unnecessary expense and all other impediments to the expeditious administration of justice.

(C)   Exceptions. These rules, to the extent that they would by their nature be clearly inapplicable, shall not apply to procedure (1) upon appeal to review any judgment, order or ruling, (2) in the appropriation of property, (3) in forcible entry and detainer, (4) in small claims matters under Chapter 1925 of the Revised Code, (5) in uniform reciprocal support actions, (6) in the commitment of the mentally ill, (7) in adoption proceedings under Chapter 3107 of the Revised Code, (8) in all other special statutory proceedings; provided, that where any statute provides for procedure by a general or specific reference to all the statutes governing procedure in civil actions such procedure shall be in accordance with these rules.

[Effective: July 1, 1970; amended effective July 1, 1971; July 1, 1975; July 1, 2015.]

Staff Note (July 1, 2015 Amendment)

Division (C) is amended to specifically include, within the exceptions to the application of the Civil Rules, Revised Code Chapter 3107 adoption proceedings, to the extent that the rules would by their nature be clearly inapplicable to those proceedings.

RULE 2.   One Form of Action

There shall be only one form of action, and it shall be known as a civil action.

[Effective: July 1, 1970.]

TITLE II. COMMENCEMENT OF ACTION AND VENUE; SERVICE OF PROCESS; SERVICE AND FILING OF PLEADINGS AND OTHER PAPERS SUBSEQUENT TO THE ORIGINAL COMPLAINT; TIME

RULE 3.   Commencement of Action; Venue

(A)   Commencement. A civil action is commenced by filing a complaint with the court, if service is obtained within one year from such filing upon a named defendant, or upon an incorrectly named defendant whose name is later corrected pursuant to Civ.R. 15(C), or upon a defendant identified by a fictitious name whose name is later corrected pursuant to Civ.R. 15(D).

(B)   Limited Appearance by Attorney. An attorney's role may be limited in scope, as authorized by Prof.Cond.R. 1.2(c), if that scope is specifically described in a "Notice of Limited Appearance" stating that the limited appearance has been authorized by the party for whom the appearance is made, and filed and served in accordance with Civ.R. 5 prior to or at the time of any such appearance. The attorney's limited appearance terminates without the necessity of leave of court, upon the attorney filing a "Notice of Completion of Limited Appearance" filed and served upon all parties, including the party for whom the appearance was made, in accordance with Civ.R. 5. If there is no objection within ten days of service of this notice, then no entry by the court is necessary for the termination of the limited appearance to take effect.

(C)   Venue: where proper. Any action may be venued, commenced, and decided in any court in any county. When applied to county and municipal courts, "county," as used in this rule, shall be construed, where appropriate, as the territorial limits of those courts. Proper venue lies in any one or more of the following counties:

(1)   The county in which the defendant resides;

(2)   The county in which the defendant has his or her principal place of business;

(3)   A county in which the defendant conducted activity that gave rise to the claim for relief;

(4)   A county in which a public officer maintains his or her principal office if suit is brought against the officer in the officer's official capacity;

(5)   A county in which the property, or any part of the property, is situated if the subject of the action is real property or tangible personal property;

(6)   The county in which all or part of the claim for relief arose; or, if the claim for relief arose upon a river, other watercourse, or a road, that is the boundary of the state, or of two or more counties, in any county bordering on the river, watercourse, or road, and opposite to the place where the claim for relief arose;

(7)   In actions described in Civ.R. 4.3, in the county where plaintiff resides;

(8)   In an action against an executor, administrator, guardian, or trustee, in the county in which the executor, administrator, guardian, or trustee was appointed;

(9)   In actions for divorce, annulment, or legal separation, in the county in which the plaintiff is and has been a resident for at least ninety days immediately preceding the filing of the complaint;

(10)   In actions for a civil protection order, in the county in which the petitioner currently or temporarily resides;

(11)   In tort actions involving asbestos claims, silicosis claims, or mixed dust disease claims, only in the county in which all of the exposed plaintiffs reside, a county where all of the exposed plaintiffs were exposed to asbestos, silica, or mixed dust, or the county in which the defendant has his or her principal place of business.

(12)   If there is no available forum in divisions (C)(1) to (C)(10) of this rule, in the county in which plaintiff resides, has his or her principal place of business, or regularly and systematically conducts business activity;

(13)   If there is no available forum in divisions (C)(1) to (C)(11) of this rule:

(a)   In a county in which defendant has property or debts owing to the defendant subject to attachment or garnishment;

(b)   In a county in which defendant has appointed an agent to receive service of process or in which an agent has been appointed by operation of law.

(D)   Change of venue.

(1)   When an action has been commenced in a county other than stated to be proper in division (C) of this rule, upon timely assertion of the defense of improper venue as provided in Civ.R. 12, the court shall transfer the action to a county stated to be proper in division (C) of this rule.

(2)   When an action is transferred to a county which is proper, the court may assess costs, including reasonable attorney fees, to the time of transfer against the party who commenced the action in a county other than stated to be proper in division (C) of this rule.

(3)   Before entering a default judgment in an action in which the defendant has not appeared, the court, if it finds that the action has been commenced in a county other than stated to be proper in division (C) of this rule, may transfer the action to a county that is proper. The clerk of the court to which the action is transferred shall notify the defendant of the transfer, stating in

the notice that the defendant shall have twenty-eight days from the receipt of the notice to answer in the transferred action.

(4)   Upon motion of any party or upon its own motion the court may transfer any action to an adjoining county within this state when it appears that a fair and impartial trial cannot be had in the county in which the suit is pending.

(E)   Venue: no proper forum in Ohio. When a court, upon motion of any party or upon its own motion, determines: (1) that the county in which the action is brought is not a proper forum; (2) that there is no other proper forum for trial within this state; and (3) that there exists a proper forum for trial in another jurisdiction outside this state, the court shall stay the action upon condition that all defendants consent to the jurisdiction, waive venue, and agree that the date of commencement of the action in Ohio shall be the date of commencement for the application of the statute of limitations to the action in that forum in another jurisdiction which the court deems to be the proper forum. If all defendants agree to the conditions, the court shall not dismiss the action, but the action shall be stayed until the court receives notice by affidavit that plaintiff has recommenced the action in the out-of-state forum within sixty days after the effective date of the order staying the original action. If the plaintiff fails to recommence the action in the out-of-state forum within the sixty day period, the court shall dismiss the action without prejudice. If all defendants do not agree to or comply with the conditions, the court shall hear the action.

If the court determines that a proper forum does not exist in another jurisdiction, it shall hear the action.

(F)   Venue: multiple defendants and multiple claims for relief. In any action, brought by one or more plaintiffs against one or more defendants involving one or more claims for relief, the forum shall be deemed a proper forum, and venue in the forum shall be proper, if the venue is proper as to any one party other than a nominal party, or as to any one claim for relief.

Neither the dismissal of any claim nor of any party except an indispensable party shall affect the jurisdiction of the court over the remaining parties.

(G)   Venue: notice of pending litigation; transfer of judgments.

(1)   When an action affecting the title to or possession of real property or tangible personal property is commenced in a county other than the county in which all of the real property or tangible personal property is situated, the plaintiff shall cause a certified copy of the complaint to be filed with the clerk of the court of common pleas in each county or additional county in which the real property or tangible personal property affected by the action is situated. If the plaintiff fails to file a certified copy of the complaint, third persons will not be charged with notice of the pendency of the action.

To the extent authorized by the laws of the United States, division (G)(1) of this rule also applies to actions, other than proceedings in bankruptcy, affecting title to or possession of real property in this state commenced in a United States District Court whenever the real property is situated wholly or partly in a county other than the county in which the permanent records of the court are kept.

(2)   After final judgment, or upon dismissal of the action, the clerk of the court that issued the judgment shall transmit a certified copy of the judgment or dismissal to the clerk of the court of common pleas in each county or additional county in which real or tangible personal property affected by the action is situated.

(3)   When the clerk has transmitted a certified copy of the judgment to another county in accordance with division (G)(2) of this rule, and the judgment is later appealed, vacated, or modified, the appellant or the party at whose instance the judgment was vacated or modified must cause a certified copy of the notice of appeal or order of vacation or modification to be filed with the clerk of the court of common pleas of each county or additional county in which the real property or tangible personal property is situated. Unless a certified copy of the notice of appeal or order of vacation or modification is so filed, third persons will not be charged with notice of the appeal, vacation, or modification.

(4)   The clerk of the court receiving a certified copy filed or transmitted in accordance with the provisions of division (G) of this rule shall number, index, docket, and file it in the records of the receiving court. The clerk shall index the first certified copy received in connection with a particular action in the indices to the records of actions commenced in the clerk's own court, but may number, docket, and file it in either the regular records of the court or in a separate set of records. When the clerk subsequently receives a certified copy in connection with that same action, the clerk need not index it, but shall docket and file it in the same set of records under the same case number previously assigned to the action.

(5)   When an action affecting title to registered land is commenced in a county other than the county in which all of such land is situated, any certified copy required or permitted by this division (G) of this rule shall be filed with or transmitted to the county recorder, rather than the clerk of the court of common pleas, of each county or additional county in which the land is situated.

(H)   Venue: collateral attack; appeal. The provisions of this rule relate to venue and are not jurisdictional. No order, judgment, or decree shall be void or subject to collateral attack solely on the ground that there was improper venue; however, nothing here shall affect the right to appeal an error of court concerning venue.

(I)   Definitions. As used in division (C)(11) of this rule:

(1)   "Asbestos claim" has the same meaning as in section 2307.91 of the Revised Code;

(2)   "Silicosis claim" and "mixed dust disease claim" have the same meaning as in section 2307.84 of the Revised Code;

(3)   In reference to an asbestos claim, "tort action" has the same meaning as in section 2307.91 of the Revised Code;

(4)   In reference to a silicosis claim or a mixed dust disease claim, "tort action" has the same meaning as in section 2307.84 of the Revised Code.

[Effective: July 1, 1970; amended effective July 1, 1971; July 1, 1986; July 1, 1991; July 1, 1998; July 1, 2005; July 1, 2018.]

Staff Note (July 1, 2018 Amendment)

New Division (B): Limited Appearance by Attorney.

This and other July 1, 2018 amendments to the Ohio Rules of Civil Procedure encourage attorneys to assist pro se parties on a limited basis without undertaking the full representation of the client on all issues related to the legal matter for which the attorney is engaged. By these amendments, the Supreme Court seeks to enlarge access to justice in Ohio's courts as recommended by a 2006 Report of the Court's Task Force on Pro Se & Indigent Litigants and by a 2015 Report of the Court's Task Force on Access to Justice.

New division (B) permits attorneys to enter a limited appearance on behalf of an otherwise unrepresented litigant. The effect of the limited appearance is to permit an attorney to represent a client on one or more matters in a lawsuit but not on all matters. While normally leave of court is required if an attorney seeks to withdraw from representation, under this provision, leave of court is not required for withdrawal from the case at the conclusion of a properly noticed limited appearance, provided the attorney files and serves the proper Notice of Completion of Limited Appearance in accordance with Civ.R. 5.

The benefits of division (B) are obtained only by filing a notice of limited appearance identified as such. The notice of limited appearance must clearly describe the scope of the limited representation and state that the limitation of appearance has been authorized by the party for whom the appearance is made. It is intended that any doubt about the scope of the limited representation be resolved in a manner that promotes the interests of justice and those of the client and opposing party.

Staff Note (July 1, 2005 Amendment)

Civ. R. 3 is amended in response to requests from the General Assembly contained in Section 3 of Am. Sub. H.B. 342 of the 125th General Assembly, effective September 1, 2004, and Section 4 of Am. Sub. H.B. 292 of the 125th General Assembly, effective September 2, 2004. These acts contain provisions governing tort claims that allege exposure and injury by persons exposed to asbestos, silica, or mixed dust. Each act includes a request that the Supreme Court amend the Rules of Civil Procedure "to specify procedures for venue and consolidation" of asbestosis, silicosis, and mixed dust disease claims.

Rule 3(B)   Venue: where proper

Civ. R. 3(B) is amended to include an exclusive venue provision that applies to the filing of actions involving asbestos, silicosis, or mixed dust disease claims. Division (B)(11) states that a civil action alleging one or more of these claims may be filed only in either the county in which all exposed plaintiffs reside, a county where all exposed plaintiffs were exposed to asbestos, silica, or mixed dust occurred, or the county in which the defendant has his or her principal place of business.

Existing divisions (B)(11) and (12) have been renumbered to reflect the addition of new division (B)(11).

Rule 3(H)   Definitions

Division (H) is added to reference the statutory definitions of "asbestos claim," "silicosis claim," "mixed dust disease claim," and "tort action" for purposes of Civ. R. 3(B)(11).

Staff Note (July 1, 1998 Amendment)

Rule 3(A) Commencement.

The style used for rule references was changed. There was no substantive amendment to this division.

Rule 3(B) Venue: where proper.

The 1998 amendment added a new division (10), and renumbered existing divisions (10) and (11) to (11) and (12), respectively. New division (10) clarifies the appropriate venue for an action seeking the entry of a civil protection order in domestic or family violence cases. The Supreme Court's Domestic Violence Task Force recommended this change in order to clarify Ohio law on this matter. Report of the Supreme Court of Ohio Domestic Violence Task Force: Increasing Safety for Victims, Increasing Accountability of Offenders 16 (October 18, 1996). The amendment uses criteria similar to other venue provisions. For example, the concept of residence is used in other divisions of Civ.R. 3(B), and the concept of a current or temporary residence is similar to the reference to plaintiff's residence in Civ.R. 3(B)(11) (renumbered from Civ. R. 3(B)(10)). See, e.g., *State, ex rel. Saunders v. Court of Common Pleas of Allen Cty*. (1987), 34 Ohio St. 3d 15, 17, 516 N.E. 2d 232 ("the term, 'resides,' as used in [prior] Civ.R. 3(B)(10) ought to be 'liberally construed and not confused with [the] requirements for domicile.'"(quoting McCormac, Ohio Civil Rules Practice). The respondent remains free to challenge venue under Civ.R. 3(D).

Nonsubstantive grammatical revisions were also made to this division.

Rule 3(C) Change of venue.

The style used for rule references was changed. There was no substantive amendment to this division.

Rule 3(F) Venue: notice of pending litigation; transfer of judgments

The style used for rule references was changed and the division was made gender-neutral. There was no substantive amendment to this division.

RULE 4. **Process: Summons**

(A) Summons: issuance. Upon the filing of the complaint the clerk shall forthwith issue a summons for service upon each defendant listed in the caption. Upon request of the plaintiff separate or additional summons shall issue at any time against any defendant.

(B) Summons: form; copy of complaint. The summons shall be signed by the clerk, contain the name and address of the court and the names and addresses of the parties, be directed to the defendant, state the name and address of the plaintiff's attorney, if any, otherwise the plaintiff's address, and the times within which these rules or any statutory provision require the defendant to appear and defend, and shall notify the defendant that in case of failure to do so, judgment by default will be rendered against the defendant for the relief demanded in the complaint. Where there are multiple plaintiffs or multiple defendants, or both, the summons may contain, in lieu of the names and addresses of all parties, the name of the first party on each side and the name and address of the party to be served.

A copy of the complaint shall be attached to each summons. The plaintiff shall furnish the clerk with sufficient copies.

(C) Summons: plaintiff and defendant defined. For the purpose of issuance and service of summons "plaintiff" shall include any party seeking the issuance and service of summons, and "defendant" shall include any party upon whom service of summons is sought.

(D) Waiver of service of summons. Service of summons may be waived in writing by any person entitled thereto under Rule 4.2 who is at least eighteen years of age and not under disability.

(E) Summons: time limit for service. If a service of the summons and complaint is not made upon a defendant within six months after the filing of the complaint and the party on whose behalf such service was required cannot show good cause why such service was not made within that period, the action shall be dismissed as to that defendant without prejudice upon the court's own initiative with notice to such party or upon motion. This division shall not apply to out-of-state service pursuant to Rule 4.3 or to service in a foreign country pursuant to Rule 4.5.

(F) Summons: revivor of dormant judgment. Upon the filing of a motion to revive a dormant judgment the clerk shall forthwith issue a summons for service upon each judgment debtor. The summons, with a copy of the motion attached, shall be in the same form and served in the same manner as provided in these rules for service of summons with complaint attached, shall command the judgment debtor to serve and file a response to the motion within the same time as provided by these rules for service and filing of an answer to a complaint, and shall notify the judgment debtor that in case of failure to respond the judgment will be revived.

[Effective: July 1, 1970; amended effective July 1, 1971; July 1, 1973; July 1, 1975; July 1, 1984; July 1, 2008.]

Staff Note (July 1, 2008 Amendment)

The adoption of the Ohio Rules of Civil Procedure in 1970 left unclear the procedure and manner of service for a motion to revive a dormant judgment, formerly governed by R.C. 2325.15 and R.C. 2325.16 which referred to statutes superseded by the Rules. Division (F) of Rule 4 has been adopted to make clear that R.C. 2325.15 and R.C. 2325.16 are superseded by this new Rule. It requires, consistent with the practice under the prior statutes, that a motion to revive a dormant judgment be served upon the judgment debtor in the same manner as service of summons with complaint attached, affording the debtor an opportunity to show cause against the revivor.

RULE 4.1   Process: Methods of Service

All methods of service within this state, except service by publication as provided in Civ.R. 4.4(A), are described in this rule. Methods of out-of-state service and for service in a foreign country are described in Civ.R. 4.3 and 4.5.

(A)   Service by clerk.

    (1)   Methods of service.

        (a)   Service by United States certified or express mail. Evidenced by return receipt signed by any person, service of any process shall be by United States certified or express mail unless otherwise permitted by these rules. The clerk shall deliver a copy of the process and complaint or other document to be served to the United States Postal Service for mailing at the address set forth in the caption or at the address set forth in written instructions furnished to the clerk as certified or express mail return receipt requested, with instructions to the delivering postal employee to show to whom delivered, date of delivery, and address where delivered.

        (b)   Service by commercial carrier service. Unless the serving party furnishes written instructions to the clerk that service be made pursuant to Civ.R. 4.1(A)(1)(a), the clerk may make service of any process by a commercial carrier service utilizing any form of delivery requiring a signed receipt. The clerk shall deliver a copy of the process and complaint or other document to be served to a commercial carrier service for delivery at the address set forth in the caption or at the address set forth in written instructions furnished to the clerk, with instructions to the carrier to return a signed receipt showing to whom delivered, date of delivery, and address where delivered.

    (2)   Docket entries; Return. The clerk shall forthwith enter on the appearance docket the fact of delivery to the United States Postal Service for mailing or the fact of delivery to a specified commercial carrier service for delivery, and make a similar entry when the return receipt is received. If the return shows failure of delivery, the clerk shall forthwith notify the attorney of record or, if there is no attorney of record, the party at whose instance process was issued and enter the fact and method of notification on the appearance docket. The clerk shall file the return receipt or returned envelope in the records of the action.

    (3)   Costs. All postage and commercial carrier service fees shall be charged to costs. If the parties to be served are numerous and the clerk determines there is insufficient security for costs, the clerk may require the party requesting service to advance an amount estimated by the clerk to be sufficient to pay the costs of delivery.

(B) **Personal service.** When the plaintiff files a written request with the clerk for personal service, service of process shall be made by that method.

When process issued from the Supreme Court, a court of appeals, a court of common pleas, or a county court is to be served personally under this division, the clerk of the court shall deliver the process and sufficient copies of the process and complaint, or other document to be served, to the sheriff of the county in which the party to be served resides or may be found. When process issues from the municipal court, delivery shall be to the bailiff of the court for service on all defendants who reside or may be found within the county or counties in which that court has territorial jurisdiction and to the sheriff of any other county in this state for service upon a defendant who resides in or may be found in that other county. In the alternative, process issuing from any of these courts may be delivered by the clerk to any person not less than eighteen years of age, who is not a party and who has been designated by order of the court to make personal service of process under this division. The person serving process shall locate the person to be served and shall tender a copy of the process and accompanying documents to the person to be served. When the copy of the process has been served, the person serving process shall endorse that fact on the process and return it to the clerk, who shall make the appropriate entry on the appearance docket.

When the person serving process is unable to serve a copy of the process within twenty-eight days, the person shall endorse that fact and the reasons therefor on the process and return the process and copies to the clerk who shall make the appropriate entry on the appearance docket. In the event of failure of service, the clerk shall follow the notification procedure set forth in division (A)(2) of this rule. Failure to make service within the twenty-eight day period and failure to make proof of service do not affect the validity of the service.

(C) **Residence service.** When the plaintiff files a written request with the clerk for residence service, service of process shall be made by that method.

When process is to be served under this division, deliver the process and sufficient copies of the process and complaint, or other document to be served, to the sheriff of the county in which the party to be served resides or may be found. When process issues from the municipal court, delivery shall be to the bailiff of the court for service on all defendants who reside or may be found within the county or counties in which that court has territorial jurisdiction and to the sheriff of any other county in this state for service upon a defendant who resides in or may be found in that county. In the alternative, process may be delivered by the clerk to any person not less than eighteen years of age, who is not a party and who has been designated by order of the court to make residence service of process under this division. The person serving process shall effect service by leaving a copy of the process and the complaint, or other document to be served, at the usual place of residence of the person to be served with some person of suitable age and discretion then residing therein. When the copy of the process has been served, the person serving process shall endorse that fact on the process and return it to the clerk, who shall make the appropriate entry on the appearance docket.

When the person serving process is unable to serve a copy of the process within twenty-eight days, the person shall endorse that fact and the reasons therefor on the process, and return the process and copies to the clerk, who shall make the appropriate entry on the appearance docket. In the event of failure of service, the clerk shall follow the notification procedure set forth in division (A)(2) of this rule. Failure to make service within the twenty-eight-day period and failure to make proof of service do not affect the validity of service.

[Effective: July 1, 1970; amended effective July 1, 1971; July 1, 1980; July 1, 1997; July 1, 2012; July 1, 2016.]

Staff Note (July 1, 1997 Amendment)

Rule 4.1 Process: Methods of Service

Prior to the 1997 amendment, service of process under this rule was permitted only by certified mail. It appears that service of process by express mail, i.e. as that sort of mail is delivered by the United States Postal Service, can always be obtained return receipt requested, and thus could accomplish the purpose of notification as well as certified mail. The amendment provides for this additional option for service.

Other amendments to this rule are nonsubstantive grammatical or stylistic changes, including lettering of the divisions (A-C) in place of the previous numbering (1-3).

Staff Note (July 1, 2012 Amendment)

Rule 4.1(A) is subdivided and amended to permit the clerk to make service of process using a commercial carrier service to make delivery by any method requiring a signed receipt. A "signed receipt" includes the return and filing of an electronic image of the signature. The amendment also removes the "by mail" limitation to the clerk's method of notifying plaintiff or plaintiff's attorney of a failure of delivery.

Divisions (B) and (C) are amended to make clear that the methods of service of process permitted to be made by a person designated by the court are limited to personal service and residence service.

Rule 4.1(C), which describes residence service, is also amended to track and incorporate where applicable the language of Civ.R. 4.1(B) which describes personal service, clarifying which portions of the two methods are the same and which portions are different.

Staff Notes (July 1, 2016 Amendment)

Division 4.1(A)(1)(b) of this rule was adopted in 2012 to provide the clerk with an option to make service of process by a commercial carrier service as an alternative to service by United States certified or express mail. Under certain circumstances, the serving party may prefer that service be made by U.S. mail. Therefore, the provisions of Civ.R. 4.1(A)(1)(b) are amended to permit the serving party to furnish written instructions to the clerk that service be made by United States certified or express mail pursuant to Civ.R. 4.1(A)(1)(a), in which case the commercial carrier option is not available to the clerk for the initial attempt to make service of process.

RULE 4.2   Process: Who May be Served

Service of process pursuant to Civ.R. 4 through Civ.R. 4.6, except service by publication as provided in Civ.R. 4.4(A), shall be made as follows:

(A)   Upon an individual, other than a person under sixteen years of age or an incompetent person, by serving the individual;

(B)   Upon a person under sixteen years of age by serving either the person's guardian or any one of the following persons with whom the person to be served lives or resides: a parent or the individual having the care of the person; or by serving the person if the person neither has a guardian nor lives or resides with a parent or a person having his or her care;

(C)   Upon an incompetent person by serving either the incompetent's guardian or the person designated in division (E) of this rule, but if no guardian has been appointed and the incompetent is not under confinement or commitment, by serving the incompetent;

(D)   Upon an individual confined to a penal institution of this state or of a subdivision of this state by serving the individual, except that when the individual to be served is a person under sixteen years of age, the provisions of division (B) of this rule shall be applicable;

(E)   Upon an incompetent person who is confined in any institution for the mentally ill or mentally deficient or committed by order of court to the custody of some other institution or person by serving the superintendent or similar official of the institution to which the incompetent is confined or committed or the person to whose custody the incompetent is committed;

(F)   Upon a corporation either domestic or foreign: by serving the agent authorized by appointment or by law to receive service of process; or by serving the corporation at any of its usual places of business by a method authorized under Civ.R. 4.1(A)(1); or by serving an officer or a managing or general agent of the corporation;

(G)   Upon a limited liability company by serving the agent authorized by appointment or by law to receive service of process; or by serving the limited liability company at any of its usual places of business by a method authorized under Civ.R. 4.1(A)(1); or by serving a manager or member;

(H)   Upon a partnership, a limited partnership, or a limited partnership association by serving the entity at any of its usual places of business by a method authorized under Civ.R. 4.1(A)(1) or by serving a partner, limited partner, manager, or member;

(I)   Upon an unincorporated association by serving it in its entity name at any of its usual places of business by a method authorized under Civ.R. 4.1(A)(1); or by serving an officer of the unincorporated association;

(J)   Upon a professional association by serving the association in its corporate name at the place where the corporate offices are maintained by a method authorized under Civ.R. 4.1(A)(1); or by serving a shareholder;

(K)   Upon this state or any one of its departments, offices and institutions as defined in division (C) of section 121.01 of the Revised Code, by serving the officer responsible for the administration of the department, office or institution or by serving the attorney general of this state;

(L)   Upon a county or upon any of its offices, agencies, districts, departments, institutions or administrative units, by serving the officer responsible for the administration of the office, agency, district, department, institution or unit or by serving the prosecuting attorney of the county;

(M)   Upon a township by serving one or more of the township trustees or the township clerk or by serving the prosecuting attorney of the county in which the township is located, unless the township is organized under Chapter 504. of the Revised Code, in which case service may be made upon the township law director;

(N)   Upon a municipal corporation or upon any of its offices, departments, agencies, authorities, institutions or administrative units by serving the officer responsible for the administration of the office, department, agency, authority, institution or unit or by serving the city solicitor or comparable legal officer;

(O)   Upon any governmental entity not mentioned above by serving the person, officer, group or body responsible for the administration of that entity or by serving the appropriate legal officer, if any, representing the entity. Service upon any person who is a member of the "group" or "body" responsible for the administration of the entity shall be sufficient.

Service of process pursuant to Civ.R. 4 through 4.6, except service by publication as provided in Civ.R. 4.4(A), may be made upon an address confidentiality "program participant," as defined by R.C. 111.41(G), by serving the Secretary of State.

[Effective: July 1, 1970; amended effective July 1, 1971; July 1, 1996; July 1, 1997; July 1, 2009; July 1, 2012; July 1, 2016; July 1, 2017.]

Staff Note (July 1, 2017 Amendment)

At the request made by the Legislature in Section 3 of 2016 Sub.H.B. No. 359, the 2017 amendment adds a final paragraph to the rule to allow service of process to be made upon an address confidentiality "program participant," as defined by R.C. 111.41(G), by serving the Secretary of State as the program participant's agent. "Program participants" include victims of domestic violence and other persons who would be at risk of harm should their addresses be disclosed.

Staff Note (July 1, 2012 Amendment)

Divisions (F) through (J) are amended to permit service of process to be made at a place of business not only by United States certified or express mail as previously authorized, but also by a commercial carrier service under the 2012 amendments to Civ.R. 4.1(A)(1).

Staff Note (July 1, 2009 Amendment)

Division (G) is inserted into Civ.R. 4.2 to provide for service on a limited liability company in a manner similar to the provisions of Civ.R. 4.2(F) for service upon a corporation, and the remaining divisions of the rule are re-lettered.

Staff Note (July 1, 1997 Amendment)

Rule 4.2 Process: Who may be served

Prior to the 1997 amendment, service of process under this rule was permitted only by certified mail. It appears that service of process by express mail, i.e. as that sort of mail is delivered by the United States Postal Service, can always be obtained return receipt requested, and thus could accomplish the purpose of notification equally well as certified mail. Therefore, the amendment provides for this additional option for service.

Other amendments to this rule are nonsubstantive grammatical or stylistic changes, including lettering of the divisions (A-N) in place of the previous numbering (1-14).

Staff Note (July 1, 1996 Amendment)

Rule 4.2 Process: Who May be Served

In 1991, the General Assembly enacted Chapter 504 of the Ohio Revised Code to give townships an option to organize the "limited self-government form" of government. Townships electing this form of government are required by law to appoint a law director who "shall be the legal advisor to the board of township trustees ... and all other township officers." R.C. 504.15. Upon attaining Chapter 504 status, then, the prosecuting attorney of the county in which the township is located no longer serves as the "legal advisor" of the township. The amendment recognizes this statutory development and should facilitate service of process in actions against Chapter 504 townships.

Staff Note (July 1, 2016 Amendments)

Division 4.2(B) of the rule is amended to substitute "a parent" for "father" and "mother" as a person upon whom service of process may be made to effectuate service of process upon a person under sixteen years of age. The amendment is made in accordance with the July 26, 2015 Administrative Action of the Ohio Supreme Court, *06/26/2015 Administrative Actions*, 2015-Ohio-2568, which ordered that the Ohio Rules of Civil Procedure be construed and amended as gender neutral where appropriate to comply with the decision of U.S. Supreme Court in *Obergefell v. Hodges*, 576 U.S. ___ , 135 S.Ct. 2584 (2015).

RULE 4.3   Process: Out-of-State Service

(A)   When service permitted. Service of process may be made outside of this state, as provided in this rule, in any action in this state, upon a person who, at the time of service of process, is a nonresident of this state or is a resident of this state who is absent from this state. "Person" includes an individual, an individual's executor, administrator, or other personal representative, or a corporation, partnership, association, or any other legal or commercial entity, who, acting directly or by an agent, has caused an event to occur out of which the claim that is the subject of the complaint arose, from the person's:

(1)   Transacting any business in this state;

(2)   Contracting to supply services or goods in this state;

(3)   Causing tortious injury by an act or omission in this state, including, but not limited to, actions arising out of the ownership, operation, or use of a motor vehicle or aircraft in this state;

(4)   Causing tortious injury in this state by an act or omission outside this state if the person regularly does or solicits business, engages in any other persistent course of conduct, or derives substantial revenue from goods used or consumed or services rendered in this state;

(5)   Causing injury in this state to any person by breach of warranty expressly or impliedly made in the sale of goods outside this state when the person to be served might reasonably have expected the person who was injured to use, consume, or be affected by the goods in this state, provided that the person to be served also regularly does or solicits business, engages in any other persistent course of conduct, or derives substantial revenue from goods used or consumed or services rendered in this state;

(6)   Having an interest in, using, or possessing real property in this state;

(7)   Contracting to insure any person, property, or risk located within this state at the time of contracting;

(8)   Living in the marital relationship within this state notwithstanding subsequent departure from this state, as to all obligations arising for spousal support, custody, child support, or property settlement, if the other party to the marital relationship continues to reside in this state;

(9)   Causing tortious injury in this state to any person by an act outside this state committed with the purpose of injuring persons, when the person to be served might reasonably have expected that some person would be injured by the act in this state;

(10)   Causing tortious injury to any person by a criminal act, any element of which takes place in this state, that the person to be served commits or in the commission of which the person to be served is guilty of complicity.

(B)   Methods of service.

(1)   Service by clerk. The clerk may make service of process or other documents to be served outside the state in the same manner as provided in Civ.R. 4.1(A)(1) through Civ.R. 4.1(A)(3).

(2)   Personal service. When ordered by the court, a "person" as defined in division (A) of this rule may be personally served with a copy of the process and complaint or other document to be served. Service under this division may be made by any person not less than eighteen years of age who is not a party and who has been designated by order of the court to make personal service of process. On request, the clerk shall deliver the summons to the plaintiff for transmission to the person who will make the service. The person serving process shall locate the person to be served and shall tender a copy of the process and accompanying documents to the person to be served.

Proof of service may be made as prescribed by Civ.R. 4.1 (B) or by order of the court. Failure to make service within the twenty-eight-day period and failure to make proof of service do not affect the validity of service.

[Effective: July 1, 1970; amended effective July 1, 1971; July 1, 1980; July 1, 1988; July 1, 1991; July 1, 1997; July 1, 2012; July 1, 2014.]

Staff Note (July 1, 2014 Amendments)

Rule 4.3(B)(2) is amended to be consistent with the provisions of Civ.R. 4.1(B) relating to personal service within the state which specify, "The person serving process shall locate the person to be served and shall tender a copy of the process and accompanying documents to the person to be served" and "Failure to make service within the twenty-eight-day period and failure to make proof of service do not affect the validity of service."

Staff Note (July 1, 2012 Amendment)

Rule 4.3(B) is amended to incorporate, rather than restate, the provisions of amended Civ.R. 4.1(A)(1) through Civ.R. 4.1(A)(3) for service by the clerk. The substantive changes (1) permit the clerk to make service of process outside the state using a commercial carrier service to make delivery by any method requiring a signed receipt and (2) make clear that the method of service of process permitted to be made by a person designated by the court is limited to personal service.

Also eliminated is a prior provision permitting service outside the state to be completed by the filing of an affidavit when service by certified or express mail is returned showing failure of delivery. Rules 4.6(C) and (D) address returns of service showing "refused" and "unclaimed" when service is attempted by U.S. mail under Civ.R. 4.1(A)(1)(a), and those provisions apply to service attempted outside the state by that method.

Staff Note (July 1, 1997 Amendment)

Rule 4.3 Process: Out-of-state service

Prior to the 1997 amendment, service of process under this rule was permitted only by certified mail. It appears that service of process by express mail, i.e. as that sort of mail is delivered by the United States Postal Service, can always be obtained return receipt requested, and thus could accomplish the purpose of notification equally well as certified mail. Therefore, the amendment provides for this additional option for service.

Other amendments to this rule are nonsubstantive grammatical or stylistic changes.

RULE 4.4   Process: Service by Publication

(A)   Residence unknown.

(1)   Service by Publication in a Newspaper. Except in an action or proceeding governed by division (A)(2) of this rule, when service of process is required upon a party whose residence is unknown, service shall be made by publication in actions where such service is authorized by law.   Before service by publication can be made, an affidavit of the party requesting service or that party's counsel shall be filed with the court. The affidavit shall aver that service of summons cannot be made because the residence of the party to be served is unknown to the affiant, all of the efforts made on behalf of the party to ascertain the residence of the party to be served, and that the residence of the party to be served cannot be ascertained with reasonable diligence.

Upon the filing of the affidavit, the clerk shall cause service of notice to be made by publication in a newspaper of general circulation in the county in which the action or proceeding is filed. If no newspaper is published in that county, then publication shall be in a newspaper published in an adjoining county. The publication shall contain the name and address of the court, the case number, the name of the first party on each side, and the name and last known address, if any, of the person or persons whose residence is unknown. The publication also shall contain a summary statement of the object of the pleading or other document seeking relief against a party whose residence is unknown, and a summary statement of the demand for relief, and shall notify the party to be served that such party is required to answer or respond either within twenty-eight days after the publication or at such other time after the publication that is set as the time to appear or within which to respond after service of such pleading or other document. The publication shall be published at least once a week for six successive weeks unless publication for a lesser number of weeks is specifically provided by law. Service of process shall be deemed complete at the date of the last publication.

After the last publication, the publisher or its agent shall file with the court an affidavit showing the fact of publication together with a copy of the notice of publication. The affidavit and copy of the notice shall constitute proof of service of process.

(2)   Service by Publication by Posting and Mail.

(a)   Actions and Proceedings other than Civil Protection Order Proceedings. In divorce, annulment, or legal separation actions, and in actions pertaining to the care, custody, and control of children whose parents are not married, and in all post-decree proceedings:

(i)   if the residence of the party upon whom service is sought is unknown; and,

(ii)   if the matter is not governed by Civ. R. 65.1; and,

(iii)   if the party requesting service upon another party is proceeding with a poverty affidavit;

service by publication shall be made by posting and mail. Before service by posting and mail can be made under this division (A)(2)(a), an affidavit of the party requesting service or that party's counsel shall be filed with the court. The affidavit shall contain the same averments required by division (A)(1) of this rule and, in addition, shall set forth the defendant's last known address.

Upon the filing of the affidavit, the clerk shall cause service of notice to be made by posting in a conspicuous place in the courthouse or courthouses in which the general and domestic relations divisions of the court of common pleas for the county are located and in two additional public places in the county that have been designated by local rule for the posting of notices pursuant to this rule. Alternatively, the postings, except for protection orders issued pursuant to Civ.R. 65.1, under this division (A)(2)(a), may be made on the website of the clerk of courts, if available, in a section designated for such purpose. The notice shall contain the same information required by division (A)(1) of this rule to be contained in a newspaper publication. The notice shall be posted for six successive weeks.

(b)   Civil Protection Order Proceedings. In civil protection order proceedings where the party's residence upon whom service is sought is unknown, service may be made by posting and mail without the necessity of a poverty affidavit. Before service by posting and mail can be made under this division (A)(2)(b), an affidavit of the party requesting service or that party's counsel shall be filed with the court. The affidavit shall contain the same averments required by division (A)(1) of this rule and, in addition, shall set forth the last known address of the party to be served.

Upon the filing of the affidavit, the clerk shall cause service of notice to be made by posting in a conspicuous place in the courthouse or courthouses within the county where Civ.R. 65.1 civil protection order proceedings may be filed and in two additional public places in the county that have been designated by local rule for the posting of notices pursuant to this rule. The postings under this division (A)(2)(b) shall not be made on the website of the clerk of courts. The notice shall contain the same information required by division (A)(1) of this rule to be contained in a newspaper publication. The notice shall be posted for six successive weeks.

(c)   Additional Requirement for Mailing. When service by publication is sought by posting and mail under either division (A)(2)(a) or division (A)(2)(b) of this rule, the clerk shall also cause the documents for service to be mailed by United States ordinary mail, address correction requested, to the last known address of the party to be served. The clerk shall obtain a certificate of mailing from the United States Postal Service. If the clerk is notified of a corrected or forwarding address of the party to be served within the six-week period that notice is posted pursuant to division (A)(2)(a) or division (A)(2)(b) of this rule, the clerk shall cause the documents for service to be mailed to the corrected or forwarding address. The clerk shall note the name, address, and date of each mailing on the docket.

(d)   Docket Entry of Posting; Completion of Service. After the last week of posting under either division (A)(2)(a) or division (A)(2)(b) of this rule, the clerk shall note on the docket where and when notice was posted. Service shall be complete upon the entry of posting.

(B)   Residence known. If the residence of a party to be served is known, and the action is one in which service by publication is authorized by law, service of process shall be effected by a method other than by publication as provided by:

(1)   Civ.R. 4.1, if the party to be served is a resident of this state,

(2)   Civ.R.4.3(B) if party to be served is not a resident of this state, or

(3)   Civ.R.4.5, in the alternative, if service on party to be served is to be effected in a foreign country.

If service of process cannot be effected under the provisions of this subdivision or Civ.R.4.6(C) or Civ.R.4.6(D), service of process shall proceed by publication.

[Effective: July 1, 1970; amended effective July 1, 1971; July 1, 1991; July 1, 2012; July 1, 2013; July 1, 2016; July 1, 2018.]

Staff Notes (July 1, 2018 Amendments)

Background to the July 1, 2018 Amendments to Civ.R. 4.4.

As initially adopted in 1970, Civ.R. 4.4(A) provided that when the defendant's residence was unknown, service could be obtained by publication, but only by publication in a newspaper.

In 1991, Civ.R. 4.4(A) was divided into two divisions -- Civ.R. 4.4(A)(1) set forth essentially the same "publication by newspaper" provisions contained in the then-existing rule, while a new Civ.R.4.4(A)(2) allowed an indigent plaintiff in a divorce, annulment, or legal separation action to obtain service by publication "by posting and mail" when the defendant's residence is unknown. In 2013, the application of the publication "by posting and mail" provisions of Civ.R. 4.4(A)(2) were expanded to include an indigent plaintiff in actions pertaining to the care, custody, and control of children whose parents are not married, and in all post-decree proceedings; and a provision for posting at a website of the clerk of courts was added.

In 2016, the application of the publication "by posting and mail" provisions of Civ.R. 4.4(A)(2) were again expanded to include an indigent plaintiff in a civil protection order proceeding pursuant to Civ.R. 65.1; but such civil protection order plaintiffs were precluded from publishing protection orders at a website of the clerk of courts since such publication is prohibited by 18 U.S.C. Section 2265(d)(3).

After the adoption of the 2016 amendments to the rule, the Supreme Court Advisory Committee on Domestic Violence requested that the rule be further amended to allow any petitioner in a civil protection order proceeding, regardless of indigency, to make use of the publication "by posting and mail" provisions of Civ.R. 4.4(A)(2) when the defendant's residence is unknown.

The July 1, 2018 amendments amend and reorganize the rule to eliminate confusion resulting from the existing structure and terminology of its provisions, and to address and account for a number of matters related to its application, including the following:

• Service by publication may be sought by parties other than plaintiffs and may be sought against parties other than defendants, particularly in divorce, annulment, or legal separation actions; in actions pertaining to the care, custody, and control of children whose parents are not married; in post-decree proceedings in such actions; and in civil protection order proceedings governed by Civ.R. 65.1;

• Service by publication may be sought for the service of documents other than complaints -- such as petitions, motions, and orders -- in divorce, annulment, or legal separation actions; in actions pertaining to the care, custody, and control of children whose parents are not married; in post-decree proceedings in such actions; and in civil protection order proceedings governed by Civ.R. 65.1;

• A time other than within twenty-eight days of service may be required to respond or appear in response to service of a document other than a complaint -- such as service of a petition, motion, or order in divorce, annulment, or legal separation actions; in actions pertaining to the care, custody, and control of children whose parents are not married; in post-decree proceedings in such actions; and in civil protection order proceedings governed by Civ.R. 65.1.

Although the basis for the 1991 exemption from the payment of court costs due to indigency, and the basis provided by R.C. 3113.31(J) for the exemption from the payment of court costs in civil protection order proceedings are decidedly different, part of the rationale which apparently supported the 1991 adoption of Civ.R. 4.4(A)(2) justifies permitting parties in civil protection order proceedings, regardless of indigency, to obtain service by publication by posting and mail, i.e., those parties are not required to pay the substantial costs of service by publication in a newspaper. See *Boddie v. Connecticut*, 401 U.S. 371, 91 S.Ct. 780, 28 L.Ed.2d 113 (1971) and *State ex rel. Blevins, v. Mowery*, 45 Ohio St.3d 20, 543 N.E.2d 99 (1989); *also see* the Staff Notes to the 1998 amendments to Juv.R. 16.

Division (A)(1). Service by Publication in a Newspaper.

The rule is amended by replacing the terms "plaintiff" and "defendant" with the terms "party requesting service" and "party to be served."

The rule is amended by replacing "where the complaint is filed" with "where the action or proceeding is filed."

The rule is amended by replacing "object of the complaint" with "object of the pleading or other document."

The rule is amended to provide "within twenty-eight days after the publication or at such other time after the publication that is set as the time to appear or within which to respond after service of such pleading or other document."

Division (A)(2). Service by Publication by Posting and Mail.

The rule is amended by further sub-dividing it into division (A)(2)(a) addressing service by publication by posting and mail in actions or proceedings other than civil protection order proceedings, and division (A)(2)(b) addressing service by publication by posting and mail in civil protection order proceedings; division (A)(2)(c) addresses the additional requirement for mailing; and division (A)(2)(d) addresses the docketing of the entry of posting and completion of service.

The rule is amended by replacing "proceeding in forma pauperis" with "proceeding with a poverty affidavit."

The rule is amended by replacing the "defendant" with the "party upon whom service is sought."

Division (A)(2)(b). Civil Protection Order Proceedings.

The new division (A)(2)(b) contains the same general requirements of division (A)(2)(a) except:

• The requirement of a poverty affidavit is eliminated.

• "Courthouses within which domestic relations divisions * * * are located" is replaced with "Courthouses within the county where Civ.R. 65.1 civil protection order proceedings may be filed[;]"

• Posting on the website of the clerk of courts is prohibited.

Division (A)(2)(c). Additional Requirements for Mailing.

The rule is amended by replacing "complaint and summons" with "documents for service."

The rule is amended by replacing "defendant's last known address" with "last known address of the party to be served."

Division (B). Residence known.

The rule is amended by replacing "defendant" with "party to be served."

Staff Note (July 1, 2016 Amendment)

Division (A): Residence unknown.

Division (A)(2) of this rule is amended to provide that publication by posting service of process is an appropriate method of service in Civ.R. 65.1 civil protection order proceedings under the conditions described in that division of the rule. As stated in division (A)(2) of the rule, a petitioner who is proceeding in forma pauperis and who requests publication by posting service of process must file an affidavit with the court containing the same averments required by division (A)(1) of the rule, i.e., that service of summons cannot be made because the residence of the defendant is unknown to the affiant, all of the efforts made on behalf of the party to ascertain the residence of the defendant, and that the residence of the defendant cannot be ascertained with reasonable diligence.

The service of process by publication by way of posting of a civil protection order shall not impact the prompt entry of such an order into the protection order file of the National Crime Information Center. It is to be noted that the alternative method of posting on the website of the clerk of courts is not available for service of protection orders issued pursuant to Civ.R. 65.1.

RULE 4.5   Process: Alternative Provisions for Service in a Foreign Country

When Civ. R. 4.3 or Civ. R. 4.4 or both allow service upon a person outside this state and service is to be effected in a foreign country, service of the summons and complaint shall be made as provided in this rule.

(A) Hague Convention Signatory. If the foreign country is a signatory to the Hague Convention on the Service Abroad of Judicial and Extrajudicial Documents in Civil or Commercial Matters, service shall be pursuant to a method allowed by the Articles of that Convention, including any method allowed by Article 8 or Article 10 to which the foreign country has not objected in accordance with Article 21.

(B) Other cases. In all cases to which division (A) does not apply, service may be made in a manner provided by Civ. R. 4.3(B)(1) or, if applicable, Civ. R. 4.4, and may also be made:

(1)   In the manner prescribed by the law of the foreign country for service in that country in an action in any of its courts of general jurisdiction when service is calculated to give actual notice;

(2)   As directed by the foreign authority in response to a letter rogatory when service is calculated to give actual notice;

(3)   Upon an individual by delivery to him or her personally;

(4)   Upon a corporation or partnership or association by delivery to an officer, a managing or general agent;

(5)   By any form of delivery requiring a signed receipt, when the clerk of the court addresses the delivery to the party to be served and delivers the summons to the person who will make the service;

(6)   As directed by order of the court.

Service under division (B)(3) or (B)(6) of this rule may be made by any person not less than eighteen years of age who is not a party and who has been designated by order of the court, or by the foreign court. On request the clerk shall deliver the summons to the plaintiff for transmission to the person or the foreign court or officer who will make the service.

(C)   Return. Proof of service may be made as prescribed by Civ.R. 4.1(B), or by the law of the foreign country, or by order of the court. Failure to make service within the twenty-eight-day period and failure to make proof of service do not affect the validity of service.

When delivery is made pursuant to division (B)(5) of this rule, proof of service shall include a receipt signed by the addressee or other evidence of delivery to the addressee satisfactory to the court.

[Effective: July 1, 1970; amended effective July 1, 1997; July 1, 2012; July 1, 2014.]

Staff Note (July 1, 2014 Amendments)

Rule 4.5(C) is amended to be consistent with the provision of Civ.R. 4.1(B) relating to personal service within the state which specifies, "Failure to make service within the twenty-eight-day period and failure to make proof of service do not affect the validity of service."

Staff Note (July 1, 2012 Amendment)

Rule 4.5 is amended to provide that when service is to be made in a foreign country that is a signatory to the Hague Convention, the provisions of that Convention supersede the other methods for service in a foreign country that are described in the rule. Pursuant to the 2012 amendments to Civ.R. 4.1(A) and Civ.R. 4.3(B)(1), delivery by commercial carrier service, requiring a signed receipt, is also authorized when the Hague Convention does not apply.

Staff Note (July 1, 1997 Amendment)

Rule 4.5 Process: Alternative Provisions for Service in a Foreign Country

The 1997 amendment changed a cross-reference in division (B) necessitated by the relettering of Civ. R. 4.1, also effective July 1, 1997. Other amendments to this rule are nonsubstantive grammatical or stylistic changes.

RULE 4.6   Process: Limits; Amendment; Service Refused; Service Unclaimed

(A)   Limits of effective service. All process may be served anywhere in this state and, when authorized by law or these rules, may be served outside this state.

(B)   Amendment. The court within its discretion and upon such terms as are just, may at any time allow the amendment of any process or proof of service thereof, unless the amendment would cause material prejudice to the substantial rights of the party against whom the process was issued.

(C)   Service refused. If attempted service of process by United States certified or express mail or by commercial carrier service within or outside the state is refused, and the certified or express mail envelope or return of the commercial carrier shows such refusal, or the return of the person serving process by personal service within or outside the state or by residence service within the state specifies that service of process has been refused, the clerk shall forthwith notify the attorney of record or, if there is no attorney of record, the party at whose instance process was issued and enter the fact and method of notification on the appearance docket. If the attorney, or serving party, after notification by the clerk, files with the clerk a written request for ordinary mail service, the clerk shall send by United States ordinary mail a copy of the summons and complaint or other document to be served to the defendant at the address set forth in the caption, or at the address set forth in written instructions furnished to the clerk. The mailing shall be evidenced by a certificate of mailing which shall be completed and filed by the clerk. Answer day shall be twenty-eight days after the date of mailing as evidenced by the certificate of mailing. The clerk shall endorse this answer date upon the summons which is sent by ordinary mail. Service shall be deemed complete when the fact of mailing is entered of record. Failure to claim United States certified or express mail or commercial carrier service is not refusal of service within the meaning of this division. This division shall not apply if any reason for failure of delivery other than "Refused" is also shown on the United States certified or express mail envelope.

(D)   United States certified or express mail service unclaimed. If a United States certified or express mail envelope attempting service within or outside the state is returned with an endorsement stating that the envelope was unclaimed, the clerk shall forthwith notify the attorney of record or, if there is no attorney of record, the party at whose instance process was issued and enter the fact and method of notification on the appearance docket. If the attorney, or serving party, after notification by the clerk, files with the clerk a written request for ordinary mail service, the clerk shall send by United States ordinary mail a copy of the summons and complaint or other document to be served to the defendant at the address set forth in the caption, or at the address set forth in written instructions furnished to the clerk. The mailing shall be evidenced by a certificate of mailing which shall be completed and filed by the clerk. Answer day shall be twenty-eight days after the date of mailing as evidenced by the certificate of mailing. The clerk shall endorse this answer date upon the summons which is sent by ordinary mail. Service shall be deemed complete when the fact of mailing is entered of record, provided that the ordinary mail envelope is not returned by the postal authorities with an endorsement showing failure of delivery. If the ordinary mail envelope is returned undelivered, the clerk shall forthwith notify the attorney, or serving party.

(E)   Duty of attorney of record or serving party. The attorney of record or the serving party shall be responsible for determining if service has been made and shall timely file written instructions with the clerk regarding completion of service notwithstanding the provisions in Civ. R. 4.1 through 4.6 which instruct a clerk to notify the attorney of record or the serving party of failure of service of process.

[Effective: July 1, 1970; amended effective July 1, 1971; July 1, 1978; July 1, 1997; July 1, 2012.]

Staff Note (July 1, 2012 Amendment)

Divisions (C) and (D) are amended (1) to specify that their provisions for service by United States ordinary mail apply to service by commercial carrier that is returned showing "Refused" but do not apply to service by commercial carrier that is returned showing "Unclaimed" and (2) to make clear that these divisions are applicable to U.S. mail service attempted both within and outside the state.

Division (C) relating to service "Refused" is also amended to specify that its provisions do not apply to ambiguous returns of U.S. certified or express mail stating other reasons for failure of delivery that suggest lack of actual notice to the defendant, such as "unable to forward". Division (D) relating to service "Unclaimed" is not similarly amended with respect to returns stating both "Unclaimed" and other reasons for failure of delivery; however, division (D) continues to apply only to U.S. Postal Service returns showing that the addressee was notified of, and failed to claim, the certified or express mail envelope.

Staff Note (July 1, 1997 Amendment)

Rule 4.6 Process: Limits; amendment; service refused; service unclaimed

Prior to the 1997 amendment, service of process under this rule was permitted only by certified mail. It appears that service of process by express mail, i.e. as that sort of mail is delivered by the United States Postal Service, can always be obtained return receipt requested, and thus could accomplish the purpose of notification equally well as certified mail. Therefore, the amendment provides for this additional option for service.

Other amendments to this rule are nonsubstantive grammatical or stylistic changes.

RULE 5.   **Service and Filing of Pleadings and Other Papers Subsequent to the Original Complaint**

(A)   **Service: When Required.** Except as otherwise provided in these rules, every order required by its terms to be served, every pleading subsequent to the original complaint unless the court otherwise orders because of numerous defendants, every paper relating to discovery required to be served upon a party unless the court otherwise orders, every written motion other than one which may be heard ex parte, and every written notice, appearance, demand, offer of judgment, and similar paper shall be served upon each of the parties. Service is not required on parties in default for failure to appear except that pleadings asserting new or additional claims for relief or for additional damages against them shall be served upon them in the manner provided for service of summons in Civ. R. 4 through Civ. R. 4.6.

(B)   **Service: how made.**

(1) Serving a party; serving an attorney. Whenever a party is not represented by an attorney, service under this rule shall be made upon the party. If a party is represented by an attorney, service under this rule shall be made on the attorney unless the court orders service on the party. Whenever an attorney has filed a notice of limited appearance pursuant to Civ.R. 3(B), service shall be made upon both that attorney and the party in connection with the proceedings for which the attorney has filed a notice of limited appearance.

(2) Service in general. A document is served under this rule by:

(a) handing it to the person;

(b) leaving it:

(i) at the person's office with a clerk or other person in charge or, if no one is in charge, in a conspicuous place in the office; or

(ii) if the person has no office or the office is closed, at the person's dwelling or usual place of abode with someone of suitable age and discretion who resides there;

(c) mailing it to the person's last known address by United States mail, in which event service is complete upon mailing;

(d) delivering it to a commercial carrier service for delivery to the person's last known address within three calendar days, in which event service is complete upon delivery to the carrier;

(e) leaving it with the clerk of court if the person has no known address; or

(f) sending it by electronic means to a facsimile number or e-mail address provided in accordance with Civ.R. 11 by the attorney or party to be served, in which event service is complete upon transmission, but is not effective if the serving party learns that it did not reach the person served.

(3) Using court facilities. If a local rule so authorizes, a party may use the court's transmission facilities to make service under Civ.R. 5(B)(2)(f).

(4) Proof of service. The served document shall be accompanied by a completed proof of service which shall state the date and manner of service, specifically identify the division of Civ.R. 5(B)(2) by which the service was made, and be signed in accordance with Civ.R. 11. Documents filed with the court shall not be considered until proof of service is endorsed thereon or separately filed.

(C)   Service: numerous defendants. In any action in which there are unusually large numbers of defendants, the court, upon motion or of its own initiative, may order that service of the pleadings of the defendants and replies thereto need not be made as between the defendants and that any cross-claim, counterclaim, or matter constituting an avoidance or affirmative defense contained therein shall be deemed to be denied or avoided by all other parties and that the filing of any such pleading and service thereof upon the plaintiff constitutes due notice of it to the parties. A copy of every such order shall be served upon the parties in such manner and form as the court directs.

(D)   Filing. Any paper after the complaint that is required to be served shall be filed with the court within three days after service. The following discovery requests and responses shall not be filed until they are used in the proceeding or the court orders filing: depositions, interrogatories, requests for documents or tangible things or to permit entry on land, and requests for admission.

(E)   Filing with the court defined. The filing of documents with the court, as required by these rules, shall be made by filing them with the clerk of court, except that the judge may permit the documents to be filed with the judge, in which event the judge shall note the filing date on the documents and transmit them to the clerk. A court may provide, by local rules adopted pursuant to the Rules of Superintendence, for the filing of documents by electronic means. If the court adopts such local rules, they shall include all of the following:

(1)   Any signature on electronically transmitted documents shall be considered that of the attorney or party it purports to be for all purposes. If it is established that the documents were transmitted without authority, the court shall order the filing stricken.

(2)   A provision shall specify the days and hours during which electronically transmitted documents will be received by the court, and a provision shall specify when documents received electronically will be considered to have been filed.

(3)   Any document filed electronically that requires a filing fee may be rejected by the clerk of court unless the filer has complied with the mechanism established by the court for the payment of filing fees.

[Effective: July 1, 1970; amended effective July 1, 1971; July 1, 1984; July 1, 1991; July 1, 1994; July 1, 2001; July 1, 2012; July 1, 2015; July 1, 2016; July 1, 2018.]

Staff Note (July 1, 2018 Amendment)

Division (B)(1): Serving a Party; Serving an Attorney.

This and other July 1, 2018 amendments to the Ohio Rules of Civil Procedure encourage attorneys to assist pro se parties on a limited basis without undertaking the full representation of the client on all issues related to the legal matter for which the attorney is engaged. By these amendments, the Supreme Court seeks to enlarge access to justice in Ohio's courts as recommended by a 2006 Report of the Court's Task Force on Pro Se & Indigent Litigants and by a 2015 Report of the Court's Task Force on Access to Justice.

The amendment to Civ.R. 5(B)(1) makes clear that when a notice of limited appearance has been filed by an attorney, an opposing party shall continue serving documents upon the party throughout the duration of the limited appearance while also serving the attorney. The purpose of the amendment is to assure appropriate service upon counsel to represented parties, but also to assure that a client being represented on a limited basis has copies of all key documents in the litigation.

Staff Note (July 1, 2016 Amendments)

Division 5(D) of this rule, the general rule for the time for filing, is amended to conform the language to the 2007 stylistic changes to Fed.R.Civ.P. 5(d) to the extent that the substance of the Ohio and Federal Rules are the same.

Staff Note (July 1, 2015 Amendments)

The rule is amended by adding a new division Civ.R. 5(B)(3) permitting a party to use a court's transmission facilities to serve other parties by electronic means if so authorized by local rule, and the subsequent division of the rule is renumbered accordingly.

The amendment eliminates a duplication of effort resulting from the 2012 amendments to Civ.R. 5(B) which permitted a party to use electronic means to fulfill the party's Civ.R. 5 duty to serve all other parties but did not authorize the party to use the facilities of a local court's electronic filing system to perform that duty—even though, under local rules, the court's facilities nevertheless serve by electronic means all parties participating in the electronic filing system. The new provision is virtually identical to Fed.R.Civ.P. 5(b)(3).

Staff Note (July 1, 2012 Amendment)

Rule 5(B)

Rule 5(B) is amended (1) to permit service of documents after the original complaint to be made by electronic means and by commercial carrier service and (2) to conform the format and language of the rule to the December 1, 2007 amendments to Fed.R.Civ.P. 5(b).

Rule 5(B)(2)(d) permits service of a document by delivering it to a commercial carrier service for delivery within three calendar days. Rule 5(B)(2)(f) adopts the language of Fed.R.Civ.P. 5(b) stating that service by electronic means is not effective if the serving party learns that the document did not reach the person to be served. Rule 5(B)(3) emphasizes a party's duty to provide a proof of service that states the date and specific manner by which the service was made, specifically identifying the division of Civ.R. 5(B)(2) by which service was made.

Rule 5(D)

The provisions of Civ.R. 5(D) relating to the duty to provide a proof of service have been moved to Civ.R. 5(B)(3) and amended to require that a serving party specifically identify the division of Civ.R. 5(B)(2) by which the service was made. Additional changes are made to substitute "document" for "paper" for consistency with other Rules of Civil Procedure.

Staff Note (July 1, 2001 Amendment)

Civil Rule 5(E) Filing with the court defined

The amendments to this rule were part of a group of amendments that were submitted by the Ohio Courts Digital Signatures Task Force to establish minimum standards for the use of information systems, electronic signatures, and electronic filing. The substantive amendment to this rule was the amendment of the second sentence and the addition of the last sentence of division (E), and the addition of divisions (E)(2) and (E)(3). Comparable amendments were made to Civil Rule 73 (for probate courts), Criminal Rule 12, Juvenile Rule 8, and Appellate Rule 13.

As part of this electronic filing and signature project, the following rules were amended effective July 1, 2001: Civil Rules 5, 11, and 73; Criminal Rule 12; Juvenile Rule 8; and Appellate Rules 13 and 18. In addition, Rule 26 of the Rules of Superintendence for Courts of Ohio was amended and Rule of Superintendence 27 was added to complement the rules of procedure. Superintendence Rule 27 establishes a process by which minimum standards for information technology are promulgated, and requires that courts submit any local rule involving the use of information technology to a technology standards committee designated by the Supreme Court for approval.

RULE 6.   Time

(A)   Time: computation. In computing any period of time prescribed or allowed by these rules, by the local rules of any court, by order of court, or by any applicable statute, the day of the act, event, or default from which the designated period of time begins to run shall not be included. The last day of the period so computed shall be included, unless it is a Saturday, a Sunday, or a legal holiday, in which event the period runs until the end of the next day which is not a Saturday, a Sunday, or a legal holiday. When the period of time prescribed or allowed is less than seven days, intermediate Saturdays, Sundays, and legal holidays shall be excluded in the computation. When a public office in which an act, required by law, rule, or order of court, is to be performed is closed to the public for the entire day which constitutes the last day for doing such an act, or before its usual closing time on such day, then such act may be performed on the next succeeding day which is not a Saturday, a Sunday, or a legal holiday.

(B)   Time: extension. When by these rules or by a notice given thereunder or by order of court an act is required or allowed to be done at or within a specified time, the court for cause shown may at any time in its discretion (1) with or without motion or notice order the period enlarged if request therefor is made before the expiration of the period originally prescribed or as extended by a previous order, or (2) upon motion made after the expiration of the specified period permit the act to be done where the failure to act was the result of excusable neglect; but it may not extend the time for taking any action under Civ.R. 50(B), Civ.R. 59(B), Civ.R. 59(D), and Civ.R. 60(B), except to the extent and under the conditions stated in them.

(C)   Time: motions.

(1)   Motion responses and movants' replies generally. Responses to a written motion, other than motions for summary judgment, may be served within fourteen days after service of the motion. Responses to motions for summary judgment may be served within twenty-eight days after service of the motion. A movant's reply to a response to any written motion may be served within seven days after service of the response to the motion.

(2)   Motions prior to hearing or trial. Unless a different period is fixed under these rules or by order of the court, a written motion for purposes of a hearing that is not a trial shall be served no later than fourteen days prior to the hearing, and a written motion for purposes of a trial shall be served no later than twenty-eight days prior to the start of trial. Responses to such motions may be served as provided by Civ.R. 6(C); however, a movant's reply to the response is not permitted.

(3)   Modification for good cause upon motion. Upon motion of a party in an action, and for good cause, the court may reduce or enlarge the periods of time provided in divisions (C)(1) and (C)(2) of this rule.

(D)   Time: additional time after service by mail or commercial carrier service. Whenever a party has the right or is required to do some act or take some proceedings within a prescribed period after the service of a notice or other document upon that party and the notice or paper is served upon that party by mail or commercial carrier service under Civ.R. 5(B)(2)(c) or (d), three days shall be added to the prescribed period. This division does not apply to responses to service of summons under Civ.R. 4 through Civ.R. 4.6.

[Effective: July 1, 1970; amended effective July 1, 1978; July 1, 2012; July 1, 2015; July 1, 2019.]

Staff Notes (July 1, 2019 Amendment)

Division 6(C)

The amendment separates Civ.R. 6(C) into three divisions.

Division (C)(1)

The provisions of Division (C)(1) supersede and replace the differing deadlines for responding to motions imposed by the numerous local rules of Ohio trial courts, thereby eliminating confusion and creating consistency by providing uniform statewide deadlines. The division establishes a twenty-eight-day deadline for service of responses to motions for summary judgment, and a fourteen-day deadline for service of responses to all other motions. A movant's reply to a response to any motion may be served within seven days after service of the response.

Division (C)(2)

The provisions of Division (C)(2) establish deadlines for serving written motions for purposes of a hearing or trial (e.g., motions in limine, motions to bifurcate, etc.). Unless a different period is fixed under another Rule of Civil Procedure or by order of the court (e.g. an scheduling order entered in accordance with Civ.R. 16) written motions for purposes of a hearing must be served not later than fourteen days prior to the hearing, while motions for purposes of trial must be served not later than twenty-eight days prior to trial.

Division (C)(3)

The provisions of Division (C)(3) permit the court to modify the periods of time provided in Division (C)(1) and Division (C)(2) in an individual action upon the filing of a motion of a party and for good cause. For example, expediting interlocutory rulings in an action for injunctive relief might constitute good cause for reducing the time for responding to certain motions in that action.

Staff Note (July 1, 2015 Amendment)

The amendment to Civ.R. 6(C) eliminates the prior requirement to serve a "notice of hearing" when serving a motion, recognizing that the requirement is inconsistent with modern practice where most courts determine motions without oral hearing—a practice permitted by Civ.R. 7(B)(2). The amendment also addresses an uncertainty existing under the prior rule as to when a response to a motion is due when there is no local rule or court order specifying a time for responding to motions, by specifying a fallback time of fourteen days after service of the motion within which to serve arguments in response. In the absence of a local rule or court order addressing replies, the amendment also permits a movant to serve reply arguments within seven days after service of the opposing party's response. The time for filing motion responses and replies is governed by Civ.R. 5(D), again in the absence of a local rule or court order specifying a different time for filing.

Staff Note (July 1, 2012 Amendment)

Former Civ.R. 6(C) has been eliminated and the remaining divisions of the rule have been re-lettered. Former division (C) was adopted in 1970 and made reference to the continuing jurisdiction of a court after expiration of a "term of court." The provision was significant at the time for clarifying a court's jurisdiction to vacate its final judgments despite prior statutes which limited a court's jurisdiction to do so "after term of court." Those procedural statutes were repealed or amended with the adoption of the Ohio Rules of Civil Procedure in 1970. However, for organizational and other purposes, R.C. 2301.05 continues to provide for one year "terms" for common pleas courts, and some non-procedural statutes refer to "term of court." Rule 6(C) does not appear to have any continuing significance for Ohio procedure. The provision is not included in Fed. R. Civ. P. 6 and its elimination makes the lettering of Civ.R. 6 consistent with that of the federal rule.

Former Civ.R. 6(E), now Civ.R. 6(D), is amended to make clear that this "three day" rule applies only when service has been made by mail or commercial carrier service under Civ.R. 5(B)(2)(c) or (d). As with the prior rule, it does not apply to responding to service of process made under Civ.R. 4 through Civ.R.4.6, nor does it apply to responding to documents served under any other divisions of Civ.R. 5.

TITLE III. PLEADINGS AND MOTIONS

RULE 7. Pleadings and Motions

(A) Pleadings. There shall be a complaint and an answer; a reply to a counterclaim denominated as such; an answer to a cross-claim, if the answer contains a cross-claim; a third-party complaint, if a person who was not an original party is summoned under the provisions of Civ.R. 14; and a third-party answer, if a third-party complaint is served. No other pleading shall be allowed, except that the court may order a reply to an answer or a third-party answer.

(B) Motions.

(1) An application to the court for an order shall be by motion which, unless made during a hearing or a trial, shall be made in writing. A motion, whether written or oral, shall state with particularity the grounds therefor, and shall set forth the relief or order sought. A written motion, and any supporting affidavits, shall be served in accordance with Civ.R. 5 unless the motion may be heard ex parte.

(2) To expedite its business, the court may make provision by rule or order not inconsistent with these rules for the submission and determination of motions without oral hearing upon brief written statements of reasons in support and opposition.

(3) The rules applicable to captions, signing, and other matters of form of pleading apply to all motions and other papers provided for by these rules.

(4) All motions shall be signed in accordance with Civ.R. 11.

[Effective: July 1, 1970; amended effective July 1, 1984; July 1, 2014; July 1, 2015; July 1, 2019.]

Staff Note (July 1, 2019 Amendment)

Division (B)(2)

Division (B)(2) of the rule is amended to ensure that any local rule or order of the court relating to the submission and determination of motions is not inconsistent with the provisions of any other Rule of Civil Procedure (e.g., Civ.R. 6).

Staff Note (July 1, 2015 Amendment)

Rule 7(B) is amended by eliminating the reference to a "notice of hearing" which is no longer required by Civ.R. 6(B).

Staff Note (July 1, 2014 Amendments)

Rule 7(C) abolishing demurrers is deleted, corresponding to the 2007 deletion of former Federal Rule 7(c). Demurrers are unknown in Ohio modern practice, having been replaced in 1970 by Civ.R. 12(B)(6) with the adoption of the Ohio Rules of Civil Procedure. As the 2007 Federal Advisory Committee Note stated: "Former Rule 7(c) is deleted because it has done its work."

RULE 8. General Rules of Pleading

(A) **Claims for relief.** A pleading that sets forth a claim for relief, whether an original claim, counterclaim, cross-claim, or third-party claim, shall contain (1) a short and plain statement of the claim showing that the party is entitled to relief, and (2) a demand for judgment for the relief to which the party claims to be entitled. If the party seeks more than twenty-five thousand dollars, the party shall so state in the pleading but shall not specify in the demand for judgment the amount of recovery sought, unless the claim is based upon an instrument required to be attached pursuant to Civ. R. 10. At any time after the pleading is filed and served, any party from whom monetary recovery is sought may request in writing that the party seeking recovery provide the requesting party a written statement of the amount of recovery sought. Upon motion, the court shall require the party to respond to the request. Relief in the alternative or of several different types may be demanded.

(B) **Defenses; Form of denials.** A party shall state in short and plain terms the party's defenses to each claim asserted and shall admit or deny the averments upon which the adverse party relies. If the party is without knowledge or information sufficient to form a belief as to the truth of an averment, the party shall so state and this has the effect of a denial. Denials shall fairly meet the substance of the averments denied. When a pleader intends in good faith to deny only a part of a qualification of an averment, the pleader shall specify so much of it as is true and material and shall deny the remainder. Unless the pleader intends in good faith to controvert all the averments of the preceding pleading, the pleader may make the denials as specific denials or designated averments or paragraphs, or the pleader may generally deny all the averments except the designated averments or paragraphs as the pleader expressly admits; but, when the pleader does intend to controvert all its averments, including averments of the grounds upon which the court's jurisdiction depends, the pleader may do so by general denial subject to the obligations set forth in Civ. R. 11.

(C) **Affirmative defenses.** In pleading to a preceding pleading, a party shall set forth affirmatively accord and satisfaction, arbitration and award, assumption of risk, contributory negligence, discharge in bankruptcy, duress, estoppel, failure of consideration, want of consideration for a negotiable instrument, fraud, illegality, injury by fellow servant, laches, license, payment, release, res judicata, statute of frauds, statute of limitations, waiver, and any other matter constituting an avoidance or affirmative defense. When a party has mistakenly designated a defense as a counterclaim or a counterclaim as a defense, the court, if justice so requires, shall treat the pleading as if there had been a proper designation.

(D) **Effect of failure to deny.** Averments in a pleading to which a responsive pleading is required, other than those as to the amount of damage, are admitted when not denied in the responsive pleading. Averments in a pleading to which no responsive pleading is required or permitted shall be taken as denied or avoided.

(E) **Pleading to be concise and direct; consistency.**

(1)   Each averment of a pleading shall be simple, concise, and direct. No technical forms of pleading or motions are required.

(2)   A party may set forth two or more statements of a claim or defense alternately or hypothetically, either in one count or defense or in separate counts or defenses. When two or more statements are made in the alternative and one of them if made independently would be sufficient, the pleading is not made insufficient by the insufficiency of one or more of the alternative statements. A party may also state as many separate claims or defenses as he has regardless of consistency and whether based on legal or equitable grounds. All statements shall be made subject to the obligations set forth in Rule 11.

(F)   Construction of pleadings.   All pleadings shall be so construed as to do substantial justice.

(G)   Pleadings shall not be read or submitted.   Pleadings shall not be read or submitted to the jury, except insofar as a pleading or portion thereof is used in evidence.

(H)   Disclosure of minority or incompetency.   Every pleading or motion made by or on behalf of a minor or an incompetent shall set forth such fact unless the fact of minority or incompetency has been disclosed in a prior pleading or motion in the same action or proceeding.

[Effective: July 1, 1970; amended effective July 1, 1994.]

RULE 9.   Pleading Special Matters

(A)   Capacity. It is not necessary to aver the capacity of a party to sue or be sued or the authority of a party to sue or be sued in a representative capacity or the legal existence of an organized association of persons that is made a party. When a party desires to raise an issue as to the legal existence of any party or the capacity of any party to sue or be sued or the authority of a party to sue or be sued in a representative capacity, he shall do so by specific negative averment, which shall include such supporting particulars as are peculiarly within the pleader's knowledge.

(B)   Fraud, mistake, condition of the mind. In all averments of fraud or mistake, the circumstances constituting fraud or mistake shall be stated with particularity. Malice, intent, knowledge, and other condition of mind of a person may be averred generally.

(C)   Conditions precedent. In pleading the performance or occurrence of conditions precedent, it is sufficient to aver generally that all conditions precedent have been performed or have occurred. A denial of performance or occurrence shall be made specifically and with particularity.

(D)   Official document or act. In pleading an official document or official act it is sufficient to aver that the document was issued or the act done in compliance with law.

(E)   Judgment. In pleading a judgment or decision of a court of this state or a foreign court, judicial or quasi-judicial tribunal, or of a board or officer, it is sufficient to aver the judgment or decision without setting forth matter showing jurisdiction to render it.

(F)   Time and place. For the purpose of testing the sufficiency of a pleading, averments of time and place are material and shall be considered like all other averments of material matter.

(G)   Special damage. When items of special damage are claimed, they shall be specifically stated.

[Effective: July 1, 1970.]

RULE 10. Form of Pleadings

(A) Caption; names of parties. Every pleading shall contain a caption setting forth the name of the court, the title of the action, the case number, and a designation as in Rule 7(A). In the complaint the title of the action shall include the names and addresses of all the parties, but in other pleadings it is sufficient to state the name of the first party on each side with an appropriate indication of other parties.

(B) Paragraphs; separate statements. All averments of claim or defense shall be made in numbered paragraphs, the contents of each of which shall be limited as far as practicable to a statement of a single set of circumstances; and a paragraph may be referred to by number in all succeeding pleadings. Each claim founded upon a separate transaction or occurrence and each defense other than denials shall be stated in a separate count or defense whenever a separation facilitates the clear presentation of the matters set forth.

(C) Adoption by reference; exhibits. Statements in a pleading may be adopted by reference in a different part of the same pleading or in another pleading or in any motion. A copy of any written instrument attached to a pleading is a part of the pleading for all purposes.

(D) Attachments to pleadings.

(1) *Account or written instrument.* When any claim or defense is founded on an account or other written instrument, a copy of the account or written instrument must be attached to the pleading. If the account or written instrument is not attached, the reason for the omission must be stated in the pleading.

(2) *Affidavit of merit; medical, dental, optometric, and chiropractic liability claims.*

(a) Except as provided in division (D)(2)(b) of this rule, a complaint that contains a medical claim, dental claim, optometric claim, or chiropractic claim, as defined in R.C. 2305.113, shall be accompanied by one or more affidavits of merit relative to each defendant named in the complaint for whom expert testimony is necessary to establish liability. Affidavits of merit shall be provided by an expert witness meeting the requirements of Evid.R. 702 and, if applicable, also meeting the requirements of Evid.R. 601(D). Affidavits of merit shall include all of the following:

(i) A statement that the affiant has reviewed all medical records reasonably available to the plaintiff concerning the allegations contained in the complaint;

(ii) A statement that the affiant is familiar with the applicable standard of care;

(iii)   The opinion of the affiant that the standard of care was breached by one or more of the defendants to the action and that the breach caused injury to the plaintiff.

(b)   The plaintiff may file a motion to extend the period of time to file an affidavit of merit. The motion shall be filed by the plaintiff with the complaint. For good cause shown and in accordance with division (c) of this rule, the court shall grant the plaintiff a reasonable period of time to file an affidavit of merit, not to exceed ninety days, except the time may be extended beyond ninety days if the court determines that a defendant or non-party has failed to cooperate with discovery or that other circumstances warrant extension.

(c)   In determining whether good cause exists to extend the period of time to file an affidavit of merit, the court shall consider the following:

(i)   A description of any information necessary in order to obtain an affidavit of merit;

(ii)   Whether the information is in the possession or control of a defendant or third party;

(iii)   The scope and type of discovery necessary to obtain the information;

(iv)   What efforts, if any, were taken to obtain the information;

(v)   Any other facts or circumstances relevant to the ability of the plaintiff to obtain an affidavit of merit.

(d)   An affidavit of merit is required to establish the adequacy of the complaint and shall not otherwise be admissible as evidence or used for purposes of impeachment. Any dismissal for the failure to comply with this rule shall operate as a failure otherwise than on the merits.

(e)   If an affidavit of merit as required by this rule has been filed as to any defendant along with the complaint or amended complaint in which claims are first asserted against that defendant, and the affidavit of merit is determined by the court to be defective pursuant to the provisions of division (D)(2)(a) of this rule, the court shall grant the plaintiff a reasonable time, not to exceed sixty days, to file an affidavit of merit intended to cure the defect.

(E)   Size of paper filed. All pleadings, motions, briefs, and other papers filed with the clerk, including those filed by electronic means, shall be on paper not exceeding 8 1/2 x 11 inches in size without backing or cover.

[Effective: July 1, 1970; amended effective July 1, 1985; July 1, 1991; July 1, 2005; July 1, 2007; July 1, 2016.]

Staff Note (July 1, 2005 Amendment)

Civ. R. 10 is amended in response to a request from the General Assembly contained in Section 3 of Sub. H.B. 215 of the 125th General Assembly, effective September 13, 2004. The act amends and enacts provisions relative to medical, dental, optometric, and chiropractic malpractice actions, and Section 3 contains a request that the Supreme Court adopt a rule that "require[s] a plaintiff filing a medical liability claim to include a certificate of expert review as to each defendant."

Rule 10(D)   Attachments to pleadings

Civ. R. 10(D) is retitled and reorganized to reflect the inclusion of a requirement in division (D)(2) that a medical liability complaint include an affidavit of merit concerning the alleged breach of the standard of care by each defendant to the action. Division (D)(2)(a) specifies three items that must be included in the affidavit and sets forth the qualifications of the person providing the affidavit of merit.

There may be instances in which multiple affidavits of merit are required as to a particular plaintiff. For example, the plaintiff may find it necessary to provide one affidavit that addresses only the issue of "standard of care" and a separate affidavit that addresses only the issue of injury caused by the breach of the standard of care.

Because there may be circumstances in which the plaintiff is unable to provide an affidavit of merit when the complaint is filed, division (D)(2)(b) of the rule requires the trial court, when good cause is shown, to provide a reasonable period of time for the plaintiff to obtain and file the affidavit. For example, "good cause" may exist in a circumstance where the plaintiff obtains counsel near the expiration of the statute of limitations, and counsel does not have sufficient time to identify a qualified health care provider to conduct the necessary review of applicable medical records and prepare an affidavit. Similarly, the relevant medical records may not have been provided to the plaintiff in a timely fashion. Further, there may be situations where the medical records do not reveal the names of all of the potential defendants and so until discovery reveals those names, it may be necessary to name a "John Doe" defendant. Once discovery has revealed the name of a previously unknown defendant and that person is added as a party, the affidavit of merit would then be required as to that newly named defendant. Under these or similar circumstances, the court must afford the plaintiff a reasonable period of time, once a qualified health care provider is identified, to have the records reviewed and submit an affidavit that satisfies the requirements set forth in the rule.

Division (D)(2)(c) provides that an affidavit of merit is intended to establish the sufficiency of the complaint filed in a medical liability action and specifies that an affidavit of merit is not otherwise admissible as evidence or for purposes of impeachment.

The amendments to Rule 10 also include nonsubstantive changes.

Staff Note (July 1, 2007 Amendments)

Rule 10(D)   Attachments to pleadings

Civ. R. 10 is amended to clarify what constitutes "good cause" to permit the plaintiff an extension of time to file an affidavit of merit and to define the effect of dismissal for failure to comply with the affidavit of merit requirement.

Rule 10(D)   Attachments to pleadings

The language of division (D)(2)(a) is amended in recognition of the fact that more than one affidavit may be required as to a particular defendant due to the number of defendants or other circumstances.

Because there may be circumstances in which the plaintiff is unable to provide an affidavit of merit when the complaint is filed, division (D)(2)(b) of the rule requires the trial court, when good cause is shown, to provide a reasonable period of time for the plaintiff to obtain and file the affidavit. Division (D)(2)(c) details the circumstances and factors which the Court should consider in determining whether good cause exists to grant the plaintiff an extension of time to file the affidavit of merit. For example, "good cause" may exist in a circumstance where the plaintiff obtains counsel near the expiration of the statute of limitations, and counsel does not have sufficient time to identify a qualified health care provider to conduct the necessary review of applicable medical records and prepare an affidavit. Similarly, the relevant medical records may not have been provided to the plaintiff in a timely fashion by the defendant or a nonparty to the litigation who possesses the records. Further, there may be situations where the medical records do not reveal the names of all of the potential defendants and so until discovery reveals those names, it may be necessary to name a "John Doe" defendant. Once discovery has revealed the name of a defendant previously designated as John Doe and that person is added as a party, the affidavit of merit is required as to that newly named defendant. The medical records might also fail to reveal how or whether medical providers who are identified in the records were involved in the care that led to the malpractice. Under these and other circumstances not described here, the court must afford the plaintiff a reasonable period of time to submit an affidavit that satisfies the requirements set forth in the rule.

It is intended that the granting of an extension of time to file an affidavit of merit should be liberally applied, but within the parameters of the "good cause" requirement. The court should also exercise its discretion to aid plaintiff in obtaining the requisite information. To accomplish these goals, the plaintiff must specifically inform the Court of the nature of the information needed as opposed to a general averment that more information is needed. The plaintiff should apprise the court, to the extent that it is known, the identity of the person who has the information and the means necessary to obtain the information, to allow the court to grant an appropriate extension of time. If medical records in the possession of a defendant or non-party must be obtained, the court may issue an order compelling the production of the records. If medical records are non-existent, incomplete, or otherwise inadequate to permit an expert to evaluate the care, the court may, in appropriate circumstances, permit a plaintiff to conduct depositions of parties or non-parties to obtain the information necessary for an expert to complete such a review and provide an affidavit.

Division (D)(2)(b) of the rule sets an outside limit of 90 days to extend the time for the filing of an affidavit of merit, unless the court determines that the defendant or a nonparty in possession of the records has failed to cooperate with discovery, and in that circumstance the court may grant an extension beyond 90 days. This division also vests the trial court with the discretion to determine whether any other circumstances justify granting an extension beyond the 90 days.

The rule is intended to make clear that the affidavit is necessary to establish the sufficiency of the complaint. The failure to comply with the rule can result in the dismissal of the complaint, and this dismissal is considered to be a dismissal otherwise than upon the merits pursuant to Civ. R. 10(D)(2)(d).

Finally, new Civ. R. 10(D)(2)(e) allows a plaintiff a reasonable time, not to exceed sixty days, to cure any defects identified by the court in any affidavit filed with a complaint.

Staff Notes (July 1, 2016 Amendments)

Division (D)(2) of this rule applies to medical, dental, optometric, and chiropractic claims, as defined by R.C. 2305.113, and was adopted in 2005 to require that, at the time of the filing of a complaint asserting any such claims, the complaint must be accompanied by certificates of expert review. The rule is amended to remedy an inaccuracy in the prior rule which incorrectly indicated that Evid.R. 601(D) applies to the qualifications of an affiant for all medical, dental, optometric, and chiropractic claims. While Evid.R. 702 applies to the qualifications of an affiant for all medical, dental, optometric, and chiropractic claims, Evid.R. 601(D) applies only to the qualifications of an affiant for certain medical claims. See Evid.R. 601(D).

RULE 11.   Signing of Pleadings, Motions, or Other Documents

Every pleading, motion, or other document of a party represented by an attorney shall be signed by at least one attorney of record in the attorney's individual name, whose address, attorney registration number, telephone number, facsimile number, if any, and business e-mail address, if any, shall be stated. A party who is not represented by an attorney shall sign the pleading, motion, or other document and state the party's address. A party who is not represented by an attorney may further state a facsimile number or e-mail address for service by electronic means under Civ.R. 5(B)(2)(f). Except when otherwise specifically provided by these rules, pleadings, as defined by Civ.R. 7(A), need not be verified or accompanied by affidavit. The signature of an attorney or *pro se* party constitutes a certificate by the attorney or party that the attorney or party has read the document; that to the best of the attorney's or party's knowledge, information, and belief there is good ground to support it; and that it is not interposed for delay. If a document is not signed or is signed with intent to defeat the purpose of this rule, it may be stricken as sham and false and the action may proceed as though the document had not been served. For a willful violation of this rule, an attorney or *pro se* party, upon motion of a party or upon the court's own motion, may be subjected to appropriate action, including an award to the opposing party of expenses and reasonable attorney fees incurred in bringing any motion under this rule. Similar action may be taken if scandalous or indecent matter is inserted.

[Effective: July 1, 1970; amended effective July 1, 1994, July 1, 1995; July 1, 2001; July 1, 2012.]

Staff Note (July 1, 1995 Amendment)

Rule 11. Signing of Pleadings, Motions, or Other Papers

The amendment of this rule that took effect July 1, 1994 contained two errors that the 1995 amendment corrects. First, in the next-to-last sentence, the word "a" was erroneously omitted and is reinserted as the second word of the sentence by this amendment. Second, the last sentence, which was contained in the original version of this rule, was erroneously omitted from the 1994 amendment and is restored with this amendment.

Staff Note (July 1, 2001 Amendment)

Civil Rule 11   Signing of Pleadings, Motions, or Other Documents

The amendments to this rule were part of a group of amendments that were submitted by the Ohio Courts Digital Signatures Task Force to establish minimum standards for the use of information systems, electronic signatures, and electronic filing. The substantive amendment to this rule was the addition of the requirement that an attorney's telefax number and e-mail address, if any, be on all documents. Also, "document" was substituted for "paper" in the title and in two places in the text, for consistency with other Rules of Civil Procedure.

As part of this electronic filing and signature project, the following rules were amended effective July 1, 2001: Civil Rules 5, 11, and 73; Criminal Rule 12; Juvenile Rule 8; and Appellate Rules 13 and 18. In addition, Rule 26 of the Rules of Superintendence for Courts of Ohio was amended and Rule of Superintendence 27 was added to complement the rules of procedure. Superintendence Rule 27 establishes a process by which minimum standards for information technology are promulgated, and requires that courts submit any local rule involving the use of information technology to a technology standards committee designated by the Supreme Court for approval.

Staff Note (July 1, 2012 Amendment)

Rule 11 has been amended to permit a party who is not represented by an attorney to designate a facsimile number or e-mail address for purposes of service by electronic means.

The amendment also highlights that the term "pleading" as used in the Ohio Rules of Civil Procedure refers to the six specific documents listed in Civ.R. 7(A), and does not refer to other documents filed or served in the action.

RULE 12.   Defenses and Objections--When and How Presented--by Pleading or Motion--Motion for Judgment on the Pleadings

(A)   When answer presented.

(1)   Generally. The defendant shall serve his answer within twenty-eight days after service of the summons and complaint upon him; if service of notice has been made by publication, he shall serve his answer within twenty-eight days after the completion of service by publication.

(2)   Other responses and motions. A party served with a pleading stating a cross-claim against him shall serve an answer thereto within twenty-eight days after the service upon him. The plaintiff shall serve his reply to a counterclaim in the answer within twenty-eight days after service of the answer or, if a reply is ordered by the court, within twenty-eight days after service of the order, unless the order otherwise directs. The service of a motion permitted under this rule alters these periods of time as follows, unless a different time is fixed by order of the court: (a) if the court denies the motion, a responsive pleading, delayed because of service of the motion, shall be served within fourteen days after notice of the court's action; (b) if the court grants a motion, a responsive pleading, delayed because of service of the motion, shall be served within fourteen days after service of the pleading which complies with the court's order.

(B)   How presented. Every defense, in law or fact, to a claim for relief in any pleading, whether a claim, counterclaim, cross-claim, or third-party claim, shall be asserted in the responsive pleading thereto if one is required, except that the following defenses may at the option of the pleader be made by motion: (1) lack of jurisdiction over the subject matter, (2) lack of jurisdiction over the person, (3) improper venue, (4) insufficiency of process, (5) insufficiency of service of process, (6) failure to state a claim upon which relief can be granted, (7) failure to join a party under Rule 19 or Rule 19.1. A motion making any of these defenses shall be made before pleading if a further pleading is permitted. No defense or objection is waived by being joined with one or more other defenses or objections in a responsive pleading or motion. If a pleading sets forth a claim for relief to which the adverse party is not required to serve a responsive pleading, he may assert at the trial any defense in law or fact to that claim for relief. When a motion to dismiss for failure to state a claim upon which relief can be granted presents matters outside the pleading and such matters are not excluded by the court, the motion shall be treated as a motion for summary judgment and disposed of as provided in Rule 56. Provided however, that the court shall consider only such matters outside the pleadings as are specifically enumerated in Rule 56. All parties shall be given reasonable opportunity to present all materials made pertinent to such a motion by Rule 56.

(C)   Motion for judgment on the pleadings. After the pleadings are closed but within such time as not to delay the trial, any party may move for judgment on the pleadings.

(D)   Preliminary hearings. The defenses specifically enumerated (1) to (7) in subdivision (B) of this rule, whether made in a pleading or by motion, and the motion for judgment mentioned in subdivision (C) of this rule shall be heard and determined before trial on application of any party.

(E)   Motion for definite statement. If a pleading to which a responsive pleading is permitted is so vague or ambiguous that a party cannot reasonably be required to frame a responsive pleading, he may move for a definite statement before interposing his responsive pleading. The motion shall point out the defects complained of and the details desired. If the motion is granted and the order of the court is not obeyed within fourteen days after notice of the order or within such other time as the court may fix, the court may strike the pleading to which the motion was directed or make such order as it deems just.

(F)   Motion to strike. Upon motion made by a party before responding to a pleading or, if no responsive pleading is permitted by these rules, upon motion made by a party within twenty-eight days after the service of the pleading upon him or upon the court's own initiative at any time, the court may order stricken from any pleading any insufficient claim or defense or any redundant, immaterial, impertinent, or scandalous matter.

(G)   Consolidation of defenses and objections. A party who makes a motion under this rule must join with it the other motions herein provided for and then available to him. If a party makes a motion under this rule and does not include therein all defenses and objections then available to him which this rule permits to be raised by motion, he shall not thereafter assert by motion or responsive pleading, any of the defenses or objections so omitted, except as provided in subdivision (H) of this rule.

(H)   Waiver of defenses and objections.

(1)   A defense of lack of jurisdiction over the person, improper venue, insufficiency of process, or insufficiency of service of process is waived (a) if omitted from a motion in the circumstances described in subdivision (G), or (b) if it is neither made by motion under this rule nor included in a responsive pleading or an amendment thereof permitted by Rule 15(A) to be made as a matter of course.

(2)   A defense of failure to state a claim upon which relief can be granted, a defense of failure to join a party indispensable under Rule 19, and an objection of failure to state a legal defense to a claim may be made in any pleading permitted or ordered under Rule 7(A), or by motion for judgment on the pleadings, or at the trial on the merits.

(3)   Whenever it appears by suggestion of the parties or otherwise that the court lacks jurisdiction on the subject matter, the court shall dismiss the action.

[Effective: July 1, 1970; amended effective July 1, 1983.]

RULE 13.   Counterclaim and Cross-Claim

(A)   Compulsory counterclaims. A pleading shall state as a counterclaim any claim which at the time of serving the pleading the pleader has against any opposing party, if it arises out of the transaction or occurrence that is the subject matter of the opposing party's claim and does not require for its adjudication the presence of third parties of whom the court cannot acquire jurisdiction. But the pleader need not state the claim if (1) at the time the action was commenced the claim was the subject of another pending action, or (2) the opposing party brought suit upon his claim by attachment or other process by which the court did not acquire jurisdiction to render a personal judgment on that claim, and the pleader is not stating any counterclaim under this Rule 13.

(B)   Permissive counterclaims. A pleading may state as a counterclaim any claim against an opposing party not arising out of the transaction or occurrence that is the subject matter of the opposing party's claim.

(C)   Counterclaim exceeding opposing claim. A counterclaim may or may not diminish or defeat the recovery sought by the opposing party. It may claim relief exceeding in amount or different in kind from that sought in the pleading of the opposing party.

(D)   Counterclaim against this state. These rules shall not be construed to enlarge beyond the limits now fixed by law the right to assert counterclaims or to claim credits against this state, a political subdivision or an officer in his representative capacity or agent of either.

(E)   Counterclaim maturing or acquired after pleading. A claim which either matured or was acquired by the pleader after serving his pleading may, with the permission of the court, be presented as a counterclaim by supplemental pleadings.

(F)   Omitted counterclaim. When a pleader fails to set up a counterclaim through oversight, inadvertence, or excusable neglect, or when justice requires, he may by leave of court set up the counterclaim by amendment.

(G)   Cross-claim against co-party. A pleading may state as a cross-claim any claim by one party against a co-party arising out of the transaction or occurrence that is the subject matter either of the original action or of a counterclaim therein or relating to any property that is the subject matter of the original action. Such cross-claim may include a claim that the party against whom it is asserted is or may be liable to the cross-claimant for all or part of a claim asserted in the action against the cross-claimant.

(H)   Joinder of additional parties. Persons other than those made parties to the original action may be made parties to a counterclaim or cross-claim in accordance with the provisions of Rule 19, Rule 19.1, and Rule 20. Such persons shall be served pursuant to Rule 4 through Rule 4.6.

(I) **Separate trials; separate judgments.** If the court orders separate trials as provided in Rule 42(B), judgment on a counterclaim or cross-claim may be rendered in accordance with the terms of Rule 54(B) when the court has jurisdiction so to do, even if the claims of the opposing party have been dismissed or otherwise disposed of.

(J) **Certification of proceedings.** In the event that a counterclaim, cross-claim, or third-party claim exceeds the jurisdiction of the court, the court shall certify the proceedings in the case to the court of common pleas.

[Effective: July 1, 1970; amended effective July 1, 1971.]

RULE 14.   Third Party Practice

(A)   When defendant may bring in third party. At any time after commencement of the action a defending party, as a third-party plaintiff, may cause a summons and complaint to be served upon a person not a party to the action who is or may be liable to him for all or part of the plaintiff's claim against him. The third-party plaintiff need not obtain leave to make the service if he files the third-party complaint not later than fourteen days after he serves his original answer. Otherwise he must obtain leave on motion upon notice to all parties to the action. The person served with the summons and third-party complaint, hereinafter called the third-party defendant, shall make his defenses to the third-party plaintiff's claim as provided in Rule 12 and his counterclaims against the third-party plaintiff and cross-claims against other third-party defendants as provided in Rule 13. The third-party defendant may assert against the plaintiff any defenses which the third-party plaintiff has to the plaintiff's claim. The third-party defendant may also assert any claim against the plaintiff arising out of the transaction or occurrence that is the subject matter of the plaintiff's claim against the third-party plaintiff. The plaintiff may assert any claim against the third-party defendant arising out of the transaction or occurrence that is the subject matter of the plaintiff's claim against the third-party plaintiff, and the third-party defendant thereupon shall assert his defenses as provided in Rule 12 and his counterclaims and cross-claims as provided in Rule 13. Any party may move to strike the third-party claim, or for its severance or separate trial. If the third-party defendant is an employee, agent, or servant of the third-party plaintiff, the court shall order a separate trial upon the motion of any plaintiff. A third-party defendant may proceed under this rule against any person not a party to the action who is or may be liable to him for all or part of the claim made in the action against the third-party defendant.

(B)   When plaintiff may bring in third party. When a counterclaim is asserted against a plaintiff, he may cause a third party to be brought in under circumstances which under this rule would entitle a defendant to do so.

[Effective: July 1, 1970.]

RULE 15.   Amended and Supplemental Pleadings

(A)   Amendments. A party may amend its pleading once as a matter of course within twenty-eight days after serving it or, if the pleading is one to which a responsive pleading is required within twenty-eight days after service of a responsive pleading or twenty-eight days after service of a motion under Civ.R. 12(B), (E), or (F), whichever is earlier. In all other cases, a party may amend its pleading only with the opposing party's written consent or the court's leave. The court shall freely give leave when justice so requires. Unless the court orders otherwise, any required response to an amended pleading must be made within the time remaining to respond to the original pleading or within fourteen days after service of the amended pleading, whichever is later.

(B)   Amendments to conform to the evidence. When issues not raised by the pleadings are tried by express or implied consent of the parties, they shall be treated in all respects as if they had been raised in the pleadings. Such amendment of the pleadings as may be necessary to cause them to conform to the evidence and to raise these issues may be made upon motion of any party at any time, even after judgment. Failure to amend as provided herein does not affect the result of the trial of these issues. If evidence is objected to at the trial on the ground that it is not within the issues made by the pleadings, the court may allow the pleadings to be amended and shall do so freely when the presentation of the merits of the action will be subserved thereby and the objecting party fails to satisfy the court that the admission of such evidence would prejudice him in maintaining his action or defense upon the merits. The court may grant a continuance to enable the objecting party to meet such evidence.

(C)   Relation back of amendments. Whenever the claim or defense asserted in the amended pleading arose out of the conduct, transaction, or occurrence set forth or attempted to be set forth in the original pleading, the amendment relates back to the date of the original pleading. An amendment changing the party against whom a claim is asserted relates back if the foregoing provision is satisfied and, within the period provided by law for commencing the action against him, the party to be brought in by amendment (1) has received such notice of the institution of the action that he will not be prejudiced in maintaining his defense on the merits, and (2) knew or should have known that, but for a mistake concerning the identity of the proper party, the action would have been brought against him.

The delivery or mailing of process to this state, a municipal corporation or other governmental agency, or the responsible officer of any of the foregoing, subject to service of process under Rule 4 through Rule 4.6, satisfies the requirements of clauses (1) and (2) of the preceding paragraph if the above entities or officers thereof would have been proper defendants upon the original pleading. Such entities or officers thereof or both may be brought into the action as defendants.

(D) **Amendments where name of party unknown.** When the plaintiff does not know the name of a defendant, that defendant may be designated in a pleading or proceeding by any name and description. When the name is discovered, the pleading or proceeding must be amended accordingly. The plaintiff, in such case, must aver in the complaint the fact that he could not discover the name. The summons must contain the words "name unknown," and a copy thereof must be served personally upon the defendant.

(E) **Supplemental pleadings.** Upon motion of a party the court may, upon reasonable notice and upon such terms as are just, permit him to serve a supplemental pleading setting forth transactions or occurrences or events which have happened since the date of the pleading sought to be supplemented. Permission may be granted even though the original pleading is defective in its statement of a claim for relief or defense. If the court deems it advisable that the adverse party plead to the supplemental pleading, it shall so order, specifying the time therefor.

[Effective: July 1, 1970; amended effective: July 1, 2013.]

Staff Notes (July 1, 2013 Amendments)

Rule 15(A) is amended to allow amendment without leave of court of a complaint, or other pleading requiring a responsive pleading, for a period of 28 days after the service of a responsive pleading or motion. Under the prior rule, amendment without leave of court was limited to pleadings not requiring a response or to which a required response had not been served.

Rule 15(A) is also amended to limit amendment without leave of court of a complaint or other pleading requiring a responsive pleading, to a period of 28 days after service of the pleading when a response has not been served. Under the prior rule, the time for amendment without leave of court under those circumstances was not limited, and could be made at any time prior to service of a response.

The 2013 changes to Civ.R. 15(A) are modeled on the 2009 amendments to Fed.R.Civ.P. 15(a) and made for the same reasons that prompted those amendments.

RULE 16.   Pretrial Procedure

In any action, the court may schedule one or more conferences before trial to accomplish the following objectives:

(1) The possibility of settlement of the action;

(2) The simplification of the issues;

(3) Itemizations of expenses and special damages;

(4) The necessity of amendments to the pleadings;

(5) The exchange of reports of expert witnesses expected to be called by each party;

(6) The exchange of medical reports and hospital records;

(7) The number of expert witnesses;

(8) The timing, methods of search and production, and the limitations, if any, to be applied to the discovery of documents and electronically stored information;

(9) The adoption of any agreements by the parties for asserting claims of privilege or for protecting designated materials after production;

(10) The imposition of sanctions as authorized by Civ. R. 37;

(11) The possibility of obtaining:

> (a) Admissions of fact;

> (b) Agreements on admissibility of documents and other evidence to avoid unnecessary testimony or other proof during trial.

(12) Other matters which may aid in the disposition of the action.

The production by any party of medical reports or hospital records does not constitute a waiver of the privilege granted under section 2317.02 of the Revised Code.

The court may, and on the request of either party shall, make a written order that recites the action taken at the conference. The court shall enter the order and submit copies to the parties. Unless modified, the order shall control the subsequent course of action.

Upon reasonable notice to the parties, the court may require that parties, or their representatives or insurers, attend a conference or participate in other pretrial proceedings.

[Effective: July 1, 1970; amended effective July 1, 1993; July 1, 2008.]

Staff Note (July 1, 2008 Amendment)

New subsections (8) and (9) are added to clarify that issues relating to discovery of documents and electronically stored information are appropriate topics for discussion and resolution during pretrial conferences. Other linguistic changes, including those made to the subsections (7), (11) and (12) and to the final paragraph of Rule 16, are stylistic rather than substantive.

TITLE IV. PARTIES

RULE 17.   Parties Plaintiff and Defendant; Capacity

(A)   Real party in interest. Every action shall be prosecuted in the name of the real party in interest. An executor, administrator, guardian, bailee, trustee of an express trust, a party with whom or in whose name a contract has been made for the benefit of another, or a party authorized by statute may sue in his name as such representative without joining with him the party for whose benefit the action is brought. When a statute of this state so provides, an action for the use or benefit of another shall be brought in the name of this state. No action shall be dismissed on the ground that it is not prosecuted in the name of the real party in interest until a reasonable time has been allowed after objection for ratification of commencement of the action by, or joinder or substitution of, the real party in interest. Such ratification, joinder, or substitution shall have the same effect as if the action had been commenced in the name of the real party in interest.

(B)   Minors or incompetent persons. Whenever a minor or incompetent person has a representative, such as a guardian or other like fiduciary, the representative may sue or defend on behalf of the minor or incompetent person. If a minor or incompetent person does not have a duly appointed representative the minor may sue by a next friend or defend by a guardian ad litem. When a minor or incompetent person is not otherwise represented in an action the court shall appoint a guardian ad litem or shall make such other order as it deems proper for the protection of such minor or incompetent person.

[Effective: July 1, 1970; amended effective July 1, 1975; July 1, 1985.]

RULE 18.   Joinder of Claims and Remedies

(A)   Joinder of claims.   A party asserting a claim to relief as an original claim, counterclaim, cross-claim, or third-party claim, may join, either as independent or as alternate claims, as many claims, legal or equitable, as he has against an opposing party.

(B) Joinder of remedies; fraudulent conveyances.   Whenever a claim is one heretofore cognizable only after another claim has been prosecuted to a conclusion, the two claims may be joined in a single action; but the court shall grant relief in that action only in accordance with the relative substantive rights of the parties. In particular, a plaintiff may state a claim for money and a claim to have set aside a conveyance fraudulent as to him, without first having obtained a judgment establishing the claim for money.

[Effective: July 1, 1970.]

RULE 19. Joinder of Persons Needed for Just Adjudication

(A) **Persons to be joined if feasible.** A person who is subject to service of process shall be joined as a party in the action if (1) in his absence complete relief cannot be accorded among those already parties, or (2) he claims an interest relating to the subject of the action and is so situated that the disposition of the action in his absence may (a) as a practical matter impair or impede his ability to protect that interest or (b) leave any of the persons already parties subject to a substantial risk of incurring double, multiple, or otherwise inconsistent obligations by reason of his claimed interest, or (3) he has an interest relating to the subject of the action as an assignor, assignee, subrogor, or subrogee. If he has not been so joined, the court shall order that he be made a party upon timely assertion of the defense of failure to join a party as provided in Rule 12(B)(7). If the defense is not timely asserted, waiver is applicable as provided in Rule 12(G) and (H). If he should join as a plaintiff but refuses to do so, he may be made a defendant, or, in a proper case, an involuntary plaintiff. In the event that such joinder causes the relief sought to exceed the jurisdiction of the court, the court shall certify the proceedings in the action to the court of common pleas.

(B) **Determination by court whenever joinder not feasible.** If a person as described in subdivision (A)(1), (2), or (3) hereof cannot be made a party, the court shall determine whether in equity and good conscience the action should proceed among the parties before it, or should be dismissed, the absent person being thus regarded as indispensable. The factors to be considered by the court include: first, to what extent a judgment rendered in the person's absence might be prejudicial to him or those already parties; second, the extent to which, by protective provisions in the judgment, by the shaping of relief, or other measures, the prejudice can be lessened or avoided; third, whether a judgment rendered in the person's absence will be adequate; fourth, whether the plaintiff will have an adequate remedy if the action is dismissed for nonjoinder.

(C) **Pleading reasons for nonjoinder.** A pleading asserting a claim for relief shall state the names, if known to the pleader, of any persons as described in subdivision (A)(1), (2), or (3) hereof who are not joined, and the reasons why they are not joined.

(D) **Exception of class actions.** This rule is subject to the provisions of Rule 23.

[Effective: July 1, 1970.]

RULE 19.1 Compulsory Joinder

(A) **Persons to be joined.** A person who is subject to service of process shall be joined as a party in the action, except as provided in division (B) of this rule, if the person has an interest in or a claim arising out of the following situations:

(1) Personal injury or property damage to the person or property of the decedent which survives the decedent's death and a claim for wrongful death to the same decedent if caused by the same wrongful act;

(2) Personal injury or property damage to a spouse and a claim of the other spouse for loss of consortium or expenses or property damage if caused by the same wrongful act;

(3) Personal injury or property damage to a minor and a claim of the parent or guardian of the minor for loss of consortium or expenses or property damage if caused by the same wrongful act;

(4) Personal injury or property damage to an employee or agent and a claim of the employer or principal for property damage if caused by the same wrongful act.

(5) Personal injury to a parent and a claim of an adult emancipated child of the parent for loss of parental consortium if caused by the same wrongful act.

If the person has not been so joined, the court, subject to division (B) of this rule, shall order that the person be made a party upon timely assertion of the defense of failure to join a party as provided in Civ.R. 12(B)(7). If the defense is not timely asserted, waiver is applicable as provided in Civ.R. 12(G) and (H). If the person should join as a plaintiff but refuses to do so, the person may be made a defendant, or, in a proper case, an involuntary plaintiff. In the event that such joinder causes the relief sought to exceed the jurisdiction of the court, the court shall certify the proceedings in the action to the court of common pleas.

(B) **Exception to compulsory joinder.** If a party to the action or a person described in s division (A) shows good cause why that person should not be joined, the court shall proceed without requiring joinder.

(C) **Pleading reasons for nonjoinder.** A pleading asserting a claim for relief shall state the names, if known to the pleader, of any persons as described in divisions (A)(1), (2), (3), or (4) of this rule who are not joined, and the reasons why they are not joined.

(D) **Exception of class actions.** This rule is subject to the provisions of Rule 23.

[Effective: July 1, 1970; amended effective July 1, 1996; July 1, 2016; July 1, 2017.]

Staff Note (July 1, 2017 Amendment)

Civ.R. 19.1(A)(5). Claims of adult emancipated children for loss of parental consortium.

In *Rolf v. Tri State Motor Transit Co.*, 91 Ohio St.3d 380, 2001-Ohio-44, the Supreme Court of Ohio held that adult emancipated children may recover under Ohio law for the loss of parental consortium caused by injuries to a parent. The 2017 amendments add those claims to the claims enumerated under Civ.R. 19.1(A). The amendments also make other nonsubstantive changes.

Staff Note (July 1, 2016 Amendments)

The rule is amended to make gender neutral language changes, including at division 19.1(A)(2) where "spouse " is substituted for "husband or wife" as a person to be joined in particular actions. The amendments are made accordance with the July 26, 2015 Administrative Action of the Ohio Supreme Court, *06/26/2015 Administrative Actions*, 2015-Ohio-2568, which ordered that the Ohio Rules of Civil Procedure be construed and amended as gender neutral where appropriate to comply with the decision of U.S. Supreme Court in *Obergefell v. Hodges*, 576 U.S. ___ , 135 S.Ct. 2584 (2015). The amendments also make non-substantive stylistic changes to the rule.

Staff Note (July 1, 1996 Amendment)

Rule 19.1(A).   Persons to be Joined

The amendment conforms the rule to a clarification of law in the Supreme Court's decision in *Gallimore v. Children's Hosp. Med. Ctr.* (1993), 67 Ohio St.3d 244, 617 N.E.2d 1052. There, the Court stated in both syllabi that "Consortium includes society, companionship, affection, comfort, guidance and counsel." Since the word "consortium" is more inclusive than the word "services," it is more appropriate to use the former term. The amendment should avoid confusion between the rule and the substantive law in this regard.

RULE 20.   Permissive Joinder of Parties

(A)   Permissive joinder. All persons may join in one action as plaintiffs if they assert any right to relief jointly, severally, or in the alternative in respect of or arising out of the same transaction, occurrence, or succession or series of transactions or occurrences and if any question of law or fact common to all these persons will arise in the action. All persons may be joined in one action as defendants if there is asserted against them jointly, severally, or in the alternative, any right to relief in respect of or arising out of the same transaction, occurrence, or succession or series of transactions or occurrences and if any question of law or fact common to all defendants will arise in the action. A plaintiff or defendant need not be interested in obtaining or defending against all the relief demanded. Judgment may be given for one or more of the plaintiffs according to their respective rights to relief, and against one or more defendants according to their respective liabilities.

(B)   Separate trials. The court may make such orders as will prevent a party from being prejudiced, delayed, or put to expense by the inclusion of a party against whom he asserts no claim and who asserts no claim against him, and may order separate trials or make other orders to prevent prejudice or delay.

[Effective: July 1, 1970.]

RULE 21.   Misjoinder and Nonjoinder of Parties

Misjoinder of parties is not ground for dismissal of an action. Parties may be dropped or added by order of the court on motion of any party or of its own initiative at any stage of the action and on such terms as are just. Any claim against a party may be severed and proceeded with separately.

[Effective: July 1, 1970.]

RULE 22.   Interpleader

Persons having claims against the plaintiff may be joined as defendants and required to interplead when their claims are such that the plaintiff is or may be exposed to double or multiple liability. It is not ground for objection to the joinder that the claims of the several claimants or the titles on which their claims depend do not have a common origin or are not identical but are adverse to and independent of one another, or that the plaintiff avers that he is not liable in whole or in part to any or all of the claimants. A defendant exposed to similar liability may obtain such interpleader by way of cross-claim or counterclaim. The provisions of this rule supplement and do not in any way limit the joinder of parties permitted in Rule 20.

In such an action in which any part of the relief sought is a judgment for a sum of money or the disposition of a sum of money or the disposition of any other thing capable of delivery, a party may deposit all or any part of such sum or thing with the court upon notice to every other party and leave of court. The court may make an order for the safekeeping, payment or disposition of such sum or thing.

[Effective: July 1, 1970.]

RULE 23.   Class Actions

(A)   Prerequisites. One or more members of a class may sue or be sued as representative parties on behalf of all members only if:

(1)   the class is so numerous that joinder of all members is impracticable,

(2)   there are questions of law or fact common to the class,

(3)   the claims or defenses of the representative parties are typical of the claims or defenses of the class,

(4)   the representative parties will fairly and adequately protect the interests of the class.

(B) Types of class actions. A class action may be maintained if Civ.R. 23(A) is satisfied, and if:

(1)   prosecuting separate actions by or against individual class members would create a risk of:

(a)   inconsistent or varying adjudications with respect to individual class members that would establish incompatible standards of conduct for the party opposing the class; or

(b)   adjudications with respect to individual class members that, as a practical matter, would be dispositive of the interests of the other members not parties to the individual adjudications or would substantially impair or impede their ability to protect their interests; or

(2)   the party opposing the class has acted or refused to act on grounds that apply generally to the class, so that final injunctive relief or corresponding declaratory relief is appropriate respecting the class as a whole; or

(3)   the court finds that the questions of law or fact common to class members predominate over any questions affecting only individual members, and that a class action is superior to other available methods for fairly and efficiently adjudicating the controversy. The matters pertinent to these findings include:

(a)   the class members' interests in individually controlling the prosecution or defense of separate actions;

(b)   the extent and nature of any litigation concerning the controversy already begun by or against class members;

(c)   the desirability or undesirability of concentrating the litigation of the claims in the particular forum; and

(d)   the likely difficulties in managing a class action.

(C) Certification order; notice to class members; judgment; issues classes; subclasses.

(1)   Certification order

(a)   Time to issue. At an early practicable time after a person sues or is sued as a class representative, the court shall determine by order whether to certify the action as a class action.

(b)   Defining the class; appointing class counsel. An order that certifies a class action shall define the class and the class claims, issues, or defenses, and shall appoint class counsel under Civ.R. 23(F).

(c)   Altering or amending the order. An order that grants or denies class certification may be altered or amended before final judgment.

(2)   Notice.

(a)   For (B)(1) or (B)(2) classes. For any class certified under Civ.R. 23(B)(1) or (B)(2), the court may direct appropriate notice to the class.

(b)   For (B)(3) classes. For any class certified under Civ.R. 23(B)(3), the court shall direct to class members the best notice that is practicable under the circumstances, including individual notice to all members who can be identified through reasonable effort. The notice shall clearly and concisely state in plain, easily understood language:

> (i)   the nature of the action;
>
> (ii)   the definition of the class certified;
>
> (iii)   the class claims, issues, or defenses;
>
> (iv)   that a class member may enter an appearance through an attorney if the member so desires;
>
> (v)   that the court will exclude from the class any member who requests exclusion;
>
> (vi)   the time and manner for requesting exclusion; and

(vii)　the binding effect of a class judgment on members under Civ.R.　23(C)(3).

(3)　Judgment. Whether or not favorable to the class, the judgment in a class action shall:

(a)　for any class certified under Civ.R. 23(B)(1) or (B)(2), include and describe those whom the court finds to be class members: and

(b)　for any class certified under Civ.R. 23(B)(3), include and specify or describe those to whom the Civ.R. 23(C)(2) notice was directed, who have not requested exclusion, and whom the court finds to be class members.

(4)　Particular issues. When appropriate, an action may be brought or maintained as a class action with respect to particular issues.

(5)　Subclasses. When appropriate, a class may be divided into subclasses that are each treated as a class under this rule.

(D)　Conducting the action.

(1)　In general. In conducting an action under this rule, the court may issue orders that:

(a)　determine the course of proceedings or prescribe measures to prevent undue repetition or complication in presenting evidence or argument;

(b)　require to protect class members and fairly conduct the action giving appropriate notice to some or all class members of:

(i)　any step in the action;

(ii)　the proposed extent of the judgment; or

(iii)　the members' opportunity to signify whether they consider the representation fair and adequate, to intervene and present claims or defenses, or to otherwise come into the action;

(c)　impose conditions on the representative parties or on intervenors;

(d)　require that the pleadings be amended to eliminate allegations about representation of absent persons, and that the action proceed accordingly; or

(e)　deal with similar procedural matters.

(2)   Combining and amending orders. An order under Civ.R. 23(D)(1) may be altered or amended from time to time and may be combined with an order under Civ.R. 16.

(E)   Settlement, voluntary dismissal, or compromise. The claims, issues, or defenses of a certified class may be settled, voluntarily dismissed, or compromised only with the court's approval. The following procedures apply to a proposed settlement, voluntary dismissal, or compromise:

(1)   The court shall direct notice in a reasonable manner to all class members who would be bound by the proposal.

(2)   If the proposal would bind class members, the court may approve it only after a hearing and on finding that it is fair, reasonable, and adequate.

(3)   The parties seeking approval shall file a statement identifying any agreement made in connection with the proposal.

(4)   If the class action was previously certified under Civ.R. 23(B)(3), the court may refuse to approve a settlement unless it affords a new opportunity to request exclusion to individual class members who had an earlier opportunity to request exclusion but did not do so.

(5)   Any class member may object to the proposal if it requires court approval under this division (E); the objection may be withdrawn only with the court's approval.

(F)   Class counsel.

(1)   Appointing class counsel. A court that certifies a class shall appoint class counsel. In appointing class counsel, the court:

    (a)   shall consider:

        (i)   the work counsel has done in identifying or investigating potential claims in the action;

        (ii)   counsel's experience in handling class actions, other complex litigation, and the types of claims asserted in the action;

        (iii)   counsel's knowledge of the applicable law; and

        (iv)   the resources that counsel will commit to representing the class;

    (b)   may consider any other matter pertinent to counsel's ability to fairly and adequately represent the interests of the class;

(c)   may order potential class counsel to provide information on any subject pertinent to the appointment and to propose terms for attorney's fees and nontaxable costs;

(d)   may include in the appointing order provisions about the award of attorney's fees or nontaxable costs under Civ.R. 23(G); and

(e)   may make further orders in connection with the appointment.

(2)   Standard for appointing class counsel. When one applicant seeks appointment as class counsel, the court may appoint that applicant only if the applicant is adequate under Civ.R. 23(F)(1) and (4). If more than one adequate applicant seeks appointment, the court shall appoint the applicant best able to represent the interests of the class.

(3)   Interim counsel. The court may designate interim counsel to act on behalf of a putative class before determining whether to certify the action as a class action.

(4)   Duty of class counsel. Class counsel shall fairly and adequately represent the interests of the class.

(G)   Attorney fees and nontaxable costs. In a certified class action, the court may award reasonable attorney's fees and nontaxable costs that are authorized by law or by the parties' agreement. The following procedures apply:

(1)   A claim for an award shall be made by motion. Notice of the motion shall be served on all parties and, for motions by class counsel, directed to class members in a reasonable manner.

(2)   A class member, or a party from whom payment is sought, may object to the motion.

(3)   The court may hold a hearing and shall state in writing the findings of fact found separately from the conclusions of law.

(4)   The court may refer issues related to the amount of the award to a magistrate as provided in Civ.R. 53.

(H)   Aggregation of claims. The claims of the class shall be aggregated in determining the jurisdiction of the court.

[Effective: July 1, 1970; July 1, 2015.]

Staff Note (July 1, 2015 Amendment)

The rule is amended to conform its provisions to the changes made to Federal Rule 23 since the 1970 adoption of the Ohio Rule. While Civ.R. 23 has remained unchanged since its adoption, the Federal rule, upon which the Ohio rule was originally modeled, has undergone significant changes to guide courts and parties in the conduct of class actions, most notably the substantive amendments made to the Federal rule in 1998 and the stylistic changes made in 2007. The changes to the Ohio rule include defining the class and appointing class counsel in the certification order; additional detail for the initial notice to Civ.R. 23(B)(3) class members and for the notice of a proposed settlement, voluntary dismissal, or compromise; and new provisions addressing the appointment of class counsel and the awarding of attorney fees and nontaxable costs.

RULE 23.1. Derivative Actions by Shareholders

In a derivative action brought by one or more legal or equitable owners of shares to enforce a right of a corporation, the corporation having failed to enforce a right which may properly be asserted by it, the complaint shall be verified and shall allege that the plaintiff was a shareholder at the time of the transaction of which he complains or that his share thereafter devolved on him by operation of law. The complaint shall also allege with particularity the efforts, if any, made by the plaintiff to obtain the action he desires from the directors and, if necessary, from the shareholders and the reasons for his failure to obtain the action or for not making the effort. The derivative action may not be maintained if it appears that the plaintiff does not fairly and adequately represent the interests of the shareholders similarly situated in enforcing the right of the corporation. The action shall not be dismissed or compromised without the approval of the court, and notice of the proposed dismissal or compromise shall be given to shareholders in such manner as the court directs.

[Effective: July 1, 1970.]

RULE 24. Intervention

(A) Intervention of right. Upon timely application anyone shall be permitted to intervene in an action: (1) when a statute of this state confers an unconditional right to intervene; or (2) when the applicant claims an interest relating to the property or transaction that is the subject of the action and the applicant is so situated that the disposition of the action may as a practical matter impair or impede the applicant's ability to protect that interest, unless the applicant's interest is adequately represented by existing parties.

(B) Permissive intervention. Upon timely application anyone may be permitted to intervene in an action: (1) when a statute of this state confers a conditional right to intervene; or (2) when an applicant's claim or defense and the main action have a question of law or fact in common. When a party to an action relies for ground of claim or defense upon any statute or executive order administered by a federal or state governmental officer or agency or upon any regulation, order, requirement or agreement issued or made pursuant to the statute or executive order, the officer or agency upon timely application may be permitted to intervene in the action. In exercising its discretion the court shall consider whether the intervention will unduly delay or prejudice the adjudication of the rights of the original parties.

(C) Procedure. A person desiring to intervene shall serve a motion to intervene upon the parties as provided in Civ.R. 5. The motion and any supporting memorandum shall state the grounds for intervention and shall be accompanied by a pleading, as defined in Civ.R. 7(A), setting forth the claim or defense for which intervention is sought. The same procedure shall be followed when a statute of this state gives a right to intervene.

[Effective: July 1, 1970; Amended July 1, 1999.]

Staff Note (July 1, 1999 Amendment)

Rule 24(A) Intervention of right

Masculine references were made gender-neutral; there were no substantive amendments to this division.

Rule 24(C) Procedure

The 1999 amendment was intended to clarify that the "pleading" to be filed with a motion to intervene requires more than just a memorandum in support of the motion to intervene. The Note following Form 17 in the Appendix of Forms was amended accordingly.

RULE 25.   Substitution of Parties

(A)   Death.

(1)   If a party dies and the claim is not thereby extinguished, the court shall, upon motion, order substitution of the proper parties. The motion for substitution may be made by any party or by the successors or representatives of the deceased party and shall be served on the parties as provided in Civ.R. 5 and upon persons not parties in the manner provided in Civ.R. 4 through Civ.R. 4.6 for the service of summons. Unless the motion for substitution is made not later than ninety days after the death is suggested upon the record by service of a statement of the fact of the death as provided herein for the service of the motion, the action shall be dismissed as to the deceased party.

(2)   In the event of the death of one or more of the plaintiffs or of one or more of the defendants in an action in which the right sought to be enforced survives only to the surviving plaintiffs or only against the surviving defendants, the action does not abate. The death shall be suggested upon the record and the action shall proceed in favor of or against the surviving parties.

(B)   Incompetency. If a party is adjudged incompetent, the court upon motion served as provided in division (A) of this rule shall allow the action to be continued by or against the party's representative.

(C)   Transfer of interest. In case of any transfer of interest, the action may be continued by or against the original party, unless the court upon motion directs the person to whom the interest is transferred to be substituted in the action or joined with the original party. Service of the motion shall be made as provided in division (A) of this rule.

(D)   Public officers; death or separation from office.

(1)   When a public officer is a party to an action in the public officer's official capacity and during its pendency dies, resigns, or otherwise ceases to hold office, the action does not abate and the public officer's successor is automatically substituted as a party. Proceedings following the substitution shall be in the name of the substituted party, but any misnomer not affecting the substantial rights of the parties shall be disregarded. An order of substitution may be entered at any time, but the omission to enter such an order shall not affect the substitution.

(2)   When a public officer sues or is sued in the public officer's official capacity, the public officer may be described as a party by official title rather than by name. The court however may require the addition of the public officer's name.

(E)   Suggestion of death or incompetency Upon the death or incompetency of a party it shall be the duty of the attorney of record for that party to suggest such fact upon the record within fourteen days after the attorney acquires actual knowledge of the death or incompetency of that party. The suggestion of death or incompetency shall be served on all other parties as provided in Civ.R. 5.

[Effective: July 1, 1970; July 1, 2015.]

Staff Note (July 1, 2015 Amendment)

Rule 25(A) is amended by eliminating the reference to a requirement for service of a "notice of hearing" which is no longer required by Civ.R. 6(B).

TITLE V. DISCOVERY

RULE 26.   General Provisions Governing Discovery

(A) Policy; discovery methods. It is the policy of these rules (1) to preserve the right of attorneys to prepare cases for trial with that degree of privacy necessary to encourage them to prepare their cases thoroughly and to investigate not only the favorable but the unfavorable aspects of such cases and (2) to prevent an attorney from taking undue advantage of an adversary's industry or efforts.

Parties may obtain discovery by one or more of the following methods: deposition upon oral examination or written questions; written interrogatories; production of documents, electronically stored information, or things or permission to enter upon land or other property, for inspection and other purposes; physical and mental examinations; and requests for admission. Unless the court orders otherwise, the frequency of use of these methods is not limited.

(B) Scope of discovery. Unless otherwise ordered by the court in accordance with these rules, the scope of discovery is as follows:

(1) In General. Parties may obtain discovery regarding any matter, not privileged, which is relevant to the subject matter involved in the pending action, whether it relates to the claim or defense of the party seeking discovery or to the claim or defense of any other party, including the existence, description, nature, custody, condition and location of any books, documents, electronically stored information, or other tangible things and the identity and location of persons having knowledge of any discoverable matter. It is not ground for objection that the information sought will be inadmissible at the trial if the information sought appears reasonably calculated to lead to the discovery of admissible evidence.

(2) Insurance agreements. A party may obtain discovery of the existence and contents of any insurance agreement under which any person carrying on an insurance business may be liable to satisfy part or all of a judgment which may be entered in the action or to indemnify or reimburse for payments made to satisfy the judgment. Information concerning the insurance agreement is not by reason of disclosure subject to comment or admissible in evidence at trial.

(3) Trial preparation: materials. Subject to the provisions of subdivision (B)(5) of this rule, a party may obtain discovery of documents, electronically stored information and tangible things prepared in anticipation of litigation or for trial by or for another party or by or for that other party's representative (including his attorney, consultant, surety, indemnitor, insurer, or agent) only upon a showing of good cause therefor. A statement concerning the action or its subject matter previously given by the party seeking the statement may be obtained without showing good cause. A statement of a party is (a) a written statement signed or otherwise adopted or approved by the party, or (b) a stenographic, mechanical, electrical, or other recording, or a transcription thereof, which is a substantially verbatim recital of an oral statement which was made by the party and contemporaneously recorded.

(4) Electronically stored information. A party need not provide discovery of electronically stored information when the production imposes undue burden or expense. On motion to compel discovery or for a protective order, the party from whom electronically stored information is sought must show that the information is not reasonably accessible because of undue burden or expense. If a showing of undue burden or expense is made, the court may nonetheless order production of electronically stored information if the requesting party shows good cause. The court shall consider the following factors when determining if good cause exists:

(a) whether the discovery sought is unreasonably cumulative or duplicative;

(b) whether the information sought can be obtained from some other source that is less burdensome, or less expensive;

(c) whether the party seeking discovery has had ample opportunity by discovery in the action to obtain the information sought; and

(d) whether the burden or expense of the proposed discovery outweighs the likely benefit, taking into account the relative importance in the case of the issues on which electronic discovery is sought, the amount in controversy, the parties' resources, and the importance of the proposed discovery in resolving the issues.

In ordering production of electronically stored information, the court may specify the format, extent, timing, allocation of expenses and other conditions for the discovery of the electronically stored information.

(5)   Trial preparation: experts.

(a) Subject to the provisions of division (B)(5)(b) of this rule and Civ.R. 35(B), a party may discover facts known or opinions held by an expert retained or specially employed by another party in anticipation of litigation or preparation for trial only upon a showing that the party seeking discovery is unable without undue hardship to obtain facts and opinions on the same subject by other means or upon a showing of other exceptional circumstances indicating that denial of discovery would cause manifest injustice.

(b) As an alternative or in addition to obtaining discovery under division (B)(5)(a) of this rule, a party by means of interrogatories may require any other party (i) to identify each person whom the other party expects to call as an expert witness at trial, and (ii) to state the subject matter on which the expert is expected to testify. Thereafter, any party may discover from the expert or the other party facts known or opinions held by the expert which are relevant to the stated subject matter. Discovery of the expert's opinions and the grounds therefor is restricted to those previously given to the other party or those to be given on direct examination at trial.

(c) Drafts of any report provided by any expert, regardless of the form in which the draft is recorded, are protected by division (B)(3) of this rule.

(d) Communications between a party's attorney and any witness identified as an expert witness under division (B)(5)(b) of this rule regardless of the form of the communications, are protected by division (B)(3) of this rule except to the extent that the communications:

(i) relate to compensation for the expert's study or testimony;

(ii) identify facts or data that the party's attorney provided and that the expert considered in forming the opinions to be expressed; or

(iii) identify assumptions that the party's attorney provided and that the expert relied on in forming the opinions to be expressed.

(e) The court may require that the party seeking discovery under division (B)(5)(b) of this rule pay the expert a reasonable fee for time spent in responding to discovery, and, with respect to discovery permitted under division (B)(5)(a) of this rule, may require a party to pay another party a fair portion of the fees and expenses incurred by the latter party in obtaining facts and opinions from the expert.

(6)   Claims of Privilege or Protection of Trial-Preparation Materials.

(a) Information Withheld. When information subject to discovery is withheld on a claim that it is privileged or subject to protection as trial preparation materials, the claim shall be made expressly and shall be supported by a description of the nature of the documents, communications, or things not produced that is sufficient to enable the demanding party to contest the claim.

(b) Information Produced. If information is produced in discovery that is subject to a claim of privilege or of protection as trial preparation material, the party making the claim may notify any party that received the information of the claim and the basis for it. After being notified, a receiving party must promptly return, sequester, or destroy the specified information and any copies within the party's possession, custody or control. A party may not use or disclose the information until the claim is resolved. A receiving party may promptly present the information to the court under seal for a determination of the claim of privilege or of protection as trial preparation material. If the receiving party disclosed the information before being notified, it must take reasonable steps to retrieve it. The producing party must preserve the information until the claim is resolved.

(C) Protective orders. Upon motion by any party or by the person from whom discovery is sought, and for good cause shown, the court in which the action is pending may make any order that justice requires to protect a party or person from annoyance, embarrassment, oppression, or undue burden or expense, including one or more of the following: (1) that the discovery not be had; (2) that the discovery may be had only on specified terms and conditions, including a designation of the time or place; (3) that the discovery may be had only by a method of discovery other than that selected by the party seeking discovery; (4) that certain matters not be inquired into or that the scope of the discovery be limited to certain matters; (5) that discovery be conducted with no one present except persons designated by the court; (6) that a deposition after being sealed be opened only by order of the court; (7) that a trade secret or other confidential research, development, or commercial information not be disclosed or be disclosed only in a designated way; (8) that the parties simultaneously file specified documents or information enclosed in sealed envelopes to be opened as directed by the court.

If the motion for a protective order is denied in whole or in part, the court, on terms and conditions as are just, may order that any party or person provide or permit discovery. The provisions of Civ. R. 37(A)(5) apply to the award of expenses incurred in relation to the motion.

Before any person moves for a protective order under this rule, that person shall make a reasonable effort to resolve the matter through discussion with the attorney or unrepresented party seeking discovery. A motion for a protective order shall be accompanied by a statement reciting the effort made to resolve the matter in accordance with this paragraph.

(D) Sequence and timing of discovery. Unless the court upon motion, for the convenience of parties and witnesses and in the interests of justice, orders otherwise, methods of discovery may be used in any sequence and the fact that a party is conducting discovery, whether by deposition or otherwise, shall not operate to delay any other party's discovery.

(E) Supplementation of responses. A party who has responded to a request for discovery with a response that was complete when made is under no duty to supplement his response to include information thereafter acquired, except as follows:

(1) A party is under a duty seasonably to supplement his response with respect to any question directly addressed to (a) the identity and location of person having knowledge of discoverable matters, and (b) the identity of each person expected to be called as an expert witness as trial and the subject matter on which he is expected to testify.

(2) A party who knows or later learns that his response is incorrect is under a duty seasonably to correct the response.

(3) A duty to supplement responses may be imposed by order of the court, agreement of the parties, or at any time prior to trial through requests for supplementation of prior responses.

[Effective: July 1, 1970; amended effective July 1, 1994; amended effective July 1, 2008; July 1, 2012.]

Staff Note (July 1, 2012 Amendment)

Civ.R. 26(B)(5) is amended to clarify the scope of expert discovery and align Ohio practice with the 2010 amendments to the Federal Rules of Civil Procedure relating to a party's ability to obtain discovery from expert witnesses who are expected to be called at trial. The amendment provides work product protection for draft reports and communications between attorneys and testifying experts, except for three categories of communications: communications that relate to compensation for the expert's study or testimony; communications containing facts or data that the party's attorney provided and that the expert considered in forming the opinions to be expressed; and communications containing any assumptions that the party's attorney provided and that the expert relied upon in forming the opinions to be expressed.

Staff Note (July 1, 2008 Amendment)

Several provisions of the rule are amended to clarify that discovery of electronically stored information is permitted.

Civ. R. 26(A), (B)(1) and (B)(3) include explicit references to discovery of electronically stored information, a type of discovery that was arguably covered in the broad definition of discoverable materials previously articulated in the rule.

Civ. R. 26(B)(4) is new language that tempers the virtually unlimited discovery traditionally authorized by Rule 26(B)(1) by providing that, as is the case with all discovery, a party is not required to produce electronically stored information if production is too burdensome or expensive compared to the potential value of the discovery. These provisions also provide guidance to trial courts for resolving disputes over claims of excessive burdensomeness and expense. The last sentence of this section reiterates the power that trial judges inherently possess to regulate discovery of electronically stored information, including allocating costs and other details related to production of electronically stored information.

Existing Rule 26(B)(4) is renumbered as 26(B)(5) but no other changes are made.

Civ. R. 26(B)(6)(a) and (b) apply to all discovery not just electronically stored information. Rule 26(B)(6)(a) establishes procedures parties must follow when withholding documents (including electronically stored information) based on privilege.

Civ. R. 26(B)(6)(b) provides a mechanism for a party to retrieve inadvertently produced documents from an opponent. This is often called a "clawback" provision. A similar provision is included in the federal rules and the rules of other states that have modified their civil rules to accommodate e-discovery. It applies to all materials produced by a party, not just electronically stored information.

The rule directs a party that has inadvertently provided privileged documents to an opponent to notify the opponent. Once notification is received, the recipient must "return, sequester, or destroy" the inadvertently proceeded information and not use the information in any way. A procedure is also provided for the court to resolve the claim of privilege relating to the materials. The amendments to Rule 26(B)(6)(b) do not conflict with the new Ohio Rule Prof. Conduct 4.4(b) requirement that an attorney who "knows or reasonably should know that the document was inadvertently sent" must "promptly notify the sender." Rather, the two rules work in concert: Rule 26(B)(6)(b) is triggered when actual notification is received from the sender that the material was inadvertently sent, and Ohio Rule Prof. Conduct 4.4(b) is animated when the recipient realizes that the material provided by an opponent is likely privileged.

RULE 27. Perpetuation of Testimony--Depositions Before Action or Pending Appeal

(A) **Before action.**

(1) **Petition.** A person who desires to perpetuate his own testimony or the testimony of another person regarding any matter that may be cognizable in any court may file a petition in the court of common pleas in the county of the residence of any expected adverse party. The petitioner shall verify that he believes the facts stated in the petition are true. The petition shall be entitled in the name of the petitioner and shall show:

(a) That the petitioner or his personal representatives, heirs, beneficiaries, successors, or assigns may be parties to an action or proceeding cognizable in a court but is presently unable to bring or defend it;

(b) The subject matter of the expected action or proceeding and his interest therein (if the validity or construction of any written instrument connected with the subject matter of the deposition may be called in question a copy shall be attached to the petition);

(c) The facts which he desires to establish by the proposed testimony and his reasons for desiring to perpetuate it;

(d) The names or, if the names are unknown, a description of the persons he expects will be adverse parties and their addresses so far as known;

(e) The names and addresses of the persons to be examined and the subject matter of the testimony which he expects to elicit from each.

The petition shall then ask for an order authorizing the petitioner to take the depositions of the persons to be examined named in the petition, for the purpose of perpetuating their testimony.

(2) **Notice and service.** The petitioner shall thereafter serve a notice upon each person named in the petition as an expected adverse party, together with a copy of the petition, stating that the petitioner will apply to the court, at a time and place named therein, for the order described in the petition. At least twenty-eight days before the date of hearing, unless the court upon application and showing of extraordinary circumstances prescribes a hearing on shorter notice, the notice shall be served either within or outside of this state by a method provided in Rule 4 through Rule 4.6 for service of summons, or in any other manner affording actual notice, as directed by order of the court. But if it appears to the court that an expected adverse party cannot be given actual notice, the court shall appoint a competent attorney to cross-examine the deponent; such attorney shall be allowed reasonable fees therefor which shall be taxed as costs. If any expected adverse party is a minor or incompetent the provisions of Rule 17(B) apply.

(3)   **Order and examination.** If the court is satisfied that the allowance of the petition may prevent a failure or delay of justice, and that the petitioner is unable to bring or defend the contemplated action, the court shall order the testimony perpetuated, designating the deponents, the subject matter of the examination, when, where, and before whom their deposition shall be taken, and whether orally or upon written questions. The depositions may then be taken in accordance with these rules; and the court may make orders of the character provided for by Rule 34, Rule 35 and Rule 37. For the purpose of applying these rules to depositions for perpetuating testimony, each reference therein to the court in which the action is pending shall be deemed to refer to the court in which the petition for such deposition was filed.

(4)   **Use of deposition.** Subject to the same limitations and objections as though the deponent were testifying at the trial in person, and to the provisions of Rule 26 and Rule 32(A) a deposition taken in accordance with this rule may be used as evidence in any action subsequently brought in any court, where the deposition is that of a party to the action, or where the issue is such that an interested party in the proceedings in which the deposition was taken had the right and opportunity for cross-examination with an interest and motive similar to that which the adverse party has in the action in which the deposition is offered. But, except where the deposition is that of a party to the action and is offered against the party, the deposition may not be used as evidence unless the deponent is unavailable as a witness at the trial.

(B)   **Pending appeal.** If an appeal has been taken from a judgment of any court, a party who desires to perpetuate testimony may make a motion in the court where the action was tried, for leave to take depositions upon the same notice and service thereof as provided in (A)(2) of this rule. The motion shall show the names and addresses of the persons to be examined, the subject matter of the testimony which he expects to elicit from each, and the reasons for perpetuating their testimony. If the court is satisfied that the motion is proper to avoid a failure or delay of justice, it may make an order allowing the deposition to be taken and may make orders of the character provided for by Rule 34, Rule 35, and Rule 37. The depositions may be taken and used in the same manner and under the same conditions as are prescribed for depositions in Rule 26 and Rule 32(A).

(C)   **Perpetuation by actions.** This rule does not limit the inherent power of a court to entertain an action to perpetuate testimony.

(D)   **Filing of depositions.** Depositions taken under this rule shall be filed with the court in which the petition is filed or the motion is made.

(E)   **Costs of deposition.** The party taking any deposition under this rule shall pay the costs thereof and of all proceedings hereunder, unless otherwise ordered by the court.

(F)   **Depositions taken in other states.** A deposition taken under similar procedure of another jurisdiction is admissible in this state to the same extent as a deposition taken under this rule.

(G)   Construction of rule. This rule shall be so construed as to effectuate the general purpose to make uniform the law of those states which have similar rules or statutes.

[Effective: July 1, 1970; amended effective July 1, 1972.]

RULE 28. Persons Before Whom Depositions May be Taken

(A) **Depositions within state.** Depositions may be taken in this state before: a person authorized to administer any oath by the laws of this state, a person appointed by the court in which the action is pending, or a person agreed upon by written stipulation of all the parties.

(B) **Depositions outside state.** Depositions may be taken outside this state before: a person authorized to administer oaths in the place where the deposition is taken, a person appointed by the court in which the action is pending, a person agreed upon by written stipulation of all the parties, or, in any foreign country, by any consular officer of the United States within his consular district.

(C) **Disqualification for interest.**

Unless the parties agree otherwise as provided in Civ. R. 29, depositions shall not be taken before a person who:

(1)   is a relative or employee of or attorney for any of the parties, or

(2)   is a relative or employee of an attorney for any of the parties, or

(3)   is financially interested in the action.

(D) **Prohibited contracts.**

(1)   Any blanket contract for private court reporting services, not related to a particular case or reporting incident, shall be prohibited between a private court reporter or any other person with whom a private court reporter has a principal and agency relationship, and any attorney, party to an action, party having a financial interest in an action, or any entity providing the services of a shorthand reporter.

(2)   "Blanket contract" means a contract under which a court reporter, court recorder, or court reporting firm agrees to perform all court reporting or court recording services for a client for two or more cases at a rate of compensation fixed in the contract.

(3)   Negotiating or bidding reasonable fees, equal to all parties, on a case-by-case basis is not prohibited.

(4)   Division (D) of this rule does not apply to the courts or the administrative tribunals of this state.

[Effective: July 1, 1970; amended effective July 1, 2001.]

Staff Note (July 1, 2001 Amendment)

Civil Rule 28   Persons Before Whom Depositions May Be Taken
Civil Rule 28(D)   Prohibited contracts

The amendment effective July 1, 2001 added division (D), Prohibited contracts. This rule was amended in response to communications from members of the bench and bar indicating that certain types of long-term financial arrangements between court reporters, court reporting firms, or other firms and litigants or other entities have given rise to concerns about the appearance of or potential for differential treatment of parties to an action. The appearance of impartiality and the existence of impartiality are no less important for those officers who take depositions than for judicial officers and other persons whose responsibilities are integral to the administration of justice.

The general prohibition of division (D) does not apply to situations where lower fees may be negotiated, provided the fees are the same for all parties and are negotiated on a case-by-case basis [division (D)(3)]. Also, the prohibition does not extend to governmental entities, which may be required by law to obtain court reporting services on a long-term basis through competitive bidding. See, e.g., sections 125.05(B) and 125.07 of the Revised Code.

The prohibition in division (D), like the pre-existing prohibitions in division (C), is enforceable by the court in which the underlying action is pending. Enforceability is implicitly recognized by Civ. R. 32(D)(2), which requires reasonable diligence of a party in raising a disqualification issue. See *Berwald v. Ford Motor Co.*, 1982 WL 5337, No. 44064 (8th Dist. Ct. App., Cuyahoga, May 6, 1982) (objection held waived); J. McCormac, Ohio Civil Rules Practice, section 10.37 at 268 (2d ed. 1992) (noting that "[c]onceivably, this objection could be made at trial if it were not discovered until that time that the officer taking the deposition was disqualified for interest under Civil Rule 28(C) and there had been no previous waiver or stipulation"). Trial courts also have extensive inherent power to control discovery. See, e.g., *State ex rel. Abner v. Elliott*, 85 Ohio St.3d 11, 16 (1999); *State ex rel. Grandview Hosp. & Med. Ctr.*, 51 Ohio St. 3d 94, 95 (1990) (citing Staff Note to Civ. R. 26(C) and Civ. R. 37); *State ex rel. Pfeiffer v. Common Pleas Ct. of Lorain Cty.*, 13 Ohio St. 2d 133, 136-37 (1968) (noting "the inherent power of courts to do all things necessary to the administration of justice and to protect its own powers and processes and the rights of those who invoke its processes" which "inheres in the constitutional grant of judicial power to the courts").

Pursuant to the effective date provisions of Civ. R. 86(Y), Civ. R. 28(D) will apply only to (1) depositions taken in actions brought after July 1, 2001, and (2) in actions pending on July 1, 2001, to depositions taken on and after July 1, 2001.

In division (C), grammatical and structural revisions were made. No substantive amendment to division (C) was intended.

RULE 29.   Stipulations Regarding Discovery Procedure

Unless the court orders otherwise, the parties may by written stipulation (1) provide that depositions may be taken before any person, at any time or place, upon any notice, and in any manner and when so taken may be used like other depositions; and (2) modify the procedures provided by these rules for other methods of discovery.

[Effective: July 1, 1970.]

RULE 30.   Depositions upon oral examination

(A)   When depositions may be taken. After commencement of the action, any party may take the testimony of any person, including a party, by deposition upon oral examination. The attendance of a witness deponent may be compelled by the use of subpoena as provided by Civ.R. 45. The attendance of a party deponent may be compelled by the use of notice of examination as provided by division (B) of this rule. The deposition of a person confined in prison may be taken only by leave of court on such terms as the court prescribes.

(B)   Notice of Examination; General Requirements; Nonstenographic Recording; Production of Documents and Things; Deposition of Organization; Deposition by Telephone or Other Means.

(1)   A party desiring to take the deposition of any person upon oral examination shall give reasonable notice in writing to every other party to the action. The notice shall state the time and place for taking the deposition and the name and address of each person to be examined, if known, and, if the name is not known, a general description sufficient to identify the person or the particular class or group to which the person belongs. If a subpoena duces tecum is to be served on the person to be examined, a designation of the materials to be produced shall be attached to or included in the notice.

(2)   If any party shows that when the party was served with notice the party was unable, through the exercise of diligence, to obtain counsel to represent the party at the taking of the deposition, the deposition may not be used against the party.

(3)   If a party taking a deposition wishes to have the testimony recorded by other than stenographic means, the notice shall specify the manner of recording, preserving, and filing the deposition. The court may require stenographic taking or make any other order to ensure that the recorded testimony will be accurate and trustworthy. With prior notice to the deponent and other parties, any party may designate another method for recording the testimony in addition to that specified in the original notice. That party bears the expense of the additional record or transcript unless the court orders otherwise.

(4)   The notice to a party deponent may be accompanied by a request made in compliance with Civ.R. 34 for the production of documents and tangible things at the taking of the deposition.

(5)   A party, in the party's notice, may name as the deponent a public or private corporation, a partnership, or an association and designate with reasonable particularity the matters on which examination is requested. The organization so named shall choose one or more of its proper employees, officers, agents, or other persons duly authorized to testify on its behalf. The persons so designated shall testify as to matters known or available to the organization. Division (B)(5) does not preclude taking a deposition by any other procedure authorized in these rules.

(6)   The parties may stipulate or the court may upon motion order that a deposition be taken by telephone or other remote means. For purposes of this rule, Civ.R. 28, and Civ.R. 45(C), a deposition taken by telephone is taken in the county and at the place where the deponent answers the questions.

(C)   Examination and cross-examination; record of examination; oath; objections; written questions.

(1) Examination and cross-examination. Each party at the deposition may examine the deponent without regard to which party served notice or called the deposition. In all other respects the examination and cross-examination of a deponent may proceed as they would at trial under the Ohio Rules of Evidence, except Evid.R. 103 and Evid.R. 615. After putting the deponent under oath or affirmation, the officer shall record the testimony by the method designated under Civ.R. 30(B)(3). The testimony shall be recorded by the officer personally or by a person acting in the presence and under the direction of the officer.

(2) Objections. An objection made at the time of the examination whether to evidence, a party's conduct, to the officer's qualifications, to the manner of taking the deposition, or to any other aspect of the deposition shall be noted on the record, but the examination still proceeds, the testimony taken subject to any objection. An objection shall be stated concisely in a nonargumentative and nonsuggestive manner. A person may instruct a deponent not to answer only when necessary to preserve a privilege, to enforce a limitation ordered by a court, or to present a motion under Civ.R. 30(D).

(3) Participating through written questions. Instead of participating in the oral examination, a party may serve written questions in a sealed envelope on the party noticing the deposition, who must deliver them to the officer. The officer must ask the deponent those questions and record the answers verbatim.

(D)   Motion to terminate or limit examinations. At any time during the taking of the deposition, on motion of any party or of the deponent and upon a showing that the examination is being conducted in bad faith or in such manner as unreasonably to annoy, embarrass, or oppress the deponent or party, the court in which the action is pending may order the officer conducting the examination to cease forthwith from taking the deposition, or may limit the scope and manner of the taking of the deposition as provided in Civ. R. 26(C). If the order made terminates the examination, it shall be resumed thereafter only upon the order of the court in which the action is pending. Upon demand of the objecting party or deponent, the taking of the deposition shall be suspended for the time necessary to make a motion for an order. The provisions of Civ. R. 37 apply to the award of expenses incurred in relation to the motion.

(E)   Submission to witness; changes; signing. When the testimony is fully transcribed, the deposition shall be submitted to the witness for examination and shall be read to or by the witness, unless examination and reading are waived by the witness and by the parties. Any changes in form or substance that the witness desires to make shall be entered upon the deposition by the officer with a statement of the reasons given by the witness for making them.

The deposition shall then be signed by the witness, unless the parties by stipulation waive the signing or the witness is ill, cannot be found, or refuses to sign. The witness shall have thirty days from submission of the deposition to the witness to review and sign the deposition. If the deposition is taken within thirty days of a trial or hearing, the witness shall have seven days from submission of the deposition to the witness to review and sign the deposition. If the trial or hearing is scheduled to commence less than seven days before the deposition is submitted to the witness, the court may establish a deadline for the witness to review and sign the deposition. If the deposition is not signed by the witness during the period prescribed in this division, the officer shall sign it and state on the record the fact of the waiver or of the illness or absence of the witness or the fact of the refusal to sign together with the reason, if any, given therefor; and the deposition may then be used as fully as though signed, unless on a motion to suppress the court holds that the reasons given for the refusal to sign require rejection of the deposition in whole or in part.

(F)   Certification and filing by officer; exhibits; copies; notice of filing.

(1)(a) Upon request of any party or order of the court, the officer shall transcribe the deposition. Provided the officer has retained an archival-quality copy of the officer's notes, the officer shall have no duty to retain paper notes of the deposition testimony. The officer shall certify on the transcribed deposition that the witness was fully sworn or affirmed by the officer and that the transcribed deposition is a true record of the testimony given by the witness. If any of the parties request or the court orders, the officer shall seal the transcribed deposition in an envelope endorsed with the title of the action and marked "Deposition of (here insert name of witness)" and, upon payment of the officer's fees, promptly shall file it with the court in which the action is pending or send it by United States certified or express mail or commercial carrier service to the clerk of the court for filing.

(b)   Unless objection is made to their production for inspection during the examination of the witness, documents and things shall be marked for identification and annexed to and returned with the deposition. The materials may be inspected and copied by any party, except that the person producing the materials may substitute copies to be marked for identification, if the person affords to all parties fair opportunity to verify the copies by comparison with the originals. If the person producing the materials requests their return, the officer shall mark them, give each party an opportunity to inspect and copy them, and return them to the person producing them, and the materials may then be used in the same manner as if annexed to and returned with the deposition.

(2)   Upon payment, the officer shall furnish a copy of the deposition to any party or to the deponent.

(3)   The party requesting the filing of the deposition shall forthwith give notice of its filing to all other parties.

(4)   As used in division (F) of this rule, "archival-quality copy" means any format of a permanent or enduring nature, including digital, magnetic, optical, or other medium, that allows an officer to transcribe the deposition.

(G)   Failure to attend or to serve subpoena; expenses.

(1)   If the party giving the notice of the taking of a deposition fails to attend and proceed with the deposition and another party attends in person or by attorney pursuant to the notice, the court may order the party giving the notice to pay to the other party the amount of the reasonable expenses incurred by the other party and the other party's attorney in so attending, including reasonable attorney's fees.

(2)   If the party giving the notice of the taking of a deposition of a witness fails to serve a subpoena upon the witness and the witness because of the failure does not attend, and another party attends in person or by attorney because the other party expects the deposition of that witness to be taken, the court may order the party giving the notice to pay to the other party the amount of the reasonable expenses incurred by the other party and the other party's attorney in so attending, including reasonable attorney's fees.

[Effective: July 1, 1970; amended effective July 1, 1976; July 1, 1985; July 1, 1992; July 1, 1994; July 1, 1997; July 1, 2006; July 1, 2012; July 1, 2015; July 1, 2017.]

Staff Notes (July 1, 2017 Amendments)

Civ.R. 30(C). Examination and cross-examination; objections.

The 2017 amendments adopt the 2007 stylistic changes to Fed.R.Civ.P. 30(c), including a nonsubstantive substitution of "deponent" for "witness." Deponents include both parties and non-parties. See Civ.R. 30(A).

The amendments provide that the Rules of Evidence shall apply at a deposition, except Evid.R. 103 and Evid.R. 615. The Federal Rules first included this provision in 1993. With respect to the exception of Evid.R. 615, the Notes of the Federal Advisory Committee included the following comments which are approved and re-stated in this Staff Note:

"[T]he revision addresses a recurring problem as to whether other potential deponents can attend a deposition. Courts have disagreed, some holding that witnesses should be excluded through invocation of Rule 615 of the evidence rules, and others holding that witnesses may attend unless excluded by an order under [Rule 26(c)]. The revision provides that other witnesses are not automatically excluded from a deposition simply by the request of a party. Exclusion, however, can be ordered under [Rule 26(c)] when appropriate; and, if exclusion is ordered, consideration should be given as to whether the excluded witnesses likewise should be precluded from reading, or being otherwise informed about, the testimony given in the earlier depositions. The revision addresses only the matter of attendance by potential deponents, and does not attempt to resolve issues concerning attendance by others, such as members of the public or press.

In adopting the 2007 federal stylistic changes, the amendments include provisions of the federal rule addressing the manner of making objections and the circumstances under which an instruction not to answer a question may be given. These additional provisions are consistent with the guidelines entitled: *Professionalism Dos and Don'ts: Depositions*, first published by the Ohio Supreme Court's Commission on Professionalism in 2012.

The amendments also add an introductory sentence to Civ.R. 30(C), which specifies that each party at the deposition may examine the deponent without regard to which party served notice or called the deposition. Although this introductory sentence is not found in the current federal rule, the provision is consistent with federal practice. See, *Powell v. Time Warner Cable, Inc.*, Case No. 2:09-CV-00600 (S.D.Ohio Nov. 2, 2010) (order partially granting motion to compel); *Smith v. Logansport Community School*, 139 F.R.D. 637, 642 (N.D.Ind 1991).

Staff Note (July 1, 2015 Amendments)

Rule 30(B)(3)

This amendment is modeled on Fed.R.Civ.P. 30(b)(3)(B) and permits a party other than the one noticing the deposition, at its own expense, after notice to the deponent and parties, to arrange for an additional method of recording the testimony, unless the court orders otherwise.

Rule 30(B)(6)

This amendment is modeled on Fed.R.Civ.P. 30(b)(4) and allows the parties to stipulate that a deposition may be taken by other remote means, such as over the Internet or using a satellite, rather than limiting the means of taking to the telephone.

Staff Note (July 1, 2006 Amendment)

The 2006 amendments contain two changes pertaining to the time period for reviewing and signing depositions and the retention of deposition notes by the court reporter who transcribed the deposition.

Rule 30(E) Submission to witness; changes; signing

Civ. R. 30(E) is amended to allow a witness thirty days to review and sign a deposition. The former rule allowed the witness only seven days to review and sign a deposition, and the Committee recognized that a careful review of a deposition in that period of time was sometimes practically or logistically difficult. When a deposition is taken close to trial, however, a quick turn-around may be necessary. Consequently, division (E) is amended to expand to thirty days the period in which a witness has to review and sign a deposition. Exceptions are provided for cases where the deposition is taken within thirty days of trial or hearing, in which case the seven-day rule still applies, or less than seven days of trial or hearing, in which case the trial judge may establish a different deadline. This amendment brings the Ohio rule closer to the Federal Rules of Civil Procedure, which give a witness thirty days to review and sign a deposition.

Rule 30(F) Certification and filing by officer; exhibits; copies; notice of filing

The 2006 amendment added division (F)(4). The amendment responds to a concern expressed by individuals charged with taking or keeping notes of depositions in light of changes in technology and the fact that most present-day court reporting machines no longer use paper but record and retain deposition testimony via electronic means. The amendment clarifies that "archival-quality copy" means any format of a permanent or enduring nature that will allow an officer to transcribe the deposition. In light of this definition, division (F)(1)(a) was revised to delete language that required the retention of paper notes of deposition testimony for a minimum of five years following the deposition.

Staff Note (July 1, 1997 Amendment)

Rule 30(F) Certification and filing by officer; exhibits; copies; notice of filing.

The 1997 amendment added the second sentence to division (F)(1). The amendment responds to a concern frequently expressed by individuals charged with taking or keeping notes of depositions, namely, what duty there is (if at all) to retain such notes. Present practice in Ohio on this matter appears to vary widely, and space and expense concerns come into play if such notes are kept in perpetuity. The amendment permits the officer to discard notes of a deposition, five years after it has taken place (whether or not the deposition has been transcribed), as long as the officer retains an archival quality copy of the notes. Archival quality would include notes maintained in magnetic, optical, or other equivalent medium. The original notes must be retained for at least five years, to provide a backup source should the archival-quality copy in any particular case not produce a usable deposition. It is anticipated that any such instances should be rare; however, in the unlikely event that such problems arise, most requests to transcribe depositions would take place within about five years of the original taking of the deposition. By that point, presumably, in most cases the litigation that gave rise to the deposition will have come to an end, as would the need for a transcribed copy of the deposition. For those few instances when a transcribed deposition is needed more than five years later, under the amendment the original notes or an archival-quality copy thereof will still be available.

Prior to the 1997 amendment, service under this rule was permitted only by certified mail. It appears that service by express mail, i.e. as that sort of mail is delivered by the United States Postal Service, can always be obtained return receipt requested, and thus could accomplish the purpose of notification equally well as certified mail. Therefore, the amendment to division (F)(1) provides for this additional option for service.

Other amendments to this rule are nonsubstantive grammatical or stylistic changes.

RULE 31.   Depositions of Witnesses Upon Written Questions

(A)   Serving questions; notice. After commencement of the action, any party may take the testimony of any person, including a party, by deposition upon written questions. The attendance of witnesses may be compelled by the use of subpoena as provided by Rule 45. The deposition of a person confined in prison may be taken only by leave of court on such terms as the court prescribes.

A party desiring to take a deposition upon written questions shall serve them upon every other party with a notice stating (1) the name and address of the person who is to answer them, if known, and if the name is not known, a general description sufficient to identify him or the particular class or group to which he belongs, and (2) the name or descriptive title and address of the officer before whom the deposition is to be taken. A deposition upon written questions may be taken of a public or private corporation or a partnership or association in accordance with the provisions of Rule 30(B)(5).

Within twenty-one days after the notice and written questions are served, a party may serve cross questions upon all other parties. Within fourteen days after being served with cross questions, a party may serve redirect questions upon all other parties. Within fourteen days after being served with redirect questions, a party may serve recross questions upon all other parties. The court may for cause shown enlarge or shorten the time.

(B)   Officer to take responses and prepare record. A copy of the notice and copies of all questions served shall be delivered by the party taking the deposition to the officer designated in the notice, who shall proceed promptly, in the manner provided by Rule 30(C), (E), and (F), to take the testimony of the witness in response to the questions and to prepare, certify, and file or mail the deposition, attaching thereto the copy of the notice and the questions received by him.

(C)   Notice of filing. The party requesting the filing of the deposition shall forthwith give notice of its filing to all other parties.

[Effective: July 1, 1970.]

RULE 32.   Use of Depositions in Court Proceedings

(A)   Use of depositions. Every deposition intended to be presented as evidence must be filed at least one day before the day of trial or hearing unless for good cause shown the court permits a later filing.

At the trial or upon the hearing of a motion or an interlocutory proceeding, any part or all of a deposition, so far as admissible under the rules of evidence applied as though the witness were then present and testifying, may be used against any party who was present or represented at the taking of the deposition or who had reasonable notice thereof, in accordance with any one of the following provisions:

(1)   Any deposition may be used by any party for the purpose of contradicting or impeaching the testimony of deponent as a witness.

(2)   The deposition of a party or of anyone who at the time of taking the deposition was an officer, director, or managing agent, or a person designated under Rule 30(B)(5) or Rule 31(A) to testify on behalf of a public or private corporation, partnership or association which is a party may be used by an adverse party for any purpose.

(3)   The deposition of a witness, whether or not a party, may be used by any party for any purpose if the court finds: (a) that the witness is dead; or (b) that the witness is beyond the subpoena power of the court in which the action is pending or resides outside of the county in which the action is pending unless it appears that the absence of the witness was procured by the party offering the deposition; or (c) that the witness is unable to attend or testify because of age, sickness, infirmity, or imprisonment; or (d) that the party offering the deposition has been unable to procure the attendance of the witness by subpoena; or (e) that the witness is an attending physician or medical expert, although residing within the county in which the action is heard; or (f) that the oral examination of a witness is not required; or (g) upon application and notice, that such exceptional circumstances exist as to make it desirable, in the interest of justice and with due regard to the importance of presenting the testimony of witnesses orally in open court, to allow the deposition to be used.

(4)   If only part of a deposition is offered in evidence by a party, an adverse party may require him to introduce all of it which is relevant to the part introduced, and any party may introduce any other parts.

Substitution of parties pursuant to Rule 25 does not affect the right to use depositions previously taken. When another action involving the same subject matter is or has been brought between the same parties or their representatives or successors in interest, all depositions lawfully taken in the one action may be used in the other as if originally taken therefor.

(B)   Objections to admissibility. Subject to the provisions of subdivision (D)(3) of this rule, objection may be made at the trial or hearing to receiving in evidence any deposition or part thereof for any reason which would require the exclusion of the evidence if the witness were then present and testifying. Upon the motion of a party, or upon its own initiative, the court shall decide such objections before the deposition is read in evidence.

(C)   Effect of taking or using depositions. A party does not make a person his own witness for any purpose by taking his deposition. The introduction in evidence of the deposition or any part thereof for any purpose other than that of contradicting or impeaching the deponent makes the deponent the witness of the party introducing the deposition, but this shall not apply to the use by an adverse party of a deposition as described in subdivision (A)(2) of this rule. The use of subdivision (A)(3)(e) of this rule does not preclude any party from calling such a witness to appear personally at the trial nor does it preclude the taking and use of any deposition otherwise provided by law. At the trial or hearing any party may rebut any relevant evidence contained in a deposition whether introduced by him or by any other party.

(D)   Effect of errors and irregularities in depositions:

(1)   As to notice. All errors and irregularities in the notice for taking a deposition are waived unless written objection stating the grounds therefor, is promptly served upon the party giving the notice.

(2)   As to disqualification of officer. Objection to taking a deposition because of disqualification of the officer before whom it is to be taken is waived unless made before the taking of the deposition begins or as soon thereafter as the disqualification becomes known or could be discovered with reasonable diligence.

(3)   As to taking of deposition.

(a)   Objections to the competency of a witness or to the competency, relevancy, or materiality of testimony are not waived by failure to make them before or during the taking of the deposition, unless the ground of the objection is one which might have been obviated or removed if presented at that time.

(b)   Errors and irregularities occurring at the oral examination in the manner of taking the deposition, in the form of the questions or answers, in the oath or affirmation, or in the conduct of parties and errors of any kind which might be obviated, removed, or cured if promptly presented, are waived unless reasonable objection thereto is made at the taking of the deposition.

(c)   Objections to the form of written questions submitted under Rule 31 are waived unless served in writing upon the party propounding them within the time allowed for serving the succeeding cross or other questions and within seven days after service of the last questions authorized.

(4) **As to completion and return of deposition.** Errors and irregularities in the manner in which the testimony is transcribed or the deposition is prepared, signed, certified, sealed, indorsed, transmitted, filed, or otherwise dealt with by the officer under Rule 30 and Rule 31 are waived unless a motion to suppress the deposition or some part thereof is made with reasonable promptness after such defect is, or with due diligence might have been, ascertained.

[Effective: July 1, 1970; amended effective July 1, 1972.]

RULE 33.   Interrogatories to Parties

(A)   Availability; procedures for use. Any party, without leave of court, may serve upon any other party up to forty written interrogatories to be answered by the party served. The party serving the interrogatories shall serve an electronic copy of the interrogatories on a shareable medium and in an editable format, by electronic mail, or by other means agreed to by the parties. A party who is unable to provide an electronic copy of the interrogatories may seek leave of court to be relieved of this requirement. A party shall not propound more than forty interrogatories to any other party without leave of court. Upon motion, and for good cause shown, the court may extend the number of interrogatories that a party may serve upon another party. For purposes of this rule, any subpart propounded under an interrogatory shall be considered a separate interrogatory.

(1)   If the party served is a public or private corporation or a partnership or association, the organization shall choose one or more of its proper employees, officers, or agents to answer the interrogatories, and the employee, officer, or agent shall furnish information as is known or available to the organization.

(2)   Interrogatories, without leave of court, may be served upon the plaintiff after commencement of the action and upon any other party after service of the summons and complaint upon the party.

(3)   Each interrogatory shall be answered separately and fully in writing under oath, unless it is objected to, in which event the reasons for objection shall be stated in lieu of an answer.   The party upon whom the interrogatories have been served shall quote each interrogatory immediately preceding the corresponding answer or objection.   When the number of interrogatories exceeds forty without leave of court, the party upon whom the interrogatories have been served need only answer or object to the first forty interrogatories.   The answers are to be signed by the person making them, and the objections signed by the attorney making them. The party upon whom the interrogatories have been served shall serve a copy of the answers and objections within a period designated by the party submitting the interrogatories, not less than twenty-eight days after the service of the interrogatories or within such shorter or longer time as the court may allow.

(B) Scope and use at trial. Interrogatories may relate to any matters that can be inquired into under Civ. R. 26(B), and the answers may be used to the extent permitted by the rules of evidence.

The party calling for such examination shall not thereby be concluded but may rebut it by evidence.

An interrogatory otherwise proper is not objectionable merely because an answer to the interrogatory involves an opinion, contention, or legal conclusion, but the court may order that such an interrogatory be answered at a later time, or after designated discovery has been completed, or at a pretrial conference.

(C) Option to produce business records. Where the answer to an interrogatory may be derived or ascertained from the business records, including electronically stored information, of the party upon whom the interrogatory has been served or from an examination, audit, or inspection of the business records, or from a compilation, abstract, or summary based on the business records, and the burden of deriving or ascertaining the answer is substantially the same for the party serving the interrogatory as for the party served, it is a sufficient answer to the interrogatory to specify the records from which the answer may be derived or ascertained and to afford to the party serving the interrogatory reasonable opportunity to examine, audit, or inspect the records and to make copies of the records or compilations, abstracts, or summaries from the records.

[Effective: July 1, 1970; amended effective July 1, 1972; July 1, 1989; July 1, 1999; July 1, 2004; July 1, 2008; July 1, 2009; July 1, 2012; July 1, 2014; July 1, 2017; July 1, 2019.]

Staff Note (2019 Amendment)

Division (A)

Recognizing the advancements in technology that have occurred since the 2004 amendment to the rule, the amendment to Division (A) changes the description of the type of electronic copy that shall be served from a copy that is "reasonably useable for word processing and provided on computer disk" to a copy "on a shareable medium and in an editable format."

Staff Note (July 1, 2017 Amendment)

Civ.R. 33(A)(2). Service of interrogatories.

The rule is amended to permit service of interrogatories on parties other than the plaintiff only after service of the summons and complaint upon that party and to disallow service of interrogatories with service of the summons and complaint.

Staff Note (July 1, 2014 Amendments)

Rule 33(A)(3) is amended to correct an oversight in the final publication of the 2012 amendments to the rule. Those prior amendments intended that interrogatories be served by electronic means making separate service of a printed copy unnecessary except for unusual circumstances. The final publication of the 2012 amendment inadvertently retained language from the prior rule stating that the designated time for responses runs from service of "a printed copy of" the interrogatories. The quoted words were not intended to be included and are stricken. A similar correction is made to Civ.R. 36 with respect to requests for admission.

Staff Note (July 1, 2012 Amendment)

The introductory paragraph of Civ.R. 33(A) and the provisions of Civ.R. 33(A)(3) are amended to eliminate difficulties raised by the 2004 amendment to Civ.R. 33(A) that requires a party serving interrogatories to "provide" an electronic copy to the served party. This amendment is enabled by the 2012 amendment to Civ.R. 5(B) which permits documents after the original complaint to be served by electronic means.

Civ.R. 5(A) requires that copies of all documents in an action be "served" on the parties. When the Civ.R. 33 requirement for an electronic copy was established in 2004, there was no provision for "service" by electronic means and it was deemed impractical to require that an electronic copy be "served" by mailing a computer disk or otherwise delivering it by one of the other methods permitted under the existing Civ.R. 5(B). Thus the 2004 amendment to Civ.R. 33 provided that a printed copy must be "served" (by one of the methods listed under Civ.R. 5(B)), and that an electronic copy also must be "'provided' on computer disk, by electronic mail, or by other means agreed to by the parties." That requirement was problematic not only because of the required dual format but also in determining a party's recourse when a paper copy was served but an electronic copy was not provided – a problem addressed by the 2009 amendment to Civ.R. 33.

The 2012 amendment simply requires that an electronic copy be served, which can be accomplished electronically under the 2012 amendment to Civ.R. 5(B), or by any other method provided under Civ.R. 5(B). Although service of a paper copy is no longer necessary, it is not prohibited and would be appropriate, for example, when a party who is unable to provide an electronic copy is relieved of that requirement by the court.

Similar amendments have been made to Civ.R. 36 relating to requests for admission.

Staff Note (July 1, 2009 Amendment)

Recognizing that computer word processors have replaced the typewriter, Rule 33 was amended in 2004 to delete the former "minimum one-inch space" requirement in favor of a requirement that the party propounding interrogatories provide the responding party with an electronic copy of the interrogatories for use in preparing a new computer-generated document containing both the questions and the answers. The 2004 amendment continued to require that the printed copy be served, and only required that the electronic copy be "provided" to the party served. The amendment further permitted the electronic copy to be provided by means other than those described in Civ. R. 5(B) for service, specifically including "by electronic mail." Finally, the amendment permitted the court to relieve a party "who is unable to provide an electronic copy" of the duty to do so.

The 2004 amendment did not specify a consequence for the failure to provide an electronic copy. Because the time designated in the interrogatories for responding runs from service, and only the printed copy is served, the amendment left uncertain the obligations and appropriate remedy for a party served with a printed copy of interrogatories, but not provided with an electronic copy. The 2009 amendment specifies the consequence and appropriate remedy for this situation.

First, the amendment specifies that the electronic copy must be "reasonably useable for word processing" to enable the responding party to transcribe the responses. Next, the amendment confirms that the period for responding, which is designated by the propounding party and cannot be less than twenty-eight days, shall run from the day of service of the printed copy, and that the failure to provide an electronic copy does not alter the response period. However, if before the designated period has expired, the responding party requests that the period be enlarged pursuant to Rule 6(B) because the propounding party has not provided an electronic copy, that reason shall constitute good cause for granting the requested extension, and the court's order may require that an electronic copy be provided.

The amendment strikes a balance between the respective duties of the parties when a provision which merely makes it easier to transcribe interrogatory answers is not followed. It enforces the duty of the party propounding interrogatories to provide an electronic copy unless otherwise relieved of that obligation by the court. At the same it time makes it clear that a responding party served with a printed copy of interrogatories cannot rely on the failure to receive an electronic copy as reason to do nothing and simply disregard the response time. A Civ. R. 6(B) request for enlargement of the period is an appropriate remedy for a responding party in this situation, and the amendment merely provides guidance in that regard. The rule states that the failure to receive an electronic copy constitutes good cause under Civ. R. 6(B). The amendment also confirms the court's discretion to relieve a party of the duty to provide an electronic copy when unable to do so, for example, when compliance would be difficult for a *pro se* party.

Similar amendments were made to Civ. R. 36, addressing the failure to provide an electronic copy of requests for admission.

Staff Note (July 1, 2008 Amendment)

The text of Civ. R. 33(A) is broken into three subparts. This is intended as a stylistic change only to make the material more accessible.

Amendments to Civ. R. 33(C) clarify that the responding party's option to produce business records in which the information sought in interrogatories may be found includes the option of producing electronically stored information.

Staff Note (July 1, 2004 Amendment)

Rule 33(A)   Availability; procedures for use

The 2004 amendment added two provisions governing the service of and response to interrogatories. New language was added to the fourth paragraph of division (A) that requires a responding party to quote the interrogatory immediately preceding the party's answer or objection. This provision ensures that the court and parties are not required to consult two documents or different parts of the same document in order to review the full text of an interrogatory and the corresponding answer or objection. The provision is similar to the second sentence of S.D. Ohio Civ. R. 26.1.

To facilitate the responding party's obligation to include the interrogatories and answers or objections in the same document, the first paragraph of division (A) was modified to require the party submitting interrogatories to provide the responding party with both a printed and an electronic copy of the interrogatories. The electronic version must be provided in a format that will enable the responding party to readily include the interrogatories and corresponding answers and objections in the same document without having to retype each interrogatory. A party who is unable to provide an electronic copy of interrogatories may seek leave of court to be relieved of the requirement.

Corresponding amendments were made to Civ. R. 36(A) relative to requests for admission.

Rule 33(D)   Form of answers and objections to interrogatories.

The 2004 amendment deleted language that required a party submitting interrogatories to allow sufficient space, not less than one inch, following each interrogatory in which the answering party could type an answer or objection. New language was added to division (A) governing the service of and response to interrogatories.

Staff Note (July 1, 1999 Amendment)

Rule 33(A) Availability, procedures for use

The 1999 amendment was to clarify that any party may file up to forty interrogatories without leave of court. Several nonsubstantive grammatical changes also were made.

Rule 33(B) Scope and use at trial

The 1999 amendment made grammatical changes only; no substantive change was made.

Rule 33(C) Option to produce business records

The 1999 amendment made grammatical changes only; no substantive change was made.

RULE 34. Producing documents, electronically stored information, and tangible things, or entering onto land, for inspection and other purposes.

(A) Scope. Subject to the scope of discovery provisions of Civ. R. 26(B), any party may serve on any other party a request to produce and permit the party making the request, or someone acting on the requesting party's behalf (1) to inspect and copy any designated documents or electronically stored information, including writings, drawings, graphs, charts, photographs, sound recordings, images, and other data or data compilations stored in any medium from which information can be obtained that are in the possession, custody, or control of the party upon whom the request is served; (2) to inspect and copy, test, or sample any tangible things that are in the possession, custody, or control of the party upon whom the request is served; (3) to enter upon designated land or other property in the possession or control of the party upon whom the request is served for the purpose of inspection and measuring, surveying, photographing, testing, or sampling the property or any designated object or operation on the property.

(B) Procedure. Without leave of court, the request may be served upon the plaintiff after commencement of the action and upon any other party after service of the summons and complaint upon that party. The request shall set forth the items to be inspected either by individual item or by category and describe each item and category with reasonable particularity. The request shall specify a reasonable time, place, and manner of making the inspection and performing the related acts. The request may specify the form or forms in which electronically stored information is to be produced, but may not require the production of the same information in more than one form. The party serving the request shall serve an electronic copy of the request on a shareable medium and in an editable format by electronic mail, or by other means agreed to by the parties. A party who is unable to provide an electronic copy of the interrogatories may seek leave of court to be relieved of this requirement.

(1) The party upon whom the request is served shall serve a written response within a period designated in the request that is not less than twenty-eight days after the service of the request or within a shorter or longer time as the court may allow. With respect to each item or category, the response shall state that inspection and related activities will be permitted as requested, unless it is objected to, including an objection to the requested form or forms for producing electronically stored information, in which event the reasons for objection shall be stated. If objection is made to part of an item or category, the part shall be specified. If objection is made to the requested form or forms for producing electronically stored information, or if no form was specified in the request, the responding party must state the form or forms it intends to use. The party submitting the request may move for an order under Civ. R. 37 with respect to any objection to or other failure to respond to the request or any part of the request, or any failure to permit inspection as requested.

(2) A party who produces documents for inspection shall, at its option, produce them as they are kept in the usual course of business or organized and labeled to correspond with the categories in the request.

(3) If a request does not specify the form or forms for producing electronically stored information, a responding party may produce the information in a form or forms in which the information is ordinarily maintained if that form is reasonably useable, or in any form that is reasonably useable. Unless ordered by the court or agreed to by the parties, a party need not produce the same electronically stored information in more than one form.

(C)   **Persons not parties.** Subject to the scope of discovery provisions of Civ. R. 26(B) and 45(F), a person not a party to the action may be compelled to produce documents, electronically stored information or tangible things or to submit to an inspection as provided in Civ. R. 45.

(D)   **Prior to filing of action.**

(1)   Subject to the scope of discovery provisions of Civ. R. 26(B) and 45(F), a person who claims to have a potential cause of action may file a petition to obtain discovery as provided in this rule. Prior to filing a petition for discovery, the person seeking discovery shall make reasonable efforts to obtain voluntarily the information from the person from whom the discovery is sought. The petition shall be captioned in the name of the person seeking discovery and be filed in the court of common pleas in the county in which the person from whom the discovery is sought resides, the person's principal place of business is located, or the potential action may be filed. The petition shall include all of the following:

    (a)   A statement of the subject matter of the petitioner's potential cause of action and the petitioner's interest in the potential cause of action;

    (b)   A statement of the efforts made by the petitioner to obtain voluntarily the information from the person from whom the discovery is sought;

    (c)   A statement or description of the information sought to be discovered with reasonable particularity;

    (d)   The names and addresses, if known, of any person the petitioner expects will be an adverse party in the potential action;

    (e)   A request that the court issue an order authorizing the petitioner to obtain the discovery.

(2)   The petition shall be served upon the person from whom discovery is sought and, if known, any person the petitioner expects will be an adverse party in the potential action, by one of the methods provided in these rules for service of summons.

(3)   The court shall issue an order authorizing the petitioner to obtain the requested discovery if the court finds all of the following:

(a) The discovery is necessary to ascertain the identity of a potential adverse party;

(b) The petitioner is otherwise unable to bring the contemplated action;

(c) The petitioner made reasonable efforts to obtain voluntarily the information from the person from whom the discovery is sought.

[Effective: July 1, 1970; amended effective July 1, 1993; July 1, 1994; July 1, 2005; July 1, 2008; July 1, 2017; July 1, 2019.]

Staff Note (July 1, 2019 Amendment)

Division (B)

Division (B) of the rule is amended to include a requirement that the party serving this form of discovery requests include an electronic copy in a word-processing format. This requirement is already found in Civ.R. 33(A) and Civ.R. 36(A) for interrogatories and requests for admissions, respectively. Its inclusion here recognizes the reality that practitioners typically respond to this form of discovery requests in writing in addition to any accompanying responsive materials.

Staff Note (July 1, 2017 Amendment)

Civ.R. 34(B). Service of requests for production.

The rule is amended to permit service of requests for production on parties other than the plaintiff only after service of the summons and complaint upon that party and to disallow service of requests for production with service of the summons and complaint.

Staff Note (July 1, 2008 Amendment)

The title of this rule is changed to reflect its coverage of electronically stored information discovery.

The amendment to Civ. R. 34(A) clarifies that discovery of electronically stored information is expressly authorized and regulated by this rule.

Amendments to the first paragraph of Civ. R. 34(B) allow the requesting party to specify the form of forms in which electronically stored information should be produced. For example, the party propounding discovery seeking electronically stored information could request that a party's internal memorandums on a particular subject be produced in Word™ format, while financial records be provided in an Excel™ spreadsheet format or other commonly used format for financial information. This provision also specifies that the requesting party cannot demand that the respondent provide the same information in more than one electronic format. If a party believes that the form or forms specified by an opponent is unduly burdensome or expensive, the party can object to the discovery under Rule 34(B)(1) and then negotiate a different, mutually acceptable form with the opponent or seek relief from the court under Rule 26(B)(4).

The remaining text of existing Civ. R. 34(B) is broken into subparts (1) and (2). This is solely a stylistic change intended to make the material more accessible.

Civ. R. 34(B)(1) requires the party responding to a request to specifically articulate its objection to the form of production of electronically stored information that the opponent has requested. It also requires a responding party to identify the form in which electronically stored information will be produced if the requesting party has not specified the format.

Civ. R. 34(B)(3) applies when a party does not specify the form in which electronically stored information should be produced; in that situation the responding party has the option of producing the materials in the form in which the information is ordinarily maintained or another form provided that the form produced is reasonable. This section also clarifies that the respondent only has to provide electronically stored information in one format unless the court orders or the parties agree to a different arrangement. Civ. R. 34(B)(3) is added to allow production of electronically stored information in more than one format if agreed to by the parties or ordered by the court.

Civ. R. 34(C) clarifies that discovery of electronically stored information from nonparties is governed by Rule 45.

Staff Note (July 1, 2005 Amendment)

Rule 34(C)   Persons not parties

Civ. R. 34(C) is amended to move a reference to notice of issuance of a subpoena directed to a nonparty to Civ. R. 45(A)(3). The amendments to Civ. R. 34 and 45 place all provisions requiring notice of issuance of most types of subpoena directed to nonparties appear in Civ. R. 45(A)(3) rather than being split between Civ. R. 34(C) and Civ. R. 45(A)(3). The prior arrangement made it easy to overlook the notice provisions of Civ. R. 34(C). See, e.g., *Neftzer v. Neftzer*, 140 Ohio App.3d 618, 621 (2000).

RULE 35.   Physical and Mental Examination of Persons

(A)   Order for examination. When the mental or physical condition (including the blood group) of a party, or of a person in the custody or under the legal control of a party, is in controversy, the court in which the action is pending may order the party to submit himself to a physical or mental examination or to produce for such examination the person in the party's custody or legal control. The order may be made only on motion for good cause shown and upon notice to the person to be examined and to all parties and shall specify the time, place, manner, conditions, and scope of the examination and the person or persons by whom it is to be made.

(B)   Examiner's report.

(1)   If requested by the party against whom an order is made under Rule 35(A) or the person examined, the party causing the examination to be made shall deliver to such party or person a copy of the detailed written report submitted by the examiner to the party causing the examination to be made. The report shall set out the examiner's findings, including results of all tests made, diagnoses and conclusions, together with like reports of all earlier examinations of the same condition. After delivery, the party causing the examination shall be entitled upon request to receive from the party against whom the order is made a like report of any examination, previously or, thereafter made, of the same condition, unless, in the case of a report of examination of a person not a party, the party shows that he is unable to obtain it. The court on motion may make an order against a party to require delivery of a report on such terms as are just. If an examiner fails or refuses to make a report, the court on motion may order, at the expense of the party causing the examination, the taking of the deposition of the examiner if his testimony is to be offered at trial.

(2)   By requesting and obtaining a report of the examination so ordered or by taking the deposition of the examiner, the party examined waives any privilege he may have in that action or any other involving the same controversy, regarding the testimony of every other person who has examined or may thereafter examine him in respect of the same mental or physical condition.

(3)   This subdivision, 35(B), applies to examinations made by agreement of the parties, unless the agreement expressly provides otherwise.

[Effective: July 1, 1970.]

RULE 36. Requests for Admission

(A) **Availability; procedures for use.** A party may serve upon any other party a written request for the admission, for purposes of the pending action only, of the truth of any matters within the scope of Civ.R. 26(B) set forth in the request, that relate to statements or opinions of fact or of the application of law to fact, including the genuineness of any documents described in the request. Copies of documents shall be served with the request unless they have been or are otherwise furnished or made available for inspection and copying. The request may, without leave of court, be served upon the plaintiff after commencement of the action and upon any other party after service of the summons and complaint upon that party. The party serving the request for admission shall serve an electronic copy of the request on a shareable medium and in an editable format, by electronic mail, or by other means agreed to by the parties. A party who is unable to provide an electronic copy of a request for admission may seek leave of court to be relieved of this requirement.

(1)   Each matter of which an admission is requested shall be separately set forth. The party to whom the requests for admissions have been directed shall quote each request for admission immediately preceding the corresponding answer or objection. The matter is admitted unless, within a period designated in the request, not less than twenty-eight days after service of the request or within such shorter or longer time as the court may allow, the party to whom the request is directed serves upon the party requesting the admission a written answer or objection addressed to the matter, signed by the party or by the party's attorney.

(2) If objection is made, the reasons therefor shall be stated. The answer shall specifically deny the matter or set forth in detail the reasons why the answering party cannot truthfully admit or deny the matter. A denial shall fairly meet the substance of the requested admission, and when good faith requires that a party qualify his or her answer, or deny only a part of the matter of which an admission is requested, the party shall specify so much of it as is true and qualify or deny the remainder. An answering party may not give lack of information or knowledge as a reason for failure to admit or deny unless the party states that the party has made reasonable inquiry and that the information known or readily obtainable by the party is insufficient to enable the party to admit or deny. A party who considers that a matter of which an admission has been requested presents a genuine issue for trial may not, on that ground alone, object to the request; the party may, subject to the provisions of Civ.R. 37(C), deny the matter or set forth reasons why the party cannot admit or deny it.

(3) The party who has requested the admissions may move for an order with respect to the answers or objections. Unless the court determines that an objection is justified, it shall order that an answer be served. If the court determines that an answer does not comply with the requirements of this rule, it may order either that the matter is admitted or that an amended answer be served. The court may, in lieu of these orders, determine that final disposition of the request be made at a pretrial conference or at a designated time prior to trial. The provisions of Civ.R. 37(A)(5) apply to the award of expenses incurred in relation to the motion.

(B) Effect of admission. Any matter admitted under this rule is conclusively established unless the court on motion permits withdrawal or amendment of the admission. Subject to the provisions of Civ. R. 16 governing modification of a pretrial order, the court may permit withdrawal or amendment when the presentation of the merits of the action will be subserved thereby and the party who obtained the admission fails to satisfy the court that withdrawal or amendment will prejudice the party in maintaining his action or defense on the merits. Any admission made by a party under this rule is for the purpose of the pending action only and is not an admission by the party for any other purpose nor may it be used against the party in any other proceeding.

(C) Document containing request for admission. If a party includes a request for admission in a document containing any other form of discovery, the party shall include a caption on the document that indicates the document contains a request for admission. A party is not required to respond to requests for admission that are not made in compliance with this division.

[Effective: July 1, 1970; amended effective July 1, 1972; July 1, 1976; July 1, 2004; July 1, 2005; July 1, 2008; July 1. 2009; July 1, 2012; July 1, 2014; July 1, 2017; July 1, 2019.]

Staff Note (July 1, 2019 Amendment)

Division (A)

Recognizing the advancements in technology that have occurred since the 2004 amendment to the rule, the amendment also changes the description of the type of electronic copy that shall be served from a copy that is "reasonably useable for word processing and provided on computer disk" to a copy "on a shareable medium and in an editable format."

Staff Note (July 1, 2017 Amendment)

Civ.R. 36(A). Requests for admission.

The rule is amended to permit service of requests for admission on parties other than the plaintiff only after service of the summons and complaint upon that party and to disallow service of requests for admission with service of the summons and complaint

Staff Note (July 1, 2014 Amendments)

Rule 36(A)(1) is amended to correct an oversight in the final publication of the 2012 amendments to the rule. Those prior amendments intended that requests for admission be served by electronic means making separate service of a printed copy unnecessary except for unusual circumstances. The final publication of the 2012 amendment inadvertently retained language from the prior rule stating that the designated time for responses runs from service of "a printed copy of" the requests. The quoted words were not intended to be included and are stricken. A similar correction is made to Civ.R. 33 with respect to interrogatories.

Staff Note (July 1, 2012 Amendment)

The introductory paragraph of Civ.R. 36(A) and the provisions of Civ.R. 36(A)(1) are amended to eliminate difficulties raised by the 2004 amendment to Civ.R. 36(A) that requires a party serving requests for admission to "provide" an electronic copy to the served party. This amendment is enabled by the 2012 amendment to Civ.R. 5(B) which permits documents after the original complaint to be served by electronic means.

Civ.R. 5(A) requires that copies of all documents in an action be "served" on the parties. When the Civ.R. 36 requirement for an electronic copy was established in 2004, there was no provision for "service" by electronic means and it was deemed impractical to require that an electronic copy be "served" by mailing a computer disk or otherwise delivering it by one of the other methods permitted under the existing Civ.R. 5(B). Thus the 2004 amendment to Civ.R. 36 provided that a printed copy must be "served" (by one of the methods listed under Civ.R. 5(B)), and that an electronic copy also must be "'provided' on computer disk, by electronic mail, or by other means agreed to by the parties." That requirement was problematic not only because of the required dual format but also in determining a party's recourse when a paper copy was served but an electronic copy was not provided – a problem addressed by the 2009 amendment to Civ.R. 36.

The 2012 amendment simply requires that an electronic copy be served, which can be accomplished electronically under the 2012 amendments to Civ.R. 5(B), or by any other method provided under Civ.R. 5(B). Although service of a paper copy is no longer necessary, it is not prohibited and would be appropriate, for example, when a party who is unable to provide an electronic copy is relieved of that requirement by the court.

Similar amendments have been made to Civ.R. 33 relating to interrogatories.

Staff Note (July 1, 2009 Amendment)

Recognizing that computer word processors have replaced the typewriter, Rule 36 was amended in 2004 to delete the former "minimum one-inch space" requirement in favor of a requirement that the party requesting admissions provide the responding party with an electronic copy of the request for use in preparing a new computer-generated document containing both the requests and the responses. The 2004 amendment continued to require that the printed copy be served, and only required that the electronic copy be "provided" to the party served. The amendment further permitted the electronic copy to be provided by means other than those described in Civ. R. 5(B) for service, specifically including "by electronic mail." Finally, the amendment permitted the court to relieve a party "who is unable to provide an electronic copy" of the duty to do so.

The 2004 amendment did not specify a consequence for the failure to provide an electronic copy. Because the time designated in the request for responding runs from service, and only the printed copy is served, the amendment left uncertain the obligations and appropriate remedy for a party served with a printed copy of requests for admission, but not provided with an electronic copy. The 2009 amendment specifies the consequence and appropriate remedy for this situation.

The amendment confirms that the period for responding, which is designated by the requesting party and cannot be less than twenty-eight days, shall run from the day of service of the printed copy, and that the failure to provide an electronic copy does not alter the response period. However, if before the designated period has expired, the responding party requests that the period be enlarged pursuant to Rule 6(B) because the requesting party has not provided an electronic copy, that reason shall constitute good cause for granting the requested extension, and the court's order may require that an electronic copy be provided.

The amendment strikes a balance between the respective duties of the parties when a provision which merely makes it easier to transcribe the responses to a request for admission is not followed. It enforces the duty of the party requesting admissions to provide an electronic copy unless otherwise relieved of that obligation by the court. At the same it time makes it clear that a responding party served with a printed copy of a request for admissions cannot rely on the failure to receive an electronic copy as reason to do nothing and simply disregard the response time. A Civ. R. 6(B) request for enlargement of the period is an appropriate remedy for a responding party in this situation, and the amendment merely provides guidance in that regard. The rule states that the failure to receive an electronic copy constitutes good cause under Civ. R. 6(B). The amendment also confirms the court's discretion to relieve a party of the duty to provide an electronic copy when unable to do so, for example, when compliance would be difficult for a *pro se* party.

Similar amendments were made to Civ. R. 33, addressing the failure to provide an electronic copy of interrogatories.

Staff Note (July 1, 2008 Amendment)

The text of Civ. R. 36(A) is broken into three subparts. This is intended as a stylistic change only to make the material more accessible.

Staff Note (July 1, 2005 Amendment)

Rule 36(C)   Document containing request for admission.

Civ. R. 36 is amended to require that a party include a specific caption on any document that includes one or more requests for admission. The amended rule recognizes that, unlike Civ. R. 33 (written interrogatories) and Civ. R. 34 (requests for production), Civ. R. 36 imposes a virtually self-executing sanction, *i.e.*, admission by default, on a party that fails timely to respond. See generally *Cleveland Trust Co. v. Willis*, 20 Ohio St.3d 66 (1985).

The Rules Advisory Committee is aware that parties intermix requests for admission with Civ. R. 33 interrogatories and Civ. R. 34 requests for production. See, e.g., *Seecharan v. Macy*, 1999 WL 980579, No. 75130 (8th Dist. Ct. App., Cuyahoga, 10-28-99) (no abuse of discretion to deny motion to deem matters admitted; "the trial court refused to countenance the obscuring of requests for admissions in the midst of other discovery requests"). The Committee believes that although there often are good reasons for combining requests for admission with other discovery requests, the nature of some discovery documents can cause requests for admission to be overlooked and result in inadvertent admissions by default. The amendment is intended to minimize this risk by requiring the propounding party to include, in the caption of the document, a clear notice that the document contains requests for admission. A party is not required to respond to requests for admission that are not made in compliance with division (C).

Staff Note (July 1, 2004 Amendment)

Rule 36(A)   Availability; procedures for use.

The 2004 amendment added two provisions governing the service of and response to requests for admissions. New language was added to the second paragraph of division (A) that requires a responding party to quote the request for admission immediately preceding the party's answer or objection. This provision ensures that the court and parties are not required to consult two documents or different parts of the same document in order to review the full text of a request for admission and the corresponding answer or objection. The provision is similar to the second sentence of S.D. Ohio Civ. R. 26.1.

To facilitate the responding party's obligation to include the request for admission and answer or objection in the same document, the first paragraph of division (A) was modified to require the party submitting requests for admissions to provide the responding party with both a printed and an electronic copy of the requests for admissions. The electronic version must be provided in a format that will enable the responding party to readily include the requests for admissions and corresponding answers and objections in the same document without having to retype each request for admission. A party who is unable to provide an electronic copy of requests for admission may seek leave of court to be relieved of the requirement.

Corresponding amendments were made to Civ. R. 33(A) relative to interrogatories.

Rule 36(C)   Form of answers and objections to requests for admissions.

The 2004 amendment deleted language that required a party submitting requests for admissions to allow sufficient space, not less than one inch, following each request for admission, in which the answering party could type an answer or objection. New language was added to division (A) governing the service of and response to requests for admissions.

RULE 37.   Failure to Make Discovery: Sanctions

(A)   Motion for an order compelling discovery.

(1)   In general. On notice to other parties and all affected persons, a party may move for an order compelling discovery. The motion shall include a certification that the movant has in good faith conferred or attempted to confer with the person or party failing to make discovery in an effort to obtain it without court action.

(2)   Appropriate court. A motion for an order to a party or a deponent shall be made to the court where the action is pending.

(3)   Specific motions.

    (a)   **To compel a discovery response.** A party seeking discovery may move for an order compelling an answer, designation, production, or inspection. This motion may be made if:

        (i)   A deponent fails to answer a question asked under Civ.R. 30 or Civ.R. 31;

        (ii)   A corporation or other entity fails to make a designation under Civ.R. 30(B)(5) or Civ.R. 31(A);

        (iii)   A party fails to answer an interrogatory submitted under Civ.R. 33;

        (iv)   A party fails to respond that inspection will be permitted—or fails to permit inspection—as requested under Civ.R. 34.

    (b)   Related to a deposition. When taking an oral deposition, the party asking a question may complete or adjourn the examination before moving for an order.

(4)   Evasive or incomplete answer or response. For purposes of division (A) of this rule, an evasive or incomplete answer or response shall be treated as a failure to answer or respond.

(5)   Payment of expenses; protective orders.

    (a)   **If the motion is granted.** If the motion is granted, the court shall, after giving an opportunity to be heard, require the party or deponent whose conduct necessitated the motion, the party or attorney advising that conduct, or both to pay the movant's reasonable expenses incurred in making the motion, including attorney's fees. But the court shall not order this payment if:

(i) The movant filed the motion before attempting in good faith to obtain the discovery without court action;

(ii) The opposing party's response or objection was substantially justified; or

(iii) Other circumstances make an award of expenses unjust.

(b) **If the motion is denied.** If the motion is denied, the court may issue any protective order authorized under Civ.R. 26(C) and shall, after giving an opportunity to be heard, require the movant, the attorney filing the motion, or both to pay the party or deponent who opposed the motion its reasonable expenses incurred in opposing the motion, including attorney's fees. But the court shall not order this payment if the motion was substantially justified or other circumstances make an award of expenses unjust.

(c) **If the motion is granted in part and denied in part.** If the motion is granted in part and denied in part, the court may issue any protective order authorized under Civ.R. 26(C) and may, after giving an opportunity to be heard, apportion reasonable expenses for the motion.

(B) **Failure to comply with order; sanctions.**

(1) **For not obeying a discovery order.** If a party or a party's officer, director, or managing agent or a witness designated under Civ.R. 30(B)(5) or Civ.R. 31(A) fails to obey an order to provide or permit discovery, including an order made under Civ.R. 35 or Civ.R. 37(A), the court may issue further just orders. They may include the following:

(a) Directing that the matters embraced in the order or other designated facts shall be taken as established for purposes of the action as the prevailing party claims;

(b) Prohibiting the disobedient party from supporting or opposing designated claims or defenses, or from introducing designated matters in evidence;

(c) Striking pleadings in whole or in part;

(d) Staying further proceedings until the order is obeyed dismissing;

(e) Dismissing the action or proceeding in whole or in part;

(f) Rendering a default judgment against the disobedient party; or

(g) Treating as contempt of court the failure to obey any orders except an order to submit to a physical or mental examination;

(2) **For not producing a person for examination.** If a party fails to comply with an order under Civ.R. 35(A) requiring it to produce another person for examination, the court may issue any of the orders listed in Civ.R. 37(B)(1), unless the disobedient party shows that it cannot produce the other person.

(3) **Payment of expenses.** Instead of or in addition to the orders above, the court shall order the disobedient party, the attorney advising that party, or both to pay the reasonable expenses, including attorney's fees, caused by the failure, unless the failure was substantially justified or other circumstances make an award of expenses unjust.

(C) **Failure to supplement an earlier response or to admit.**

(1) **Failure to supplement.** If a party fails to provide information or identify a witness as required by Civ.R. 26(E), the party is not allowed to use that information or witness to supply evidence on a motion, at a hearing, or at a trial, unless the failure was substantially justified or is harmless. In addition to or instead of this sanction, the court, on motion and after giving an opportunity to be heard:

(a) may order payment of the reasonable expenses, including attorney's fees, caused by the failure;

(b) may inform the jury of the party's failure; and

(c) may impose other appropriate sanctions, including any of the orders listed in Civ.R. 37(B)(1)(a) through (f).

(2) **Failure to admit.** If a party fails to admit what is requested under Civ.R. 36, and if the requesting party later proves a document to be genuine or the matter true, the requesting party may move that the party who failed to admit pay the reasonable expenses, including attorney's fees, incurred in making that proof. The court shall so order unless:

(a) The request was held objectionable under Civ.R. 36(A);

(b) The admission sought was of no substantial importance;

(c) The party failing to admit had a reasonable ground to believe that it might prevail on the matter; or

(d) There was other good reason for the failure to admit.

(D) **Party's failure to attend its own deposition, serve answers to interrogatories, or respond to a request for inspection.**

(1) **In general.**

(a) **Motion; grounds for sanctions.** The court may, on motion, order sanctions if:

(i) A party or a party's officer, director, or a managing agent or a person designated under Civ.R. 30(B)(5) or Civ.R. 31(A) fails, after being served with a proper notice, to appear for that person's deposition; or

(ii) A party, after being properly served with interrogatories under Civ.R. 33 or a request for inspection under Civ.R. 34, fails to serve its answers, objections, or written response.

(b) **Certification.** A motion for sanctions for failing to answer or respond shall include a certification that the movant has in good faith conferred or attempted to confer with the party failing to act in an effort to obtain the answer or response without court action.

(2) **Unacceptable excuse for failing to act.** A failure described in Civ.R. 37(D)(1)(a) is not excused on the ground that the discovery sought was objectionable, unless the party failing to act has a pending motion for a protective order under Civ.R. 26(C).

(3) **Types of sanctions.** Sanctions may include any of the orders listed in Civ.R. 37(B)(1)(a) through (f). Instead of or in addition to these sanctions, the court shall require the party failing to act, the attorney advising that party, or both to pay the reasonable expenses, including attorney's fees, caused by the failure, unless the failure was substantially justified or other circumstances make an award of expenses unjust.

(E) **Failure to provide electronically stored information.**

Absent exceptional circumstances, a court may not impose sanctions under these rules on a party for failing to provide electronically stored information lost as a result of the routine, good-faith operation of an electronic information system. The court may consider the following factors in determining whether to impose sanctions under this division:

(1) Whether and when any obligation to preserve the information was triggered;

(2) Whether the information was lost as a result of the routine alteration or deletion of information that attends the ordinary use of the system in issue;

(3) Whether the party intervened in a timely fashion to prevent the loss of information;

(4) Any steps taken to comply with any court order or party agreement requiring preservation of specific information;

(5) Any other facts relevant to its determination under this division.

[Effective: July 1, 1970; amended effective July 1, 1994; amended effective July 1, 2008; July 1, 2016.]

Staff Note (July 1, 2008 Amendment)

Civ. R. 37(F) provides factors for judges to consider when a party seeks sanctions against an opponent who has lost potentially relevant electronically stored information. This rule does not attempt to address the larger question of when the duty to preserve electronically stored information is triggered. That matter is addressed by case law and is generally left to the discretion of the trial judge.

Staff Notes (July 1, 2016 Amendments)

The rule is amended to adopt the 2007 stylistic changes to Fed.R.Civ.P. 37. In adopting those federal stylistic changes, the amendments also add provisions of the Federal rule that make the following substantive changes to existing Civ.R. 37:

1. Including within the scope of amended Civ.R. 37(A)(3), "a corporation or other entity fails to make a designation under Civ.R. 30(B)(5) or Civ.R. 31(A)";

2. Adding to the exceptions to amended Civ.R. 37(A)(5), "the movant filed the motion before attempting in good faith to obtain the discovery without court action";

3. Adding to the remedies available under amended Civ.R. 37(A)(5)(b) and Civ.R. 37(A)(5)(c), "the court may issue any protective order authorized under Rule 26(C)"; and

4. Adding amended Civ.R. 37(C)(1) addressing failure to supplement an earlier response.

The 2016 amendments to the Ohio rule do not incorporate the 2015 changes made to Fed.R.Civ.P. 37.

TITLE VI. TRIALS

RULE 38.   Jury Trial of Right

(A)   Right preserved.   The right to trial by jury shall be preserved to the parties inviolate.

(B)   Demand.   Any party may demand a trial by jury on any issue triable of right by a jury by serving upon the other parties a demand therefor at any time after the commencement of the action and not later than fourteen days after the service of the last pleading directed to such issue. Such demand shall be in writing and may be indorsed upon a pleading of the party. If the demand is indorsed upon a pleading the caption of the pleading shall state "jury demand endorsed hereon." In an action for appropriation of a right of way brought by a corporation pursuant to Article XIII, Section 5, of the Ohio Constitution, the jury shall be composed of twelve members unless the demand specifies a lesser number; and in the event of timely demand by more than one party in such action the jury shall be composed of the greater number not to exceed twelve. In all other civil actions the jury shall be composed of eight members unless the demand specifies a lesser number; and in the event of timely demand by more than one party in such actions the jury shall be composed of the greater number not to exceed eight.

(C)   Specification of issues.   In his demand a party may specify the issues which he wishes so tried; otherwise he shall be deemed to have demanded trial by jury for all the issues so triable. If he has demanded trial by jury for only some of the issues, any other party within fourteen days after service of the demand or such lesser time as the court may order, may serve a demand for trial by jury of any other or all of the issues of fact in the action.

(D)   Waiver.   The failure of a party to serve a demand as required by this rule and to file it as required by Rule 5(D) constitutes a waiver by him of trial by jury. A demand for trial by jury made as herein provided may not be withdrawn without the consent of the parties.

[Effective: July 1, 1970; amended effective July 1, 1972; July 1, 1976.]

RULE 39. Trial by Jury or by the Court

(A) By jury. When trial by jury has been demanded as provided in Rule 38, the action shall be designated upon the docket as a jury action. The trial of all issues so demanded shall be by jury, unless (1) the parties or their attorneys of record, by written stipulation filed with the court or by an oral stipulation made in open court and entered in the record, consent to trial by the court sitting without a jury or (2) the court upon motion or of its own initiative finds that a right of trial by jury of some or all of those issues does not exist. The failure of a party or his attorney of record either to answer or appear for trial constitutes a waiver of trial by jury by such party and authorizes submission of all issues to the court.

(B) By the court. Issues not demanded for trial by jury as provided in Rule 38 shall be tried by the court; but, notwithstanding the failure of a party to demand a jury in an action in which such a demand might have been made of right, the court in its discretion upon motion may order a trial by a jury of any or all issues.

(C) Advisory jury and trial by consent. In all actions not triable of right by a jury (1) the court upon motion or on its own initiative may try any issue with an advisory jury or (2) the court, with the consent of both parties, may order a trial of any issue with a jury, whose verdict has the same effect as if trial by jury had been a matter of right.

[Effective: July 1, 1970; amended effective July 1, 1971.]

RULE 40. Pre-Recorded Testimony

All of the testimony and such other evidence as may be appropriate may be presented at a trial by video recording, subject to the provisions of the Rules of Superintendence.

[Effective: July 1, 1972; amended effective July 1, 2013.]

Staff Notes (July 1, 2013 Amendments)

Rule 40 is amended to reflect that modern technology now encompasses digital video recording. The amendment is intended to clarify that presentation by video, analog or digital, is permissible provided that the recording complies with the provisions of the Rules of Superintendence for the Courts of Ohio.

RULE 41.   Dismissal of Actions

(A)   Voluntary dismissal: effect thereof.

(1)   By plaintiff; by stipulation. Subject to the provisions of Civ. R. 23(E), Civ. R. 23.1, and Civ. R. 66, a plaintiff, without order of court, may dismiss all claims asserted by that plaintiff against a defendant by doing either of the following:

(a)   filing a notice of dismissal at any time before the commencement of trial unless a counterclaim which cannot remain pending for independent adjudication by the court has been served by that defendant;

(b)   filing a stipulation of dismissal signed by all parties who have appeared in the action.

Unless otherwise stated in the notice of dismissal or stipulation, the dismissal is without prejudice, except that a notice of dismissal operates as an adjudication upon the merits of any claim that the plaintiff has once dismissed in any court.

(2)   By order of court. Except as provided in division (A)(1) of this rule, a claim shall not be dismissed at the plaintiff's instance except upon order of the court and upon such terms and conditions as the court deems proper. If a counterclaim has been pleaded by a defendant prior to the service upon that defendant of the plaintiff's motion to dismiss, a claim shall not be dismissed against the defendant's objection unless the counterclaim can remain pending for independent adjudication by the court. Unless otherwise specified in the order, a dismissal under division (A)(2) of this rule is without prejudice.

(B)   Involuntary dismissal: effect thereof.

(1)   Failure to prosecute. Where the plaintiff fails to prosecute, or comply with these rules or any court order, the court upon motion of a defendant or on its own motion may, after notice to the plaintiff's counsel, dismiss an action or claim.

(2)   Dismissal; non-jury action. After the plaintiff, in an action tried by the court without a jury, has completed the presentation of the plaintiff's evidence, the defendant, without waiving the right to offer evidence in the event the motion is not granted, may move for a dismissal on the ground that upon the facts and the law the plaintiff has shown no right to relief. The court as trier of the facts may then determine them and render judgment against the plaintiff or may decline to render any judgment until the close of all the evidence. If the court renders judgment on the merits against the plaintiff, the court shall make findings as provided in Civ. R. 52 if requested to do so by any party.

(3) **Adjudication on the merits; exception.** A dismissal under division (B) of this rule and any dismissal not provided for in this rule, except as provided in division (B)(4) of this rule, operates as an adjudication upon the merits unless the court, in its order for dismissal, otherwise specifies.

(4) **Failure other than on the merits.** A dismissal for either of the following reasons shall operate as a failure otherwise than on the merits:

      (a)   lack of jurisdiction over the person or the subject matter;

      (b)   failure to join a party under Civ. R. 19 or Civ. R. 19.1.

(C) **Dismissal of counterclaim, cross-claim, or third-party claim.** The provisions of this rule apply to the dismissal of any counterclaim, cross-claim, or third-party claim. A voluntary dismissal by the claimant alone pursuant to division (A)(1) of this rule shall be made before the commencement of trial.

(D) **Costs of previously dismissed action.** If a plaintiff who has once dismissed a claim in any court commences an action based upon or including the same claim against the same defendant, the court may make such order for the payment of costs of the claim previously dismissed as it may deem proper and may stay the proceedings in the action until the plaintiff has complied with the order.

[Effective: July 1, 1970; amended effective July 1, 1971; July 1, 1972; July 1, 2001.]

Staff Note (July 1, 2001 Amendment)

Civil Rule 41   Dismissal of Actions

This rule was amended (1) to reflect more precisely its interpretation by the Supreme Court in *Denham v. City of New Carlisle*, 86 Ohio St. 3d 594 (1999); (2) to conform Civ. R. 41(D) with Civ. R. 41(A) as amended; and (3) to reflect that Civ. R. 23.1 provides that a shareholder derivative action "shall not be dismissed or compromised without the approval of the court."

In divisions (B) and (C), masculine references were changed to gender-neutral language, the style used for rule references was changed, and other grammatical changes were made. No substantive amendment to divisions (B) and (C) was intended.

RULE 42. Consolidation; Separate Trials

(A)   Consolidation.

(1)   *Generally.* If actions before the court involve a common question of law or fact, the court may:

> (a) join for hearing or trial any or all matters at issue in the actions;

> (b) consolidate the actions; or

> (c) issue any other orders to avoid unnecessary cost or delay.

(2)   *Asbestos, silicosis, or mixed dust disease actions.* In tort actions involving an asbestos claim, a silicosis claim, or a mixed dust disease claim, the court may consolidate pending actions for case management purposes. For purposes of trial, the court may consolidate pending actions only with the consent of all parties. Absent the consent of all parties, the court may consolidate, for purposes of trial, only those pending actions relating to the same exposed person and members of the exposed person's household.

(3)   As used in division (A)(2) of this rule:

> (a)   "Asbestos claim" has the same meaning as in R.C. 2307.91;

> (b)   "Silicosis claim" and "mixed dust disease claim" have the same meaning as in R.C. 2307.84;

> (c)   In reference to an asbestos claim, "tort action" has the same meaning as in R.C. 2307.91;

> (d)   In reference to a silicosis claim or a mixed dust disease claim, "tort action" has the same meaning as in R.C. 2307.84.

(B)   Separate trials. For convenience, to avoid prejudice, or to expedite or economize, the court may order a separate trial of one or more separate issues, claims, cross-claims, counterclaims, or third-party claims. When ordering a separate trial, the court shall preserve any right to a jury trial.

[Effective: July 1, 1970; amended effective July 1, 2005; July 1, 2015.]

Staff Notes (July 1, 2015 Amendments)

Stylistic Changes

The rule is amended to conform the provisions of Civ.R. 42(A)(1) and Civ.R. 42(B) to the 2007 stylistic changes to Federal Rule 42. The amendments are nonsubstantive. Rule 42(A)(2), not found in the federal rule, remains unchanged.

Rule 42(B)   R.C. 2315.21(B)(1) Bifurcation

R.C. 2315.21(B)(1) requires a two-stage bifurcation of the trial upon the motion of any party in a tort action that is tried to a jury and in which a plaintiff makes a claim for compensatory damages and a claim for punitive or exemplary damages. In *Havel v. Villa St. Joseph,* 131 Ohio St.3d 235, 2012-Ohio-552, the Ohio Supreme Court held that the statute creates a substantive right and, therefore, takes precedence over the discretion conferred by Civ.R. 42(B) to grant or deny bifurcation. In cases governed by R.C. 2315.21(B), upon the motion of any party the trial court must grant the two-stage bifurcation required by the statute.

Staff Note (July 1, 2005 Amendment)

Civ. R. 42 is amended in response to requests from the General Assembly contained in Section 3 of Am. Sub. H.B. 342 of the 125th General Assembly, effective September 1, 2004, and Section 4 of Am. Sub. H.B. 292 of the 125th General Assembly, effective September 2, 2004. These acts contain provisions governing tort claims that allege exposure and injury by persons exposed to asbestos, silica, or mixed dust. Each act includes a request that the Supreme Court amend the Rules of Civil Procedure "to specify procedures for venue and consolidation" of asbestosis, silicosis, and mixed dust disease claims.

Rule 42(A)   Consolidation

Civ. R. 42(A)(2) provides that a trial court must have the consent of the parties before consolidating actions for trial that involve an asbestos claim, a silicosis claim, or a mixed dust disease claim. Absent the consent of the parties, the court may consolidate for trial only those claims that involve the same exposed person and members of the exposed person's household. The rule expressly permits the consolidation of pending actions for case management purposes. Division (A)(3) incorporates the statutory definitions of "asbestos claim," "silicosis claim," "mixed dust disease claim," and "tort action" for purposes of Civ. R. 42(A)(2).

RULE 43.   Taking Testimony

(A)   In open court. At trial or hearing, the witnesses' testimony shall be taken in open court unless a statute, the Rules of Evidence, these rules, or other rules adopted by the Supreme Court provide otherwise. For good cause in compelling circumstances and with appropriate safeguards, the court may permit testimony in open court by contemporaneous transmission from a different location.

(B)   Evidence on a motion. When a motion relies on facts outside the record, the court may hear the matter on affidavits or may hear it wholly or partly on oral testimony or on depositions.

[Effective: July 1, 2015.]

Staff Note (July 1, 2015 Amendment)

The July 1, 2015 amendment adopts a new rule – Civ.R. 43 – heretofore designated within the Ohio rules as "Reserved". The new rule is modeled on Fed.R.Civ.P. 43. Division (A) recognizes the availability of modern electronic transmission facilities by specifically authorizing live open court testimony from a location outside the courtroom. Consistent with Fed.R.Civ.P. 43(c) division (B) provides that a court may, in its discretion, consider facts presented by affidavit in deciding a motion.

RULE 44.   **Proof of Official Record**

(A)   **Authentication.**

(1)   **Domestic.** An official record, or an entry therein, kept within a state or within the United States or within a territory or other jurisdiction of the United States, when admissible for any purpose, may be evidenced by an official publication thereof or by a copy attested by the officer having the legal custody of the record, or by his deputy, and accompanied by a certificate that such officer has the custody. The certificate may be made by a judge of a court of record in which the record is kept or may be made by any public officer having a seal of office and having official duties in the political subdivision in which the record is kept, authenticated by the seal of his office.

(2)   **Foreign.** A foreign official record, or an entry therein, when admissible for any purpose, may be evidenced by an official publication thereof; or a copy thereof, attested by a person authorized to make the attestation, and accompanied by a final certification as to the genuineness of the signature and official position (a) of the attesting person or (b) of any foreign official whose certificate of genuineness of signature and official position relates to the attestation or is in a chain of certificates of genuineness of signature and official position relating to the attestation. A final certification may be made by a secretary of embassy or legation, consul general, consul, vice consul, or consular agent of the United States, or a diplomatic or consular official of the foreign country assigned or accredited to the United States. If reasonable opportunity has been given to all parties to investigate the authenticity and accuracy of the documents, the court may, for good cause shown, (a) admit an attested copy without final certification or (b) permit the foreign official record to be evidenced by an attested summary with or without a final certification.

(B)   **Lack of record.** A written statement that after diligent search no record or entry of a specified tenor is found to exist in the records designated by the statement, authenticated as provided in subdivision (A)(1) of this rule in the case of a domestic record, or complying with the requirements of subdivision (A)(2) of this rule for a summary in the case of a foreign record, is admissible as evidence that the records contain no such record or entry.

(C)   **Other proof.** This rule does not prevent the proof of official records or of entry or lack of entry therein by any other method authorized by law.

[Effective: July 1, 1970.]

RULE 44.1. Judicial Notice of Certain Law; Determination of Foreign Law

(A) Judicial notice of certain law.

(1) Judicial notice shall be taken of the rules of the supreme court of this state and of the decisional, constitutional, and public statutory law of this state.

(2) A party who intends to rely on a municipal ordinance, a local rule of court, or an administrative regulation within this state shall give notice in his pleading or other reasonable written notice. The court in taking judicial notice of a municipal ordinance, a local rule of court, or an administrative regulation within this state may inform itself in such manner as it deems proper, and may call upon counsel to aid in obtaining such information. The court's determination shall be treated as a ruling on a question of law and shall be made by the court and not the jury. A court may, however, take judicial notice of its own rules or of a municipal ordinance within the territorial jurisdiction of the court without advance notice in the pleading of a party or other written notice.

(3) A party who intends to rely on the decisional, constitutional, public statutory law, rules of court, municipal ordinances, or administrative regulations of any other state, territory, and jurisdiction of the United States shall give notice in his pleading or other reasonable notice. The court in taking judicial notice of the decisional, constitutional, public statutory law, rules of court, municipal ordinances, or administrative regulations of any other state, territory, and jurisdiction of the United States may inform itself in such manner as it deems proper, and may call upon counsel to aid in obtaining such information. The court's determination shall be treated as a ruling on a question of law, and shall be made by the court and not the jury.

(B) Determination of foreign law. A party who intends to rely on the law of a foreign country shall give notice in his pleadings or other reasonable written notice. The court in determining the law of a foreign country may consider any relevant material or source, including testimony, whether or not submitted by a party. The court's determination shall be treated as a ruling on a question of law and shall be made by the court and not the jury.

[Effective: July 1, 1970.]

RULE 45. Subpoena

(A) Form; Issuance; Notice.

(1) Every subpoena shall do all of the following:

    (a) state the name of the court from which it is issued, the title of the action, and the case number;

    (b) command each person to whom it is directed, at a time and place specified in the subpoena, to:

        (i) attend and give testimony at a trial or hearing at any place within this state;

        (ii) attend and give testimony at a deposition in the county where the deponent resides or is employed or transacts business in person, or at such other convenient place as is fixed by an order of court;

        (iii) produce documents, electronically stored information, or tangible things at a trial, hearing, or deposition;

        (iv) produce and permit inspection and copying of any designated documents or electronically stored information that are in the possession, custody, or control of the person;

        (v) produce and permit inspection and copying, testing, or sampling of any tangible things that are in the possession, custody, or control of the person; or

        (vi) permit entry upon designated land or other property that is in the possession or control of the person for the purposes described in Civ.R. 34(A)(3).

    (c) set forth the text of divisions (C) and (D) of this rule.

A command to produce and permit inspection may be joined with a command to attend and give testimony, or may be issued separately. A subpoena may specify the form or forms in which electronically stored information is to be produced, but may not require the production of the same information in more than one form.

A subpoena may not be used to obtain the attendance of a party or the production of documents by a party in discovery. Rather, a party's attendance at a deposition may be obtained only by notice under Civ.R. 30, and documents or electronically stored information may be obtained from a party in discovery only pursuant to Civ.R. 34.

(2) The clerk shall issue a subpoena, signed, but otherwise in blank, to a party requesting it, who shall complete it before service. An attorney who has filed an appearance on behalf of a party in an action may also sign and issue a subpoena on behalf of the court in which the action is pending.

(3) A party on whose behalf a subpoena is issued under division (A)(1)(b)(ii), (iii), (iv), (v), or (vi) of this rule shall serve prompt written notice, including a copy of the subpoena, on all other parties as provided in Civ.R. 5. If the issuing attorney modifies a subpoena issued under division (A)(1)(b)(ii), (iii), (iv), (v), or (vi) of this rule in any way, the issuing attorney shall give prompt written notice of the modification, including a copy of the subpoena as modified, to all other parties.

(B) Service

A subpoena may be served by a sheriff, bailiff, coroner, clerk of court, constable, or a deputy of any, by an attorney at law, or by any other person designated by order of court who is not a party and is not less than eighteen years of age. Service of a subpoena upon a person named therein shall be made by delivering a copy of the subpoena to the person, by reading it to him or her in person, by leaving it at the person's usual place of residence, or by placing a sealed envelope containing the subpoena in the United States mail as certified or express mail return receipt requested with instructions to the delivering postal authority to show to whom delivered, date of delivery and address where delivered, and by tendering to the person upon demand the fees for one day's attendance and the mileage allowed by law. The person responsible for serving the subpoena shall file a return of the subpoena with the clerk. When the subpoena is served by mail delivery, the person filing the return shall attach the signed receipt to the return. If the witness being subpoenaed resides outside the county in which the court is located, the fees for one day's attendance and mileage shall be tendered without demand. The return may be forwarded through the postal service or otherwise.

(C) Protection of persons subject to subpoenas.

(1) A party or an attorney responsible for the issuance and service of a subpoena shall take reasonable steps to avoid imposing undue burden or expense on a person subject to that subpoena.

(2)(a) A person commanded to produce under divisions (A)(1)(b), (iii), (iv), (v), or (vi) of this rule need not appear in person at the place of production or inspection unless commanded to attend and give testimony at a deposition, hearing, or trial.

(b) Subject to division (D)(2) of this rule, a person commanded to produce under divisions (A)(1)(b), (iii), (iv), (v), or (vi) of this rule may, within fourteen days after service of the subpoena or before the time specified for compliance if such time is less than fourteen days after service, serve upon the party or attorney designated in the subpoena written objections to production. If objection is made, the party serving the subpoena shall not be entitled to production except pursuant to an order of the court by which the subpoena was issued. If objection has been made, the party serving the subpoena, upon notice to the person commanded to produce, may move at any time for an order to compel the production. An order to compel production shall protect any person who is not a party or an officer of a party from significant expense resulting from the production commanded.

(3) On timely motion, the court from which the subpoena was issued shall quash or modify the subpoena, or order appearance or production only under specified conditions, if the subpoena does any of the following:

    (a)   Fails to allow reasonable time to comply;

    (b)   Requires disclosure of privileged or otherwise protected matter and no exception or waiver applies;

    (c)   Requires disclosure of a fact known or opinion held by an expert not retained or specially employed by any party in anticipation of litigation or preparation for trial as described by Civ.R. 26(B)(5), if the fact or opinion does not describe specific events or occurrences in dispute and results from study by that expert that was not made at the request of any party;

    (d)   Subjects a person to undue burden.

(4) Before filing a motion pursuant to division (C)(3)(d) of this rule, a person resisting discovery under this rule shall attempt to resolve any claim of undue burden through discussions with the issuing attorney. A motion filed pursuant to division (C)(3)(d) of this rule shall be supported by an affidavit of the subpoenaed person or a certificate of that person's attorney of the efforts made to resolve any claim of undue burden.

(5) If a motion is made under division (C)(3)(c) or (C)(3)(d) of this rule, the court shall quash or modify the subpoena unless the party in whose behalf the subpoena is issued shows a substantial need for the testimony or material that cannot be otherwise met without undue hardship and assures that the person to whom the subpoena is addressed will be reasonably compensated.

(D) Duties in responding to subpoena.

(1) A person responding to a subpoena to produce documents shall, at the person's option, produce them as they are kept in the usual course of business or organized and labeled to correspond with the categories in the subpoena. A person producing documents or electronically stored information pursuant to a subpoena for them shall permit their inspection and copying by all parties present at the time and place set in the subpoena for inspection and copying.

(2) If a request does not specify the form or forms for producing electronically stored information, a person responding to a subpoena may produce the information in a form or forms in which the information is ordinarily maintained if that form is reasonably useable, or in any

form that is reasonably useable. Unless ordered by the court or agreed to by the person subpoenaed, a person responding to a subpoena need not produce the same electronically stored information in more than one form.

(3) A person need not provide discovery of electronically stored information when the production imposes undue burden or expense. On motion to compel discovery or for a protective order, the person from whom electronically stored information is sought must show that the information is not reasonably accessible because of undue burden or expense. If a showing of undue burden or expense is made, the court may nonetheless order production of electronically stored information if the requesting party shows good cause. The court shall consider the factors in Civ. R. 26(B)(4) when determining if good cause exists. In ordering production of electronically stored information, the court may specify the format, extent, timing, allocation of expenses and other conditions for the discovery of the electronically stored information.

(4) When information subject to a subpoena is withheld on a claim that it is privileged or subject to protection as trial preparation materials, the claim shall be made expressly and shall be supported by a description of the nature of the documents, communications, or things not produced that is sufficient to enable the demanding party to contest the claim.

(5) If information is produced in response to a subpoena that is subject to a claim of privilege or of protection as trial-preparation material, the person making the claim may notify any party that received the information of the claim and the basis for it. After being notified, a receiving party must promptly return, sequester, or destroy the specified information and any copies within the party's possession, custody or control. A party may not use or disclose the information until the claim is resolved. A receiving party may promptly present the information to the court under seal for a determination of the claim of privilege or of protection as trial-preparation material. If the receiving party disclosed the information before being notified, it must take reasonable steps to retrieve it. The person who produced the information must preserve the information until the claim is resolved.

(E) Sanctions. Failure by any person without adequate excuse to obey a subpoena served upon that person may be deemed a contempt of the court from which the subpoena issued. A subpoenaed person or that person's attorney who frivolously resists discovery under this rule may be required by the court to pay the reasonable expenses, including reasonable attorney's fees, of the party seeking the discovery. The court from which a subpoena was issued may impose upon a party or attorney in breach of the duty imposed by division (C)(1) of this rule an appropriate sanction, which may include, but is not limited to, lost earnings and reasonable attorney's fees.

(F) Privileges. Nothing in this rule shall be construed to authorize a party to obtain information protected by any privilege recognized by law, or to authorize any person to disclose such information.

[Effective: July 1, 1970; amended effective July 1, 1971; July 1, 1972; July 1, 1993; July 1, 1994; July 1, 2005; amended effective July 1, 2008; July 1, 2012; July 1, 2014.]

Staff Note (July 1, 2014 Amendments)

Rule 45(C)(3)(c) is amended to account for the 2008 renumbering of Civ.R. 26(B) which changed the section of that rule addressing experts from Civ.R. 26(B)(4) to Civ.R. 26(B)(5).

Staff Note (July 1, 2012 Amendment)

Rule 45 is amended to return language from Civ.R. 45 (D)(2) before the 1993 amendments. Under the 2012 amendment a deponent no longer may be compelled by subpoena to appear for a deposition anywhere in the state, but only in the county where the deponent resides or is employed or transacts business in person, or at such other convenient place as is fixed by an order of court. A person may still be compelled to appear for trial or hearing at any place within the state.

Staff Note (July 1, 2008 Amendment)

Rule 45 allows discovery to be obtained from nonparties in a manner that closely parallels Rule 34 discovery of parties. Civ. R. 45(A) and 45(D)(2) clarify that a party may use subpoenas to obtain electronically stored information from nonparties. It allows the party issuing the subpoena to specify the form or forms of production for electronically stored information while prohibiting the requesting party from demanding that the subpoenaed person provide the same information in more than one electronic format. For example, the party issuing the subpoena may request that a party's internal memorandums on a particular subject be produced in a Word™ file, while financial records be provided in an Excel™ spreadsheet format or other format commonly used for financial matters.

Civ. R. 45(B) is amended in light of court decisions holding that service of a subpoena by a mail carrier was not authorized under the prior language of the Rule. Consistent with Civ. R. 4.1(A) relating to service of process for a complaint and summons, the amendment allows a person, otherwise authorized by the Rule to perform service of a subpoena, to do so by means of United States certified or United States express mail.

Civ. R. 45(D)(2) parallels Rule 34(B) and applies when a party serving the subpoena does not specify the form in which electronically stored information should be produced; in that situation the person subpoenaed has the option of producing the materials in the form in which the information is ordinarily maintained or another form provided that the form produced is reasonable. This section also clarifies that the respondent only has to provide electronically stored information in one format unless the court orders or the parties agree to a different arrangement.

Staff Note (July 1, 2005 Amendment)

Rule 45(A)   Form; Issuance; Notice

Civ. R. 45(A)(3) is amended so that provisions requiring notice of issuance of most types of subpoena directed to nonparties appear in Civ. R. 45(A)(3) rather than being split between Civ. R. 45(A)(3) and Civ. R. 34(C). Civ. R. 34(C) is concurrently amended to eliminate any reference to notice of issuance of a subpoena directed to a nonparty. The prior arrangement made it easy to overlook the notice provisions of Civ. R. 34(C). See, e.g., *Neftzer v. Neftzer*, 140 Ohio App.3d 618, 621 (2000).

The amendment adds a new first sentence to Civ. R. 45(A)(3) to require service as provided in Civ. R. 5 on all other parties of prompt written notice of any subpoena issued under Civ. R. 45(A)(1)(b)(ii), (iii), (iv), or (v). Unlike former Civ. R. 34(C), amended Civ. R. 45(a)(3) requires that notice include a copy of the subpoena.

Notice of the taking of a deposition upon oral examination, whether of a party or nonparty, is required by Civ. R. 30(B)(1) and service of questions for a deposition upon written questions, whether of a party or nonparty, is required by Civ. R. 31(B). See, e.g., *Standring v. Xerox Corp.*, 1992 WL 90726 at *3-4, No. 60426 (8th Dist. Ct. App., Cuyahoga, 4-30-92). Subpoenas issued under Civ. R. 45(A)(1)(b)(i) for trial or hearing are excluded from the notice requirement of amended Civ. R. 45(A)(3) to permit a trial court to decide, pursuant to local rule, customary practice, or otherwise, whether to require prior disclosure by parties of the identity of witnesses to be called during a trial or hearing.

The notice requirement of amended Civ. R. 45(A)(3), like its counterpart in Rule 45(b)(1), Federal Rules of Civil Procedure, is intended "to afford other parties an opportunity to object to the production or inspection, or to serve a demand for additional documents or things." Advisory Committee's Note to 1991 Amendments to the Federal Rules of Civil Procedure; see, e.g., *Spencer v. Steinman*, 179 F.R.D. 484, 488 (E.D. Pa. 1998).

The title of Civ. R. 45(A) is amended to call attention to the fact that it deals with notice of issuance of subpoenas as well as with the form and issuance of subpoenas.

RULE 46.   Exceptions Unnecessary

An exception at any stage or step of the case or matter is unnecessary to lay a foundation for review whenever a matter has been called to the attention of the court by objection, motion, or otherwise and the court has ruled thereon.

[Effective: July 1, 1970; amended effective July 1, 1975.]

RULE 47.   Jurors

(A)   Brief introduction of case. To assist prospective jurors in understanding the general nature of the case, the court, in consultation with the parties, may give jurors a brief introduction to the case. The brief introduction may include a general description of the legal claims and defenses of the parties.

(B)   Examination of prospective jurors. Any person called as a prospective juror for the trial of any cause shall be examined under oath or upon affirmation as to the prospective juror's qualifications. The court may permit the parties or their attorneys to conduct the examination of the prospective jurors or may itself conduct the examination. In the latter event, the court shall permit the parties or their attorneys to supplement the examination by further inquiry. Nothing in this rule shall limit the court's discretion to allow the examination of all prospective jurors in the array or, in the alternative, to permit individual examination of each prospective juror seated on a panel, prior to any challenges for cause or peremptory challenges.

(C)   Challenges to prospective jurors. In addition to challenges for cause provided by law, each party peremptorily may challenge three prospective jurors. If the interests of multiple litigants are essentially the same, "each party" shall mean "each side."

Peremptory challenges shall be exercised alternately, with the first challenge exercised by the plaintiff. The failure of a party to exercise a peremptory challenge constitutes a waiver of that challenge, but does not constitute a waiver of any subsequent challenge. However, if all parties or sides, alternately and in sequence, fail to exercise a peremptory challenge, the joint failure constitutes a waiver of all peremptory challenges.

A prospective juror peremptorily challenged by either party shall be excused.

Nothing in this rule shall limit the court's discretion to allow challenges to be made outside the hearing of prospective jurors.

(D)   Alternate jurors.

(1)   Selection; powers. The court may direct that no more than four jurors in addition to the regular jury be called and impaneled to sit as alternate jurors. Alternate jurors in the order in which they are called shall replace jurors who, prior to the time the jury retires to consider its verdict, become or are found to be unable or disqualified to perform their duties. Alternate jurors shall be drawn in the same manner, shall have the same qualifications, shall be subject to the same examination and challenges, shall take the same oath, and shall have the same functions, powers, facilities, and privileges as the regular jurors. Each party is entitled to one peremptory challenge in addition to those otherwise allowed by law if one or two alternate jurors are to be impaneled, and two peremptory challenges if three or four alternate jurors are to be impaneled. The additional peremptory challenges may be used against an alternate juror.

(2)   Retention; discharge. The court may retain alternate jurors after the jury retires. The court must ensure that a retained alternate does not discuss the case with anyone until that alternate replaces a juror or is discharged. If an alternate replaces a juror after deliberations have begun, the court must instruct the jury to begin its deliberations anew. If the court does not retain alternate jurors after the jury retires and instead discharges the alternate jurors, the alternate jurors cannot be recalled as jurors.

(E)   Taking of notes by jurors. The court, after providing appropriate cautionary instructions, may permit jurors who wish to do so to take notes during a trial. If the court permits the taking of notes, notes taken by a juror may be carried into deliberations by that juror. The court shall require that all juror notes be collected and destroyed promptly after the jury renders a verdict.

(F)   Juror questions to witnesses. The court may permit jurors to propose questions for the court to ask of the witnesses. If the court permits jurors to propose questions, the court shall use procedures that minimize the risk of prejudice, including all of the following:

(1)   Require jurors to propose any questions to the court in writing;

(2)   Retain a copy of each proposed question for the record;

(3)   Instruct the jurors that they shall not display or discuss a proposed question with other jurors;

(4)   Before reading a question to a witness, provide counsel with an opportunity to object to each question on the record and outside the hearing of the jury;

(5)   Read the question, either as proposed or rephrased, to the witness;

(6)   Permit counsel to reexamine the witness regarding a matter addressed by a juror question;

(7)   If a question proposed by a juror is not asked, instruct the jurors that they should not draw any adverse inference from the court's refusal to ask any question proposed by a juror.

[Effective: July 1, 1970; amended effective July 1, 1971; July 1, 1972; July 1, 1975; July 1, 2005; July 1, 2006; July 1, 2009; July 1, 2012; July 1, 2019.]

Staff Note (July 1, 2019 Amendment)

Division (D)

The amendment divides the prior, undivided Division (D) into two parts.

The language of the existing rule addressing the selection and powers of alternate jurors, including the language relating to the procedure for selecting alternate jurors and the use of peremptory challenges in the selection of alternate jurors, is moved, unchanged, to Division (D)(1).

Division (D)(2) retains the language of the existing rule permitting the court, in its discretion, to retain alternate jurors when the jury retires to deliberate, but also adds a provision addressing a situation not addressed by the existing rule — the recalling of alternate jurors who are discharged after the jury retires to deliberate. The amendment specifically prohibits the court from recalling discharged alternate jurors.

Retention. A retained alternate juror has not been discharged. A retained (i.e. not "discharged") alternate juror continues to be subject to the court's instructions and admonitions, and thus may not discuss the case with anyone "until that alternate replaces a juror or is discharged." The rule does not address whether a "retained" alternate juror may be free to leave — a matter left to the court's discretion — but good practice suggests that the court ensure that a retained alternate juror remain readily available to appear before the court to replace an alternate juror if necessary.

Discharge. "Discharge" occurs when the court does not retain, but instead "discharges" an alternate juror. A discharged (i.e. not "retained") alternate juror cannot be recalled as a juror.

Staff Note (July 1, 2012 Amendment)

Civ.R. 47(D) is amended to parallel Crim.R. 24 (C) (1), the alternate juror rule for non-capital cases. The difference between the two rules is that six alternates are permitted under the criminal rule.

Staff Note (July 1, 2009 Amendment)

Prior to 2006, Civ. R. 47 appeared to require judges to empanel a prospective jury and examine each one individually, a process referred to as the "strike and replace" method. In 2006, Civ. R. 47(B) was amended with the intent to clarify that examination of prospective jurors in an array (sometimes referred to as the "struck" method of juror examination) was also permitted. Civ. R. 47(C), however, which was not changed in 2006, retained language that arguably applied apply only to examination of jurors seated on a panel. The 2009 amendments add language to Civ. R. 47(B) and delete language from Civ. R. 47(C) to further clarify that prospective jurors may be examined either in the array or after being seated on a panel.

Staff Note (July 1, 2006 Amendment)

Civ. R. 47 is amended to recognize the existence of alternative methods of jury selection and expressly permit the use of these methods in Ohio courts. The amendments are consistent with recommendations contained in the February 2004 *Report and Recommendations of the Supreme Court of Ohio Task Force on Jury Service*, at pp. 10-11.

The Task Force identified two primary methods of jury selection and encouraged the use of a selection process that is efficient and enhances juror satisfaction. The Rules Advisory Committee learned that some judges and lawyers believe that the pre-2006 version of Civ. R. 47 precluded the use of a selection method, commonly referred to as the "struck" method, whereby prospective jurors are examined as a group and then the trial judge and attorneys meet privately to challenge jurors for cause and exercise peremptory challenges. Two amendments to Civ. R. 47 are added to expressly permit alternative selection methods.

Rule 47(B)   Examination of prospective jurors

The last sentence of Civ. R. 47(B) is added to expressly permit the examination of prospective jurors in an array.

Rule 47(C)   Challenges to prospective jury

The last sentence of Civ. R. 47(C) is added to expressly afford the trial court the discretion to allow the exercise of challenges for cause and peremptory challenges outside the hearing of the jury.

Staff Note (July 1, 2005 Amendment)

Civ. R. 47 is amended to reflect four recommendations of the Task Force on Jury Service. See *Report and Recommendations of the Supreme Court of Ohio Task Force on Jury Service* (February 2004).

Rule 47(A)   Preliminary statement of case

A new Civ. R. 47(A) is added to permit the trial judge, prior to jury selection, to provide a brief introduction to the case to persons called as prospective jurors. See *Report and Recommendations, supra,* at 1 (recommending "a brief statement of the case by the court or counsel prior to the beginning of voir dire" and inclusion of "the legal claims and defenses of the parties' in the list of instructions the court may give at the commencement of trial"). The Rules Advisory Committee shares the views of the Task Force that the preliminary statement may "help the jury selection process run smoothly" and "increase the satisfaction of jurors." *Report and Recommendations, supra,* at 9. The preliminary statement is intended to help prospective jurors to understand why certain questions are asked during voir dire, recognize personal bias, and give candid responses to questions during voir dire.

The Committee recognizes that there may be instances in which the brief introduction is unnecessary; thus the rule vests discretion with the trial judge as to whether an introduction will be provided in a particular case. The rule also requires the trial judge to consult with the parties as to whether to provide the introduction and the content of the introduction. The consultation is required in recognition that the parties can aid the trial judge in determining whether a statement is necessary, developing the content of the statement, and ascertaining the claims and defenses the parties will put forth during trial.

Former divisions (A), (B), and (C) of Civ. R. 47 are relettered as divisions (B), (C), and (D), respectively.

Rule 47(C)   Challenges to prospective jurors

New Civ. R. 47(C) (formerly Civ. R. 47(B)) is amended to make two related principles regarding peremptory challenges more clear. One principle is that failure of a party to exercise a given peremptory challenge waives that challenge but does not waive any other peremptory challenges to which the party may otherwise be entitled. As the 1972 Staff Notes to Civ. R. 47 explained:

> Thus, assume that plaintiff waives [plaintiff's] first opportunity to exercise a peremptory challenge. Defendant exercises [defendant's] first peremptory challenge. If plaintiff, in turn, now exercises a peremptory challenge, the challenge will be [plaintiff's] second challenge because [plaintiff] has waived [plaintiff's] first challenge.

The other principle is that consecutive passes by all parties or sides waives all remaining peremptory challenges. As the 1972 Staff Notes likewise pointed out, "a double pass' ends the procedure even though peremptory challenges might remain." The Task Force concluded that, contrary to the language and intent of former Civ. R. 47(B), "often courts and attorneys will assume that once a peremptory challenge is waived all remaining peremptory challenges are waived." *Report and Recommendations, supra,* at 22. The amended language is designed to deter the incorrect assumption perceived by the Task Force.

Rule 47(E)   Taking of notes by jurors

A new Civ. R. 47(E) is added to explicitly authorize trial courts, after providing appropriate cautionary instructions, to permit jurors who wish to do so to take notes during trial and to take notes into deliberations. The Rules Advisory Committee agrees with the Task Force that allowing jurors to take notes potentially promotes the fact-finding process and aids juror comprehension and recollection.

The reference in sentence one of new division (E) to "appropriate cautionary instructions" reflects the apparent requirements of *State v. Waddell,* 75 Ohio St.3d 163 (1996), which held that "[a] trial court has the discretion to permit or prohibit note-taking by jurors," *Waddell*, 75 Ohio St.3d at 163 (syl. 1), and explained that "[i]f a trial court determines that a particular case warrants note-taking, the court can, *sua sponte*, furnish jurors with materials for taking notes and instruct the jurors that they are permitted to take notes during the trial." *Id.* at 170. The *Waddell* opinion appears to condition the permitting of note-taking on the giving of instructions to jurors that (1) "they are not required to take notes;" *id.* (syl. 2), (2) "their notes are to be confidential;" (3) "note-taking should not divert their attention from hearing the evidence in the case;" (4) "a juror who has not taken notes should not be influenced by those jurors who decided to take notes;" and (5) "notes taken by jurors are to be used solely as memory aids and should not be allowed to take precedence over their independent memory of facts." *Id.* (syl. 3); see also *State v. Blackburn*, 1996 WL 570869 at *3 and n.1, No. 93 CA 10 (5th Dist. Ct. App., Fairfield, 9-26-96) (finding no plain error in the trial court's decision to permit juror note-taking despite lack of instruction on items (3) through (5) but noting that "in the future, it would be better practice for trial courts to instruct and caution the jury as suggested by the Ohio Supreme Court in *Waddell*"); *cf.* 1 Ohio Jury Instructions 2.52, § 1 ("Note-taking Prohibited") and § 2 ("Note-taking Permitted") (2002). The Task Force noted that many of the judges who participated in the pilot project that it sponsored "instructed jurors to make notes only when there was a break in the testimony (e.g., while judge and attorneys are busy at sidebar)." *Report and Recommendations, supra*, at 14.

Sentence two of new division (E) explicitly authorizes a practice perhaps only implicitly approved in *Waddell*, i.e., the carrying into deliberations by a juror of any notes taken pursuant to permission of the court. See Markus, *Trial Handbook for Ohio Lawyers* § 37:6 (2003) (citing *Waddell* for the proposition that "[w]hen the court permits the jurors to take notes during the trial, it may allow the jurors to retain those notes during their deliberations").

The requirement of sentence three of new division (E) that the court require that all juror notes be collected and destroyed promptly after verdict reflects in part the *Waddell* prescription that "notes are to be confidential." *See also State v. Williams*, 80 Ohio App.3d 648, 654 (1992) (cited with apparent approval by the Court in *Waddell* and rejecting the argument that notes taken by jurors should have been preserved for review rather than destroyed).

Rule 47(F)   Juror questions to witnesses

A new Civ. R. 47(F) is added to set forth a procedure to be followed if the trial court permits jurors to propose questions to be asked of witnesses during trial. See *Report and Recommendations, supra*, at 15-16 and *State v. Fisher* 99 Ohio St.3d 127, 2003-Ohio-2761. The rule incorporates the holding of the Supreme Court in *State v. Fisher, supra*, by stating that the practice of allowing jurors to propose questions to witnesses is discretionary with the trial judge, and codifies procedures that have been sanctioned by the Supreme Court. See *State v. Fisher* 99 Ohio St.3d at 135. In addition to the procedures outlined in *Fisher*, the rule provides that the court must retain a copy of all written questions proposed by the jury for the record and that the court may rephrase any question proposed by the jury before posing it to a witness. These added procedures ensure the existence of a proper record, should an issue regarding juror questions be raised on appeal, and recognize that a question proposed by a juror may need to be rephrased for clarity, to address an objection from a party, or for some other reason appropriate under the circumstances.

The amendments to Civ. R. 47 also include nonsubstantive changes that include gender-neutral language and uniform usage of the term "prospective juror."

RULE 48. Juries: Majority Verdict; Stipulation of Number of Jurors

In all civil actions, a jury shall render a verdict upon the concurrence of three-fourths or more of their number. The verdict shall be in writing and signed by each of the jurors concurring therein. All jurors shall then return to court where the judge shall cause the verdict to be read and inquiry made to determine if the verdict is that of three-fourths or more of the jurors. Upon request of either party, the jury shall be polled by asking each juror if the verdict is that of the juror; if more than one-fourth of the jurors answer in the negative, or if the verdict in substance is defective, the jurors must be sent out again for further deliberation. If three-fourths or more of the jurors answer affirmatively, the verdict is complete and the jury shall be discharged from the case. If the verdict is defective in form only, with the assent of the jurors and before their discharge, the court may correct it.

The parties may stipulate that the jury shall consist of any number less than the maximum number provided by Rule 38(B). For the purpose of rendering a verdict, whenever three-fourths of the jury does not consist of an integral number, the next higher number shall be construed to represent three-fourths of the jury. For juries with less than four members, the verdict must be unanimous.

[Effective: July 1, 1970; amended effective July 1, 1971; July 1, 1972.]

RULE 49.   Verdicts; Interrogatories

(A)   General verdict. A general verdict, by which the jury finds generally in favor of the prevailing party, shall be used.

(B)   General verdict accompanied by answer to interrogatories. The court shall submit written interrogatories to the jury, together with appropriate forms for a general verdict, upon request of any party prior to the commencement of argument. Counsel shall submit the proposed interrogatories to the court and to opposing counsel at such time. The court shall inform counsel of its proposed action upon the requests prior to their arguments to the jury, but the interrogatories shall be submitted to the jury in the form that the court approves. The interrogatories may be directed to one or more determinative issues whether issues of fact or mixed issues of fact and law.

The court shall give such explanation or instruction as may be necessary to enable the jury both to make answers to the interrogatories and to render a general verdict, and the court shall direct the jury both to make written answers and to render a general verdict.

When the general verdict and the answers are consistent, the appropriate judgment upon the verdict and answers shall be entered pursuant to Rule 58. When one or more of the answers is inconsistent with the general verdict, judgment may be entered pursuant to Rule 58 in accordance with the answers, notwithstanding the general verdict, or the court may return the jury for further consideration of its answers and verdict or may order a new trial.

(C)   Special verdicts abolished. Special verdicts shall not be used.

[Effective: July 1, 1970; amended effective July 1, 1980.]

RULE 50. Motion for a Directed Verdict, for Judgment, or for Judgment Notwithstanding the Verdict or in Lieu of Verdict

(A) Motion for directed verdict.

(1) When made. A motion for a directed verdict may be made on the opening statement of the opponent, at the close of the opponent's evidence or at the close of all the evidence.

(2) When not granted. A party who moves for a directed verdict at the close of the evidence offered by an opponent may offer evidence in the event that the motion is not granted, without having reserved the right so to do and to the same extent as if the motion had not been made. A motion for a directed verdict which is not granted is not a waiver of trial by jury even though all parties to the action have moved for directed verdicts.

(3) Grounds. A motion for a directed verdict shall state the specific grounds therefor.

(4) When granted on the evidence. When a motion for a directed verdict has been properly made, and the trial court, after construing the evidence most strongly in favor of the party against whom the motion is directed, finds that upon any determinative issue reasonable minds could come to but one conclusion upon the evidence submitted and that conclusion is adverse to such party, the court shall sustain the motion and direct a verdict for the moving party as to that issue.

(5) Jury assent unnecessary. The order of the court granting a motion for a directed verdict is effective without any assent of the jury.

(B) Post-trial motion for judgment or for judgment notwithstanding the verdict or in lieu of verdict.

(1) Whether or not a motion to direct a verdict has been made or overruled, a party may serve a motion to have the verdict and any judgment entered thereon set aside and to have judgment entered in accordance with the party's motion. Such a motion shall be served within twenty-eight days of the entry of judgment or, if the clerk has not completed service of the notice of judgment within the three-day period described in Civ.R. 58(B), within twenty-eight days of the date when the clerk actually completes service. If a verdict was not returned, a party may serve a motion for judgment in accordance with the party's motion within twenty-eight days of the jury's discharge. A motion for a new trial may be joined with either motion, or a new trial may be requested in the alternative.

(2) Unless otherwise provided by local rule or by order of the court, arguments in response to the motion shall be served within fourteen days of service of the motion, and a movant's reply may be served within seven days of service of the response to the motion.

(3)   If a verdict was returned, the court may allow the judgment to stand or may reopen the judgment. If the judgment is reopened, the court shall either order a new trial or direct the entry of judgment, but no judgment shall be rendered by the court on the ground that the verdict is against the weight of the evidence. If no verdict was returned the court may direct the entry of judgment or may order a new trial.

(C)   Conditional rulings on motion for judgment notwithstanding verdict.

(1)   If the motion for judgment notwithstanding the verdict, provided for in division (B) of this rule, is granted, the court shall also rule on the motion for a new trial, if any, by determining whether it should be granted if the judgment is thereafter vacated or reversed. If the motion for a new trial is thus conditionally granted, the order thereon does not affect the finality of the judgment. In case the motion for a new trial has been conditionally granted and the judgment is reversed on appeal, the new trial shall proceed unless the appellate court has otherwise ordered. In case the motion for a new trial has been conditionally denied, the appellee on appeal may assert error in that denial; and if the judgment is reversed on appeal, subsequent proceedings shall be in accordance with the order of the appellate court.

(2)   The party whose verdict has been set aside on motion for judgment notwithstanding the verdict may serve a motion for a new trial pursuant to Civ.R. 59 not later than twenty-eight days after entry of the judgment notwithstanding the verdict.

(D)   Denial of motion for judgment notwithstanding verdict. If the motion for judgment notwithstanding the verdict is denied, the party who prevailed on that motion may, as appellee, assert grounds entitling him to a new trial in the event the appellate court concludes that the trial court erred in denying the motion for judgment notwithstanding the verdict. If the appellate court reverses the judgment, nothing in this rule precludes it from determining that the appellee is entitled to a new trial, or from directing the trial court to determine whether a new trial shall be granted.

(E)   Statement of basis of decision. When in a jury trial a court directs a verdict or grants judgment without or contrary to the verdict of the jury, the court shall state the basis for its decision in writing prior to or simultaneous with the entry of judgment. Such statement may be dictated into the record or included in the entry of judgment.

[Effective: July 1, 1970; July 1, 2013; July 1, 2015; July 1, 2018.]

Staff Note (July 1, 2018 Amendment)

Division (B): Post-trial motion for judgment or for judgment in lieu of verdict.

The amendment provides that if the clerk fails to serve the parties with notice of a judgment in the three-day period contemplated by Civ.R. 58(B), the time to serve a post-trial motion for judgment in favor of the movant does not begin to run until after the clerk does so. The purpose of the amendment is to avoid the harsh result that otherwise can occur if a would-be movant does not receive notice of the judgment. *See, e.g., Wing v. Haaff*, 1st Dist. Hamilton No. C-160257, 2016-Ohio-8258. This amendment brings the timing of post-trial motions under Civ.R. 50 in line with the timing of a notice of appeal in civil cases under App.R. 4(A)(3).

Staff Note (July 1, 2015 Amendments)

Consistent with the provisions of Civ.R. 59(B) addressing motions for new trial, Civ.R. 50(B) is amended to make clear that the motion must be served within the required time. The time for filing the motion is governed by Civ.R. 5(D).

Consistent with a similar amendment to Civ.R. 6(B), the provisions of Civ.R. 50(B) are also amended to specify, in the absence of a local rule or court order providing a time for responding to a motion for judgment notwithstanding the verdict, a fallback time of fourteen days after service of the motion within which to serve responsive arguments. In the absence of a local rule or court order addressing replies, the amendment also permits the movant to serve reply arguments within seven days after service of the adverse party's response. The time for filing responsive arguments and replies is governed by Civ.R. 5(D), again in the absence of a local rule or order of the court specifying a different time for filing.

Staff Notes (July 1, 2013 Amendments)

Rule 50(B) is amended to extend the time for filing a motion for judgment notwithstanding the verdict to 28 days after entry of judgment, or within 28 days after the jury has been discharged if a verdict was not returned. These changes are modeled on the 2009 amendments to Fed.R.Civ.P. 50(b) and are made for the same reasons that prompted the amendments to the federal rule.

RULE 51. Instructions to the Jury; Objection

(A) Instructions; error; record. At the close of the evidence or at such earlier time during the trial as the court reasonably directs, any party may file written requests that the court instruct the jury on the law as set forth in the requests. Copies shall be furnished to all other parties at the time of making the requests. The court shall inform counsel of its proposed action on the requests prior to counsel's arguments to the jury and shall give the jury complete instructions after the arguments are completed. The court also may give some or all of its instructions to the jury prior to counsel's arguments. The court shall reduce its final instructions to writing or make an audio, electronic, or other recording of those instructions, provide at least one written copy or recording of those instructions to the jury for use during deliberations, and preserve those instructions for the record.

On appeal, a party may not assign as error the giving or the failure to give any instruction unless the party objects before the jury retires to consider its verdict, stating specifically the matter objected to and the grounds of the objection. Opportunity shall be given to make the objection out of the hearing of the jury.

(B) Cautionary instructions. At the commencement and during the course of the trial, the court may give the jury cautionary and other instructions of law relating to trial procedure, credibility and weight of the evidence, and the duty and function of the jury and may acquaint the jury generally with the nature of the case.

[Effective: July 1, 1970; amended effective July 1, 1972; July 1, 1975; July 1, 1992; July 1, 2005.]

Staff Note (July 1, 2005 Amendment)

Rule 51(A)   Instructions; error; record

Civ. R. 51 is amended to reflect a recommendation of the Task Force on Jury Service. See *Report and Recommendations of the Supreme Court of Ohio Task Force on Jury Service* at 1 and 12-13 (February 2004). The amendment mandates practices that trial courts have frequently chosen to adopt in particular civil actions: (1) reducing final jury instructions to writing or making an audio, electronic, or other recording of those instructions; (2) providing at least one written copy or recording of those instructions to the jury for use during deliberations; and (3) preserving those instructions for the record.

R.C. 2315.01(G) provides that (1) "[a]ny charge shall be reduced to writing by the court if either party, before the argument to the jury is commenced, requests it;" (2) "[a]ll written charges and instructions shall be taken by the jurors in their retirement;" and (3) "[a]ll written charges and instructions ... shall remain on file with the papers of the case." The Modern Courts Amendment, art. IV, § 5(B), of the Ohio Constitution, provides that "[a]ll laws in conflict with [valid Civil Rules] shall be of no further force or effect after such rules have taken effect." Some aspects of R.C. 2315.01 appear to have survived promulgation of the Civil Rules. *Phung v. Waste Mgt., Inc.*, 71 Ohio St.3d 408, 410 (1994) (R.C. 2315.01(C)); *State v. Jenkins*, 15 Ohio St.3d 164, 214 and n.43 (1984) (R.C. 2315.01(C), 2315.01(F)). However, to the extent that any of the provisions of R.C. 2315.01(G) quoted above are interpreted as conflicting with amended Civ. R. 51, the rule presumably supersedes the code section by virtue of art. IV, § 5(B). *See generally* 1 Klein and Darling, *Baldwin's Ohio*

Practice, Civil Practice § 1:96 (2d ed. 2004) and Harper and Solimine, 4 *Anderson's Ohio Civil Practice* § 147.01 (1996); *cf. Kinzer v. Wilson*, 1986 WL 8182 at *2, No. 1247 (4th Dist. Ct. App., Ross, 7-22-86) ("appellants admit that R.C. 2315.01(G) has been superseded by Civ. R. 51;" "The staff note of 7-1-72 under Civ. R. 51 clearly states that Civ. R. 51(A) supersedes R.C. 2315.01(G)"); *Cole v. Bollinger*, 1983 WL 6936 at *3-4, No C.A. WD-83-26 (6th Dist. Ct. App., Wood, 9-2-83).

The practices mandated by the amendment are intended to increase juror comprehension of jury instructions, reduce juror questions of the court during deliberations, and help juries structure their deliberations. The Task Force recommended that "each individual juror be given a copy of written instructions but, in the event of budgetary constraints, one copy of written instructions be provided to the jury to use during the deliberation process." *Report and Recommendations, supra,* at 13.

RULE 52. Findings by the Court

When questions of fact are tried by the court without a jury, judgment may be general for the prevailing party unless one of the parties in writing requests otherwise before the entry of judgment pursuant to Civ. R. 58, or not later than seven days after the party filing the request has been given notice of the court's announcement of its decision, whichever is later, in which case, the court shall state in writing the findings of fact found separately from the conclusions of law.

When a request for findings of fact and conclusions of law is made, the court, in its discretion, may require any or all of the parties to submit proposed findings of fact and conclusions of law; however, only those findings of fact and conclusions of law made by the court shall form part of the record.

Findings of fact and conclusions of law required by this rule and by Civ.R. 41(B)(2) and Civ.R. 23(G)(3) are unnecessary upon all other motions including those pursuant to Civ.R. 12, Civ.R. 55 and Civ.R. 56.

An opinion or memorandum of decision filed in the action prior to judgment entry and containing findings of fact and conclusions of law stated separately shall be sufficient to satisfy the requirements of this rule and Civ.R. 41(B)(2).

[Effective: July 1, 1970; amended effective July 1, 1971; July 1, 1989; July 1, 2015.]

Staff Note (July 1, 2015 Amendments)

The rule is amended to (1) replace "conclusions of fact" with "findings of fact" in the first paragraph of the rule and (2) include a reference to the findings of fact and conclusions of law required by Civ.R. 23(G)(3).

RULE 53.   Magistrates

(A)   Appointment. A court of record may appoint one or more magistrates who shall have been engaged in the practice of law for at least four years and be in good standing with the Supreme Court of Ohio at the time of appointment. A magistrate appointed under this rule may also serve as a magistrate under Crim. R. 19 or as a traffic magistrate.

(B)   Compensation. The compensation of magistrates shall be fixed by the court, and no part of the compensation shall be taxed as costs under Civ. R. 54(D).

(C)   Authority.

(1)   *Scope.* To assist courts of record and pursuant to reference under Civ. R. 53(D)(1), magistrates are authorized, subject to the terms of the relevant reference, to do any of the following:

(a)   Determine any motion in any case;

(b)   Conduct the trial of any case that will not be tried to a jury;

(c)   Upon unanimous written consent of the parties, preside over the trial of any case that will be tried to a jury;

(d)   Conduct proceedings upon application for the issuance of a temporary protection order as authorized by law;

(e)   Exercise any other authority specifically vested in magistrates by statute and consistent with this rule.

(2)   *Regulation of proceedings.* In performing the responsibilities described in Civ. R. 53(C)(1), magistrates are authorized, subject to the terms of the relevant reference, to regulate all proceedings as if by the court and to do everything necessary for the efficient performance of those responsibilities, including but not limited to, the following:

(a)   Issuing subpoenas for the attendance of witnesses and the production of evidence;

(b)   Ruling upon the admissibility of evidence;

(c)   Putting witnesses under oath and examining them;

(d)   Calling the parties to the action and examining them under oath;

(e)   When necessary to obtain the presence of an alleged contemnor in cases involving direct or indirect contempt of court, issuing an attachment for the alleged contemnor and setting the type, amount, and any conditions of bail pursuant to Crim. R. 46;

(f)   Imposing, subject to Civ. R. 53(D)(8), appropriate sanctions for civil or criminal contempt committed in the presence of the magistrate.

(D)   Proceedings in Matters Referred to Magistrates.

(1)   *Reference by court of record.*

(a)   *Purpose and method.* A court of record may, for one or more of the purposes described in Civ. R. 53(C)(1), refer a particular case or matter or a category of cases or matters to a magistrate by a specific or general order of reference or by rule.

(b)   *Limitation.*   A court of record may limit a reference by specifying or limiting the magistrate's powers, including but not limited to, directing the magistrate to determine only particular issues, directing the magistrate to perform particular responsibilities, directing the magistrate to receive and report evidence only, fixing the time and place for beginning and closing any hearings, or fixing the time for filing any magistrate's decision on the matter or matters referred.

(2)   *Magistrate's order; motion to set aside magistrate's order.*

(a)   *Magistrate's order.*

(i)   *Nature of order.* Subject to the terms of the relevant reference, a magistrate may enter orders without judicial approval if necessary to regulate the proceedings and if not dispositive of a claim or defense of a party.

(ii)   *Form, filing, and service of magistrate's order.* A magistrate's order shall be in writing, identified as a magistrate's order in the caption, signed by the magistrate, filed with the clerk, and served by the clerk on all parties or their attorneys.

(b)   *Motion to set aside magistrate's order.* Any party may file a motion with the court to set aside a magistrate's order. The motion shall state the moving party's reasons with particularity and shall be filed not later than ten days after the magistrate's order is filed. The pendency of a motion to set aside does not stay the effectiveness of the magistrate's order, though the magistrate or the court may by order stay the effectiveness of a magistrate's order.

(3)   *Magistrate's decision; objections to magistrate's decision.*

(a)   *Magistrate's decision.*

(i) *When required.* Subject to the terms of the relevant reference, a magistrate shall prepare a magistrate's decision respecting any matter referred under Civ. R. 53(D)(1).

(ii) *Findings of fact and conclusions of law.* Subject to the terms of the relevant reference, a magistrate's decision may be general unless findings of fact and conclusions of law are timely requested by a party or otherwise required by law. A request for findings of fact and conclusions of law shall be made before the entry of a magistrate's decision or within seven days after the filing of a magistrate's decision. If a request for findings of fact and conclusions of law is timely made, the magistrate may require any or all of the parties to submit proposed findings of fact and conclusions of law.

(iii) *Form; filing, and service of magistrate's decision.* A magistrate's decision shall be in writing, identified as a magistrate's decision in the caption, signed by the magistrate, filed with the clerk, and served by the clerk on all parties or their attorneys no later than three days after the decision is filed. A magistrate's decision shall indicate conspicuously that a party shall not assign as error on appeal the court's adoption of any factual finding or legal conclusion, whether or not specifically designated as a finding of fact or conclusion of law under Civ. R. 53(D)(3)(a)(ii), unless the party timely and specifically objects to that factual finding or legal conclusion as required by Civ. R. 53(D)(3)(b).

(b) *Objections to magistrate's decision.*

(i) *Time for filing.* A party may file written objections to a magistrate's decision within fourteen days of the filing of the decision, whether or not the court has adopted the decision during that fourteen-day period as permitted by Civ. R. 53(D)(4)(e)(i). If any party timely files objections, any other party may also file objections not later than ten days after the first objections are filed. If a party makes a timely request for findings of fact and conclusions of law, the time for filing objections begins to run when the magistrate files a decision that includes findings of fact and conclusions of law.

(ii) *Specificity of objection.* An objection to a magistrate's decision shall be specific and state with particularity all grounds for objection.

(iii) *Objection to magistrate's factual finding; transcript or affidavit.* An objection to a factual finding, whether or not specifically designated as a finding of fact under Civ. R. 53(D)(3)(a)(ii), shall be supported by a transcript of all the evidence submitted to the magistrate relevant to that finding or an affidavit of that evidence if a transcript is not available. With leave of court, alternative technology or manner of reviewing the relevant evidence may be considered. The objecting party shall file the transcript or affidavit with the court within thirty days after filing objections unless the court extends the time in writing for preparation of the transcript or other good cause. If a party files timely objections prior to the date on which a transcript is prepared, the party may seek leave of court to supplement the objections.

        (iv)   Waiver of right to assign adoption by court as error on appeal. Except for a claim of plain error, a party shall not assign as error on appeal the court's adoption of any factual finding or legal conclusion, whether or not specifically designated as a finding of fact or conclusion of law under Civ. R. 53(D)(3)(a)(ii), unless the party has objected to that finding or conclusion as required by Civ. R. 53(D)(3)(b).

    (4)   *Action of court on magistrate's decision and on any objections to magistrate's decision; entry of judgment or interim order by court.*

        (a)   *Action of court required.* A magistrate's decision is not effective unless adopted by the court.

        (b)   *Action on magistrate's decision.* Whether or not objections are timely filed, a court may adopt or reject a magistrate's decision in whole or in part, with or without modification. A court may hear a previously-referred matter, take additional evidence, or return a matter to a magistrate.

        (c)   *If no objections are filed.* If no timely objections are filed, the court may adopt a magistrate's decision, unless it determines that there is an error of law or other defect evident on the face of the magistrate's decision.

        (d)   *Action on objections.* If one or more objections to a magistrate's decision are timely filed, the court shall rule on those objections. In ruling on objections, the court shall undertake an independent review as to the objected matters to ascertain that the magistrate has properly determined the factual issues and appropriately applied the law. Before so ruling, the court may hear additional evidence but may refuse to do so unless the objecting party demonstrates that the party could not, with reasonable diligence, have produced that evidence for consideration by the magistrate.

        (e)   *Entry of judgment or interim order by court.* A court that adopts, rejects, or modifies a magistrate's decision shall also enter a judgment or interim order.

        (i)   *Judgment.* The court may enter a judgment either during the fourteen days permitted by Civ. R. 53(D)(3)(b)(i) for the filing of objections to a magistrate's decision or after the fourteen days have expired. If the court enters a judgment during the fourteen days permitted by Civ. R. 53(D)(3)(b)(i) for the filing of objections, the timely filing of objections to the magistrate's decision shall operate as an automatic stay of execution of the judgment until the court disposes of those objections and vacates, modifies, or adheres to the judgment previously entered.

(ii)   *Interim order.* The court may enter an interim order on the basis of a magistrate's decision without waiting for or ruling on timely objections by the parties where immediate relief is justified. The timely filing of objections does not stay the execution of an interim order, but an interim order shall not extend more than twenty-eight days from the date of entry, subject to extension by the court in increments of twenty-eight additional days for good cause shown. An interim order shall comply with Civ. R. 54(A), be journalized pursuant to Civ. R. 58(A), and be served pursuant to Civ. R. 58(B).

(5)   *Extension of time.* For good cause shown, the court shall allow a reasonable extension of time for a party to file a motion to set aside a magistrate's order or file objections to a magistrate's decision. "Good cause" includes, but is not limited to, a failure by the clerk to timely serve the party seeking the extension with the magistrate's order or decision.

(6)   *Disqualification of a magistrate.* Disqualification of a magistrate for bias or other cause is within the discretion of the court and may be sought by motion filed with the court.

(7)   *Recording of proceedings before a magistrate.* Except as otherwise provided by law, all proceedings before a magistrate shall be recorded in accordance with procedures established by the court.

(8)   *Contempt in the presence of a magistrate.*

(a)   *Contempt order.* Contempt sanctions under Civ. R. 53(C)(2)(f) may be imposed only by a written order that recites the facts and certifies that the magistrate saw or heard the conduct constituting contempt.

(b)   *Filing and provision of copies of contempt order.* A contempt order shall be filed and copies provided forthwith by the clerk to the appropriate judge of the court and to the subject of the order.

(c)   *Review of contempt order by court; bail.* The subject of a contempt order may by motion obtain immediate review by a judge. A judge or the magistrate entering the contempt order may set bail pending judicial review of the order.

[Effective: July 1, 1970; amended effective July 1, 1975; July 1, 1985; July 1, 1992; July 1, 1993; July 1, 1995; July 1, 1996; July 1, 1998; July 1, 2003; July 1, 2006; July 1, 2011.]

Staff Note (July 1, 2006 Amendment)

Civ. R. 53 has been reorganized in an effort to make it more helpful to bench and bar and reflective of developments since the rule was last substantially revised effective July 1, 1995. The relatively-few significant changes included in the reorganization are noted below.

Rule 53(A)   Appointment

Civ. R. 53(A) is taken verbatim from sentence one of former Civ. R. 53(A). Sup. R. 19 requires that all municipal courts having more than two judges appoint one or more magistrates to hear specified matters. See also Crim. R. 19 and Traf. R. 14.

Rule 53(B)   Compensation

Civ. R. 53(B) refers to Civ. R. 54(D) so as to more clearly harmonize Civ. R. 53 with statutory provisions that authorize courts to collect funds from litigants generally and to use the collected funds for purposes that include employment of magistrates. See, *e.g.,* R.C. 1901.26(B)(1), 1907.24(B)(1), 2303.201(E)(1), and 2501.16(B).

Rule 53(C)   Authority

Civ. R. 53(C) is drawn largely from former Civ. R. 53(C)(1) and (2) and reflects the admonition of the Supreme Court that "a [magistrate's] oversight of an issue or issues, or even an entire trial, is not a *substitute* for the judicial functions but only an *aid* to them." *Hartt v. Munobe* (1993), 67 Ohio St.3d 3, 6, 615 N.E.2d 617 (emphases added). Civ. R. 53(C)(1)(d) is added to parallel Crim. R. 19(C)(1)(g) and recognize that magistrates have authority to conduct temporary protection order proceedings in accordance with law. Consistent with the admonition in *Hartt*, however, any temporary protection order issued as a result of such proceedings must be signed by a judge.

Rule 53(D)   Proceedings in Matters Referred to Magistrates

Civ. R. 53(D)(1) through (4) treat each of the steps that potentially occur if a magistrate participates: (1) reference to a magistrate; (2) magistrate's orders and motions to set aside magistrate's orders; (3) magistrate's decisions and objections to magistrate's decisions; and (4) action of the court on magistrate's decisions and on any objections to magistrate's decisions and entry of judgment or interim order by the court. Civ. R. 53(D)(5) through (8) deal with good cause extensions of time, disqualification of a magistrate, recording of proceedings before a magistrate, and contempt in the presence of a magistrate.

Reference by court of record

Civ. R. 53(D)(1), unlike former Civ. R. 53(C)(1)(b), specifically authorizes reference of types of matters by rule as well as by a specific or general order of reference. In so doing, it recognizes existing practice in some courts. See, e.g., Loc. R. 99.02, Franklin Cty. Ct. of Common Pleas; Loc. R. 23(B), Hamilton Cty. Ct. of Common Pleas; *State ex rel. Nalls v. Russo,* 96 Ohio St.3d 410, 412-13, 2002-Ohio-4907 at ¶¶ 20-24, 775 N.E.2d 522; *Davis v. Reed* (Aug. 31, 2000), 8th Dist. App. No. 76712, 2000 WL 1231462 at *2 (citing *White v. White* (1977), 50 Ohio App.2d 263, 266-268, 362 N.E.2d 1013), and *Partridge v. Partridge* (Aug. 27, 1999), 2nd Dist. App. No. 98 CA 38, 1999 WL 945046 at *2, (treating a local rule of the Greene Cty. Ct. of Common Pleas, Dom. Rel. Div., as a standing order of reference).

Magistrate's order; motion to set aside magistrate's order

Civ. R. 53(D)(2)(a)(i) generally authorizes a magistrate to enter orders without judicial approval if necessary to regulate the proceedings and, adapting language from Crim. R. 19(B)(5)(a), if "not dispositive of a claim or defense of a party." The new language removes the arguably limiting title of former Civ. R. 53(C)(3)(a) ["Pretrial orders"] and is intended to more accurately reflect proper and existing practice. This language is not intended to narrow the power of a magistrate to enter pretrial orders without judicial approval on matters related to (1) pretrial management under Civ. R. 16; (2) discovery conducted pursuant to Civ. R. 26-37; (3) temporary orders issued pursuant to Civ. R. 75(N); (4) temporary restraining order governing marital property under Civ. R. 75(I) (2); or (5) any other orders necessary to the regulation of proceedings before a magistrate. All temporary protection orders, however, including orders issued to avoid bodily harm pursuant to Civ. R. 75(I)(2), must be signed by a judge and comply fully with the procedures set forth in R.C. 3113.31 and related sections. Civ. R. 53(D)(2)(b) replaces language in former Civ. R. 53(C)(3)(b), which purported to authorize "[a]ny person" to "appeal to the court" from any order of a magistrate "by filing a motion to set the order aside." The new language refers to the appropriate challenge to a magistrate's order as solely a "motion to set aside" the order. Civ. R. 53(D)(2)(b) likewise limits the authorization to file a motion to "any *party*," though an occasional nonparty may be entitled to file a motion to set aside a magistrate's order. Sentence two of Civ. R. 53(D)(2)(b) changes the trigger for the ten days permitted to file a motion to set aside a magistrate's order from entry of the order to filing of the order, as the latter date is definite and more easily available to counsel.

Magistrate's decision; objections to magistrate's decision

Civ. R. 53(D)(3) prescribes procedures for preparation of a magistrate's decision and for any objections to a magistrate's decision.

Civ. R. 53(D)(3)(a)(ii), unlike former Civ. R. 53(E)(2), adapts language from Civ. R. 52 rather than simply referring to Civ. R. 52. The change is intended to make clear that, e.g., a request for findings of fact and conclusions of law in a referred matter should be directed to the magistrate rather than to the court. Civ. R. 53(D)(3)(a)(ii) explicitly authorizes a magistrate's decision, subject to the terms of the relevant reference, to be general absent a timely request for findings of fact and conclusions of law or a provision of law that provides otherwise. Occasional decisions under former Civ. R. 53 said as much. See, *e.g., In re Chapman* (Apr. 21, 1997), 12th Dist. App. No. CA96-07-127, 1997 WL 194879 at *2; *Burke v. Brown*, 4th Dist. App. No. 01CA731, 2002-Ohio-6164 at ¶ 21; and *Rush v. Schlagetter* (Apr. 15, 1997), 4th Dist. App. No. 96CA2215, 1997 WL 193169 at *3. For a table of sections of the Ohio Revised Code that purport to make findings of fact by judicial officers mandatory in specified circumstances, see 2 Klein-Darling, Ohio Civil Practice § 52-4, 2002 Pocket Part at 136 (West Group 1997).

Civ. R. 53(D)(3)(a)(iii) now requires that the magistrate's decision be served on the parties or their attorneys no later than three days after the decision was filed. The former rule contained no specific time requirement. The provision further requires that a magistrate's decision include a conspicuous warning of the waiver rule prescribed by amended Civ. R. 53(D)(3)(b)(iv). The latter rule now provides that a party shall not assign as error on appeal a court's adoption of any factual finding or legal conclusion of a magistrate, whether or not specifically designated as a finding of fact or conclusion of law under Civ. R. 53(D)(3)(a)(ii), unless that party has objected to that finding or conclusion as required by Civ. R. 53(D)(3)(b). While the prior waiver rule, prescribed by former Civ. R. 53(E)(3)(b) (effective July 1, 1995) and former Civ. R. 53(E)(3)(d) (effective July 1, 2003), arguably applied only to findings of fact or conclusions of law specifically designated as such, the amended waiver rule applies to any factual finding or legal conclusion in a magistrate's decision and the required warning is broadened accordingly.

Civ. R. 53(D)(3)(b)(i) retains the fourteen-day time for filing written objections to a magistrate's decision. While the rule continues to authorize filing of objections by a "party," it has been held that a nonparty attorney can properly object to a magistrate's decision imposing sanctions on the attorney. *All Climate Heating & Cooling, Inc. v. Zee Properties, Inc.* (May 17, 2001), 10th Dist. App. No. 00AP-1141, 2001 WL 521408 at *3.

Sentence one of Civ. R. 53(D)(3)(b)(iii) requires that an objection to a factual finding in a magistrate's decision, whether or not specifically designated as a finding of fact under Civ. R. 53(D)(3)(a)(ii), be supported by a transcript of all the evidence submitted to the magistrate relevant to that fact or by an affidavit of that evidence if a transcript is not available. The Supreme Court has prescribed the consequences on appeal of failure to supply the requisite transcript or affidavit as follows: (1) "appellate review of the court's findings is limited to whether the trial court abused its discretion in adopting the [magistrate's decision]" and (2) "the appellate court is precluded from considering the transcript of the hearing submitted with the appellate record." *State ex rel. Duncan v. Chippewa Twp. Trustees* (1995), 73 Ohio St.3d 728, 730, 654 N.E.2d 1254.

Sentence two of Civ. R. 53(D)(3)(b)(iii) adds a new requirement, adapted from Loc. R. 99.05, Franklin Cty. Ct. of Common Pleas, that the requisite transcript or affidavit be filed within thirty days after filing objections unless the court extends the time in writing for preparation of the transcript or other good cause. The last sentence of Civ. R. 53(D)(3)(b)(iii) allows an objecting party to seek leave of court to supplement previously filed objections where the additional objections become apparent after a transcript has been prepared.

Civ. R. 53(D)(3)(b)(iv), as noted above, expands the "waiver rule" prescribed by former Civ. R. 53(E)(3)(b) (effective July 1, 1995) and former Civ. R. 53(E)(3)(d) (effective July 1, 2003) to include any factual finding or legal conclusion in a magistrate's decision, whether or not specifically designated as a finding of fact or conclusion of law under Civ. R. 53(D)(3)(a)(ii). The Rules Advisory Committee was unable to discern a principled reason to apply different requirements to, e.g., a factual finding depending on whether or not that finding is specifically designated as a finding of fact under Civ. R. 53(D)(3)(a)(ii). An exception to the "waiver rule" exists for plain error, which cannot be waived based on a party's failure to object to a magistrate's decision.

Action of court on magistrate's decision and on any objections to magistrate's decision; entry of judgment or interim order by the court

Civ. R. 53(D)(4)(a), like sentence one of former Civ. R. 53(E)(4)(a), confirms that a magistrate's decision is not effective unless adopted by the court.

Civ. R. 53(D)(4)(b) provides that a court may properly choose among a wide range of options in response to a magistrate's decision, whether or not objections are timely filed. See, e.g., *Johnson v. Brown* 2nd Dist. App. No. 2002 CA 76, 2003-Ohio-1257 at ¶ 12 (apparently concluding that former Civ. R. 53(E)(4)(b) permitted the trial court to modify an aspect of the magistrate's decision to which no objection had been made).

Civ. R. 53(D)(4)(c) provides that if no timely objections are filed, the court may adopt a magistrate's decision unless the court determines that there is an error of law or other defect evident on the face of the decision. A similar result was reached under sentence two of former Civ. R. 53(E)(4)(a). See, e.g., *Perrine v. Perrine*, 9th Dist. App. No. 20923, 2002-Ohio-4351 at ¶ 9; *City of Ravenna Police Dept. v. Sicuro* (Apr. 30, 2002), 11th Dist. App. No. 2001-P-0037; and *In re Weingart* (Jan. 17, 2002), 8th Dist. App. No. 79489, 2002 WL 68204 at *4. The language of Civ. R. 53(D)(4)(c) has been modified in an attempt to make clear that the obligation of the court does not extend to any "error of law" whatever but is limited to errors of law that are evident on the face of the decision. To the extent that decisions such as *In re Kelley*, 11th Dist. App. No. 2002-A-0088, 2003-Ohio-194 at ¶ 8 suggest otherwise, they are rejected. The "evident on the face" standard does not require that the court conduct an independent analysis of the magistrate's decision. The amended rule does not speak to the effect, if any, on the waiver rule prescribed by amended Civ. R. 53(D)(3)(b)(iv) of the "evident on the face" requirement. At least two courts have explicitly held that the "evident on the face" standard generates an exception to the waiver rule. *Dean-Kitts v. Dean*, 2nd Dist. App. No. 2002CA18, 2002-Ohio-5590 at ¶ 13 and *Hennessy v. Hennessy* (Mar. 24, 2000), 6th Dist. App. No. L-99-1170, 2000 WL 299450 at *1. Other decisions have indicated that the standard may generate an exception to the waiver rule. *Ohlin v. Ohlin* (Nov. 12, 1999), 11th Dist. App. No. 98-PA-87, 1999 WL 1580977 at *2; *Group One Realty, Inc. v. Dixie Intl. Co.* (1998), 125 Ohio App.3d 767, 769, 709 N.E.2d 589; *In re Williams* (Feb. 25, 1997), 10th Dist. App. No. 96APF06-778, 1997 WL 84659 at *1. However, the Supreme Court applied the waiver rule three times without so much as referring to the "evident on the face" standard as a possible exception. *State ex rel. Wilson v. Industrial Common.* (2003), 100 Ohio St. 3d 23, 24, 2003-Ohio-4832 at ¶ 4, 795 N.E.2d 662; *State ex rel. Abate v. Industrial Comm'n.* (2002), 96 Ohio St.3d 343, 2002-Ohio-4796, 774 N.E.2d 1212; *State ex rel. Booher v. Honda of America Mfg. Co., Inc.* (2000), 88 Ohio St.3d 52, 2000-Ohio-269, 723 N.E.2d 571.

As noted above, even if no timely objection is made, a court may, pursuant to Civ. R. 53(D)(4)(b), properly choose a course of action other than adopting a magistrate's decision even if there is no error of law or other defect evident on the face of the magistrate's decision.

Sentence one of Civ. R. 53(D)(4)(d), like sentence one of former Civ.R. 53(E)(4)(b), requires that the court rule on timely objections. Sentence two of Civ. R. 53(D)(4)(d) requires that, if timely objection is made to a magistrate's decision, the court give greater scrutiny than if no objections are made. The "independent review as to the objected matters" standard that applies if timely objection is made should be distinguished from the lesser scrutiny permitted if no objections to a magistrate's decision are timely filed, the latter standard having been first adopted by former Civ.R. 53(E)(4)(a), effective July 1, 1995, and retained by new Civ. R. 53(D)(4)(c), discussed above.

The "independent review as to the objected matters" standard is intended to exclude the more limited appellate standards of review and codify the practice approved by most courts of appeals. The Second District Court of Appeals has most clearly and consistently endorsed and explained that standard. *See, e.g., Crosby v. McWilliam*, 2nd Dist. App. No. 19856, 2003-Ohio-6063; *Quick v. Kwiatkowski* (Aug. 3, 2001), 2nd Dist. App. No. 18620, 2001 WL 871406 (acknowledging that "Magistrates truly do the 'heavy lifting' on which we all depend"); *Knauer v. Keener* (2001), 143 Ohio App.3d 789, 758 N.E.2d 1234. Other district courts of appeal have followed suit. *Reese v. Reese*, 3rd Dist. App. No. 14-03-42, 2004-Ohio-1395; *Palenshus v. Smile Dental Group, Inc.*, 3rd Dist. App. No. 3-02-46, 2003-Ohio-3095,; *Huffer v. Chafin*, 5th Dist. App. No. 01 CA 74, 2002-Ohio-356; *Rhoads v. Arthur* (June 30, 1999), 5th Dist. App. No. 98CAF10050, 1999 WL 547574; *Barker v. Barker* (May 4, 2001), 6th Dist. App. No. L-00-1346, 2001 WL 477267; *In re Day*, 7th Dist. App. No. 01 BA 28, 2003-Ohio-1215; *State ex rel. Ricart Auto. Personnel, Inc. v. Industrial Comm'n. of Ohio*, 10th Dist. App. No. 03AP-246, 2003-Ohio-7030; *Holland v. Holland* (Jan. 20, 1998), 10th Dist. App. No. 97APF08-974, 1998 WL 30179; *In re Gibbs* (Mar. 13, 1998), 11th Dist. App. No. 97-L-067, 1998 WL 257317.

Only one court of appeals appears consistently and knowingly to have taken a different approach. *Lowery v. Keystone Bd. of Ed.* (May 9, 2001), 9th Dist. App. No. 99CA007407, 2001 WL 490017; *Weber v. Weber* (June 30, 1999), 9th Dist. App. No. 2846-M, 1999 WL 459359; *Meadows v. Meadows* (Feb. 11, 1998), 9th Dist. App. No. 18382, 1998 WL 78686; *Rogers v. Rogers* (Dec. 17, 1997), 9th Dist. App. No. 18280, 1997 WL 795820.

The Rules Advisory Committee believes that the view adopted by the majority of courts of appeals is correct and that no change was made by the 1995 amendments to Civ. R. 53 in the review required of a trial judge upon the filing of timely objections to a magistrate's decision.

The phrase "as to the objected matters" permits a court to choose to limit its independent review to those matters raised by proper objections. If a court need apply only the "defect evident on the face" standard if no objections are filed at all, then, if one or more objections *are* filed, a court logically need apply the more stringent independent review only to those aspects of the magistrate's decision that are challenged by that objection or those objections.

Sentence three of Civ. R. 53(D)(4)(d) provides that, before ruling on objections, a court may hear additional evidence and that it may refuse to hear additional evidence unless the objecting party demonstrates that the party could not, with reasonable diligence, have produced that evidence for consideration by the magistrate.

Civ. R. 53(D)(4)(e) requires that a court that adopts, rejects, or modifies a magistrate's decision also enter a judgment or interim order. Civ. R. 53 (D)(4)(e)(i) permits the court to enter a judgment during the fourteen days permitted for the filing of objections to a magistrate's decision but provides that the timely filing of objections operates as an automatic stay of execution of the judgment until the court disposes of those objections and vacates, modifies, or adheres to the judgment previously entered. Civ. R. 53(D)(4)(e)(ii) permits the court, if immediate relief is justified, to enter an interim order based on the magistrate's decision without waiting for or ruling on timely objections. The timely filing of objections does not stay such an interim order, but the order may not properly extend more than twenty-eight days from the date of entry, subject to extension by the court in increments of twenty-eight additional days for good cause shown. New sentence three of Civ. R. 53(D)(4)(e)(ii) provides that an interim order shall comply with Civ. R. 54(A), be journalized pursuant to Civ. R. 58(A), and be served pursuant to Civ. R. 58(B). See *Hall v. Darr,* 6th Dist. App. No. OT-03-001, 2003-Ohio-1035.

Extension of time

Civ. R. 53(D)(5) is new and requires the court, for good cause shown, to provide an objecting party with a reasonable extension of time to file a motion to set aside a magistrate's order or file objections to a magistrate's decision. "Good cause" would include the failure of a party to receive timely service of the magistrate's order or decision.

Disqualification of a magistrate

Civ. R. 53(D)(6) has no counterpart in former Civ. R. 53. The statutory procedures for affidavits of disqualification apply to judges rather than magistrates. Rev. Code §§ 2101.39, 2501.13, 2701.03, 2701.131; *In re Disqualification of Light* (1988), 36 Ohio St.3d 604, 522 N.E.2d 458. The new provision is based on the observation of the Chief Justice of the Supreme Court that "[t]he removal of a magistrate is within the discretion of the judge who referred the matter to the magistrate and should be brought by a motion filed with the trial court." *In re Disqualification of Wilson* (1996), 77 Ohio St. 3d 1250, 1251, 674 N.E.2d 260; see also *Mascorro v. Mascorro* (June 9, 2000), 2nd Dist. App. No. 17945, 2000 WL 731751 at *3 (citing *In re Disqualification of Wilson*); *Reece v. Reece* (June 22, 1994), 2nd Dist. App. No. 93-CA-45, 1994 WL 286282 at *2 ("Appointment of a referee is no different from any other process in which the trial court exercises discretion it is granted by statute or rule. * * * If the defect concerns possible bias or prejudice on the part of the referee, that may be brought to the attention of the court by motion."); *Moton v. Ford Motor Credit Co.,* 5th Dist. App. No. 01CA74, 2002-Ohio-2857, appeal not allowed (2002), 95 Ohio St.3d 1422, 2002-Ohio-1734, 766 N.E.2d 163, reconsideration denied (2002), 95 Ohio St.3d 1476, 2002-Ohio-244, 768 N.E.2d 1183; *Walser v. Dominion Homes, Inc.* (June 11, 2001), 5th Dist. App. No. 00-CA-G-11-035, 2001 WL 704408 at *5; *Unger v. Unger* (Dec. 29, 2000), 12th Dist. App. No. CA2000-04-009, 2000 WL 1902196 at *2 (citing *In re Disqualification of Wilson, supra)*; *Jordan v. Jordan* (Nov. 15, 1996), 4th Dist. App. No. 1427, 1990 WL 178162 at *5 ("Although referees are not judges and arguably, are not bound by Canon 3(C)(1) of the Code of Judicial Conduct, it would appear axiomatic that a party should be able to petition the court to have a referee removed from the case if the referee is unable to render a fair and impartial decision."); *In re Reiner* (1991), 74 Ohio App.3d 213, 220, 598 N.E.2d 768 ("where a referee affirmatively states that he is biased on the matter before him, it is an abuse of the court's discretion to fail to recuse the referee"). Particularly because "a [magistrate's] oversight of an issue or issues, or even an entire trial, is not a *substitute* for the judicial functions but only an *aid* to them," *Hartt v. Munobe* (1993), 67 Ohio St.3d 3, 6, 1993-Ohio-177, 615 N.E.2d 617 (emphases added), Civ. R. 53(D)(6) contemplates that disqualification on a ground other than bias may sometimes be appropriate.

Recording of proceedings before a magistrate

Civ. R. 53(D)(7), generally requiring recording of proceedings before a magistrate, is taken verbatim from former Civ. R. 53(D)(2).

Contempt in the presence of a magistrate

Civ. R. 53(D)(8) is adapted from sentences two, three, and four of former Civ. R. 53(C)(3)(c). Civ. R. 53(D)(8)(b), unlike its predecessor, explicitly requires that the clerk provide a copy of a contempt order to the subject of the order.

Staff Note (July 1, 2012 Adoption of Civ.R. 65.1(F))

Rule 65.1(F), effective July 1, 2012, relates to the reference to a magistrate of civil protection order proceedings under R.C. 3113.31, R.C. 2151.34, and R.C. 2903.214. Rule 65.1(A) states that the provisions of the rule shall be interpreted and applied in a manner consistent with the intent and purposes of the protection order statutes, and supersede and make inapplicable in those proceedings the provisions of any other rules to the extent that their application is inconsistent with Civ.R. 65.1. Provisions of Civ.R. 65.1(F) which affect Civ.R. 53 include:

Civ.R. 65.1(F)(2)(b)(ii): A magistrate's denial or granting of an ex parte protection order without judicial approval does not constitute a magistrate's order or a magistrate's decision under Civ.R. 53(D)(2) or (3) and is not subject to the requirements of those rules.

Civ.R. 65.1(F)(2)(b)(iii): The court's approval and signing of a magistrate's denial or granting of an ex parte protection order does not constitute a judgment or interim order under Civ.R. 53(D)(4)(e) and is not subject to the requirements of that rule;

Civ.R. 65.1(F)(3)(b): A magistrate's denial or granting of a protection order after a full hearing does not constitute a magistrate's order or a magistrate's decision under Civ.R. 53(D)(2) or (3) and Is not subject to the requirements of those rules;

Civ.R. 65.1(F)(3)(c)(iv): A court's adoption, modification, or rejection of a magistrate's denial or granting of a protection order after a full hearing does not constitute a judgment or interim order under Civ.R. 53(D)(4)(e) and is not subject to the requirements of that rule.

The adoption of Civ.R. 65.1(F) also nullifies comments in the 2006 Staff Note to Civ.R. 53(D)(2)(a)(i) relating to the entry of temporary protection orders under R.C. 3113.31.

The listing above is not exclusive or comprehensive. Additional provisions of Civ.R. 53 relating to such matters as the authority and responsibilities of a magistrate are also affected by Civ.R. 65.1(F). As indicated in the Staff Notes to Rule 65.1, the rule was adopted to provide a set of provisions uniquely applicable to civil protection order proceedings and to provide the court with the discretion to suspend the application in such proceedings of any other rules to the extent that their application interferes with the statutory process or are inconsistent with its purposes.

Staff Note (July 1, 2003 amendment)

Rule 53 Magistrates

Rule 53(E)   Decisions in referred matters

The amendment to this rule is identical to an amendment to Juv. R. 40(E), also effective July 1, 2003.

It was suggested to the Rules Advisory Committee that the waiver rule prescribed by sentence four of former Civ. R. 53(E)(3)(b) [now division (E)(3)(d)] sometimes surprised counsel and *pro se* litigants because they did not expect to be required to object to a finding of fact or conclusion of law in a magistrate's decision in order to assign its adoption by the trial court as error on appeal. A review of relevant appellate decisions seemed to confirm that suggestion.

It was further suggested that counsel or a *pro se* litigant was particularly likely to be surprised by the waiver rule of sentence four of former Civ. R. 53(E)(3)(b) if a trial court, as authorized by sentence two of Civ. R. 53(E)(4)(a), adopted a magistrate's decision prior to expiration of the fourteen days permitted for the filing of objections. See, e.g., *Riolo v. Navin*, 2002 WL 502408, 2002-Ohio-1551 (8th Dist. Ct. App., 4-19-2002).

Since 1995, the potential for surprise posed by the waiver rule may have been exacerbated by the fact that, under the original version of Civ. R. 53, a party did not, by failing to file an objection, waive the right to assign as error on appeal the adoption by a trial court of a finding of fact or conclusion of law of a referee. *Normandy Place Associates v. Beyer*, 2 Ohio St.3d 102, 103 (1982) (syl. 1). As of July 1, 1985, sentence one of Civ. R. 53(E)(6) was amended to read "[a] party may not assign as error the court's adoption of a referee's *finding of fact* unless an objection to that finding is contained in that party's written objections to the referee's report" (emphasis added). See *State ex rel. Donah v. Windham Exempted Village Sch. Dist. Bd. of Ed.*, 69 Ohio St.3d 114, 118 (1994)(confirming that the waiver rule of sentence one of the 1985 version of Civ. R. 53 applied only to findings of fact by a magistrate). The present waiver rule, which applies to both findings of fact and conclusions of law, took effect July 1, 1995, and represents a complete reversal of the no waiver position of the original Civ. R. 53. See *State ex rel. Booher v. Honda of America Mfg., Inc.*, 88 Ohio St.3d 52 (2000)(confirming that the waiver rule now applies to conclusions of law as well as to findings of fact by a magistrate).

The amendment thus makes three changes in Civ. R. 53(E), none of which are intended to modify the substantive scope or effect of the waiver rule contained in sentence four of former Civ. R. 53(E)(3)(b) [now division (E)(3)(d)]. First, the amendment retains, but breaks into three appropriately-titled subdivisions, the four sentences which comprised former Civ. R. 53(E)(3)(b). Sentences two and three of former Civ. R. 53(E)(3)(b) are included in a new subdivision (c) entitled "Objections to magistrate's findings of fact." Sentence four of former Civ. R. 53(E)(3)(b), which prescribes the waiver rule, is a new subdivision (d) entitled "Waiver of right to assign adoption by court as error on appeal."

Second, new language is inserted at the beginning of Civ. R. 53(E)(3)(a) to make it more evident that a party may properly file timely objections to a magistrate's decision even if the trial court has previously adopted that decision as permitted by Civ. R. 53(E)(4)(c).

Third, the amendment adds a new sentence to Civ. R. 53(E)(2), which sentence requires that a magistrate who files a decision which includes findings of fact and conclusions of law also provide a conspicuous warning that timely and specific objection as required by Civ. R. 53(E)(3) is necessary to assign as error on appeal adoption by the trial court of any finding of fact or conclusion of law. It is ordinarily assumed that rule language that prescribes a procedural requirement (see, e.g., sentence six of Civ. R. 51(A), which is analogous to the waiver rule of Civ. R. 53(E)(3)) constitutes sufficient notice to counsel and to *pro se* litigants of that requirement. The Committee nonetheless concluded that the additional provision requiring that a magistrate's decision which includes findings of fact and conclusions of law call attention of counsel and *pro se* litigants to the waiver rule is justified because, as noted above, the original version of Civ. R. 53 imposed no waiver at all and even the 1985 version imposed waiver only as to findings of fact by referees.

Staff Note (July 1, 1998 Amendment)

Rule 53(A) Appointment.

The 1998 amendment to this division changed "traffic referee" to "traffic magistrate" to conform to the 1996 amendment of Rule 14 of the Ohio Traffic Rules. No substantive change is intended.

Rule 53(C) Reference and powers.

The 1998 amendment to division (C)(3)(a) was to change cross-references to Civ. R. 75 necessitated by 1998 amendments to that rule. Division (C)(3)(d) was amended to change "referee" to "magistrate" to conform to the 1996 amendment of Rule 14 of the Ohio Traffic Rules. No substantive change is intended.

Rule 53(E) Decisions in referred matters.

The 1998 amendment was to division (E)(4)(b) of this rule. The amendment was made because some trial judges apparently had avoided ruling upon objections to magistrates' reports since the previous rule appeared to require only "consideration" of the objections. The amendment should clarify that the judge is to rule upon, not just consider, any objections.

An identical amendment was made to division (E)(4)(b) of Juv.R. 40, also effective July 1, 1998.

Staff Note (July 1, 1996 Amendment)

Rule 53(E) Decisions in referred matters

The 1996 amendment corrected the first sentence of division (E)(2), which erroneously stated that a magistrate's decision was to include "proposed" findings of fact and conclusions of law. The amendment deleted the word "proposed". The amendment is technical only and no substantive change is intended

Staff Note (July 1, 1995 Amendment)

Rule 53(A) Appointment

Changes the title of "referee" to "magistrate" and makes clear that the same person may exercise magisterial authority under the Civil and Criminal Rules. By limiting the power of appointment to courts of record, the rule eliminates any authority implicit in the prior rule for appointment of referees by mayor's courts.

Rule 53(B) Compensation

Eliminates the prior authority to tax the compensation of a referee appointed on an interim basis as part of court costs. The Supreme Court Rules Advisory Committee is of the opinion that the salaries of judicial officers should be borne by the taxpayers generally, rather than by the parties to cases.

Rule 53(C) Reference and Powers

(C)(1) Order of Reference. This division replaces language previously found in Rule 53(A). It makes clear that magistrates have authority to act only on matters referred to them by a judge in an order of reference, but permits that order of reference to be categorical or specific to a particular case or motion in a case. Rule 53(C)(1)(a)(iii) codifies in part the result in *Hartt v. Munobe* (1993), 67 Ohio St. 3d 3, but requires that consent to a magistrate's presiding at a jury trial must be written. Division (C)(1)(c) largely tracks prior language, which makes it clear that a particular judge in a given order of reference may limit the powers generally provided in this rule for magistrates.

(C)(2) General Powers. Only stylistic changes are made, except that the provision for recording proceedings before magistrates is moved to Rule 53(D) and changed. (See Staff Note for Rule 53(D) below)

(C)(3) Power to Enter Orders. Division (C)(3)(a) clarifies the authority of magistrates to enter orders that are effective without being approved by a judge. It codifies existing practice in some courts in the state. Division (C)(3)(b) provides that any party may move to set the order aside, but the order remains effective unless a stay is granted.

(C)(3)(b) Contempt in the Magistrate's Presence. This division codifies the inherent power of magistrates, as judicial officers, to deal with contempt of court which occurs in their actual presence. The core purpose of the contempt power is to permit courts to deal with disruptions of proceedings and to maintain order. This power is as much needed in proceedings before magistrates as before other judicial officers. The rule follows Fed. R. Crim. P. 42 in requiring that the magistrate certify in writing what he or she perceived that constitutes contempt. The clerk is to provide an immediate copy of any magistrate contempt order to an appropriate judge so that there can be prompt judicial review of any contempt order.

(C)(3)(d) Other Orders. The General Assembly has recognized the existence of the referee system and from time to time conferred authority directly on referees, particularly in juvenile matters. This rule is necessary to prevent any inference of intent to override those statutes by adoption of this revised rule.

(C)(3)(e) Form of Magistrate's Orders. This division clarifies the form in which magistrate's orders are to be prepared so that they will be easily identified as such by parties and on the dockets.

Rule 53(D) Proceedings

Prior language largely drawn from Federal Civil Rule 53 relative to special masters and largely applicable to situations where special masters were appointed for individual cases and were not court employees is eliminated. To prevent any implication that proceedings before magistrates are to follow any different procedure from other civil proceedings, division (D)(1) is added. Division (D)(2) requires that proceedings before magistrates be recorded by whatever method a particular court deems appropriate. The rule is not meant to limit courts to particular recording means, but to emphasize that, as judicial officers of courts of record, magistrates should conduct proceedings before them on the record.

Rule 53(E) Decisions in Referred Matters

New division (E) entirely replaces the prior language which required preparation of reports by referees. Experience throughout the state demonstrated that often the report writing requirement substantially slowed the decision of cases without adding anything of value to the decision-making process. The new rule preserves the authority of judges to require reports by so specifying in orders of reference. In the absence of such a requirement, however, magistrates will now prepare a magistrate's decision [division (E)(1)]. If a party desires that the magistrate's decision embody the detail characteristic of a referee's report, the party may make a request for findings of fact and conclusions of law under Civ. R. 52, either before or after the magistrate's decision is filed [division (E)(2)]. The fourteen-day time period for objections is preserved and it begins to run only when a magistrate's decision embodying findings and conclusions is filed, if they have been appropriately requested [division(E)(3)(a)].

Division (E)(3)(b) prescribes the form of objections and requires that they be specific; a general objection is insufficient to preserve an issue for judicial consideration. The rule permits the parties to tailor the objection process by providing that a magistrate's findings of fact will be final. The rule reinforces the finality of trial court proceedings by providing that failure to object constitutes a waiver on appeal of a matter which could have been raised by objection. Compare *United States v. Walters*, 638 F.2d 947 (6th Cir. 1981); *Thomas v. Arn*, 474 U.S. 140(1985).

Division (E)(4) prescribes the procedure to be followed by the court with respect to a magistrate's decision. Proposed decisions are effective only when adopted by the court. However, a magistrate's decision to which no objection is made may be adopted unless there is apparent error; the judge is no longer required to conduct an independent review and make a determination himself or herself. The last sentence of division (E)(4)(b), paralleling Civ. R. 59, permits a court to refuse to hear new evidence on objections unless the evidence would not have been obtained in time to present it to the magistrate.

Division (E)(4)(c) conforms existing law on interim orders to the new style of "magistrate's decision" as opposed to reports. No substantive change is intended.

TITLE VII. JUDGMENT

RULE 54. Judgments; Costs

(A) Definition; Form. "Judgment" as used in these rules means a written entry ordering or declining to order a form of relief, signed by a judge, and journalized on the docket of the court.

(B) Judgment upon multiple claims or involving multiple parties. When more than one claim for relief is presented in an action whether as a claim, counterclaim, cross-claim, or third-party claim, and whether arising out of the same or separate transactions, or when multiple parties are involved, the court may enter final judgment as to one or more but fewer than all of the claims or parties only upon an express determination that there is no just reason for delay. In the absence of a determination that there is no just reason for delay, any order or other form of decision, however designated, which adjudicates fewer than all the claims or the rights and liabilities of fewer than all the parties, shall not terminate the action as to any of the claims or parties, and the order or other form of decision is subject to revision at any time before the entry of judgment adjudicating all the claims and the rights and liabilities of all the parties.

(C) Demand for judgment. A judgment by default shall not be different in kind from or exceed in amount that prayed for in the demand for judgment. Except as to a party against whom a judgment is entered by default, every final judgment shall grant the relief to which the party in whose favor it is rendered is entitled, even if the party has not demanded the relief in the pleadings.

(D) Costs. Except when express provision therefor is made either in a statute or in these rules, costs shall be allowed to the prevailing party unless the court otherwise directs.

(E) Attorney Fees. Whenever a provision of these rules authorizes a court to award attorney fees, including attorney fees described in the provision as "caused" or "incurred," the court may award the reasonable value of the services performed by the attorney, whether or not the party represented by that attorney actually paid or is obligated to pay the attorney for such services performed.

[Effective: July 1, 1970; amended effective July 1, 1989; July 1, 1992; July 1, 1994; July 1, 1996; July 1, 2016; July 1, 2019.]

Staff Notes (July 1, 2019 Amendment)

Division (A)

The amendment to division (A) deletes the circular reference to the final-order statute, which often could not be reconciled with how the term "judgment" is used in the civil rules or with evolving final-order jurisprudence. Not every judgment constitutes a final order, and some judgments are final under statutes other than R.C. 2505.02. The amendment now places the finality analysis squarely on the apposite statutes, where it rightly belongs.

The amendment also deletes the last sentence of the rule, which unnecessarily circumscribed the contents of a judgment. The original purpose of this language appears, at least in part, to be to distinguish between decisions (which "announce[] what the judgment will be") and judgments (which "unequivocally order[] the relief"). *See, e.g., Downard v. Gilliland*, 4th Dist. Jackson No. 10CA2, 2011-Ohio-1783, ¶ 11, citing *St. Vincent Charity Hosp. v. Mintz*, 33 Ohio St.3d 121, 123, 515 N.E.2d 917 (1987). The amendment now specifies that a judgment must order or decline to order a form of relief; what a judgment includes beyond that requirement should be left in the discretion of the issuing court.

Staff Notes (July 1, 2016 Amendment)

A new division (E) is added to address awards of attorney fees. The purpose of the new division is to supersede any application of the decision in *State ex rel. Citizens for Open, Responsive & Accountable Govt. v. Register*, 116 Ohio St.3d 88, 2007–Ohio–5542 to an award of attorney fees under the rules by specifying that when any provision of the rules authorizes an award of attorney fees, the court may award the reasonable value of the services performed by the attorney, whether or not the party actually paid or is obligated to pay the attorney for such services. The heading of the rule is also amended to indicate that, in addition to "Judgments" and "Cost," the rule now also addresses the separate subject of "Attorney Fees."

Staff Note (July 1, 1996 Amendment)

Rule 54(A) Definition; Form

The amendment changed the rule's reference from "report of a referee" to "magistrate's decision" in division (A) in order to harmonize the rule with the language adopted in the 1995 amendments to Civ. R. 53. The amendment is technical only and no substantive change is intended.

RULE 55.   Default

(A)   Entry of judgment. When a party against whom a judgment for affirmative relief is sought has failed to plead or otherwise defend as provided by these rules, the party entitled to a judgment by default shall apply in writing or orally to the court therefor; but no judgment by default shall be entered against a minor or an incompetent person unless represented in the action by a guardian or other such representative who has appeared therein. If the party against whom judgment by default is sought has appeared in the action, he (or, if appearing by representative, his representative) shall be served with written notice of the application for judgment at least seven days prior to the hearing on such application. If, in order to enable the court to enter judgment or to carry it into effect, it is necessary to take an account or to determine the amount of damages or to establish the truth of any averment by evidence or to make an investigation of any other matter, the court may conduct such hearings or order such references as it deems necessary and proper and shall when applicable accord a right of trial by jury to the parties.

(B)   Setting aside default judgment. If a judgment by default has been entered, the court may set it aside in accordance with Rule 60(B).

(C)   Plaintiffs, counterclaimants, cross-claimants. The provisions of this rule apply whether the party entitled to the judgment by default is a plaintiff, a third-party plaintiff or a party who has pleaded a cross-claim or counterclaim. In all cases a judgment by default is subject to the limitations of Rule 54(C).

(D)   Judgment against this state. No judgment by default shall be entered against this state, a political subdivision, or officer in his representative capacity or agency of either unless the claimant establishes his claim or right to relief by evidence satisfactory to the court.

[Effective: July 1, 1970; amended effective July 1, 1971.]

RULE 56. Summary Judgment

(A) **For party seeking affirmative relief.** A party seeking to recover upon a claim, counterclaim, or cross-claim or to obtain a declaratory judgment may move with or without supporting affidavits for a summary judgment in the party's favor as to all or any part of the claim, counterclaim, cross-claim, or declaratory judgment action. A party may move for summary judgment at any time after the expiration of the time permitted under these rules for a responsive motion or pleading by the adverse party, or after service of a motion for summary judgment by the adverse party. If the action has been set for pretrial or trial, a motion for summary judgment may be made only with leave of court.

(B) **For defending party.** A party against whom a claim, counterclaim, or cross-claim is asserted or a declaratory judgment is sought may, at any time, move with or without supporting affidavits for a summary judgment in the party's favor as to all or any part of the claim, counterclaim, cross-claim, or declaratory judgment action. If the action has been set for pretrial or trial, a motion for summary judgment may be made only with leave of court.

(C) **Motion and proceedings.** The motion together with all affidavits and other materials in support shall be served in accordance with Civ.R. 5. Responsive arguments, together with all affidavits and other materials in opposition, and a movant's reply arguments may be served as provided by Civ.R. 6(C). Summary judgment shall be rendered forthwith if the pleadings, depositions, answers to interrogatories, written admissions, affidavits, transcripts of evidence, and written stipulations of fact, if any, timely filed in the action, show that there is no genuine issue as to any material fact and that the moving party is entitled to judgment as a matter of law. No evidence or stipulation may be considered except as stated in this rule. A summary judgment shall not be rendered unless it appears from the evidence or stipulation, and only from the evidence or stipulation, that reasonable minds can come to but one conclusion and that conclusion is adverse to the party against whom the motion for summary judgment is made, that party being entitled to have the evidence or stipulation construed most strongly in the party's favor. A summary judgment, interlocutory in character, may be rendered on the issue of liability alone although there is a genuine issue as to the amount of damages.

(D) **Case not fully adjudicated upon motion.** If on motion under this rule summary judgment is not rendered upon the whole case or for all the relief asked and a trial is necessary, the court in deciding the motion, shall examine the evidence or stipulation properly before it, and shall if practicable, ascertain what material facts exist without controversy and what material facts are actually and in good faith controverted. The court shall thereupon make an order on its journal specifying the facts that are without controversy, including the extent to which the amount of damages or other relief is not in controversy, and directing such further proceedings in the action as are just. Upon the trial of the action the facts so specified shall be deemed established, and the trial shall be conducted accordingly.

(E) **Form of affidavits; further testimony; defense required.** Supporting and opposing affidavits shall be made on personal knowledge, shall set forth such facts as would be admissible in evidence, and shall show affirmatively that the affiant is competent to testify to the matters stated in the affidavit. Sworn or certified copies of all papers or parts of papers referred to in an affidavit shall be attached to or served with the affidavit. The court may permit affidavits to be supplemented or opposed by depositions or by further affidavits. When a motion for summary judgment is made and supported as provided in this rule, an adverse party may not rest upon the mere allegations or denials of the party's pleadings, but the party's response, by affidavit or as otherwise provided in this rule, must set forth specific facts showing that there is a genuine issue for trial. If the party does not so respond, summary judgment, if appropriate, shall be entered against the party.

(F)   **When affidavits unavailable.** Should it appear from the affidavits of a party opposing the motion for summary judgment that the party cannot for sufficient reasons stated present by affidavit facts essential to justify the party's opposition, the court may refuse the application for judgment or may order a continuance to permit affidavits to be obtained or discovery to be had or may make such other order as is just.

(G)   **Affidavits made in bad faith.** Should it appear to the satisfaction of the court at any time that any of the affidavits presented pursuant to this rule are presented in bad faith or solely for the purpose of delay, the court shall forthwith order the party employing them to pay to the other party the amount of the reasonable expenses which the filing of the affidavits caused the other party to incur, including reasonable attorney's fees, and any offending party or attorney may be adjudged guilty of contempt.

[Effective: July 1, 1970; amended effective July 1, 1976; July 1, 1997; July 1, 1999; July 1, 2015; July 1, 2019.]

Staff Note (July 1, 2019 Amendment)

Division (C)

Recognizing that provisions of Civ.R.6(C) govern the requirements for service of responses to motions for summary judgment and for service of a movant's reply to such responses, the amendment to Civ.R. 56(C) eliminates the prior provisions addressing those matters.

Division (C) is also amended to specify that the materials in support of a motion for summary judgment shall be served when the motion is served.

Staff Note (July 1, 2015 Amendment)

Consistent with a similar amendment to Civ.R. 6(C), the amendment to Civ.R. 56(C) deletes the reference in the prior rule to "the time fixed for hearing." The amendment also specifies, in the absence of a local rule or court order specifying a time for responding to a motion for summary judgment, a fallback time of twenty-eight days after service of the motion within which to serve responsive arguments and opposing affidavits. In the absence of a local rule or court order addressing replies, the amendment also permits the movant to serve reply arguments within fourteen days after service of the adverse party's response. The time for filing the motion, responses, and replies is governed by Civ.R. 5(D), again in the absence of a local rule or court order specifying a different time for filing. The rule applies only in the absence of a local rule or court order providing times for briefing motions, whether or not the rule or order specifically addresses summary judgment motions, and does not supersede or affect the application of local rules or orders addressing briefing on motions.

Staff Note (July 1, 1999 Amendment)

Rule 56(C) Motion and proceedings thereon

The prior rule provided that "transcripts of evidence in the pending case" was one of the items that could be considered in deciding a motion for summary judgment. The 1999 amendment deleted "in the pending case" so that transcripts of evidence from another case can be filed and considered in deciding the motion.

Staff Note (July 1, 1997 Amendment)

Rule 56(A) For party seeking affirmative relief.

The 1997 amendment to division (A) divided the previous first sentence into two separate sentences for clarity and ease of reading, and replaced a masculine reference with gender-neutral language. The amendment is grammatical only and no substantive change is intended.

Rule 56(B) For defending party.

The 1997 amendment to division (B) added a comma after the "may" in the first sentence and replaced a masculine reference with gender-neutral language. The amendment is grammatical only and no substantive change is intended.

Rule 56(C) Motion and proceedings thereon.

The 1997 amendment to division (C) changed the word "pleading" to "pleadings" and replaced a masculine reference with gender-neutral language. The amendment is grammatical only and no substantive change is intended.

Rule 56(E) Form of affidavits; further testimony; defense required.

The 1997 amendment to division (E) replaced several masculine references with gender-neutral language. The amendment is grammatical only and no substantive change is intended.

Rule 56(F) When affidavits unavailable.

The 1997 amendment to division (F) replaced several masculine references with gender-neutral language. The amendment is grammatical only and no substantive change is intended.

Rule 56(G) Affidavits made in bad faith.

The 1997 amendment to division (G) replaced a masculine reference with gender-neutral language. The amendment is grammatical only and no substantive change is intended.

RULE 57.   Declaratory Judgments

The procedure for obtaining a declaratory judgment pursuant to Sections 2721.01 to 2721.15, inclusive, of the Revised Code, shall be in accordance with these rules. The existence of another adequate remedy does not preclude a judgment for declaratory relief in cases where it is appropriate. The court may advance on the trial list the hearing of an action for a declaratory judgment.

[Effective: July 1, 1970.]

RULE 58.   Entry of Judgment

(A)   Preparation; entry; effect; approval.

(1) Subject to the provisions of Rule 54(B), upon a general verdict of a jury, upon a decision announced, or upon the determination of a periodic payment plan, the court shall promptly cause the judgment to be prepared and, the court having signed it, the clerk shall thereupon enter it upon the journal. A judgment is effective only when entered by the clerk upon the journal.

(2) Approval of a judgment entry by counsel or a party indicates that the entry correctly sets forth the verdict, decision, or determination of the court and does not waive any objection or assignment of error for appeal.

(B)   Notice of filing.
When the court signs a judgment, the court shall endorse thereon a direction to the clerk to serve upon all parties not in default for failure to appear notice of the judgment and its date of entry upon the journal. Within three days of entering the judgment upon the journal, the clerk shall serve the parties in a manner prescribed by Civ.R. 5(B) and note the service in the appearance docket. Upon serving the notice and notation of the service in the appearance docket, the service is complete. The failure of the clerk to serve notice does not affect the validity of the judgment or the running of the time for appeal except as provided in App.R. 4(A).

(C)   Costs.
Entry of the judgment shall not be delayed for the taxing of costs.

[Effective: July 1, 1970; amended effective July 1, 1971; July 1, 1989; July 1, 2012.]

Staff Note (July 1, 2012 Amendment)

Division (A) has been subdivided in order to add Civ.R. 58(A)(2) which is a restatement of Rule 7(B) of the Rules of Superintendence for the Courts of Ohio. The provision is more appropriately included within the civil rules governing the conduct of actions.

The July 1, 1997 Commentary to Sup. R. 7 stated in pertinent part:

[T]he rule was added in 1995 and is intended to address the decision of the Eighth District Court of Appeals in *Paletta v. Paletta* (1990), 68 Ohio App.3d 507. In *Paletta*, the court of appeals held that the appellant waived any objection to the judgment of the trial court when his attorney signed a proposed judgment entry and failed to file objections as required by local rule of court, notwithstanding the attorney's assertion that he did not intend to approve the entry but only to acknowledge its receipt. The 1995 amendment indicates that a party's approval of a proposed judgment entry only reflects agreement that the entry correctly sets forth the decision of the court and does not constitute a waiver of any error or objection for purposes of appeal.

RULE 59.   New Trials

(A)   Grounds for new trial. A new trial may be granted to all or any of the parties and on all or part of the issues upon any of the following grounds:

(1)   Irregularity in the proceedings of the court, jury, magistrate, or prevailing party, or any order of the court or magistrate, or abuse of discretion, by which an aggrieved party was prevented from having a fair trial;

(2)   Misconduct of the jury or prevailing party;

(3)   Accident or surprise which ordinary prudence could not have guarded against;

(4)   Excessive or inadequate damages, appearing to have been given under the influence of passion or prejudice;

(5)   Error in the amount of recovery, whether too large or too small, when the action is upon a contract or for the injury or detention of property;

(6)   The judgment is not sustained by the weight of the evidence; however, only one new trial may be granted on the weight of the evidence in the same case;

(7)   The judgment is contrary to law;

(8)   Newly discovered evidence, material for the party applying, which with reasonable diligence he could not have discovered and produced at trial;

(9)   Error of law occurring at the trial and brought to the attention of the trial court by the party making the application.

In addition to the above grounds, a new trial may also be granted in the sound discretion of the court for good cause shown.

When a new trial is granted, the court shall specify in writing the grounds upon which such new trial is granted.

On a motion for a new trial in an action tried without a jury, the court may open the judgment if one has been entered, take additional testimony, amend findings of fact and conclusions of law or make new findings and conclusions, and enter a new judgment.

(B)   Time for certain post-trial motions, responsive briefs, and replies. Except as otherwise provided by statute, a motion for a new trial, remitter, additur, prejudgment interest, or attorney's fees must be served within twenty-eight days of the entry of judgment or, if the clerk has not completed service of the notice of judgment within the three-day period described in Civ.R. 58(B), within twenty-eight days of the date when the clerk actually completes service.

Unless otherwise provided by local rule or by order of the court, briefs in response to the motion shall be served within fourteen days of service of the motion, and a movant's reply may be served within seven days of service of the response to the motion.

(C) **Time for serving affidavits.** When a motion for a new trial is based upon affidavits they shall be served with the motion. The opposing party has fourteen days after such service within which to serve opposing affidavits, which period may be extended for an additional period not exceeding twenty-one days either by the court for good cause shown or by the parties by written stipulation. The court may permit supplemental and reply affidavits.

(D) **On initiative of court.** Not later than twenty-eight days after entry of judgment the court of its own initiative may order a new trial for any reason for which it might have granted a new trial on motion of a party.

The court may also grant a motion for a new trial, timely served by a party, for a reason not stated in the party's motion. In such case the court shall give the parties notice and an opportunity to be heard on the matter. The court shall specify the grounds for new trial in the order.

[Effective: July 1, 1970; amended effective July 1, 1996; July 1, 2013; July 1, 2015; July 1, 2018.]

Staff Note (July 1, 2018 Amendment)

Division (B): Time for Certain Post-Trial Motions, Responsive Briefs, and Replies.

The amendment makes two substantive changes.

First, it provides that if the clerk fails to serve the parties with notice of a judgment in the three-day period contemplated by Civ.R. 58(B), the time to serve a post-trial motion for judgment in favor of the movant does not begin to run until after the clerk does so. The purpose of the amendment is to avoid the harsh result that otherwise can occur if a would-be movant does not receive notice of the judgment. *See, e.g., Wing v. Haaff*, 1st Dist. Hamilton No. C-160257, 2016- Ohio-8258. This amendment brings the timing of post-trial motions under Civ.R. 59 in line with the timing of a notice of appeal in civil cases under App.R. 4(A)(3).

Staff Notes (July 1, 2015 Amendments)

Consistent with a similar amendment to Civ.R. 6(B), the amendment to Civ.R. 59(B) specifies, in the absence of a local rule or court order specifying a time for responding to a motion for new trial, a fallback time of fourteen days after service of the motion within which to serve responsive arguments. In the absence of a local rule or court order addressing replies, the amendment also permits the movant to serve reply arguments within seven days after service of the adverse party's response. The time for filing responsive arguments and replies is governed by Civ.R. 5(D), again in the absence of a local rule or order of the court specifying a different time for filing.

Staff Notes (July 1, 2013 Amendments)

Rule 59(B) is amended to extend the time for serving a motion for new trial to 28 days after the entry of the judgment. This change is modeled on the 2009 amendment to Fed.R.Civ.P. 59(b) and is made for the same reasons that prompted the amendment to the federal rule.

Staff Note (July 1, 1996 Amendment)

Rule 59(A) Grounds

The amendment changed the rule's reference from "referee" to "magistrate" in division (A)(1) in order to harmonize the rule with the language adopted in the 1995 amendments to Civ. R. 53. The amendment is technical only and no substantive change is intended.

RULE 60.   Relief From Judgment or Order

(A)   Clerical mistakes. Clerical mistakes in judgments, orders or other parts of the record and errors therein arising from oversight or omission may be corrected by the court at any time on its own initiative or on the motion of any party and after such notice, if any, as the court orders. During the pendency of an appeal, such mistakes may be so corrected before the appeal is docketed in the appellate court, and thereafter while the appeal is pending may be so corrected with leave of the appellate court.

(B)   Mistakes; inadvertence; excusable neglect; newly discovered evidence; fraud; etc. On motion and upon such terms as are just, the court may relieve a party or his legal representative from a final judgment, order or proceeding for the following reasons: (1) mistake, inadvertence, surprise or excusable neglect; (2) newly discovered evidence which by due diligence could not have been discovered in time to move for a new trial under Rule 59(B); (3) fraud (whether heretofore denominated intrinsic or extrinsic), misrepresentation or other misconduct of an adverse party; (4) the judgment has been satisfied, released or discharged, or a prior judgment upon which it is based has been reversed or otherwise vacated, or it is no longer equitable that the judgment should have prospective application; or (5) any other reason justifying relief from the judgment. The motion shall be made within a reasonable time, and for reasons (1), (2) and (3) not more than one year after the judgment, order or proceeding was entered or taken. A motion under this subdivision (B) does not affect the finality of a judgment or suspend its operation.

The procedure for obtaining any relief from a judgment shall be by motion as prescribed in these rules.

[Effective: July 1, 1970.]

RULE 61.   Harmless Error

No error in either the admission or the exclusion of evidence and no error or defect in any ruling or order or in anything done or omitted by the court or by any of the parties is ground for granting a new trial or for setting aside a verdict or for vacating, modifying or otherwise disturbing a judgment or order, unless refusal to take such action appears to the court inconsistent with substantial justice. The court at every stage of the proceeding must disregard any error or defect in the proceeding which does not affect the substantial rights of the parties.

[Effective: July 1, 1970.]

RULE 62.   Stay of Proceedings to Enforce a Judgment

(A)   Stay on motion after judgment. In its discretion and on such conditions for the security of the adverse party as are proper, the court may, upon motion made any time after judgment, stay the execution of that judgment or stay any proceedings to enforce the judgment until the time for moving for a new trial under Civ.R. 59, moving for relief from a judgment or order under Civ.R. 60, moving for judgment notwithstanding the verdict under Civ. R. 50, or filing a notice of appeal, and during the pendency of any motion under Civ.R. 50, Civ.R. 59, or Civ.R. 60.

(B)   Stay upon appeal. When an appeal is taken the appellant may obtain a stay of execution of a judgment or any proceedings to enforce a judgment by giving an adequate supersedeas bond. The bond may be given at or after the time of filing the notice of appeal. The stay is effective when the supersedeas bond is approved by the court.

(C)   Stay in favor of the government. When an appeal is taken by this state or political subdivision, or administrative agency of either, or by any officer thereof acting in his representative capacity and the operation or enforcement of the judgment is stayed, no bond, obligation or other security shall be required from the appellant.

(D)   Power of appellate court not limited. The provisions in this rule do not limit any power of an appellate court or of a judge or justice thereof to stay proceedings during the pendency of an appeal or to suspend, modify, restore, or grant an injunction during the pendency of an appeal or to make any order appropriate to preserve the status quo or the effectiveness of the judgment subsequently to be entered.

(E)   Stay of judgment as to multiple claims or multiple parties. When a court has ordered a final judgment under the conditions stated in Rule 54(B), the court may stay enforcement of that judgment until the entering of a subsequent judgment or judgments and may prescribe such conditions as are necessary to secure the benefit thereof to the party in whose favor the judgment is entered.

[Effective: July 1, 1970; amended effective July 1, 2017.]

Staff Note (July 1, 2017 Amendments)

Civ.R. 62(A). Stay on motion after judgment.

The rule is amended to allow a party to move to stay execution of judgment, or any proceedings to enforce the judgment, at any time after entry of judgment, including before any relief under Civ.R. 50, 59, or 60 is sought or an appeal is filed, as well as during the pendency of any motion seeking relief under Civ.R. 50, 59, or 60.

RULE 63.   Disability of a Judge

(A)   During trial. If for any reason the judge before whom a jury trial has commenced is unable to proceed with the trial, another judge designated by the administrative judge, or in the case of a single-judge division by the chief justice of the supreme court, may proceed with and finish the trial upon certifying in the record that he has familiarized himself with the record of the trial; but if such other judge is satisfied that he cannot adequately familiarize himself with the record, he may in his discretion grant a new trial.

(B)   If for any reason the judge before whom an action has been tried is unable to perform the duties to be performed by the court after a verdict is returned or findings of fact and conclusions of law are filed, another judge designated by the administrative judge, or in the case of a single-judge division by the Chief Justice of the Supreme Court, may perform those duties; but if such other judge is satisfied that he cannot perform those duties, he may in his discretion grant a new trial.

[Effective: July 1, 1970; amended effective July 1, 1972; July 1, 1973; July 1, 1994.]

TITLE VIII. PROVISIONAL AND FINAL REMEDIES

RULE 64.   Seizure of Person or Property

At the commencement of and during the course of an action, all remedies providing for seizure of person or property for the purpose of securing satisfaction of the judgment ultimately to be entered in the action are available under the circumstances and in the manner provided by law.   The remedies thus available include arrest, attachment, garnishment, replevin, sequestration, and other corresponding or equivalent remedies, however designated and regardless of whether the remedy is ancillary to an action or must be obtained by independent action.

[Effective: July 1, 1970.]

RULE 65. Injunctions

(A) Temporary restraining order; notice; hearing; duration. A temporary restraining order may be granted without written or oral notice to the adverse party or his attorney only if (1) it clearly appears from specific facts shown by affidavit or by the verified complaint that immediate and irreparable injury, loss or damage will result to the applicant before the adverse party or his attorney can be heard in opposition, and (2) the applicant's attorney certifies to the court in writing the efforts, if any, which have been made to give notice and the reasons supporting his claim that notice should not be required. The verification of such affidavit or verified complaint shall be upon the affiant's own knowledge, information or belief; and so far as upon information and belief, shall state that he believes this information to be true. Every temporary restraining order granted without notice shall be filed forthwith in the clerk's office; shall define the injury and state why it is irreparable and why the order was granted without notice; and shall expire by its terms within such time after entry, not to exceed fourteen days, as the court fixes, unless within the time so fixed the order, for good cause shown, is extended for one like period or unless the party against whom the order is directed consents that it may be extended for a longer period. The reasons for the extension shall be set forth in the order of extension. In case a temporary restraining order is granted without notice, the motion for a preliminary injunction shall be set down for hearing at the earliest possible time and takes precedence over all matters except older matters of the same character. When the motion comes on for hearing the party who obtained the temporary restraining order shall proceed with the application for a preliminary injunction and, if he does not do so, the court shall dissolve the temporary restraining order. On two days' notice to the party who obtained the temporary restraining order without notice or on such shorter notice to that party as the court may prescribe, the adverse party may appear and move its dissolution or modification, and in that event the court shall proceed to hear and determine such motion as expeditiously as the ends of justice require.

(B) Preliminary injunction.

(1) Notice. No preliminary injunction shall be issued without reasonable notice to the adverse party. The application for preliminary injunction may be included in the complaint or may be made by motion.

(2) Consolidation of hearing with trial on merits. Before or after the commencement of the hearing of an application for a preliminary injunction, the court may order the trial of the action on the merits to be advanced and consolidated with the hearing of the application. Even when this consolidation is not ordered, any evidence received upon an application for a preliminary injunction which would be admissible upon the trial on the merits becomes part of the record on the trial and need not be repeated upon the trial. This subdivision (B)(2) shall be so construed and applied as to save to the parties any rights they may have to trial by jury.

(C) **Security.** No temporary restraining order or preliminary injunction is operative until the party obtaining it gives a bond executed by sufficient surety, approved by the clerk of the court granting the order or injunction, in an amount fixed by the court or judge allowing it, to secure to the party enjoined the damages he may sustain, if it is finally decided that the order or injunction should not have been granted.

The party obtaining the order or injunction may deposit, in lieu of such bond, with the clerk of the court granting the order or injunction, currency, cashier's check, certified check or negotiable government bonds in the amount fixed by the court.

Before judgment, upon reasonable notice to the party who obtained an injunction, a party enjoined may move the court for additional security. If the original security is found to be insufficient, the court may vacate the injunction unless, in reasonable time, sufficient security is provided.

No security shall be required of this state or political subdivision, or agency of either, or of any officer thereof acting in his representative capacity.

A surety upon a bond or undertaking under this rule submits himself to the jurisdiction of the court and irrevocably appoints the clerk of the court as his agent upon whom any papers affecting his liability on the bond or undertaking may be served. His liability as well as the liability of the party obtaining the order or injunction may be enforced by the court without jury on motion without the necessity for an independent action. The motion and such notice of the motion as the court prescribes may be served on the clerk of the court who shall forthwith mail copies to the persons giving the security if their addresses are known.

(D) **Form and scope of restraining order or injunction.** Every order granting an injunction and every restraining order shall set forth the reasons for its issuance; shall be specific in terms; shall describe in reasonable detail, and not by reference to the complaint or other document, the act or acts sought to be restrained; and is binding upon the parties to the action, their officers, agents, servants, employees, attorneys and those persons in active concert or participation with them who receive actual notice of the order whether by personal service or otherwise.

(E) **Service of temporary restraining orders and injunctions.** Restraining orders which are granted ex parte shall be served in the manner provided for service of process under Rule 4 through Rule 4.3 and Rule 4.6; or in manner directed by order of the court. If the restraining order is granted upon a pleading or motion accompanying a pleading the order may be served with the process and pleading. When service is made pursuant to Rule 4 through Rule 4.3 and Rule 4.6 the sheriff or the person designated by order of the court shall forthwith make his return.

Restraining orders or injunctions which are granted with notice may be served in the manner provided under Rule 4 through Rule 4.3 and Rule 4.6, in the manner provided in Rule 5 or in the manner designated by order of the court. When service is made pursuant to Rule 4 through Rule 4.3 and Rule 4.6 the sheriff or the person designated by order of the court shall forthwith make his return.

[Effective: July 1, 1970.]

RULE 65.1. Civil Protection Orders

(A) Applicability; construction; other rules. The provisions of this rule apply to special statutory proceedings under R.C. 3113.31, R.C. 2151.34, and R.C. 2903.214 providing for domestic violence, stalking, and sexually oriented offense civil protection orders, shall be interpreted and applied in a manner consistent with the intent and purposes of those protection order statutes, and supersede and make inapplicable in such proceedings the provisions of any other rules of civil procedure to the extent that such application is inconsistent with the provisions of this rule.

(B) Definitions. Any terms used in this rule which are also specifically defined in R.C. 3113.31, R.C. 2151.34, and R.C. 2903.214 shall have the same definition in applying the provisions of this rule in those special statutory proceedings.

(C) Service.

(1) Service by clerk. The clerk shall cause service to be made of a copy of the petition, and all other documents required by the applicable protection order statute to be served on the Respondent and, if applicable, on the parent, guardian, or legal custodian of the Respondent.

(2)   Initial service. Initial service, and service of any ex parte protection order that is entered, shall be made in accordance with the provisions for personal service of process within the state under Civ. R. 4.1(B) or outside the state under Civ. R. 4.3(B)(2). Upon failure of such personal service, or in addition to such personal service, service may be made in accordance with any applicable provision of Civ. R. 4 through Civ. R 4.6.

(3)   Subsequent service. After service has been made in accordance with division (C)(2) of this rule, any additional service required to be made during the course of the proceedings on Respondent and, if applicable, on the parent, guardian, or legal custodian of Respondent, shall be made in accordance with the provisions of Civ.R. 5(B).

(4)   Modification; contempt; renewal; termination.

(a)   Service of a motion for modification, contempt, renewal, or termination of a civil protection order issued after a full hearing or an approved consent agreement shall be made in the manner provided for service of process under Civ. R. 4 through Civ. R. 4.6.

(b)   After service has been made in accordance with division (C)(4)(a) of this rule, any additional service required to be made on the Respondent and, if applicable, on the parent, guardian, or legal custodian of the Respondent, shall be made in accordance with provisions of Civ. R. 5(B).

(5)   Confidentiality. Upon request of the Petitioner, any method of service provided by Civ. R. 4 through 4.6 or by Civ. R. 5(B) may be limited or modified by the court to protect the confidentiality of the Petitioner's address in making service under this division.

(D) Discovery.

(1) Time. Discovery under this rule shall be completed prior to the time set for the full hearing.

(2) Discovery Order. Discovery may be had only upon the entry of an order containing all of the following to the extent applicable:

(a) The time and place of the discovery;

(b) The identities of the persons permitted to be present, which shall include any victim advocate; and

(c) Such terms and conditions deemed by the court to be necessary to assure the safety of the Petitioner, including if applicable, maintaining the confidentiality of the Petitioner's address.

(E) Appointed counsel for minor at full hearing. In a special statutory proceeding under R.C. 2151.34, the court, in its discretion, may determine if the Respondent is entitled to court-appointed counsel at the full hearing.

(F) Proceedings in matters referred to magistrates.

(1) Reference by court. A court may refer the proceedings under these special statutory proceedings to a magistrate.

(2) Ex parte proceedings. The following shall apply when these special statutory proceedings are referred to a magistrate for determination of a petitioner's request for an ex parte protection order:

(a) Authority. The magistrate shall conduct the ex parte hearing and, upon conclusion of the hearing, deny or grant an ex parte protection order.

(b) Nature of order.

(i) A magistrate's denial or granting of an ex parte protection order does not require judicial approval, shall otherwise comply with the statutory requirements relating to an ex parte protection order, shall be effective when signed by the magistrate and filed with the clerk, and shall have the same effect as an ex parte protection order entered by the court without reference to a magistrate.

(ii) A magistrate's denial or granting of an ex parte protection order without judicial approval under this division does not constitute a magistrate's order or a magistrate's decision under Civ.R. 53(D)(2) or (3) and is not subject to the requirements of those rules.

(iii) The court's approval and signing of a magistrate's denial or granting of an ex parte protection order entered under this division does not constitute a judgment or interim order under Civ.R. 53(D)(4)(e) and is not subject to the requirements of that rule.

(3) Full hearing proceedings. The following shall apply when these special statutory proceedings are referred to a magistrate for full hearing and determination:

(a) Authority. The magistrate shall conduct the full hearing and, upon conclusion of the hearing, deny or grant a protection order.

(b) Nature of order. A magistrate's denial or granting of a protection order after full hearing under this division does not constitute a magistrate's order or a magistrate's decision under Civ.R. 53(D)(2) or (3) and is not subject to the requirements of those rules.

(c) Court adoption; modification; rejection.

(i) A magistrate's denial or granting of a protection order after a full hearing shall comply with the statutory requirements relating to such orders and is not effective unless adopted by the court.

(ii) When a magistrate has denied or granted a protection order after a full hearing, the court may adopt the magistrate's denial or granting of the protection order upon review of the order and a determination that there is no error of law or other defect evident on the face of the order.

(iii) Upon review of a magistrate's denial or granting of a protection order after a full hearing, the court may modify or reject the magistrate's order.

(iv) A court's adoption, modification, or rejection of a magistrate's denial or granting of a protection order after a full hearing under this division does not constitute a judgment or interim order under Civ.R. 53(D)(4)(e) and is not subject to the requirements of that rule.

(v) A court's adoption, modification, or rejection of a magistrate's denial or granting of a protection order after a full hearing shall be effective when signed by the court and filed with the clerk.

(d) Objections.

(i) A party may file written objections to a court's adoption, modification, or rejection of a magistrate's denial or granting of a protection order after a full hearing, or any terms of such an order, within fourteen days of the court's filing of the order. If any party timely files objections, any other party may also file objections not later than ten days after the first objections are filed.

(ii) The timely filing of objections under this division shall not stay the execution of the order.

(iii) A party filing objections under this division has the burden of showing that an error of law or other defect is evident on the face of the order, or that the credible evidence of record is insufficient to support the granting or denial of the protection order, or that the magistrate abused the magistrate's discretion in including or failing to include specific terms in the protection order.

(iv) Objections based upon evidence of record shall be supported by a transcript of all the evidence submitted to the magistrate or an affidavit of that evidence if a transcript is not available. With leave of court, alternative technology or manner of reviewing the relevant evidence may be considered. The objecting party shall file the transcript or affidavit with the court within thirty days after filing objections unless the court extends the time in writing for preparation of the transcript or other good cause. If a party files timely objections prior to the date on which a transcript is prepared, the party may seek leave of court to supplement the objections.

(e) **Motions for modification, contempt, renewal, or termination of civil protection orders.** When a motion for modification, contempt, renewal, or termination of a civil protection order is referred to a magistrate for determination, the provisions of this division (F)(3) of this rule relating to full hearing proceedings shall apply unless such provisions would by their nature be clearly inapplicable.

(G) **Final order; objections prior to appeal; stay of appeal.** Notwithstanding the provisions of any other rule, an order entered by the court under division (F)(3)(c) or division (F)(3)(e) of this rule is a final, appealable order. However, a party must timely file objections to such an order under division (F)(3)(d) of this rule prior to filing an appeal, and the timely filing of such objections shall stay the running of the time for appeal until the filing of the court's ruling on the objections.

[Effective: July 1, 2012; amended effective July 1, 2016.]

Staff Note (July 1, 2012 Amendment)

The special statutory proceedings established by R.C. 3113.31, R.C. 2151.34, and R.C. 2903.214 provide regulations and requirements for the entry of civil protection orders against adults and juveniles for the protection of victims of domestic violence, stalking, and sexually oriented offenses. Each of those statutes provides that the proceedings, which customarily proceed pro se, "shall be conducted in accordance with the Rules of Civil Procedure." Rule 65.1 is adopted to provide a set of provisions uniquely applicable to those statutory proceedings because application of the existing rules, particularly with respect to service, discovery, and reference to magistrates, interferes with the statutory process and is inconsistent with its purposes.

Division (A): Applicability; construction; other rules

Division (A) provides that the rule applies to protection order proceedings under the three specified statutes, and specifies that the provisions of the rule are to be interpreted and applied consistently with the intent and purpose of those statutes and supersede any inconsistent Rules of Civil Procedure.

Division (B): Definitions

The statutes contain defined terms. Division (B) incorporates those definitions in construing any of the same terms included in the rule.

Division (C): Service

The statutes each provide for obtaining an ex parte protection order, followed by service on the Respondent of the petition, any ex parte order that has been entered, and notice of the date scheduled for the full hearing.

Division (C) provides that it is the responsibility of the clerk to cause service to be made of all documents required to be served on the Respondent. Initial service, and service of any ex parte order that is entered, is to be made in the same manner as personal service of process. In addition to personal service, or upon failure of that service, service may be made by other methods of service of process. The relevant statutes require that a Respondent be served with a protection order on the same day the order is entered, and therefore, an initial attempt by personal service is necessary. Although other methods of service are permitted in the event of failure of personal service, until the Respondent has actual notice of a protection order, the order could not be enforced against that Respondent, nor could the Respondent be prosecuted for violations occurring prior to such actual notice.

Once initial service has been made, further service during the course of the proceedings is to be made in accordance with Civ.R. 5(B).

Division (D): Discovery

The statutes do not address discovery. Division (D) provides for discovery only upon a court order containing accommodations and protections deemed necessary for the protection of the Petitioner.

Division (D)(1) states that discovery shall be completed prior to the date set for the full hearing. Since the statutes provide for a relatively short period of time between the entry of an ex parte order and the date of the full hearing, there may not be sufficient time for meaningful discovery in such cases, and a statutory request for a continuance of the full hearing would be appropriate.

Division (E): Appointed counsel for minor at full hearing

The entry of a protection order against a minor is addressed by R.C. 2151.34. That statute provides that "the court, in its discretion, may determine if the respondent is entitled to court-appointed counsel at the full hearing." Division (E) restates that provision.

Division (F): Proceedings in matters referred to magistrates

The statutes provide expedited processes for obtaining an ex parte protection order and for obtaining a protection order after a full hearing. When the proceedings are referred to a magistrate, several of the provisions of Civ.R. 53 are incompatible with those processes, particularly with respect to temporary magistrate "orders" to regulate the proceedings, independent review by the court of magistrate "decisions" rendered after hearing, and the filing and consideration of objections to those magistrate "decisions"

Divisions (F)(2)(b)(ii) and (F)(3)(b) exempt these protection order proceedings from the Civ.R. 53 requirements for magistrate temporary "orders" to regulate the proceedings and magistrate "decisions" rendered after hearing. Divisions (F)(2)(b)(iii) and (F)(3)(c)(iv) exempt the proceedings from the requirements applicable to orders entered by the court after referral to magistrates.

Division (F)(2)(b)(1) provides that a magistrate may enter an ex parte protection order without judicial approval, and that the ex parte order is effective when signed by the magistrate and filed with the clerk.

Division (F)(3)(c) provides that a magistrate's ruling after a full hearing is not effective until adopted by the court, permits adoption upon a determination that "there is no error of law or other defect evident on the face of the order," and also permits the court to modify or reject the magistrate's ruling. Adoption, modification, or rejection is effective when signed by the court and filed with the clerk.

Division (F)(3)(d)(i) is intended to encourage the parties, as an alternative to immediate appeal, to allow the trial court to review a court's adoption, modification, or rejection of a magistrate's protection order ruling based on the record, by filing objections in the trial court. Pursuant to division (F)(3)(d)(ii) the filing of objections does not stay execution of the protection order (but pursuant to division (G) the filing of objections does stay the time for appeal). Division (F)(3)(d)(iii) provides that the objecting party has the burden of showing either "that an error of law or other defect is evident on the face of the order, or that the credible evidence of record is insufficient to support the granting or denial of the protection order or that the magistrate abused the magistrate's discretion in including or failing to include specific terms in the protection order.

Division G: Final order; stay of appeal

Each statute provides that the granting or denial of a protection order, other than an ex parte order, is a final appealable order. Consistent with that provision, division (G) states that such rulings are final and appealable, notwithstanding the provisions of any other rule, such as Civ.R. 60(B). However, division (G) also provides that the timely filing of objections to the court's adoption or modification of a magistrate's protection order ruling stays the running of the time for appeal until the filing of the court's ruling on the objections.

Staff Notes (July 1, 2016 Amendment)

Division (C): Service

It is well-established that all proceedings under R.C. 3113.31, R.C. 2151.34, and R.C. 2903.214 must follow the Rules of Civil Procedure. See, e.g., *State v. Smith*, 136 Ohio St. 3d 1, 2013-Ohio-1698 at ¶21. Accordingly, division (C) of this rule provides clear direction regarding the methods of service in civil protection order proceedings. Division (C)(2) of this rule directs the clerk of court to cause the first attempt at initial service in these proceedings, including service of a copy of the petition and an ex parte order, by personal service of process. This method of service provides the respondent expeditious notice consistent with the urgent nature of these proceedings. Notwithstanding, division (C)(2) of this rule also recognizes, only upon failure of personal service, the other methods of service of process in the Rules of Civil Procedure, i.e., Civ. R. 4 through 4.6, provide similar reliable form of notice for the initial service.

The plain language of division (C)(3) of this rule indicates that subsequent service in civil protection order proceedings after the petition and ex parte order has been served, including service of a protection order entered after full hearing, must follow Civ.R. 5(B). In following the authority of Civ.R. 5(B), division (C)(3) of this rule fosters consistency regarding service subsequent to the original complaint, provides a clear direction and discretion regarding the methods of service appropriate for subsequent service in civil protection order proceedings under Civ.R. 5(B), and ensures the Respondent receives reliable notice of full hearing civil protection orders. Additionally, Civ.R. 5(B)(3) requires a proof of service record be created, which includes the date and specific manner by which the service was made under Civ.R. 5(B)(2).

Consistent with R.C. 3113.31, R.C. 2151.34, and R.C. 2903.214, division (C)(4)(a) of this rule recognizes that the statutory urgency of adjudicating a civil protection order petition is not part of a motion for renewal, contempt, modification, or termination of a full hearing civil protection order or an approved consent agreement. Accordingly, an initial attempt by personal service is not required and any of the methods of service under Civ.R. 4 through Civ.R. 4.6 is appropriate for such a motion.

Division (C)(4)(b) aligns with division (C)(3) of this rule and clarifies that subsequent service in proceedings for renewal, contempt, modification, or termination of a full hearing civil protection order or an approved consent agreement is to be made in accordance with Civ.R. 5(B).

Division (F): Proceedings in matters referred to magistrates.

A new division (F)(3)(e) of this rule is also added to address issues discussed in *Schneider v. Razek*, 2015-Ohio-410 (8th Dist.) relating to proceedings on motions for renewal, contempt, modification, or termination of civil protection orders.

Division (G): Final order; objections prior to appeal; stay of appeal.

Division (G) of this rule is amended to require that a party must file objections prior to filing an appeal from a trial court's otherwise appealable adoption, modification, or rejection of a magistrate's ruling. This amendment is grounded on two key principles. First, it promotes the fair administration of justice, including affording the trial court an opportunity to review the transcript and address any insufficiency of evidence or abuse of discretion that would render the order or a term of the order unjust. Second, it creates a more robust record upon which the appeal may proceed.

RULE 66.   Receivers

An action wherein a receiver has been appointed shall not be dismissed except by order of the court. Receiverships shall be administered in the manner provided by law and as provided by rules of court.

[Effective: July 1, 1970.]

RULE 67.   **[RESERVED]**

RULE 68.   Offer of Judgment

An offer of judgment by any party, if refused by an opposite party, may not be filed with the court by the offering party for purposes of a proceeding to determine costs.

This rule shall not be construed as limiting voluntary offers of settlement made by any party.

[Effective: July 1, 1970.]

RULE 69.   Execution

Process to enforce a judgment for the payment of money shall be a writ of execution, unless the court directs otherwise. The procedure on execution, in proceedings supplementary to and in aid of a judgment, and in proceedings on and in aid of execution shall be as provided by law. In aid of the judgment or execution, the judgment creditor or his successor in interest when that interest appears of record, may also obtain discovery from any person, including the judgment debtor, in the manner provided in these rules.

[Effective: July 1, 1970.]

RULE 70.   Judgment for Specific Acts; Vesting Title

If a judgment directs a party to execute a conveyance of land, to transfer title or possession of personal property, to deliver deeds or other documents, or to perform any other specific act, and the party fails to comply within the time specified, the court may, where necessary, direct the act to be done at the cost of the disobedient party by some other person appointed by the court, and the act when so done has like effect as if done by the party. On application of the party entitled to performance, the clerk shall issue a writ of attachment against the property of the disobedient party to compel obedience to the judgment. The court may also in proper cases adjudge the party in contempt. If real or personal property is within this state, the court in lieu of directing a conveyance thereof may enter a judgment divesting the title of any party and vesting it in others, and such judgment has the effect of a conveyance executed in due form of law. When any order or judgment is for the delivery of possession, the party in whose favor it is entered is entitled to a writ of execution upon application to the clerk.

[Effective: July 1, 1970.]

RULE 71.   Process in Behalf of and Against Persons Not Parties

When an order is made in favor of a person who is not a party to the action, he may enforce obedience to the order by the same process as if he were a party; and, when obedience to an order may be lawfully enforced against a person who is not a party, he is liable to the same process for enforcing obedience to the order as if he were a party.

[Effective: July 1, 1970.]

RULE 72. [RESERVED]

TITLE IX. PROBATE, JUVENILE, AND DOMESTIC RELATIONS PROCEEDINGS

RULE 73. **Probate Division of the Court of Common Pleas**

(A) **Applicability.** These Rules of Civil Procedure shall apply to proceedings in the probate division of the court of common pleas as indicated in this rule. Additionally, all of the Rules of Civil Procedure, though not specifically mentioned in this rule, shall apply except to the extent that by their nature they would be clearly inapplicable.

(B) **Venue.** Civ. R. 3(B) shall not apply to proceedings in the probate division of the court of common pleas, which shall be venued as provided by law. Proceedings under Chapters 2101. through 2131. of the Revised Code, which may be venued in the general division or the probate division of the court of common pleas, shall be venued in the probate division of the appropriate court of common pleas.

Proceedings that are improperly venued shall be transferred to a proper venue provided by law and division (B) of this rule, and the court may assess costs, including reasonable attorney fees, to the time of transfer against the party who commenced the action in an improper venue.

(C) **Service of summons.** Civ. R. 4 through 4.6 shall apply in any proceeding in the probate division of the court of common pleas requiring service of summons.

(D) **Service and filing of pleadings and papers subsequent to original pleading.** In proceedings requiring service of summons, Civ. R. 5 shall apply to the service and filing of pleadings and papers subsequent to the original pleading.

(E) **Service of notice.** In any proceeding where any type of notice other than service of summons is required by law or deemed necessary by the court, and the statute providing for notice neither directs nor authorizes the court to direct the manner of its service, notice shall be given in writing and may be served by or on behalf of any interested party without court intervention by one of the following methods:

(1)   By delivering a copy to the person to be served;

(2)   By leaving a copy at the usual place of residence of the person to be served;

(3)   By United States certified or express mail return receipt requested, or by a commercial carrier service utilizing any form of delivery requiring a signed receipt, addressed to the person to be served at the person's usual place of residence with instructions to the delivering postal employee or to the carrier to show to whom delivered, date of delivery, and address where delivered, provided that the certified or express mail envelope or return of the commercial carrier is not returned showing failure of delivery;

(4)   By United States ordinary mail after a returned United States certified or express mail envelope or return of the commercial carrier shows that it was refused;

(5)   By United States ordinary mail after a United States certified or express mail envelope is returned with an endorsement stating that it was unclaimed, provided that the United States ordinary mail envelope is not returned by the postal authorities showing failure of delivery;

(6)   By publication once each week for three consecutive weeks in some newspaper of general circulation in the county when the name, usual place of residence, or existence of the person to be served is unknown and cannot with reasonable diligence be ascertained; provided that before publication may be utilized, the person giving notice shall file an affidavit which states that the name, usual place of residence, or existence of the person to be served is unknown and cannot with reasonable diligence be ascertained;

(7)   By other method as the court may direct.

Civ.R. 4.2 shall apply in determining who may be served and how particular persons or entities must be served.

(F)   Proof of service of notice; when service of notice complete. When service is made through the court, proof of service of notice shall be in the same manner as proof of service of summons.

When service is made without court intervention, proof of service of notice shall be made by affidavit. When service is made by United States certified or express mail or by commercial carrier service, the return receipt which shows delivery shall be attached to the affidavit. When service is made by United States ordinary mail, the prior returned certified or express mail envelope which shows that the mail was refused or unclaimed shall be attached to the affidavit.

Service of notice by United States ordinary mail shall be complete when the fact of mailing is entered of record except as stated in division (E)(5) of this rule. Service by publication shall be complete at the date of the last publication.

(G)   Waiver of service of notice. Civ. R. 4(D) shall apply in determining who may waive service of notice.

(H)   Forms used in probate practice. Forms used in proceedings in the probate division of the courts of common pleas shall be those prescribed in the rule applicable to standard probate forms in the Rules of Superintendence. Forms not prescribed in such rule may be used as permitted in that rule.

Blank forms reproduced for use in probate practice for any filing to which the rule applicable to specifications for printing probate forms of the Rules of Superintendence applies shall conform to the specifications set forth in that rule.

No pleading, application, acknowledgment, certification, account, report, statement, allegation, or other matter filed in the probate division of the courts of common pleas shall be required to be executed under oath, and it is sufficient if it is made upon the signature alone of the person making it.

(I)   Notice of Filing of Judgments. Civ. R. 58(B) shall apply to all judgments entered in the probate division of the court of common pleas in any action or proceeding in which any party other than a plaintiff, applicant, or movant has filed a responsive pleading or exceptions. Notice of the judgment shall be given to each plaintiff, applicant, or movant, to each party filing a responsive pleading or exceptions, and to other parties as the court directs.

(J)   Filing with the court defined. The filing of documents with the court, as required by these rules, shall be made by filing them with the probate judge as the *ex officio* clerk of the court.   A court may provide, by local rules adopted pursuant to the Rules of Superintendence, for the filing of documents by electronic means. If the court adopts such local rules, they shall include all of the following:

(1)   Any signature on electronically transmitted documents shall be considered that of the attorney or party it purports to be for all purposes. If it is established that the documents were transmitted without authority, the court shall order the filing stricken.

(2)   A provision shall specify the days and hours during which electronically transmitted documents will be received by the court, and a provision shall specify when documents received electronically will be considered to have been filed.

(3)   Any document filed electronically that requires a filing fee may be rejected by the clerk of court unless the filer has complied with the mechanism established by the court for the payment of filing fees.

[Effective: July 1, 1970; amended effective July 1, 1971; July 1, 1975; July 1, 1977; July 1, 1980; July 1, 1996; July 1, 1997; July 1, 2001; July 1, 2012.]

Staff Note (July 1, 2012 Amendment)

Divisions (E) and (F) are amended so that they are consistent with the 2012 amendments to Civ.R. 4.1 relating to service of process by commercial carrier service and Civ.R. 4.6 relating to returns of service showing "refused" or "unclaimed" when service of process is attempted by U.S. certified or express mail or by commercial carrier service.

Staff Note (July 1, 2001 Amendment)

Civil Rule 73   Probate Division of the Court of Common Pleas

The amendments to this rule were part of a group of amendments that were submitted by the Ohio Courts Digital Signatures Task Force to establish minimum standards for the use of information systems, electronic signatures, and electronic filing. The substantive amendment to this rule was the addition of division (J). Comparable amendments were made to Civil Rule 5, Criminal Rule 12, Juvenile Rule 8, and Appellate Rule 13.

As part of this electronic filing and signature project, the following rules were amended effective July 1, 2001: Civil Rules 5, 11, and 73; Criminal Rule 12; Juvenile Rule 8; and Appellate Rules 13 and 18. In addition, Rule 26 of the Rules of Superintendence for Courts of Ohio was amended and Rule of Superintendence 27 was added to complement the rules of procedure. Superintendence Rule 27 establishes a process by which minimum standards for information technology are promulgated, and requires that courts submit any local rule involving the use of information technology to a technology standards committee designated by the Supreme Court for approval.

Staff Note (July 1, 1997 Amendment)

Rule 73 Probate division of the court of common pleas

Prior to the 1997 amendment, service of process under this rule was permitted only by certified mail. It appears that service of process by express mail, i.e. as that sort of mail is delivered by the United States Postal Service, can always be obtained return receipt requested, and thus could accomplish the purpose of notification equally well as certified mail. Therefore, the amendment provides for this additional option for service.

Division (H) was amended to delete the specific reference to Rule 16 of the Rules of Superintendence for Courts of Common Pleas, and instead a generic reference is made to the applicable rule. This amendment was made because the rules of superintendence were being revised and renumbered in 1997, and the rule number that will apply to probate forms was not known at the time of this amendment.

Other amendments to this rule are nonsubstantive grammatical or stylistic changes.

Staff Note (July 1, 1996 Amendment)

Rule 73(I), Notice of Filing of Judgments

In 1989, Civ. R. 58 was amended to, among other things, make clear that a clerk of courts shall serve signed judgments upon parties. After that amendment, there apparently has been some confusion as to the effect of that amendment upon probate proceedings. The amendment to division (I) makes clear that Civ. R. 58(B) does apply to probate proceedings, in the manner indicated.

RULE 74.   [RESERVED]

[Former Rule 74, adopted effective July 1, 1970 and amended effective July 1, 1971 and July 1, 1972, was repealed effective July 1, 1977.]

RULE 75.   Divorce, Annulment, and Legal Separation Actions

(A)   Applicability. The Rules of Civil Procedure shall apply in actions for divorce, annulment, legal separation, and related proceedings, with the modifications or exceptions set forth in this rule.

(B)   Joinder of parties. Civ.R. 14, 19, 19.1, and 24 shall not apply in divorce, annulment, or legal separation actions, however:

(1)   A person or corporation having possession of, control of, or claiming an interest in property, whether real, personal, or mixed, out of which a party seeks a division of marital property, a distributive award, or an award of spousal support or other support, may be made a party defendant;

(2)   When it is essential to protect the interests of a child, the court may join the child of the parties as a party defendant and appoint a guardian ad litem and legal counsel, if necessary, for the child and tax the costs;

(3)   The court may make any person or agency claiming to have an interest in or rights to a child by rule or statute, including but not limited to R.C. 3109.04 and R.C. 3109.051, a party defendant;

(4)   When child support is ordered, the court, on its own motion or that of an interested person, after notice to the party ordered to pay child support and to his or her employer, may make the employer a party defendant.

(C)   Trial by court or magistrate. In proceedings under this rule there shall be no right to trial by jury. All issues may be heard either by the court or by a magistrate as the court on the request of any party or on its own motion, may direct. Civ. R. 53 shall apply to all cases or issues directed to be heard by a magistrate.

(D)   Investigation. On the filing of a complaint for divorce, annulment, or legal separation, where minor children are involved, or on the filing of a motion for the modification of a decree allocating parental rights and responsibilities for the care of children, the court may cause an investigation to be made as to the character, family relations, past conduct, earning ability, and financial worth of the parties to the action. The report of the investigation shall be made available to either party or their counsel of record upon written request not less than seven days before trial. The report shall be signed by the investigator and the investigator shall be subject to cross-examination by either party concerning the contents of the report. The court may tax as costs all or any part of the expenses for each investigation.

(E)   Subpoena where custody involved. In any case involving the allocation of parental rights and responsibilities for the care of children, the court, on its own motion, may cite a party to the action from any point within the state to appear in court and testify.

(F) **Judgment.** The provisions of Civ.R. 55 shall not apply in actions for divorce, annulment, legal separation, or civil protection orders. For purposes of Civ.R. 54(B), the court shall not enter final judgment as to a claim for divorce, dissolution of marriage, annulment, or legal separation unless one of the following applies:

(1)   The judgment also divides the property of the parties, determines the appropriateness of an order of spousal support, and, where applicable, either allocates parental rights and responsibilities, including payment of child support, between the parties or orders shared parenting of minor children;

(2)   Issues of property division, spousal support, and allocation of parental rights and responsibilities or shared parenting have been finally determined in orders, previously entered by the court, that are incorporated into the judgment;

(3)   The court includes in the judgment the express determination required by Civ.R. 54(B) and a final determination that either of the following applies:

(a)   The court lacks jurisdiction to determine such issues;

(b)   In a legal separation action, the division of the property of the parties would be inappropriate at that time.

(G) **Civil protection order.** A claim for a civil protection order based upon an allegation of domestic violence shall be a separate claim from a claim for divorce, dissolution of marriage, annulment, or legal separation.

(H) **Relief pending appeal.** A motion to modify, pending appeal, either a decree allocating parental rights and responsibilities for the care of children, a spousal or other support order, shall be made to the trial court in the first instance, whether made before or after a notice of appeal is filed. The trial court may grant relief upon terms as to bond or otherwise as it considers proper for the security of the rights of the adverse party and in the best interests of the children involved. Civ. R. 62(B) does not apply to orders allocating parental rights and responsibilities for the care of children or a spousal or other support order. An order entered upon motion under this rule may be vacated or modified by the appellate court. The appellate court has authority to enter like orders pending appeal, but an application to the appellate court for relief shall disclose what has occurred in the trial court regarding the relief.

(I) **Temporary restraining orders.**

(1) **Restraining order: exclusion.** The provisions of Civ. R. 65(A) shall not apply in divorce, annulment, or legal separation actions.

(2) **Restraining order: grounds, procedure.** When it is made to appear to the court by affidavit of a party sworn to absolutely that a party is about to dispose of or encumber property, or any part thereof of property, so as to defeat another party in obtaining an equitable division of marital property, a distributive award, or spousal or other support, or that a party to the action or a child of any party is about to suffer physical abuse, annoyance, or bodily injury by the other party, the court may allow a temporary restraining order, with or without bond, to prevent that action. A temporary restraining order may be issued without notice and shall remain in force during the pendency of the action unless the court or magistrate otherwise orders.

(J) **Continuing jurisdiction.** The continuing jurisdiction of the court shall be invoked by motion filed in the original action, notice of which shall be served in the manner provided for the service of process under Civ. R. 4 to 4.6. When the continuing jurisdiction of the court is invoked pursuant to this division, the discovery procedures set forth in Civ. R. 26 to 37 shall apply.

(K) **Hearing.** No action for divorce, annulment, or legal separation may be heard and decided until the expiration of forty-two days after the service of process or twenty-eight days after the last publication of notice of the complaint, and no action for divorce, annulment, or legal separation shall be heard and decided earlier than twenty-eight days after the service of a counterclaim, which under this rule may be designated a cross-complaint, unless the plaintiff files a written waiver of the twenty-eight day period.

(L) **Notice of trial.** In all cases where there is no counsel of record for the adverse party, the court shall give the adverse party notice of the trial upon the merits. The notice shall be made by regular mail to the party's last known address, and shall be mailed at least seven days prior to the commencement of trial.

(M) **Testimony.** Judgment for divorce, annulment, or legal separation shall not be granted upon the testimony or admission of a party not supported by other credible evidence. No admission shall be received that the court has reason to believe was obtained by fraud, connivance, coercion, or other improper means. The parties, notwithstanding their marital relations, shall be competent to testify in the proceeding to the same extent as other witnesses.

(N) **Temporary Orders of spousal support, child support, and custody.**

(1) When requested in the complaint, answer, or counterclaim, or by motion served with the pleading, upon satisfactory proof by affidavit duly filed with the clerk of the court, the court or magistrate, without oral hearing and for good cause shown, may grant a temporary order regarding spousal support to either of the parties for the party's sustenance and expenses during the suit and may make a temporary order regarding the support, maintenance, and allocation of parental rights and responsibilities for the care of children of the marriage, whether natural or adopted, during the pendency of the action for divorce, annulment, or legal separation.

(2) Counter affidavits may be filed by the other party within fourteen days from the service of the complaint, answer, counterclaim, or motion, all affidavits to be used by the court or magistrate in making a temporary spousal support order, child support order, and order allocating parental rights and responsibilities for the care of children. Upon request, in writing, after any temporary spousal support, child support, or order allocating parental rights and responsibilities

for the care of children is journalized, the court shall grant the party so requesting an oral hearing within twenty-eight days to modify the temporary order. A request for oral hearing shall not suspend or delay the commencement of spousal support or other support payments previously ordered or change the allocation of parental rights and responsibilities until the order is modified by journal entry after the oral hearing.

(O) Delay of decree. When a party who is entitled to a decree of divorce or annulment is ordered to pay spousal support or child support for a child not in his or her custody, or to deliver a child to the party to whom parental rights and responsibilities for the care of the child are allocated, the court may delay entering a decree for divorce or annulment until the party, to the satisfaction of the court, secures the payment of the spousal support or the child support for the child, or delivers custody of the child to the party to whom parental rights and responsibilities are allocated.

[Effective: July 1, 1970; amended effective July 1, 1971; July 1, 1972; July 1, 1977; July 1, 1978; July 1, 1991; July 1, 1996; July 1, 1997; July 1, 1998; July 1, 2001; July 1, 2014; July 1, 2018.]

Staff Note (July 1, 2018 Amendment)

Division (N): Temporary Orders.

Reflecting contemporary terminology, the former term "pendente lite" is replaced with the term "temporary."

Staff Note (July 1, 2014 Amendments)

The rule is amended by inserting a new Civ.R. 75(B)(3) and renumbering the following provision. The new provision expressly grants courts the authority and discretion to join persons or agencies claiming to have an interest in or rights with respect to a child. This would include agencies such as child support enforcement and children services boards. This would also include third parties seeking the designation of residential parent or being granted parenting time rights.

Staff Note (July 1, 2001 Amendment)

Civil Rule 75(B)   Joinder of parties

Civ. R. 75(B) provides that Civ. R. 14 (third-party practice), Civ. R. 19 (joinder of parties needed for just adjudication), Civ. R. 19.1 (compulsory joinder), and Civ. R. 24 (intervention) are generally inapplicable in divorce, annulment, or legal separation actions. Division (1) of Rule 75(B), however, permits a corporation or person to be made a party defendant to such an action if that corporation or person has possession or control of or claims an interest in property out of which another seeks an award. Civ. R. 75(B)(1) thus permits the court to protect both the person seeking an award and the corporation or person who has possession or control of or claims an interest in property. See *Huener v. Huener*, 110 Ohio App. 3d 322, 327, 674 N.E. 2d 389, 393 (1996) (trial court abused its discretion by attempting to divest parents of party of legal title to property without joining them as parties; purpose of Civ. R. 75(B)(1) joinder "is to allow individuals to join whose interests need to be protected").

Division (B)(1) was amended effective July 1, 2001 to track more precisely the language of R.C. 3105.171, which provides for division of marital property and, in appropriate circumstances, a distributive award, and R.C. 3105.18, which provides for spousal support. The amendment is intended to make clear that the joinder of a corporation or person is proper whether a division of marital property, a distributive award, or an award of spousal support is the underlying issue. The reference to "other support" is retained in order to avoid foreclosing the use of Civ. R. 75(B)(1) when, e.g., child support is the underlying issue.

Rule 75(I)   Temporary restraining orders

Civ. R. 75(I)(1) provides that Civ. R. 65(A), which prescribes general conditions for the issuance of a temporary restraining order, is inapplicable to divorce, annulment, or legal separation actions. Civ. R. 75(I)(2), however, permits a court to issue a temporary restraining order in such an action without notice, which order may remain in effect during the pendency of the action, so as to protect a party from action by another party who is about to dispose of or encumber property so as to defeat the other party in obtaining a fair award. See *Addy v. Addy*, 97 Ohio App. 3d 204, 210, 646 N.E. 2d 513, 517 (1994) ("Rule 75(H) [now 75(I)] is intended to protect the interests of the parties and preserve the authority of the court to make meaningful final orders for support"); see also Civ. R. 53(C)(3) (power of magistrate to enter orders; Civ. R. 75(I) incorporated by reference).

Civ. R. 75(I)(2) was amended effective July 1, 2001 to track more precisely the language of R.C. 3105.171, which provides for division of marital property and, in appropriate circumstances, a distributive award, and R.C. 3105.18, which provides for spousal support. Though courts appear properly to have rejected an overly-literal reading of Civ. R. 75(I)(2), see *Sherban v. Sherban*, 1985 WL 4710, Nos. CA-6688, CA-6695, CA-6696, and CA-6683 (5th Dist. Ct. App., Stark, 12-23-85) (restraining order under Civ. R. 75(H) [now 75(I)] proper in support of division of property), the amendment is intended to make clear that a temporary restraining order may properly be entered if necessary to prevent a party from defeating another party's right to an equitable division of marital property, a distributive award, or an award of spousal support. The reference to "other support" is retained in order to avoid foreclosing the use of Civ. R. 75(I)(2) to prevent a party from defeating the right of another party to, e.g., child support.

Staff Note (July 1, 1998 Amendment)

Rule 75(F) Judgment

Division (F) was amended to require that the final judgment in a domestic relations case include all relevant claims except the domestic violence protection order: divorce, property settlement, and parental rights and responsibilities. The amendment was suggested by the Ohio State Bar Association Family Law Committee and the Ohio Gender Fairness Task Force. The amendment also changed the title of this division from "Default." Division (G) was added and the remainder of the divisions were relettered accordingly.

Staff Note (July 1, 1997 Amendment)

Rule 75(G) Relief pending appeal.

The amendment clarifies the procedure to be followed when parental rights, spousal support, and similar issues are sought to be modified while an appeal is pending. The rule prior to the amendment was unclear on which court or courts had authority to entertain motions to modify such orders, leading to a split of authority among Ohio courts. Compare *Rahm v. Rahm* (1974), 39 Ohio App.2d 74, 315 N.E. 2d 495 (trial court could only grant such relief prior to the filing of an appeal) with *Buckles v. Buckles* (1988), 46 Ohio App.3d 118, 546 N.E.2d 950 (declines to follow *Rahm*, holds that trial court retains jurisdiction to grant relief pending appeal as long as the exercise of that jurisdiction did not interfere with appellate review).

The amendment follows the *Buckles* case by requiring a motion to modify to be made in the first instance to the trial court, with that court's decision subject to review and modification, if appropriate, in the appellate court. The trial court is the most appropriate forum to consider such a motion in the first instance, given that the trial judge is already familiar with the issues, and the likelihood that further factual presentations and inquiry will be necessary for the court to dispose of the motion.

Staff Note (July 1, 1996 Amendment)

Rule 75 Divorce, Annulment, and Legal Separation Actions

The amendment changed the rule's reference from "referee" to "magistrate" in divisions (C), (H)(2), and (M) in order to harmonize the rule with the language adopted in the 1995 amendments to Civ. R. 53. Also, in divisions (B), (C), (F), (H)(1), and (I) the style used for citations to other rules was amended. The amendment is technical only and no substantive change is intended.

RULE 76.   [RESERVED]

[Former Rule 76, adopted effective July 1, 1970 and amended effective July 1, 1971, was repealed effective July 1, 1972.]

RULE 77 TO 80.   [RESERVED]

RULE 81.   References to Ohio Revised Code

A reference in these Rules to a section of the Revised Code shall mean the section as amended from time to time including the enactment of additional sections the numbers of which are subsequent to the section referred to in the rules.

[Effective: July 1, 1970.]

TITLE X. GENERAL PROVISIONS

RULE 82.   **Jurisdiction Unaffected**

These rules shall not be construed to extend or limit the jurisdiction of the courts of this state.

[Effective: July 1, 1970.]

RULE 83.   Rule of Court

(A)   A court may adopt local rules of practice which shall not be inconsistent with these rules or with other rules promulgated by the Supreme Court and shall file its local rules of practice with the Clerk of the Supreme Court.

(B)   Local rules of practice shall be adopted only after the court gives appropriate notice and an opportunity for comment. If a court determines that there is an immediate need for a rule, it may adopt the rule without prior notice and opportunity for comment, but promptly shall afford notice and opportunity for comment.

[Effective: July 1, 1970; amended effective July 1, 1994; July 1, 2000.]

Staff Note (July 1, 2000 Amendment)

Rule 83 Local Rules of Practice

The title of Civ. R. 83 and the text of division (A) were amended to more accurately reflect the intent of the original Civ. R. 83, which was to (1) restate the rule-making power of local courts as granted by sentence five of Section 5(B), Art. IV, Ohio Constitution and (2) require that rules adopted by local courts be filed with the Supreme Court. Civ. R. 83 was previously entitled Rule of Court. Although the previous rule did not reflect that intent as accurately as it might have, courts had generally accorded it treatment consistent with that intent. See 2 J. Klein & S. Darling, *Baldwin's Ohio Practice: Civil Practice*, Section 83-1 through 83-4 at 786-92 (West Group 1997).

The amendment was intended to (1) remove any doubt about the intent of the rule, (2) serve as a reminder that local rules of practice must be consistent with the Civil Rules and with other rules promulgated by the Supreme Court, and (3) make Civ. R. 83(A) more clearly consistent with Sup. R. 5(A).

Division (B) was amended in technical respects only; no substantive change was intended.

RULE 84.   Forms

The forms contained in the Appendix of Forms which the Supreme Court from time to time may approve are sufficient under these rules and shall be accepted for filing by courts of this state. Forms adopted by local courts that are substantially similar to the forms in the Appendix of Forms may also be accepted for filing. The forms in the Appendix of Forms are intended to indicate the simplicity and brevity of statement which these rules contemplate.

[Effective: July 1, 1970; amended effective July 1, 2011.]

Staff Note (July 1, 2011 Amendment)

Civil Rule 84 is amended to indicate that forms contained in the Appendix of Forms provide a "safe haven" for litigants. The forms must be accepted by local courts as sufficient under the rules. Local courts may continue, however, to adopt local forms which can also be accepted for filing. The amendment is intended to make it easier for pro se litigants and practitioners to access courts and justice by allowing for standardized forms in certain proceedings.

RULE 85.   Title

These rules shall be known as the Ohio Rules of Civil Procedure and may be cited as "Civil Rules" or "Civ.R. _."

[Effective: July 1, 1970; amended effective July 1, 1971.]

RULE 86.   Effective Date

(A)   Effective date of rules. These rules shall take effect on the first day of July, 1970. They govern all proceedings in actions brought after they take effect and also all further proceedings in actions then pending, except to the extent that in the opinion of the court their application in a particular action pending when the rules take effect would not be feasible or would work injustice, in which event the former procedure applies.

(B)   Effective date of amendments. The amendments submitted by the Supreme Court to the General Assembly on January 15, 1971, on April 14, 1971, and on April 30, 1971, shall take effect on the first day of July, 1971. They govern all proceedings in actions brought after they take effect and also all further proceedings in actions then pending, except to the extent that in the opinion of the court their application in a particular action pending when the rules take effect would not be feasible or would work injustice, in which event the former procedure applies.

(C)   Effective date of amendments. The amendments submitted by the Supreme Court to the General Assembly on January 15, 1972, and on May 1, 1972, shall take effect on the first day of July, 1972. They govern all proceedings in actions brought after they take effect and also all further proceedings in actions then pending, except to the extent that their application in a particular action pending when the rules take effect would not be feasible or would work injustice, in which event the former procedure applies.

(D)   Effective date of amendments. The amendments submitted by the supreme court to the general assembly on January 12, 1973, shall take effect on the first day of July 1973. They govern all proceedings in actions brought after they take effect and also all further proceedings in actions then pending, except to the extent that their application in a particular action pending when the rules take effect would not be feasible or would work injustice, in which event the former procedure applies.

(E)   Effective date of amendments. The amendments submitted by the Supreme Court to the General Assembly on January 10, 1975 and on April 29, 1975, shall take effect on July 1, 1975. They govern all proceedings in actions brought after they take effect and also all further proceedings in actions then pending, except to the extent that their application in a particular action pending when the amendments take effect would not be feasible or would work injustice, in which event the former procedure applies.

(F)   Effective date of amendments. The amendments submitted by the Supreme Court to the General Assembly on January 9, 1976, shall take effect on July 1, 1976. They govern all proceeding in actions brought after they take effect and also all further proceedings in actions then pending, except to the extent that their application in a particular action pending when the amendments take effect would not be feasible, or would work injustice, in which event the former procedure applies.

(G) **Effective date of amendments.** The amendments submitted by the Supreme Court to the General Assembly on January 12, 1978, and on April 28, 1978, shall take effect on July 1, 1978. They govern all proceedings in actions brought after they take effect and also all further proceedings in actions then pending, except to the extent that their application in a particular action pending when the amendments take effect would not be feasible or would work injustice, in which event the former procedure applies.

(H) **Effective date of amendments.** The amendments submitted by the Supreme Court to the General Assembly on January 14, 1980 shall take effect on July 1, 1980. They govern all proceedings in actions brought after they take effect and also all further proceedings in actions then pending, except to the extent that their application in a particular action pending when the amendments take effect would not be feasible or would work injustice, in which event the former procedure applies.

(I) **Effective date of amendments.** The amendments submitted by the Supreme Court to the General Assembly on January 12, 1983 shall take effect on July 1, 1983. They govern all proceedings in actions brought after they take effect and also all further proceedings in actions then pending, except to the extent that their application in a particular action pending when the amendments take effect would not be feasible or would work injustice, in which event the former procedure applies.

(J) **Effective date of amendments.** The amendments submitted by the Supreme Court to the General Assembly on January 12, 1984 shall take effect on July 1, 1984. They govern all proceedings in actions brought after they take effect and also all further proceedings in actions then pending, except to the extent that their application in a particular action pending when the amendments take effect would not be feasible or would work injustice, in which event the former procedure applies.

(K) **Effective date of amendments.** The amendments submitted by the Supreme Court to the General Assembly on December 24, 1984 and January 8, 1985 shall take effect on July 1, 1985. They govern all proceedings in actions brought after they take effect and also all further proceedings in actions then pending, except to the extent that their application in a particular action pending when the amendments take effect would not be feasible or would work injustice, in which event the former procedure applies.

(L) **Effective date of amendments.** The amendments submitted by the Supreme Court to the General Assembly on January 9, 1986 shall take effect on July 1, 1986. They govern all proceedings in actions brought after they take effect and also all further proceedings in actions then pending, except to the extent that their application in a particular action pending when the amendments take effect would not be feasible or would work injustice, in which event the former procedure applies.

(M) **Effective date of amendments.** The amendments submitted by the Supreme Court to the General Assembly on January 14, 1988 shall take effect on July 1, 1988. They govern all proceedings in actions brought after they take effect and also all further proceedings in actions then pending, except to the extent that their application in a particular action pending when the amendments take effect would not be feasible or would work injustice, in which event the former procedure applies.

(N) **Effective date of amendments.** The amendments submitted by the Supreme Court to the General Assembly on January 6, 1989 shall take effect on July 1, 1989. They govern all proceedings in actions brought after they take effect and also all further proceedings in actions then pending, except to the extent that their application in a particular action pending when the amendments take effect would not be feasible or would work injustice, in which event the former procedure applies.

(O) **Effective date of amendments.** The amendments submitted by the Supreme Court to the General Assembly on January 10, 1991 and further revised and submitted on April 29, 1991, shall take effect on July 1, 1991. They govern all proceedings in actions brought after they take effect and also all further proceedings in actions then pending, except to the extent that their application in a particular action pending when the amendments take effect would not be feasible or would work injustice, in which event the former procedure applies.

(P) **Effective date of amendments.** The amendments filed by the Supreme Court with the General Assembly on January 14, 1992 and further revised and filed on April 30, 1992, shall take effect on July 1, 1992. They govern all proceedings in actions brought after they take effect and also all further proceedings in actions then pending, except to the extent that their application in a particular action pending when the amendments take effect would not be feasible or would work injustice, in which event the former procedure applies.

(Q) **Effective date of amendments.** The amendments submitted by the Supreme Court to the General Assembly on January 8, 1993 and further revised and filed on April 30, 1993 shall take effect on July 1, 1993. They govern all proceedings in actions brought after they take effect and also all further proceedings in actions then pending, except to the extent that their application in a particular action pending when the amendments take effect would not be feasible or would work injustice, in which event the former procedure applies.

(R) **Effective date of amendments.** The amendments submitted by the Supreme Court to the General Assembly on January 14, 1994 and further revised and filed on April 29, 1994 shall take effect on July 1, 1994. They govern all proceedings in actions brought after they take effect and also all further proceedings in actions then pending, except to the extent that their application in a particular action pending when the amendments take effect would not be feasible or would work injustice, in which event the former procedure applies.

(S) **Effective date of amendments.** The amendments to Rules 11 and 53 filed by the Supreme Court with the General Assembly on January 11, 1995 shall take effect on July 1, 1995. They govern all proceedings in actions brought after they take effect and also all further proceedings in actions then pending, except to the extent that their application in a particular action pending when the amendments take effect would not be feasible or would work injustice, in which event the former procedure applies.

(T) **Effective Date of Amendments.** The amendments to Rules 4.2, 19.1, 53, 54, 59, 73, and 75 filed by the Supreme Court with the General Assembly on January 5, 1996 and refiled on April 26, 1996 shall take effect on July 1, 1996. They govern all proceedings in actions brought after they take effect and also all further proceedings in actions then pending, except to the extent that their application in a particular action pending when the amendments take effect would not be feasible or would work injustice, in which event the former procedure applies.

(U) **Effective date of amendments.** The amendments to Rules 4.1, 4.2, 4.3, 4.5, 4.6, 30, 56, 73, and 75 filed by the Supreme Court with the General Assembly on January 10, 1997 and refiled on April 24, 1997 shall take effect on July 1, 1997. They govern all proceedings in actions brought after they take effect and also all further proceedings in actions then pending, except to the extent that their application in a particular action pending when the amendments take effect would not be feasible or would work injustice, in which event the former procedure applies.

(V) **Effective date of amendments.** The amendments to Rules 3, 53, and 75 filed by the Supreme Court with the General Assembly on January 15, 1998 and further revised and refiled on April 30, 1998 shall take effect on July 1, 1998. They govern all proceedings in actions brought after they take effect and also all further proceedings in actions then pending, except to the extent that their application in a particular action pending when the amendments take effect would not be feasible or would work injustice, in which event the former procedure applies.

(W) **Effective date of amendments.** The amendments to Rules 24, 33, and 56 filed by the Supreme Court with the General Assembly on January 13, 1999 shall take effect on July 1, 1999. They govern all proceedings in actions brought after they take effect and also all further proceedings in actions then pending, except to the extent that their application in a particular action pending when the amendments take effect would not be feasible or would work injustice, in which event the former procedure applies.

(X) **Effective date of amendments.** The amendments to Civil Rule 83 filed by the Supreme Court with the General Assembly on January 13, 2000 and refiled on April 27, 2000 shall take effect on July 1, 2000. They govern all proceedings in actions brought after they take effect and also all further proceedings in actions then pending, except to the extent that their application in a particular action pending when the amendments take effect would not be feasible or would work injustice, in which event the former procedure applies.

(Y)   Effective date of amendments. The amendments to Civil Rules 5, 11, 28, 41, 73, and 75 filed by the Supreme Court with the General Assembly on January 12, 2001, and revised and refiled on April 26, 2001, shall take effect on July 1, 2001. They govern all proceedings in actions brought after they take effect and also all further proceedings in actions then pending, except to the extent that their application in a particular action pending when the amendments take effect would not be feasible or would work injustice, in which event the former procedure applies.

(Z)   Effective date of amendments. The amendments to Civil Rule 53 filed by the Supreme Court with the General Assembly on January 9, 2003 and refiled on April 28, 2003, shall take effect on July 1, 2003. They govern all proceedings in actions brought after they take effect and also all further proceedings in actions then pending, except to the extent that their application in a particular action pending when the amendments take effect would not be feasible or would work injustice, in which event the former procedure applies.

(AA)   Effective date of amendments. The amendments to Civil Rule 33 and 36 filed by the Supreme Court with the General Assembly on January 7, 2004 and refiled on April 28, 2004 shall take effect on July 1, 2004. They govern all proceedings in actions brought after they take effect and also all further proceedings in actions then pending, except to the extent that their application in a particular action pending when the amendments take effect would not be feasible or would work injustice, in which event the former procedure applies.

(BB)   Effective date of amendments. The amendments to Civil Rules 3, 10, 34, 36, 42, 45, 47, and 51 filed by the Supreme Court with the General Assembly on January 14, 2005 and revised and refiled on April 20, 2005 shall take effect on July 1, 2005. They govern all proceedings in actions brought after they take effect and also all further proceedings in actions then pending, except to the extent that their application in a particular action pending when the amendments take effect would not be feasible or would work injustice, in which event the former procedure applies.

(CC)   Effective date of amendments. The amendments to Civil Rules 30, 47, and 53 filed by the Supreme Court with the General Assembly on January 12, 2006 shall take effect on July 1, 2006. They govern all proceedings in actions brought after they take effect and also all further proceedings in actions then pending, except to the extent that their application in a particular action pending when the amendments take effect would not be feasible or would work injustice, in which event the former procedure applies.

(DD)   Effective date of amendments. The amendments to Civil Rule 10 filed by the Supreme Court with the General Assembly on January 11, 2007 and refiled April 30, 2007 shall take effect on July 1, 2007. They govern all proceedings in actions brought after they take effect and also all further proceedings in actions then pending, except to the extent that their application in a particular action pending when the amendments take effect would not be feasible or would work injustice, in which event the former procedure applies.

(EE) Effective date of amendments. The amendments to Civil Rules 4, 16, 26, 33, 34, 36, 37, and 45 filed by the Supreme Court with the General Assembly on January 14, 2008 and refiled on April 28, 2008 shall take effect on July 1, 2008. They govern all proceedings in actions brought after they take effect and also all further proceedings in actions then pending, except to the extent that their application in a particular action pending when the amendments take effect would not be feasible or would work injustice, in which event the former procedure applies.

(FF)   Effective date of amendments. The amendments to Civil Rules 4.2, 33, 36 and 47 filed by the Supreme Court with the General Assembly on January 14, 2009 and revised and refiled on April 30, 2009 shall take effect on July 1, 2009. They govern all proceedings in actions brought after they take effect and also all further proceedings in actions then pending, except to the extent that their application in a particular action pending when the amendments take effect would not be feasible or would work injustice, in which event the former procedure applies.

(GG)   Effective date of amendments. The amendments to the Uniform Domestic Relations Forms (Affidavits 1 through 5), approved on May 25, 2010 by the Supreme Court pursuant to Ohio Rule of Civil Procedure 84 are effective July 1, 2010.

(HH)   Effective date of amendments. The amendments to Civil Rule 53 and 84 filed by the Supreme Court with the General Assembly on January 5, 2011 and refiled on April 21, 2011 shall take effect on July 1, 2011. They govern all proceedings in actions brought after they take effect and also all further proceedings in actions then pending, except to the extent that their application in a particular action pending when the amendments take effect would not be feasible or would work injustice, in which event the former procedure applies.

(II)   Effective date of amendments. The amendments to Civil Rules 4.1, 4.2, 4.3, 4.4, 4.5, 4.6, 5, 6, 11, 26, 30, 33, 36, 45, 47, 58, 65.1, 73, and 86 filed by the Supreme Court with the General Assembly on January 13, 2012 and revised and refiled on April 30, 2012 shall take effect on July 1, 2012. They govern all proceedings in actions brought after they take effect and also all further proceedings in actions then pending, except to the extent that their application in a particular action pending when the amendments take effect would not be feasible or would work injustice, in which event the former procedure applies.

(JJ)   Effective date of amendments. The amendments to Civil Rules 4.4, 15, 40, 50, 59, and 86 filed by the Supreme Court with the General Assembly on January 15, 2013 and revised and refiled on April 29, 2013 shall take effect on July 1, 2013. They govern all proceedings in actions brought after they take effect and also all further proceedings in actions then pending, except to the extent that their application in a particular action pending when the amendments take effect would not be feasible or would work injustice, in which event the former procedure applies.

(KK) Effective date of amendments. New Uniform Domestic Relations Forms (6-28), approved on April 11, 2013 by the Supreme Court pursuant to Ohio Rule of Civil Procedure 84 are effective July 1, 2013.

(LL) Effective date of amendments. The amendment to the Appendix of Forms (Repeal of Form 20) of the Ohio Rules of Civil Procedure is effective September 1, 2013, pursuant to the Court's authority under Civil Rule 84.

(MM) Effective date of amendments. The amendments to Civil Rules 4.3, 4.5, 4.6, 7, 33, 36, 45, 75, and 86 filed by the Supreme Court with the General Assembly on January 15, 2014 and revised and refiled on April 30, 2014 shall take effect on July 1, 2014. They govern all proceedings in actions brought after they take effect and also all further proceedings in actions then pending, except to the extent that their application in a particular action pending when the amendments take effect would not be feasible or would work injustice, in which event the former procedure applies.

(NN) Effective date of amendments. The amendments to Civil Rules 1, 5, 6, 7, 23, 25, 30, 42, 43, 50, 52, 56, 59, and 86 filed by the Supreme Court with the General Assembly on January 15, 2015 and refiled on April 30, 2015 shall take effect on July 1, 2015. They govern all proceedings in actions brought after they take effect and also all further proceedings in actions then pending, except to the extent that their application in a particular action pending when the amendments take effect would not be feasible or would work injustice, in which event the former procedure applies.

(OO) Effective date of amendments. The amendments to the Uniform Domestic Relations Forms (Affidavits 1, 2, 4, and 5 and Forms 6 through 12 and 14 through 20), approved on February 23, 2016, by the Supreme Court pursuant to Ohio Rule of Civil Procedure 84 are effective March 15, 2016.

(PP) Effective date of amendments. The amendments to Civil Rules 4.1, 4.2, 4.4, 5, 10, 19.1, 37, 54, 65.1, and 86 filed by the Supreme Court with the General Assembly on January 13, 2016 and refiled on April 29, 2016 shall take effect on July 1, 2016. They govern all proceedings in actions brought after they take effect and also all further proceedings in actions then pending, except to the extent that their application in a particular action pending when the amendments take effect would not be feasible or would work injustice, in which event the former procedure applies.

(QQ) Effective date of amendments. The amendments to Civil Rules 4.2, 19.1, 30, 33, 34, 36 and 62 filed by the Supreme Court with the General Assembly on January 6, 2017 and refiled on April 26, 2017 shall take effect on July 1, 2017. They govern all proceedings in actions brought after they take effect and also all further proceedings in actions then pending, except to the extent that their application in a particular action pending when the amendments take effect would not be feasible or would work injustice, in which event the former procedure applies.

(RR) **Effective date of amendments.** The amendments to Civil Rules 3, 4.4, 5, 50, 59, and 75 filed by the Supreme Court with the General Assembly on January 9, 2018 and refiled on April 24, 2018 shall take effect on July 1, 2018. They govern all proceedings in actions brought after they take effect and also all further proceedings in actions then pending, except to the extent that their application in a particular action pending when the amendments take effect would not be feasible or would work injustice, in which event the former procedure applies.

(SS) **Effective date of amendments.** The amendments to Civil Rules 6, 7, 33, 34, 36, 47, 54, and 56 filed by the Supreme Court with the General Assembly on January 9, 2019 and refiled on April 24, 2019 shall take effect on July 1, 2019. They govern all proceedings in actions brought after they take effect and also all further proceedings in actions then pending, except to the extent that their application in a particular action pending when the amendments take effect would not be feasible or would work injustice, in which event the former procedure applies.

APPENDIX OF FORMS

FORMS 1 THROUGH 19: GENERAL CIVIL FORMS

APPENDIX OF FORMS
(See Rule 84)

INTRODUCTORY STATEMENT

The forms which follow are intended for illustration only. They are limited in number inasmuch as no attempt is made to furnish a manual of forms.

The forms are expressly declared by Rule 84 to be sufficient under the rules.

Departures from the forms shall not void papers which are otherwise sufficient, and the forms may be varied when necessary to meet the facts of a particular case.

Where appropriate, the forms assume that the action has been brought in the Court of Common Pleas, Franklin County, Ohio.

FORM 1. CAPTION AND SUMMONS

COURT OF COMMON PLEAS
_____ COUNTY, OHIO

_____	) Case No. _____
[Street Address]	) Judge _____
[City, State Zip]	)
Plaintiff	)
v.	) SUMMONS
	)
_____	)
[Street Address]	)
[City, State Zip]	)
Defendant	)

To the following named defendant(s):

Name: Address:

_____   _____

_____   _____

_____   _____

You have been named as a defendant in this Court. The Plaintiff(s) has filed a lawsuit against you. A copy of the Complaint is attached. The Plaintiff's attorney and that attorney's address are: _____

_____

_____

You must deliver to the Plaintiff's attorney (or the Plaintiff if not represented by an attorney) a written Answer to the Complaint within 28 days; Civil Rule 5 explains the ways that you may deliver the Answer (http://www.supremecourt.ohio.gov/LegalResources/Rules/civil/Civil Procedure.pdf). You must then file a copy of the Answer with this Court within three days after you serve it on the Plaintiff(s). If you fail to serve and file an Answer, the Court may enter judgment against you for the relief requested in the Complaint.

You may wish to hire an attorney to represent you. Because this is a civil suit, the Court cannot appoint an attorney for you. If you need help to find a lawyer, contact a local bar association and request assistance.

Date: _____   Clerk: _____

Note

The caption above designates the particular paper as a "SUMMONS." The particular pleading or paper should contain an appropriate designation, thus: "COMPLAINT," "ANSWER," etc. A more specific designation in a caption is also appropriate, thus: "MOTION TO INTERVENE AS A DEFENDANT."

* *

***Multilingual notice:

You have been named as a defendant in this Court. You must file an answer within 28 days; if you fail to answer, the Court may enter judgment against you for the relief stated in the Complaint. Seek assistance from both an interpreter and an attorney. Your inability to understand, write, or speak English will not be a defense to possible judgment against you.

1. Spanish (US)

***Aviso multilingüe:

Este Tribunal lo ha declarado como acusado. Debe presentar una respuesta en un plazo de 28 días. Si no contesta en dicho plazo, el Tribunal podrá dictar sentencia en su contra por el amparo que se detalla en la demanda. Solicite la ayuda de un intérprete y de un abogado. Su incapacidad para comprender, escribir o hablar inglés no se considerará como defensa ante una posible sentencia en su contra.

2. Somali

***Ogeysiis luqadda badan ah:

Waxaa laguu magacaabay sida eedeysane gudaha Maxkamadan. Waa in aad ku soo gudbisaa jawaab 28 maalmood gudahood; haddii aad ku guuldareysto jawaabta, Maxkamada laga yaabo in ay gasho xukun adiga kaa soo horjeedo ee ka nasashada lagu sheegay Cabashada. Raadi caawinta ka timid labadaba turjubaanka iyo qareenka. Karti la'aantaada aad ku fahmo, ku qoro, ama ku hadasho Af Ingiriisiga ma noqon doonto difaacida xukunkaaga suuralka ah ee adiga kugu lidka ah.

3. Russian

***Уведомление на разных языках:

Вы были названы в качестве ответчика в данном суде. Вы должны предоставить ответ в течение 28 дней; если Ваш ответ не будет получен, суд может вынести решение против Вас и удовлетворить содержащиеся в жалобе требования. Воспользуйтесь услугами переводчика и адвоката. Тот факт, что Вы не понимаете английскую речь и не можете читать и писать по-английски, не является препятствием для возможного вынесения судебного решения против Вас.

4. Arabic

***ملاحظة متعددة اللغات:

لقد تم اعتبارك مدعى عليه في هذه المحكمة. يجب أن تقدم ردًا خلال 28 يومًا؛ وإذا لم تقم بالرد، فقد تصدر المحكمة حكمًا ضدك بالتعويض المنصوص عليه في هذه الشكوى القضائية. اطلب المساعدة من مترجم فوري ومحامٍ. فلن تُعد عدم قدرتك على فهم اللغة الإنجليزية أو كتابتها أو تحدثها دفاعًا لك أمام الحكم المحتمل ضدك.

5. Chinese (Simplified)

***多語版本通知:

您在本法庭已被列为被告。您必须于 28 日内递交答辩状；如果没有递交答辩状，法庭会针对诉状中声明的补救措施对您作出不利判决。请向口译人员和律师寻求帮助。您无法理解、书写或说英语的情况不能作为对您可能作出不利判决的辩护理由。

INSTRUCTIONS FOR PERSONAL OR RESIDENCE SERVICE

To:_____

You are instructed to make personal--residence [cross out one] service upon defendant(s)
_____
                                    (name)

at _____
           (address for service if different from body of summons).

_____

Special instructions for server:_____

_____

_____

* *

RETURN OF SERVICE OF SUMMONS
(PERSONAL)

Fees	
Service$_____	
Mileage	$_____
Copy	$_____
Docket	$_____
Return	$_____
Total	$_____

I received this summons on _____, 20____, at _____ o'clock, ___.m., and made personal service of it upon _____ by locating him -- them (cross out one) and tendering a copy of the summons and accompanying documents, on _____, 20 ___.

_____
Sheriff -- Bailiff -- Process Server
By _____
Deputy

* *

RETURN OF SERVICE OF SUMMONS
(RESIDENCE)

	Fees
Service	$_____
Mileage	$_____
Copy	$_____
Docket	$_____
Return	$_____
Total	$_____

I received this summons on _____, 20____, at _____ o'clock, ___.m., and made residence service of it upon _____ by leaving it at his - - their (cross out one) usual place of residence with _____, a person of suitable age and discretion then residing therein, a copy of the summons, a copy of the complaint and accompanying documents, on _____, 20 ___.

_____

Sheriff -- Bailiff -- Process Server

By _____

Deputy

* *

FORM 2. COMPLAINT ON A PROMISSORY NOTE

COURT OF COMMON PLEAS
FRANKLIN COUNTY, OHIO

A.B., Plaintiff)
(address))

          v.   )   No._____

C.D., Defendant)
(address))   COMPLAINT

1. Defendant on or about _____, 20____, executed and delivered to plaintiff a promissory note, a copy of which is hereto attached as Exhibit A.

2. Defendant owes to plaintiff the amount of said note and interest.

Wherefore plaintiff demands judgment against defendant for the sum of _____dollars, interest, and costs.

_____
(Attorney for Plaintiff)

_____
(Address)

_____

Note

1. The pleader should follow the form above if he has possession of a copy of the note. The pleader should attach a copy of the note to the pleading. See Rule 10(D).

2. Under the rules free joinder of claims is permitted. See Rule 8(E) and Rule 18. Consequently the claims set forth in each and all of the following forms may be joined with this complaint or with each other. Ordinarily each claim should be stated in a separate division of the complaint, and the divisions should be designated as counts successively numbered (i.e., COUNT ONE, COUNT TWO, etc.). See Rule 10(B). In particular the rules permit alternative and inconsistent pleading. See Rule 8(E)(2).

3. The attorney must sign the pleading. See Rule 11. The pleading need not be verified. See Rule 11.

[Effective: July 1, 1970.]

FORM 2A. COMPLAINT ON A PROMISSORY NOTE
(REASON FOR OMISSION OF COPY STATED)

1. Defendant on or about _____, 20____, executed and delivered to plaintiff a promissory note

[in the following words and figures: (here set out the note verbatim)]

or

[whereby defendant promised to pay plaintiff or order on_____, 20 _____, the sum of _____ dollars with interest thereon at the rate of _____ percent per annum].

2. Plaintiff is unable to attach a copy of the said note because (here set out the reason for failure to attach the note).

3. Defendant owes to plaintiff the amount of said note and interest.

Wherefore (etc. as in Form 2).

Note

1. The pleader states why, under Rule 10(D), he is unable to attach a copy of the note.

2. If pleader can set forth the note verbatim from information at hand, he may do so.

3. Or pleader may plead the legal effect of the note, he being unable to attach a copy of the note.

4. This type form may be used in other situations whenever pleader is required to attach a copy of an instrument, but a copy of the instrument is not available to him.

[Effective: July 1, 1970.]

FORM 3. COMPLAINT ON AN ACCOUNT

Defendant owes plaintiff _____ dollars according to the account hereto annexed as Exhibit A.

Wherefore (etc. as in Form 2).

[Effective: July 1, 1970.]

FORM 4. COMPLAINT FOR GOODS SOLD AND DELIVERED

Defendant owes plaintiff _____ dollars for goods sold and delivered by plaintiff to defendant between_____, 20_____, and_____, 20_____.

Wherefore (etc. as in Form 2).

Note

This form may be used where the action is for an agreed price or for the reasonable value of the goods.

[Effective: July 1, 1970.]

FORM 5. COMPLAINT FOR MONEY LENT

 Defendant owes plaintiff _____ dollars for money lent by plaintiff to defendant on_____, 20____.

 Wherefore (etc. as in Form 2).

 [Effective: July 1, 1970.]

FORM 6. COMPLAINT FOR MONEY PAID BY MISTAKE

Defendant owes plaintiff _____ dollars for money paid by plaintiff to defendant by mistake on_____, 20____, under the following circumstances: [here state the circumstances with particularity--see Rule 9(B)].

Wherefore (etc. as in Form 2).

[Effective: July 1, 1970.]

FORM 7. COMPLAINT FOR MONEY HAD AND RECEIVED

  Defendant owes plaintiff _____ dollars for money had and received from one G.H. on_____, 20_____, to be paid by defendant to plaintiff.

  Wherefore (etc. as in Form 2).

[Effective: July 1, 1970.]

FORM 8. COMPLAINT FOR NEGLIGENCE

1.   On_____, 20_____, in a public highway called _____Street in_____, Ohio, defendant negligently drove a motor vehicle against plaintiff who was then crossing said highway.

2. As a result plaintiff was thrown down and had his leg broken and was otherwise injured, was prevented from transacting his business, suffered great pain of body and mind, and incurred expenses for medical attention and hospitalization in the sum of one thousand dollars.

Wherefore plaintiff demands judgment against defendant in the sum of_____ dollars and costs.

Note

Since contributory negligence is an affirmative defense, the complaint need contain no allegation of due care of plaintiff.

[Effective: July 1, 1970.]

FORM 9. COMPLAINT FOR NEGLIGENCE WHERE PLAINTIFF
IS UNABLE TO DETERMINE DEFINITELY WHETHER
THE PERSON RESPONSIBLE IS C.D. OR E.F.
OR WHETHER BOTH ARE RESPONSIBLE AND
WHERE HIS EVIDENCE MAY JUSTIFY A FINDING
OF WILFULNESS OR OF RECKLESSNESS OR OF NEGLIGENCE

A.B., Plaintiff   )
(address)   )   No. _____

      v.   )

C.D. and E.F., Defendants   )   COMPLAINT
(addresses)   )

     1. On ____, 19_, in a public highway called ____Street in ____, Ohio, defendant C.D. or defendant E.F., or both defendants C.D. and E.F. wilfully or recklessly or negligently drove or caused to be driven a motor vehicle against plaintiff who was then crossing said highway.

     2. As a result plaintiff was thrown down and had his leg broken and was otherwise injured, was prevented from transacting his business, suffered great pain of body and mind, and incurred expenses for medical attention and hospitalization in the sum of one thousand dollars.

     Wherefore plaintiff demands judgment against C.D. or against E.F. or against both in the sum of _____ dollars and costs.

[Effective: July 1, 1970.]

FORM 10. COMPLAINT FOR CONVERSION

On or about ____, 19_, defendant converted to his own use ten bonds of the ____ Company (here insert brief identification as by number and issue) of the value of ____dollars, the property of plaintiff.

Wherefore plaintiff demands judgment against defendant in the sum of ___ dollars, interest, and costs.

[Effective: July 1, 1970.]

FORM 11. COMPLAINT FOR SPECIFIC PERFORMANCE
OF CONTRACT TO CONVEY LAND

1. On our about ____, 19_, plaintiff and defendant entered into an agreement in writing a copy of which is hereto annexed as Exhibit A.

2. In accord with the provisions of said agreement plaintiff tendered to defendant the purchase price and requested a conveyance of the land, but defendant refused to accept the tender and refused to make the conveyance.

3. Plaintiff now offers to pay the purchase price.

Wherefore plaintiff demands (1) that defendant be required specifically to perform said agreement, (2) damages in the sum of one thousand dollars, and (3) that if specific performance is not granted plaintiff have judgment against defendant in the sum of ____ dollars.

Note

The demand for relief seeks specific performance as well as ancillary damages resulting from the delay. In addition the demand for relief seeks damages in a certain sum if the court finds it impossible to grant specific performance as where, in the interim, defendant has conveyed the property to a purchaser for value without notice.

[Effective: July 1, 1970.]

FORM 12. COMPLAINT ON CLAIM FOR DEBT
AND TO SET ASIDE FRAUDULENT CONVEYANCE UNDER RULE 18(B)

A.B., Plaintiff	)
(address)	) No. _____
	)
v.	)
	)
C.D. and E.F., Defendants	) COMPLAINT
(addresses)	)

1. Defendant C.D. on or about ____ executed and delivered to plaintiff a promissory note, a copy of which is hereto annexed as Exhibit A.

2. Defendant C.D. owes to plaintiff the amount of said note and interest.

3. Defendant C.D. on or about ____ conveyed all his property, real and personal [or specify and describe] to defendant E.F. for the purpose of defrauding plaintiff and hindering and delaying the collection of the indebtedness evidenced by the note above referred to.

Wherefore plaintiff demands:

(1) That plaintiff have judgment against defendant C.D. for ____ dollars and interest; (2) that the aforesaid conveyance to defendant E.F. be declared void and the judgment herein be declared a lien on said property; (3) that plaintiff have judgment against the defendants for costs.

[Effective: July 1, 1970.]

FORM 13. COMPLAINT FOR INTERPLEADER AND DECLARATORY RELIEF

1. On or about ____, 19_, plaintiff issued to G.H. a policy of life insurance, a copy of which is attached as Exhibit A, whereby plaintiff promised to pay to K.L. as beneficiary the sum of ____ dollars upon the death of G.H. The policy required the payment by G.H. of a stipulated premium on ____, 19_, and annually thereafter as a condition precedent to its continuance in force.

2. No part of the premium due ____, 19_, was ever paid and the policy ceased to have any force or effect on ____, 19_.

3. Thereafter, on _____, 19_, G.H. and K.L. died as the result of a collision between a locomotive and the automobile in which G.H. and K.L. were riding.

4. Defendant C.D. is the duly appointed and acting executor of the will of G.H.; defendant E.F. is the duly appointed and acting executor of the will of K.L.; defendant X.Y. claims to have been duly designated as beneficiary of said policy in place of K.L.

5. Each of defendants, C.D., E.F., and X.Y. is claiming that the abovementioned policy was in full force and effect at the time of the death of G.H.; each of them is claiming to be the only person entitled to receive payment of the amount of the policy and has made demand for payment thereof.

6. By reason of these conflicting claims of the defendants, plaintiff is in great doubt as to which defendant is entitled to be paid the amount of the policy, if it was in force at the death of G.H.

Wherefore plaintiff demands that the court adjudge:

(1) That none of the defendants is entitled to recover from plaintiff the amount of said policy or any part thereof.

(2) That each of the defendants be restrained from instituting any action against plaintiff for the recovery of the amount of said policy or any part thereof.

(3) That, if the court shall determine that said policy was in force at the death of G.H., the defendants be required to interplead and settle between themselves their rights to the money due under said policy, and that plaintiff be discharged from all liability in the premises except to the person whom the court shall adjudge entitled to the amount of said policy.

(4) That plaintiff recover its costs.

[Effective: July 1, 1970.]

FORM 14. MOTION TO DISMISS, PRESENTING DEFENSES OF FAILURE TO STATE A CLAIM, OF LACK OF SERVICE OF PROCESS, AND OF LACK OF JURISDICTION UNDER RULE 12(B)

COURT OF COMMON PLEAS
FRANKLIN COUNTY, OHIO

A.B., Plaintiff   )
(address)   )   No. _____

        v.   )

C.D. Corporation, Defendant   )   MOTION TO DISMISS
(address)   )

The defendant moves the court as follows:

1. To dismiss the action because the complaint fails to state a claim against defendant upon which relief can be granted.

2. To dismiss the action or in lieu thereof to quash the return of service of summons on the grounds (a) that the defendant is a corporation organized under the laws of Delaware and was not and is not subject to service of process within this state, and (b) that the defendant has not been properly served with process in this action, all of which more clearly appears in the affidavits of M.N. and X.Y. hereto attached as Exhibit A and Exhibit B, respectively.

3. To dismiss the action on the ground that the court lacks jurisdiction because [here state the reasons why the court lacks jurisdiction].

                         _____
                         (Attorney for Defendant)

                         _____
                         (Address)

                         _____

SERVICE OF COPY

A copy hereof was served upon X.Y., attorney for plaintiff, by mailing it to him on June 1, 19 [or set forth other method of service upon X.Y.].

_____
(Attorney for Defendant)

Note

1. The form gives various examples of defenses which may be raised by motion under Rule 12(B).

2. Whether the motion should be accompanied by a notice of hearing on the motion or whether the motion should be accompanied by a memorandum brief depends upon the rules of a particular local court. See Rule 7(B) and the rules of the local court regarding motion practice.

3. All papers after the original pleading required to be served upon an opposite party shall have endorsed thereon, when filed with the court, a statement setting forth the date and method of service. See Rule 5.

[Effective: July 1, 1970; amended effective July 1, 1971.]

FORM 15. ANSWER PRESENTING DEFENSES UNDER RULE 12(B)

A.B., Plaintiff (address)	)) No. _____
v.	)
C.D. and E.F., Defendants (addresses)	) ANSWER, COUNTERCLAIM,) AND CROSS-CLAIM

FIRST DEFENSE

The complaint fails to state a claim against defendant C.D. upon which relief can be granted.

SECOND DEFENSE

If defendant C.D. is indebted to plaintiff for the goods mentioned in the complaint, he is indebted to him jointly with G.H.   G.H. is alive, is a resident of this state, is subject to the jurisdiction of this court and can be made a party but has not been made one.

THIRD DEFENSE

Defendant C.D. admits the allegation contained in paragraphs 1 and 4 of the complaint; alleges that he is without knowledge or information sufficient to form a belief as to the truth of the allegations contained in paragraph 2 of the complaint; and denies each and every other allegation contained in the complaint.

FOURTH DEFENSE

The right of action set forth in the complaint did not accrue within ____ years next before the commencement of this action.

COUNTERCLAIM

[Here set forth any claim as a counterclaim in the manner in which a claim is pleaded in a complaint.]

CROSS-CLAIM AGAINST DEFENDANT M.N.

[Here set forth the claim constituting a cross-claim against defendant M.N. in the manner in which a claim is pleaded in a complaint.]

_____

(Attorney for Defendant, C.D.)

_____

(Address)

_____

(Service of Copy as in Form 14)

Note

1. The above form contains examples of certain defenses provided for in Rule 12(B). The first defense challenges the legal sufficiency of the complaint. It is a substitute for a motion to dismiss; that is, under former practice the issue raised by the first defense would have been raised by demurrer, and under present practice the same issue might have been raised by motion at the option of the defendant. See Rule 12(B).

2. The second defense embodies the old plea in abatement. The decision thereon, however, may, for example, well provide under Rule 19(A) or Rule 21 for the citing in of the party rather than an abatement of the action.

3. The third defense is an answer on the merits.

4. The fourth defense is one of the affirmative defenses provided for in Rule 8(C).

5. The answer also includes a counterclaim and a cross-claim. See Rule 12(B).

[Effective: July 1, 1970.]

FORM 16. SUMMONS AGAINST THIRD-PARTY DEFENDANT

COURT OF COMMON PLEAS
FRANKLIN COUNTY, OHIO

A.B., Plaintiff)
(address))
   v.)
C.D., Defendant and Third-Party) No. _____
Plaintiff)
(address)) SUMMONS
   v.)
E.F., Third-Party Defendant)
(address))

To the above-named Third-Party Defendant:

  You are hereby summoned and required to serve upon _____, plaintiff's attorney whose address is ____ and upon ____, who is attorney for C.D., defendant and third-party plaintiff, and whose address is ____, an answer to the third-party complaint which is herewith served upon you within twenty-eight days after the service of this summons upon you exclusive of the day of service. If you fail to do so, judgment by default will be taken against you for the relief demanded in the third-party complaint. There is also served upon you herewith a copy of the complaint of the plaintiff which you may but are not required to answer. Your answer to the third-party complaint and your answer to the plaintiff's complaint must also be filed with the court.

             _____
             (Clerk of Court)
             By _____ Deputy Clerk
Dated _____

Note

  It may be necessary, depending upon when the third-party complaint is served, to seek leave of court by motion to bring in a third-party defendant. See Rule 14(A).

[Effective: July 1, 1970.]

FORM 16A. COMPLAINT AGAINST THIRD-PARTY DEFENDANT

COURT OF COMMON PLEAS
FRANKLIN COUNTY, OHIO

A.B., Plaintiff
(address)
     v.
C.D., Defendant and Third-Party
Plaintiff
(address)
     v.
E.F., Third-Party Defendant
(address)
	)
	)
	)
	) No. _____
	)
	) THIRD-PARTY COMPLAINT
	)
	)
	)

1. Plaintiff A.B. has filed against defendant C.D. a complaint, a copy of which is hereto attached as Exhibit A.

2. [Here state the grounds upon which C.D. is entitled to recover from E.F., all or part of what A.B. may recover from C.D. The statement should be framed as in an original complaint.]

Wherefore C.D. demands judgment against third-party defendant E.F. for all sums [make appropriate change where C.D. is entitled to only partial recovery over against E.F.] that may be adjudged against defendant C.D. in favor of plaintiff A.B.

_____
(Attorney for C.D.,
Third-Party Plaintiff)

_____
(Address)

_____

Note

It is necessary to comply with Rule 5 regarding service of third-party papers on plaintiff.

[Effective: July 1, 1970.]

FORM 17. MOTION TO INTERVENE AS A DEFENDANT UNDER RULE 24

COURT OF COMMON PLEAS
FRANKLIN COUNTY, OHIO

A.B., Plaintiff   )
(address)   ) No. ____
       v.   )
C.D., Defendant   ) MOTION TO INTERVENE
(address)   ) AS A DEFENDANT
E.F., Applicant for Intervention   )
(address)   )

      E.F. moves for leave to intervene as a defendant in this action in order to assert the defenses set forth in his proposed answer, of which a copy is hereto attached, on the ground that [here insert the appropriate grounds of intervention].

_____

(Attorney for E.F.,
Applicant for Intervention)

_____

(Address)

(Adopted eff. 7-1-70)

Note (Amended Effective July 1, 1999)

      It is necessary that a motion to intervene be accompanied by a pleading as required in Civ.R. 24(C). It is also necessary to comply with Civ.R. 5 regarding service of the motion on the parties to the action.

FORM 18. JUDGMENT ON JURY VERDICT

COURT OF COMMON PLEAS
FRANKLIN COUNTY OHIO

A.B., Plaintiff)
(address)) No. _____
   v.)
C.D., Defendant) JUDGMENT
(address))

This action came on for trial before the Court and a jury, and the issues having been duly tried and the jury having duly rendered its verdict,

It is ordered and adjudged [that the plaintiff A.B. recover of the defendant C.D. the sum of ___, with interest thereon at the rate of ___ percent as provided by law, and his costs of action.]

[that the plaintiff take nothing, that the action be dismissed on the merits, and that the defendant C.D. recover of the plaintiff A.B. his costs of action.]

Dated at ____, Ohio, this ____ day of ___ , 19_

_____
Judge, Court of Common Pleas

Journalized this ____ day of ___, 19_

_____
Clerk of Court

By _____ Deputy Clerk

Note

This form is illustrative of the judgment to be entered upon the general verdict of a jury. It deals with the cases where there is a general jury verdict awarding the plaintiff money damages or finding for the defendant, but is adaptable to other situations of jury verdict.

[Effective: July 1, 1970.]

FORM 19. JUDGMENT ON DECISION BY THE COURT

COURT OF COMMON PLEAS
FRANKLIN COUNTY, OHIO

A.B., Plaintiff) (address)) v.) C.D., Defendant) (address))	No. _____ JUDGMENT

      This action came on for [trial] [hearing] before the Court, and the issues having been duly [tried] [heard] and a decision having been duly rendered,

      It is ordered and adjudged [that the plaintiff A.B. recover of the defendant C.D. the sum of ___, with interest thereon at the rate of ___ percent as provided by law, and his costs of action.]

      [that the plaintiff take nothing, that the action be dismissed on the merits, and that the defendant C.D. recover of the plaintiff A.B. his costs of action.]

Dated at ___, Ohio, this ___ day of ___, 19_

_____
Judge, Court of Common Pleas

Journalized this ___ day of ___, 19_

_____
Clerk of Court

By _____ Deputy Clerk

Note

    This form is illustrative of the judgment to be entered upon a decision of the court. It deals with the cases of decisions by the court awarding a party only money damages or costs, but is adaptable to other decisions by the court.

[Effective: July 1, 1970.]

FORMS 1 THROUGH 28: DOMESTIC RELATIONS FORMS

COURT OF COMMON PLEAS
_____ COUNTY, OHIO

_____
Plaintiff/Petitioner 1

v./and

_____
Defendant/Petitioner 2

Case No. _____

Judge _____

Magistrate _____

Instructions: Check local court rules to determine when this form must be filed.
This affidavit is used to make complete disclosure of income, expenses and money owed. It is used to determine child and spousal support amounts. Do not leave any category blank. Write "none" where appropriate. If you do not know exact figures for any item, give your best estimate and put "EST." **If you need more space, add additional pages.**

AFFIDAVIT OF INCOME AND EXPENSES

Affidavit of _____
(Print Your Name)

Date of marriage _____ Date of separation _____

SECTION I - INCOME

	_____ Your Name	_____ Spouse's Name
Employed	☐ Yes ☐ No	☐ Yes ☐ No
Employer	_____	_____
Payroll address	_____	_____
Payroll city, state, zip	_____	_____
Scheduled paychecks per year	☐ 12 ☐ 24 ☐ 26 ☐ 52	☐ 12 ☐ 24 ☐ 26 ☐ 52

A. <u>YEARLY INCOME, OVERTIME, COMMISSIONS AND BONUSES FOR PAST THREE YEARS</u>

	_____ Your Name		_____ Spouse's Name
Base yearly income	$ _____	3 years ago	20 ____ $ _____
	$ _____	2 years ago	20 ____ $ _____
	$ _____	Last year	20 ____ $ _____
Yearly overtime, commissions and/or bonuses	$ _____	3 years ago	20 ____ $ _____
	$ _____	2 years ago	20 ____ $ _____
	$ _____	Last year	20 ____ $ _____

Supreme Court of Ohio
Uniform Domestic Relations Form – Affidavit 1
Affidavit of Income and Expenses
Approved under Ohio Civil Rule 84
Amended: March 15, 2016

Page 1 of 7

B. COMPUTATION OF CURRENT INCOME

	_____ **Your Name**	_____ **Spouse's Name**
Base yearly income	$ _____	$ _____
Average yearly overtime, commissions and/or bonuses over last 3 years (from part A)	$ _____	$ _____
Unemployment compensation	$ _____	$ _____
Disability benefits		
☐ Workers' Compensation		
☐ Social Security		
☐ Other: _____	$ _____	$ _____
Retirement benefits		
☐ Social Security		
☐ Other: _____	$ _____	$ _____
Spousal support received	$ _____	$ _____
Interest and dividend income (source) _____ _____	$ _____	$ _____
Other income (type and source) _____ _____	$ _____	$ _____
TOTAL YEARLY INCOME	$ _____	$ _____
Supplemental Security Income (SSI) or public assistance	$ _____	$ _____
Court-ordered child support that you receive for minor and/or dependent child(ren) not of the marriage or relationship	$ _____	$ _____

Supreme Court of Ohio
Uniform Domestic Relations Form – Affidavit 1
Affidavit of Income and Expenses
Approved under Ohio Civil Rule 84
Amended: March 15, 2016

Page 2 of 7

SECTION II – CHILDREN AND HOUSEHOLD RESIDENTS

Minor and/or dependent child(ren) who are from this marriage or relationship:

Name	Date of birth	Living with
_____	_____	_____
_____	_____	_____
_____	_____	_____
_____	_____	_____

In addition to the above children there is/are in your household:

_____ adult(s)

_____ other minor and/or dependent child(ren).

SECTION III – EXPENSES

List monthly expenses below for your present household.

A.   MONTHLY HOUSING EXPENSES

Rent or first mortgage (including taxes and insurance)	$ _____
Real estate taxes (if not included above)	$ _____
Real estate/homeowner's insurance (if not included above)	$ _____
Second mortgage/equity line of credit	$ _____
Utilities	
o Electric	$ _____
o Gas, fuel oil, propane	$ _____
o Water and sewer	$ _____
o Telephone	$ _____
o Trash collection	$ _____
o Cable/satellite television	$ _____
Cleaning, maintenance, repair	$ _____
Lawn service, snow removal	$ _____
Other: _____	$ _____
_____	$ _____
TOTAL MONTHLY :	$ _____

Supreme Court of Ohio
Uniform Domestic Relations Form – Affidavit 1
Affidavit of Income and Expenses
Approved under Ohio Civil Rule 84
Amended: March 15, 2016

Page 3 of 7

B. OTHER MONTHLY LIVING EXPENSES

Food

     o   Groceries (including food, paper, cleaning products, toiletries, other) $ _____

     o   Restaurant $ _____

Transportation

     o   Vehicle loans, leases $ _____

     o   Vehicle maintenance (oil, repair, license) $ _____

     o   Gasoline $ _____

     o   Parking, public transportation $ _____

Clothing

     o   Clothes (other than children's) $ _____

     o   Dry cleaning, laundry $ _____

Personal grooming

     o   Hair, nail care $ _____

     o   Other _____ $ _____

Cell phone $ _____

Internet (if not included elsewhere) $ _____

Other _____ $ _____

                                         TOTAL MONTHLY $ _____

C. MONTHLY CHILD-RELATED EXPENSES
(for children of the marriage or relationship)

Work/education-related child care $ _____

Other child care $ _____

Unusual parenting time travel $ _____

Special and unusual needs of child(ren) (not included elsewhere) $ _____

Clothing $ _____

School supplies $ _____

Child(ren)'s allowances $ _____

Extracurricular activities, lessons $ _____

School lunches $ _____

Other _____ $ _____

                                         TOTAL MONTHLY $ _____

Supreme Court of Ohio
Uniform Domestic Relations Form – Affidavit 1
Affidavit of Income and Expenses
Approved under Ohio Civil Rule 84
Amended: March 15, 2016

Page 4 of 7

D.   INSURANCE PREMIUMS

Life $ _____

Auto $ _____

Health $ _____

Disability $ _____

Renters/personal property (if not included in part A above) $ _____

Other _____ $ _____

                                   TOTAL MONTHLY $ _____

E.   MONTHLY EDUCATION EXPENSES

Tuition

  o   Self $ _____

  o   Child(ren) $ _____

Books, fees, other $ _____

College loan repayment $ _____

Other _____ $ _____

_____ $ _____

                                   TOTAL MONTHLY: $ _____

F.   MONTHLY HEALTH CARE EXPENSES
     (not covered by insurance)

Physicians $ _____

Dentists $ _____

Optometrists/opticians $ _____

Prescriptions $ _____

Other _____ $ _____

_____ $ _____

                                   TOTAL MONTHLY: $ _____

G.   MISCELLANEOUS MONTHLY EXPENSES

Extraordinary obligations for other minor/handicapped child(ren) (not stepchildren) $ _____

Child support for children who were not born of this marriage or relationship and were
not adopted of this marriage $ _____

Spousal support paid to former spouse(s) $ _____

Subscriptions, books $ _____

Entertainment $ _____

Supreme Court of Ohio
Uniform Domestic Relations Form – Affidavit 1
Affidavit of Income and Expenses
Approved under Ohio Civil Rule 84
Amended: March 15, 2016

Page 5 of 7

Charitable contributions	$	_____
Memberships (associations, clubs)	$	_____
Travel, vacations	$	_____
Pets	$	_____
Gifts	$	_____
Bankruptcy payments	$	_____
Attorney fees	$	_____
Required deductions from wages (excluding taxes, Social Security and Medicare) (type) _____	$	_____
Additional taxes paid (not deducted from wages) (type) _____	$	_____
Other _____	$	_____
_____	$	_____
TOTAL MONTHLY:	$	_____

H.   MONTHLY INSTALLMENT PAYMENTS
      (Do not repeat expenses already listed.)
      Examples: car, credit card, rent-to-own, cash advance payments

To whom paid	Purpose	Balance due	Monthly payment
_____	_____	$ _____	$ _____
_____	_____	$ _____	$ _____
_____	_____	$ _____	$ _____
_____	_____	$ _____	$ _____
_____	_____	$ _____	$ _____
_____	_____	$ _____	$ _____
_____	_____	$ _____	$ _____
_____	_____	$ _____	$ _____
_____	_____	$ _____	$ _____
_____	_____	$ _____	$ _____
_____	_____	$ _____	$ _____
_____	_____	$ _____	$ _____
_____	_____	$ _____	$ _____
_____	_____	$ _____	$ _____
	TOTAL MONTHLY:	$ _____	

GRAND TOTAL MONTHLY EXPENSES (Sum of A through H): $ _____

Supreme Court of Ohio
Uniform Domestic Relations Form – Affidavit 1
Affidavit of Income and Expenses
Approved under Ohio Civil Rule 84
Amended: March 15, 2016

Page 6 of 7

OATH

(Do not sign until notary is present.)

I, (print name) _____ , swear or affirm that I have read this document and, to the best of my knowledge and belief, the facts and information stated in this document are true, accurate and complete. I understand that if I do not tell the truth, I may be subject to penalties for perjury.

_____
Your Signature

Sworn before me and signed in my presence this _____ day of _____ , _____ .

_____
Notary Public
My Commission Expires:

_____

Supreme Court of Ohio
Uniform Domestic Relations Form – Affidavit 1
Affidavit of Income and Expenses
Approved under Ohio Civil Rule 84
Amended: March 15, 2016

Page 7 of 7

COURT OF COMMON PLEAS

_____ COUNTY, OHIO

_____	Case No. _____
Plaintiff/Petitioner 1	Judge _____
v./and	Magistrate _____
_____	
Respondent/Petitioner 2	

Instructions: Check local court rules to determine when this form must be filed.
List ALL OF YOUR PROPERTY AND DEBTS, the property and debts of your spouse, and any joint property or debts. Do not leave any category blank. For each item, if none, put "NONE." If you do not know exact figures for any item, give your best estimate, and put "EST." **If more space is needed, add additional pages.**

AFFIDAVIT OF PROPERTY

Affidavit of _____

(Print Your Name)

I. REAL ESTATE INTERESTS

	Address	Present Fair Market Value	Titled To	Mortgage Balance	Equity (as of date)
1.	_____	$ _____	☐ _____ Your Name ☐ _____ Spouse's Name ☐ Both	$ _____	$ _____
	_____		☐ _____		_____
2.	_____	$ _____	Your Name ☐ _____ Spouse's Name ☐ Both	$ _____	$ _____
	_____				_____

TOTAL SECTION I: REAL ESTATE INTERESTS $ _____

Supreme Court of Ohio
Uniform Domestic Relations Form – Affidavit 2
Affidavit of Property
Approved under Ohio Civil Rule 84
Amended: March 15, 2016

II. OTHER ASSETS

Category	Description (List who has possession)	Titled To	Value/Date of Value
A. Vehicles and Other Certificate of Title Property	(Include model and year of automobiles, trucks, motorcycles, boats, motors, motor homes, etc.)		
1. _____	_____	☐ _____ Your Name ☐ _____ Spouse's Name ☐ Both	$ _____
2. _____	_____	☐ _____ Your Name ☐ _____ Spouse's Name ☐ Both	$ _____
3. _____	_____	☐ _____ Your Name ☐ _____ Spouse's Name ☐ Both	$ _____
4. _____	_____	☐ _____ Your Name ☐ _____ Spouse's Name ☐ Both	$ _____
5. _____	_____	☐ _____ Your Name ☐ _____ Spouse's Name ☐ Both	$ _____
6. _____	_____	☐ _____ Your Name ☐ _____ Spouse's Name ☐ Both	$ _____
B. Financial Accounts	(Include checking, savings, CDs, POD accounts, money market accounts, etc.)		
1. _____	_____	☐ _____ Your Name ☐ _____ Spouse's Name ☐ Both	$ _____
2. _____	_____	☐ _____ Your Name ☐ _____ Spouse's Name ☐ Both	$ _____
3. _____	_____	☐ _____ Your Name ☐ _____ Spouse's Name ☐ Both	$ _____
4. _____	_____	☐ _____ Your Name ☐ _____ Spouse's Name ☐ Both	$ _____

Supreme Court of Ohio
Uniform Domestic Relations Form – Affidavit 2
Affidavit of Property
Approved under Ohio Civil Rule 84
Amended: March 15, 2016

Page 2 of 7

Category	Description (List who has possession)	Titled To	Value/Date of Value
C. Pensions & Retirement plans	(Include profit-sharing, IRAs, 401k plans, etc.; Describe each type of plan)		
		☐ _____ Your Name	$ _____
1. _____	_____	☐ _____ Spouse's Name ☐ Both	_____
		☐ _____ Your Name	$ _____
2. _____	_____	☐ _____ Spouse's Name ☐ Both	_____
		☐ _____ Your Name	$ _____
3. _____	_____	☐ _____ Spouse's Name ☐ Both	_____
		☐ _____ Your Name	$ _____
4. _____	_____	☐ _____ Spouse's Name ☐ Both	_____
D. Publicly Held Stocks, Bonds, Securities, & Mutual Funds			
		☐ _____ Your Name	$ _____
1. _____	_____	☐ _____ Spouse's Name ☐ Both	_____
		☐ _____ Your Name	$ _____
2. _____	_____	☐ _____ Spouse's Name ☐ Both	_____
		☐ _____ Your Name	$ _____
3. _____	_____	☐ _____ Spouse's Name ☐ Both	_____
		☐ _____ Your Name	$ _____
4. _____	_____	☐ _____ Spouse's Name ☐ Both	_____

Category	Description (List who has possession)	Titled To	Value/Date of Value
E. Closely Held Stocks & Other Business Interests and Name of Company	(Type of ownership and number)		
		☐ _____ Your Name	$ _____
1. _____	_____	☐ _____ Spouse's Name ☐ Both	_____
		☐ _____ Your Name	$ _____
2. _____	_____	☐ _____ Spouse's Name ☐ Both	_____

Supreme Court of Ohio
Uniform Domestic Relations Form – Affidavit 2
Affidavit of Property
Approved under Ohio Civil Rule 84
Amended: March 15, 2016

Page 3 of 7

F. Life Insurance Type
(Term/Whole Life)   (Any cash value or loans)   (Insured party
                                                                                             & value upon death)

1. _____   _____   ☐ _____ $ _____
                                                             Your Name
                                                             ☐
                                                             Spouse's Name
   _____   _____   ☐ Both

2. _____   _____   ☐ _____ $ _____
                                                             Your Name
                                                             ☐
                                                             Spouse's Name
                                                             ☐ Both

3. _____   _____   ☐ _____ $ _____
                                                             Your Name
                                                             ☐
                                                             Spouse's Name
   _____   _____   ☐ Both

4. _____   _____   ☐ _____ $ _____
                                                             Your Name
                                                             ☐
                                                             Spouse's Name
   _____   _____   ☐ Both

Category	Description	Who Has Possession	Value/Date of Value

G. Furniture &   (Estimate value of those in your
Appliances   possession and value of those in your
                             spouse's possession)

1. _____   _____   ☐ _____ $ _____
                                                             Your Name
                                                             ☐
                                                             Spouse's Name
                                                             ☐ Both

2. _____   _____   ☐ _____ $ _____
                                                             Your Name
                                                             ☐
                                                             Spouse's Name
                                                             ☐ Both

3. _____   _____   ☐ _____ $ _____
                                                             Your Name
                                                             ☐
                                                             Spouse's Name
                                                             ☐ Both

4. _____   _____   ☐ _____ $ _____
                                                             Your Name
                                                             ☐
                                                             Spouse's Name
                                                             ☐ Both

H. Safe Deposit Box   (Give location and describe contents)   Titled To

1. _____   _____   ☐ _____ $ _____
                                                             Your Name
                                                             ☐
                                                             Spouse's Name
                                                             ☐ Both

2. _____   _____   ☐ _____ $ _____
                                                             Your Name
                                                             ☐
                                                             Spouse's Name
                                                             ☐ Both

Supreme Court of Ohio
Uniform Domestic Relations Form – Affidavit 2
Affidavit of Property
Approved under Ohio Civil Rule 84
Amended: March 15, 2016

Page 4 of 7

I. Transfer of Assets

Explanation: List the name and address of any person (other than creditors listed on your Affidavit) who has received money or property from you exceeding $300 in value in the past 12 months and the reason for each transfer.

1. _____ _____

☐ _____
Your Name $ _____
☐ _____
Spouse's Name
☐ Both

2. _____ _____

☐ _____
Your Name $ _____
☐ _____
Spouse's Name
☐ Both

3. _____ _____

☐ _____
Your Name $ _____
☐ _____
Spouse's Name
☐ Both

4. _____ _____

☐ _____
Your Name $ _____
☐ _____
Spouse's Name
☐ Both

Category	Description (Also list who has possession)	Titled To	Value/Date of Value

J. All Other Assets Not Listed Above

Explanation: List any item you have not listed above that is considered an asset.

1. _____ _____

☐ _____
Your Name $ _____
☐ _____
Spouse's Name
☐ Both

2. _____ _____

☐ _____
Your Name $ _____
☐ _____
Spouse's Name
☐ Both

TOTAL SECTION II: OTHER ASSETS $ _____

III. SEPARATE PROPERTY CLAIMS: Pre-marital assets, gifts to one spouse only, inheritances

If you are making any claims in any of the categories below, explain the nature and amount of your claim. **This includes, but is not limited to, inheritances, property owned before marriage, and any pre-marital agreements.**

Category (Pre-marital Gift, Inheritance, etc., acquired after separation)	Description	Why do you claim this as a separate property?	Present Fair Market Value
1. _____	_____	_____	$ _____
2. _____	_____	_____	$ _____
3. _____	_____	_____	$ _____
4. _____	_____	_____	$ _____
5. _____	_____	_____	$ _____

TOTAL SECTION III: SEPARATE PROPERTY CLAIMS $ _____

Supreme Court of Ohio
Uniform Domestic Relations Form – Affidavit 2
Affidavit of Property
Approved under Ohio Civil Rule 84
Amended: March 15, 2016

Page 5 of 7

IV. DEBT

List ALL OF YOUR DEBTS, the debts of your spouse, and any joint debts. Do not leave any category blank. For each item, if none, put "NONE." If you don't know exact figures for any item, give your best estimate, and put "EST." **If more space is needed to explain, please attach an additional page with the explanation and identify which question you are answering.**

Type	Name of Creditor/Purpose of Debt	Account Name	Name(s) on Account	Total Debt Due	Monthly Payment

A. Secured Debt (Mortgages, Car, etc.)

1. _____ _____ _____ ☐ Your Name ☐ Spouse's Name ☐ Joint $ _____ $ _____

2. _____ _____ _____ ☐ Your Name ☐ Spouse's Name ☐ Joint $ _____ $ _____

3. _____ _____ _____ ☐ Your Name ☐ Spouse's Name ☐ Joint $ _____ $ _____

4. _____ _____ _____ ☐ Your Name ☐ Spouse's Name ☐ Joint $ _____ $ _____

5. _____ _____ _____ ☐ Your Name ☐ Spouse's Name ☐ Joint $ _____ $ _____

B. Unsecured Debt, including credit cards

1. _____ _____ _____ ☐ Your Name ☐ Spouse's Name ☐ Joint $ _____ $ _____

2. _____ _____ _____ ☐ Your Name ☐ Spouse's Name ☐ Joint $ _____ $ _____

3. _____ _____ _____ ☐ Your Name ☐ Spouse's Name ☐ Joint $ _____ $ _____

Supreme Court of Ohio
Uniform Domestic Relations Form – Affidavit 2
Affidavit of Property
Approved under Ohio Civil Rule 84
Amended: March 15, 2016

Page 6 of 7

			☐ _____ Your Name			
			☐ _____ Spouse's Name			
4. _____	_____	_____	☐ Joint	$ _____	$ _____	
			☐ _____ Your Name			
			☐ _____ Spouse's Name			
5. _____	_____	_____	☐ Joint	$ _____	$ _____	

TOTAL SECTION IV: DEBT $ _____

V. BANKRUPTCY

Filed by:

☐ _____
Your Name

☐ _____
Spouse's Name

☐ Both

	Date of Filing: Case Number	Date of Discharge or Relief from Stay	Type of Case (Ch. 7, 11, 12, 13)	Current Monthly Payments
1. ☐ _____ Your Name ☐ _____ Spouse's Name ☐ Both	_____	_____	_____	$ _____
2. ☐ _____ Your Name ☐ _____ Spouse's Name ☐ Both	_____	_____	_____	$ _____

TOTAL SECTION V: BANKRUPTCY $ _____

OATH

(Do Not Sign Until Notary is Present)

I, (print name) _____ swear or affirm that I have read this document and, to the best of my knowledge and belief, the facts and information stated in this document are true, accurate and complete. I understand that if I do not tell the truth, I may be subject to penalties for perjury.

_____
Your Signature

Sworn before me and signed in my presence this ____ day of _____ , _____ .

_____
Notary Public

My Commission Expires:

_____

Supreme Court of Ohio
Uniform Domestic Relations Form – Affidavit 2
Affidavit of Property
Approved under Ohio Civil Rule 84
Amended: March 15, 2016

Page 7 of 7

COURT OF COMMON PLEAS
_____ COUNTY, OHIO

_____
Plaintiff/Petitioner

Case No. _____

Judge _____

v./and

Magistrate _____

_____
Defendant/Petitioner

> **Instructions:** Check local court rules to determine when this form must be filed.
> This affidavit is used to make complete disclosure of income, expenses and money owed. It is used to determine child and spousal support amounts. Do not leave any category blank. Write "none" where appropriate. If you do not know exact figures for any item, give your best estimate, and put "EST." **If you need more space, add additional pages.**

AFFIDAVIT OF INCOME AND EXPENSES

Affidavit of _____
(Print Your Name)

Date of marriage _____ Date of separation _____

SECTION I - INCOME

	Husband	**Wife**
Employed	☐ Yes ☐ No	☐ Yes ☐ No
Employer	_____	_____
Payroll address	_____	_____
Payroll city, state, zip	_____	_____
Scheduled paychecks per year	☐ 12 ☐ 24 ☐ 26 ☐ 52	☐ 12 ☐ 24 ☐ 26 ☐ 52

A. YEARLY INCOME, OVERTIME, COMMISSIONS AND BONUSES FOR PAST THREE YEARS

	Husband				**Wife**
Base yearly income	$ _____	3 years ago	20 ___	$ _____	
	$ _____	2 years ago	20 ___	$ _____	
	$ _____	Last year	20 ___	$ _____	
Yearly overtime, commissions and/or bonuses	$ _____	3 years ago	20 ___	$ _____	
	$ _____	2 years ago	20 ___	$ _____	
	$ _____	Last year	20 ___	$ _____	

Supreme Court of Ohio
Uniform Domestic Relations Form – Affidavit 1
Affidavit of Income and Expenses
Approved under Ohio Civil Rule 84
Effective Date: July 1, 2010

Page 1 of 7

B. COMPUTATION OF CURRENT INCOME

	Husband	**Wife**
Base yearly income	$ _____	$ _____
Average yearly overtime, commissions and/or bonuses over last 3 years (from part A)	$ _____	$ _____
Unemployment compensation	$ _____	$ _____
Disability benefits ☐ Workers' Compensation ☐ Social Security ☐ Other: _____	$ _____	$ _____
Retirement benefits ☐ Social Security ☐ Other: _____	$ _____	$ _____
Spousal support received	$ _____	$ _____
Interest and dividend income (source) _____ _____	$ _____	$ _____
Other income (type and source) _____ _____	$ _____	$ _____
TOTAL YEARLY INCOME	$ _____	$ _____
Supplemental Security Income (SSI) or public assistance	$ _____	$ _____
Court-ordered child support that you receive for minor and/or dependent child(ren) not of the marriage or relationship	$ _____	$ _____

Supreme Court of Ohio
Uniform Domestic Relations Form – Affidavit 1
Affidavit of Income and Expenses
Approved under Ohio Civil Rule 84
Effective Date: July 1, 2010

Page 2 of 7

SECTION II – CHILDREN AND HOUSEHOLD RESIDENTS

Minor and/or dependent child(ren) who are adopted or born of this marriage or relationship:

Name	Date of birth	Living with
_____	_____	_____
_____	_____	_____
_____	_____	_____
_____	_____	_____

In addition to the above children there is/are in your household:

_____ adult(s)

_____ other minor and/or dependent child(ren).

SECTION III – EXPENSES

List monthly expenses below for your present household.

A.   MONTHLY HOUSING EXPENSES

Rent or first mortgage (including taxes and insurance)	$	_____
Real estate taxes (if not included above)	$	_____
Real estate/homeowner's insurance (if not included above)	$	_____
Second mortgage/equity line of credit	$	_____
Utilities		
○ Electric	$	_____
○ Gas, fuel oil, propane	$	_____
○ Water and sewer	$	_____
○ Telephone	$	_____
○ Trash collection	$	_____
○ Cable/satellite television	$	_____
Cleaning, maintenance, repair	$	_____
Lawn service, snow removal	$	_____
Other: _____	$	_____
	$	_____
TOTAL MONTHLY :	$	_____

Supreme Court of Ohio
Uniform Domestic Relations Form – Affidavit 1
Affidavit of Income and Expenses
Approved under Ohio Civil Rule 84
Effective Date: July 1, 2010

Page 3 of 7

B. OTHER MONTHLY LIVING EXPENSES

Food

    ○   Groceries (including food, paper, cleaning products, toiletries, other) $ _____

    ○   Restaurant $ _____

Transportation

    ○   Vehicle loans, leases $ _____

    ○   Vehicle maintenance (oil, repair, license) $ _____

    ○   Gasoline $ _____

    ○   Parking, public transportation $ _____

Clothing

    ○   Clothes (other than children's) $ _____

    ○   Dry cleaning, laundry $ _____

Personal grooming

    ○   Hair, nail care $ _____

    ○   Other _____ $ _____

Cell phone $ _____

Internet (if not included elsewhere) $ _____

Other _____ $ _____

                                  TOTAL MONTHLY $ _____

C. MONTHLY CHILD-RELATED EXPENSES
    (for children of the marriage or relationship)

Work/education-related child care $ _____

Other child care $ _____

Unusual parenting time travel $ _____

Special and unusual needs of child(ren) (not included elsewhere) $ _____

Clothing $ _____

School supplies $ _____

Child(ren)'s allowances $ _____

Extracurricular activities, lessons $ _____

School lunches $ _____

Other _____ $ _____

                                  TOTAL MONTHLY $ _____

Supreme Court of Ohio
Uniform Domestic Relations Form – Affidavit 1
Affidavit of Income and Expenses
Approved under Ohio Civil Rule 84
Effective Date: July 1, 2010

Page 4 of 7

D. INSURANCE PREMIUMS

Life	$	
Auto	$	
Health	$	
Disability	$	
Renters/personal property (if not included in part A above)	$	
Other _____	$	
TOTAL MONTHLY	$	

E. MONTHLY EDUCATION EXPENSES

Tuition

○ Self	$	
○ Child(ren)	$	
Books, fees, other	$	
College loan repayment	$	
Other _____	$	
_____	$	
TOTAL MONTHLY:	$	

F. MONTHLY HEALTH CARE EXPENSES
(not covered by insurance)

Physicians	$	
Dentists	$	
Optometrists/opticians	$	
Prescriptions	$	
Other _____	$	
_____	$	
TOTAL MONTHLY:	$	

G. MISCELLANEOUS MONTHLY EXPENSES

Extraordinary obligations for other minor/handicapped child(ren) (not stepchildren)	$	
Child support for children who were not born of this marriage or relationship and were not adopted of this marriage	$	
Spousal support paid to former spouse(s)	$	
Subscriptions, books	$	
Entertainment	$	

Supreme Court of Ohio
Uniform Domestic Relations Form – Affidavit 1
Affidavit of Income and Expenses
Approved under Ohio Civil Rule 84
Effective Date: July 1, 2010

Page 5 of 7

Charitable contributions $ _____

Memberships (associations, clubs) $ _____

Travel, vacations $ _____

Pets $ _____

Gifts $ _____

Bankruptcy payments $ _____

Attorney fees $ _____

Required deductions from wages (excluding taxes, Social Security and Medicare)
(type) _____ $ _____

Additional taxes paid (not deducted from wages) (type) _____ $ _____

Other _____ $ _____

_____ $ _____

TOTAL MONTHLY: $ _____

H. **MONTHLY INSTALLMENT PAYMENTS**
(Do not repeat expenses already listed.)
Examples: car, credit card, rent-to-own, cash advance payments

To whom paid	Purpose	Balance due	Monthly payment
_____	_____	$ _____	$ _____
_____	_____	$ _____	$ _____
_____	_____	$ _____	$ _____
_____	_____	$ _____	$ _____
_____	_____	$ _____	$ _____
_____	_____	$ _____	$ _____
_____	_____	$ _____	$ _____
_____	_____	$ _____	$ _____
_____	_____	$ _____	$ _____
_____	_____	$ _____	$ _____
_____	_____	$ _____	$ _____
_____	_____	$ _____	$ _____
_____	_____	$ _____	$ _____
_____	_____	$ _____	$ _____
_____	_____	$ _____	$ _____

TOTAL MONTHLY: $ _____

GRAND TOTAL MONTHLY EXPENSES (Sum of A through H): $ _____

Supreme Court of Ohio
Uniform Domestic Relations Form – Affidavit 1
Affidavit of Income and Expenses
Approved under Ohio Civil Rule 84
Effective Date: July 1, 2010

Page 6 of 7

OATH

(Do not sign until notary is present.)

I, (print name) _____ , swear or affirm that I have read this document and, to the best of my knowledge and belief, the facts and information stated in this document are true, accurate and complete. I understand that if I do not tell the truth, I may be subject to penalties for perjury.

_____
Your Signature

Sworn before me and signed in my presence this _____ day of _____ , _____ .

_____
Notary Public
My Commission Expires:

_____

Supreme Court of Ohio
Uniform Domestic Relations Form – Affidavit 1
Affidavit of Income and Expenses
Approved under Ohio Civil Rule 84
Effective Date: July 1, 2010

Page 7 of 7

COURT OF COMMON PLEAS

_____ COUNTY, OHIO

_____ Plaintiff/Petitioner	Case No. _____
	Judge _____
v./and	Magistrate _____
_____ Respondent/Petitioner	

> **Instructions:** Check local court rules to determine when this form must be filed.
> List ALL OF YOUR PROPERTY AND DEBTS, the property and debts of your spouse, and any joint property or debts. Do not leave any category blank. For each item, if none, put "NONE." If you do not know exact figures for any item, give your best estimate, and put "EST." **If more space is needed, add additional pages.**

AFFIDAVIT OF PROPERTY

Affidavit of _____
(Print Your Name)

I. REAL ESTATE INTERESTS

	Address	Present Fair Market Value	Titled To	Mortgage Balance	Equity (as of date)
1.	_____	$ _____	☐ Husband ☐ Wife ☐ Both	$ _____	$ _____
	_____				_____
2.	_____	$ _____	☐ Husband ☐ Wife ☐ Both	$ _____	$ _____
	_____				_____

TOTAL SECTION I: REAL ESTATE INTERESTS $ _____

Supreme Court of Ohio
Uniform Domestic Relations Form – Affidavit 2
Affidavit of Property
Approved under Ohio Civil Rule 84
Effective Date: July 1, 2010

Page 1 of 7

II. OTHER ASSETS

Category	Description (List who has possession)	Titled To	Value/Date of Value
A. Vehicles and Other Certificate of Title Property	(Include model and year of automobiles, trucks, motorcycles, boats, motors, motor homes, etc.)		
1. _____	_____	☐ Husband ☐ Wife ☐ Both	$ _____ _____
2. _____	_____	☐ Husband ☐ Wife ☐ Both	$ _____ _____
3. _____	_____	☐ Husband ☐ Wife ☐ Both	$ _____ _____
4. _____	_____	☐ Husband ☐ Wife ☐ Both	$ _____ _____
5. _____	_____	☐ Husband ☐ Wife ☐ Both	$ _____ _____
6. _____	_____	☐ Husband ☐ Wife ☐ Both	$ _____ _____
B. Financial Accounts	(Include checking, savings, CDs, POD accounts, money market accounts, etc.)		
1. _____	_____	☐ Husband ☐ Wife ☐ Both	$ _____ _____
2. _____	_____	☐ Husband ☐ Wife ☐ Both	$ _____ _____
3. _____	_____	☐ Husband ☐ Wife ☐ Both	$ _____ _____
4. _____	_____	☐ Husband ☐ Wife ☐ Both	$ _____ _____

Supreme Court of Ohio
Uniform Domestic Relations Form – Affidavit 2
Affidavit of Property
Approved under Ohio Civil Rule 84
Effective Date: July 1, 2010

Page 2 of 7

Category	Description (List who has possession) (Include profit-sharing, IRAs, 401k plans, etc.; Describe each type of plan)	Titled To	Value/Date of Value
C. Pensions & Retirement plans			
1. _____	_____	☐ Husband ☐ Wife ☐ Both	$ _____ _____
2. _____	_____	☐ Husband ☐ Wife ☐ Both	$ _____ _____
3. _____	_____	☐ Husband ☐ Wife ☐ Both	$ _____ _____
4. _____	_____	☐ Husband ☐ Wife ☐ Both	$ _____ _____
D. Publicly Held Stocks, Bonds, Securities & Mutual Funds			
1. _____	_____	☐ Husband ☐ Wife ☐ Both	$ _____ _____
2. _____	_____	☐ Husband ☐ Wife ☐ Both	$ _____ _____
3. _____	_____	☐ Husband ☐ Wife ☐ Both	$ _____ _____
4. _____	_____	☐ Husband ☐ Wife ☐ Both	$ _____ _____

Category	Description (List who has possession) (Type of ownership and number)	Titled To	Value/Date of Value
E. Closely Held Stocks & Other Business Interests and Name of Company			
1. _____ _____	_____ _____	☐ Husband ☐ Wife ☐ Both	$ _____ _____
2. _____ _____	_____ _____	☐ Husband ☐ Wife ☐ Both	$ _____ _____

Supreme Court of Ohio
Uniform Domestic Relations Form – Affidavit 2
Affidavit of Property
Approved under Ohio Civil Rule 84
Effective Date: July 1, 2010

Page 3 of 7

F. Life Insurance Type (Term/Whole Life)	(Any cash value or loans)		(Insured party & value upon death)
1. _____	_____	☐ Husband ☐ Wife ☐ Both	$ _____
			_____
2. _____		☐ Husband ☐ Wife ☐ Both	$ _____
			_____
3. _____	_____	☐ Husband ☐ Wife ☐ Both	$ _____
			_____
4. _____	_____	☐ Husband ☐ Wife ☐ Both	$ _____
			_____

Category	Description	Who Has Possession	Value/Date of Value
G. Furniture & Appliances	(Estimate value of those in your possession, and value of those in your spouse's possession)		
1. _____	_____	☐ Husband ☐ Wife ☐ Both	$ _____
2. _____	_____	☐ Husband ☐ Wife ☐ Both	$ _____
3. _____	_____	☐ Husband ☐ Wife ☐ Both	$ _____
4. _____	_____	☐ Husband ☐ Wife ☐ Both	$ _____

H. Safe Deposit Box	(Give location and describe contents)	Titled To	
1. _____	_____	☐ Husband ☐ Wife ☐ Both	$ _____
2. _____	_____	☐ Husband ☐ Wife ☐ Both	$ _____

Supreme Court of Ohio
Uniform Domestic Relations Form – Affidavit 2
Affidavit of Property
Approved under Ohio Civil Rule 84
Effective Date: July 1, 2010

Page 4 of 7

I. Transfer of Assets

Explanation: List the name and address of any person (other than creditors listed on your Affidavit) who has received money or property from you exceeding $300 in value in the past 12 months and the reason for each transfer.

1. _____ _____ ☐ Husband ☐ Wife ☐ Both $ _____

2. _____ _____ ☐ Husband ☐ Wife ☐ Both $ _____

3. _____ _____ ☐ Husband ☐ Wife ☐ Both $ _____

4. _____ _____ ☐ Husband ☐ Wife ☐ Both $ _____

Category	Description (Also list who has possession)	Titled To	Value/Date of Value
J. All Other Assets Not Listed Above	Explanation: List any item you have not listed above that is considered an asset.		

1. _____ _____ ☐ Husband ☐ Wife ☐ Both $ _____

2. _____ _____ ☐ Husband ☐ Wife ☐ Both $ _____

TOTAL SECTION II: OTHER ASSETS $ _____

III. SEPARATE PROPERTY CLAIMS: Pre-marital assets, gifts to one spouse only, inheritances

If you are making any claims in any of the categories below, explain the nature and amount of your claim. **This includes, but is not limited to, inheritances, property owned before marriage, and any pre-marital agreements.**

Category (Pre-marital Gift, Inheritance, etc., acquired after separation)	Description	Why do you claim this as a separate property?	Present Fair Market Value
1. _____	_____	_____	$ _____
2. _____	_____	_____	$ _____
3. _____	_____	_____	$ _____
4. _____	_____	_____	$ _____
5. _____	_____	_____	$ _____

TOTAL SECTION III: SEPARATE PROPERTY CLAIMS $ _____

IV. DEBT

List ALL OF YOUR DEBTS, the debts of your spouse, and any joint debts. Do not leave any category blank. For each item, if none, put "NONE." If you don't know exact figures for any item, give your best estimate, and put "EST." **If more space is needed to explain, please attach an additional page with the explanation and identify which question you are answering.**

Type	Name of Creditor/Purpose of Debt	Account Name	Name(s) on Account	Total Debt Due	Monthly Payment
A. Secured Debt (Mortgages, Car, etc.)					
1. _____	_____	_____	☐ Husband ☐ Wife ☐ Joint	$ _____	$ _____
2. _____	_____	_____	☐ Husband ☐ Wife ☐ Joint	$ _____	$ _____
3. _____	_____	_____	☐ Husband ☐ Wife ☐ Joint	$ _____	$ _____
4. _____	_____	_____	☐ Husband ☐ Wife ☐ Joint	$ _____	$ _____
5. _____	_____	_____	☐ Husband ☐ Wife ☐ Joint	$ _____	$ _____
B. Unsecured Debt, including credit cards					
1. _____	_____	_____	☐ Husband ☐ Wife ☐ Joint	$ _____	$ _____
2. _____	_____	_____	☐ Husband ☐ Wife ☐ Joint	$ _____	$ _____
3. _____	_____	_____	☐ Husband ☐ Wife ☐ Joint	$ _____	$ _____
4. _____	_____	_____	☐ Husband ☐ Wife ☐ Joint	$ _____	$ _____
5. _____	_____	_____	☐ Husband ☐ Wife ☐ Joint	$ _____	$ _____

TOTAL SECTION IV: DEBT $ _____

Supreme Court of Ohio
Uniform Domestic Relations Form – Affidavit 2
Affidavit of Property
Approved under Ohio Civil Rule 84
Effective Date: July 1, 2010

Page 6 of 7

V. BANKRUPTCY

Filed by: Wife, Husband, Both	Date of Filing: Case Number	Date of Discharge or Relief from Stay	Type of Case (Ch. 7, 11, 12, 13)	Current Monthly Payments
1. ☐ Husband ☐ Wife ☐ Both	_____			
	_____	_____	_____	$ _____
2. ☐ Husband ☐ Wife ☐ Both	_____			
	_____	_____	_____	$ _____

TOTAL SECTION V: BANKRUPTCY $ _____

OATH

(Do Not Sign Until Notary is Present)

I, (print name) _____ swear or affirm that I have read this document and, to the best of my knowledge and belief, the facts and information stated in this document are true, accurate and complete. I understand that if I do not tell the truth, I may be subject to penalties for perjury.

_____
Your Signature

Sworn before me and signed in my presence this _____ day of _____ , _____ .

_____
Notary Public

My Commission Expires:

_____

COURT OF COMMON PLEAS

_____ COUNTY, OHIO

_____	Case No. _____
Plaintiff/Petitioner	Judge _____
v./and	Magistrate _____
_____	
Defendant/Petitioner/Respondent	

Instructions: Check local court rules to determine when this form must be filed.
By law, an affidavit must be filed and served with the first pleading filed by each party in every parenting (custody/visitation) proceeding in this Court, including Dissolutions, Divorces and Domestic Violence Petitions. Each party has a continuing duty while this case is pending to inform the Court of any parenting proceeding concerning the child(ren) in any other court in this or any other state. **If more space is needed, add additional pages.**

PARENTING PROCEEDING AFFIDAVIT (R.C. 3127.23(A))

Affidavit of _____
(Print Your Name)

Check and complete ALL THAT APPLY:

1. ☐ I request that the court not disclose my current address or that of the child(ren). My address is confidential pursuant to R.C. 3127.23(D) and should be placed under seal to protect the health, safety, or liberty of myself and/or the child(ren).

2. ☐ Minor child(ren) are subject to this case as follows:

Insert the information requested below for all minor or dependent children of this marriage. You must list the residences for all places where the children have lived for the last **FIVE** years.

a. **Child's Name:** _____   **Place of Birth:** _____

Date of Birth: _____

Sex: ☐ Male ☐ Female

Period of Residence			Check if Confidential	Person(s) With Whom Child Lived (name & address)	Relationship
	to	present	☐ Address Confidential?	_____	_____
	to		☐ Address Confidential?	_____	_____
	to		☐ Address Confidential?	_____	_____
	to		☐ Address Confidential?	_____	_____

Supreme Court of Ohio
Uniform Domestic Relations Form – Affidavit 3
Parenting Proceeding Affidavit
Approved under Ohio Civil Rule 84
Effective Date: July 1, 2010

b.   **Child's Name:**   **Place of Birth:**

     Date of Birth: **Sex:**   ☐ Male ☐ Female

☐ Check this box if the information requested below would be the same as in subsection 2a and skip to the next question.

Period of Residence			Check if Confidential	Person(s) With Whom Child Lived (name & address)	Relationship
	to	present	☐ Address Confidential?		
	to		☐ Address Confidential?		
	to		☐ Address Confidential?		
	to		☐ Address Confidential?		

c.   **Child's Name:**   **Place of Birth:**

     Date of Birth: **Sex:**   ☐ Male ☐ Female

☐ Check this box if the information requested below would be the same as in subsection 2a and skip to the next question.

Period of Residence			Check if Confidential	Person(s) With Whom Child Lived (name & address)	Relationship
	to	present	☐ Address Confidential?		
	to		☐ Address Confidential?		
	to		☐ Address Confidential?		
	to		☐ Address Confidential?		

IF MORE SPACE IS NEEDED FOR ADDITIONAL CHILDREN, ATTACH A SEPARATE PAGE AND CHECK THIS BOX ☐.

3.   **Participation in custody case(s): (Check only one box.)**

    ☐   I **HAVE NOT** participated as a party, witness, or in any capacity in any other case, in this or any other state, concerning the custody of, or visitation (parenting time), with any child subject to this case.

    ☐   I **HAVE** participated as a party, witness, or in any capacity in any other case, in this or any other state, concerning the custody of, or visitation (parenting time), with any child subject to this case. For each case in which you participated, give the following information:

a.   Name of each child: _____ _____

_____ _____ _____

b.   Type of case: _____

c.   Court and State: _____

d.   Date and court order or judgment (if any): _____

_____

IF MORE SPACE IS NEEDED FOR ADDITIONAL CUSTODY CASES, ATTACH A SEPARATE PAGE AND CHECK THIS BOX ☐.

4.   **Information about other civil case(s) that could affect this case: (Check only one box.)**

☐   I **HAVE NO INFORMATION** about any other civil cases that could affect the current case, including any cases relating to custody, domestic violence or protection orders, dependency, neglect or abuse allegations or adoptions concerning any child subject to this case.

☐   I **HAVE THE FOLLOWING INFORMATION** concerning other civil cases that could affect the current case, including any cases relating to custody, domestic violence or protection orders, dependency, neglect or abuse allegations or adoptions concerning a child subject to this case. Do not repeat cases already listed in Paragraph 3. Explain:

a.   Name of each child: _____ _____

_____ _____ _____

b.   Type of case: _____

c.   Court and State: _____

d.   Date and court order or judgment (if any): _____

_____

IF MORE SPACE IS NEEDED FOR ADDITIONAL CASES, ATTACH A SEPARATE PAGE AND CHECK THIS BOX ☐.

5.   **Information about criminal case(s):**

List all of the criminal convictions, including guilty pleas, for you and the members of your household for the following offenses: any criminal offense involving acts that resulted in a child being abused or neglected; any domestic violence offense that is a violation of R.C. 2919.25; any sexually oriented offense as defined in R.C. 2950.01; and any offense involving a victim who was a family or household member at the time of the offense and caused physical harm to the victim during the commission of the offense.

Name	Case Number	Court/State/County	Convicted of What Crime?
_____	_____	_____	_____
_____	_____	_____	_____
_____	_____	_____	_____
_____	_____	_____	_____

IF MORE SPACE IS NEEDED FOR ADDITIONAL CASES, ATTACH A SEPARATE PAGE AND CHECK THIS BOX ☐.

Supreme Court of Ohio
Uniform Domestic Relations Form – Affidavit 3
Parenting Proceeding Affidavit
Approved under Ohio Civil Rule 84
Effective Date: July 1, 2010

Page 3 of 4

6. **Persons not a party to this case who has physical custody or claims to have custody or visitation rights to children subject to this case: (Check only one box.)**

    ☐   I **DO NOT KNOW OF ANY PERSON(S)** not a party to this case who has/have physical custody or claim(s) to have custody or visitation rights with respect to any child subject to this case.

    ☐   I **KNOW THAT THE FOLLOWING NAMED PERSON(S)** not a party to this case has/have physical custody or claim(s) to have custody or visitation rights with respect to any child subject to this case.

a.   Name/Address of Person

☐ Has physical custody   ☐ Claims custody rights   ☐ Claims visitation rights

Name of each child:

b.   Name/Address of Person

☐ Has physical custody   ☐ Claims custody rights   ☐ Claims visitation rights

Name of each child:

c.   Name/Address of Person

☐ Has physical custody   ☐ Claims custody rights   ☐ Claims visitation rights

Name of each child:

OATH

(Do Not Sign Until Notary is Present)

I, (print name) _____ , swear or affirm that I have read this document and, to the best of my knowledge and belief, the facts and information stated in this document are true, accurate and complete. I understand that if I do not tell the truth, I may be subject to penalties for perjury.

_____
Your Signature

Sworn before me and signed in my presence this _____ day of _____ , _____ .

_____
Notary Public

My Commission Expires:

_____

COURT OF COMMON PLEAS
_____ COUNTY, OHIO

_____
Plaintiff/Petitioner

v./and

_____
Defendant/Petitioner

Case No. _____

Judge _____

Magistrate _____

Instructions: Check local court rules to determine when this form must be filed.
This affidavit is used to disclose health insurance coverage that is available for children. It is also used to determine child support. It must be filed if there are minor children of the relationship. **If more space is needed, add additional pages.**

HEALTH INSURANCE AFFIDAVIT

Affidavit of _____
(Print Your Name)

	Mother	**Father**
Are your child(ren) currently enrolled in a low-income government-assisted health care program (Healthy Start/Medicaid)?	☐ Yes ☐ No	☐ Yes ☐ No
Are you enrolled in an individual (non-group or COBRA) health insurance plan?	☐ Yes ☐ No	☐ Yes ☐ No
Are you enrolled in a health insurance plan through a group (employer or other organization)?	☐ Yes ☐ No	☐ Yes ☐ No
If you are not enrolled, do you have health insurance available through a group (employer or other organization)?	☐ Yes ☐ No	☐ Yes ☐ No
Does the available insurance cover primary care services within 30 miles of the child(ren)'s home?	☐ Yes ☐ No	☐ Yes ☐ No

Supreme Court of Ohio
Uniform Domestic Relations Form – Affidavit 4
Health Insurance Affidavit
Approved under Ohio Civil Rule 84
Effective Date: July 1, 2010

Page 1 of 2

	Mother	**Father**

Under the available insurance, what would be the annual premium for a plan covering you and the child(ren) of this relationship (not including a spouse)? $ _____ $ _____

Under the available insurance, what would be the annual premium for a plan covering you alone (not including children or spouse)? $ _____ $ _____

If you are enrolled in a health insurance plan through a group (employer or other organization) or individual insurance plan, which of the following people is/are covered:

	Mother	Father
Yourself?	☐ Yes ☐ No	☐ Yes ☐ No
Your spouse?	☐ Yes ☐ No	☐ Yes ☐ No
Minor child(ren) of this relationship?	☐ Yes ☐ No Number _____	☐ Yes ☐ No Number _____
Other individuals?	☐ Yes ☐ No Number _____	☐ Yes ☐ No Number _____

Name of group (employer or organization) that provides health insurance   _____   _____

Address   _____   _____

Phone number   _____   _____

OATH

(Do not sign until notary is present.)

I, (print name) _____ , swear or affirm that I have read this document and, to the best of my knowledge and belief, the facts and information stated in this document are true, accurate and complete. I understand that if I do not tell the truth, I may be subject to penalties for perjury.

_____
Your Signature

Sworn before me and signed in my presence this _____ day of _____ , _____ .

_____
Notary Public
My Commission Expires:

_____

Supreme Court of Ohio
Uniform Domestic Relations Form – Affidavit 4
Health Insurance Affidavit
Approved under Ohio Civil Rule 84
Effective Date: July 1, 2010

Page 2 of 2

COURT OF COMMON PLEAS

_____ COUNTY, OHIO

_____
Plaintiff

v.

_____
Defendant

Case No. _____

Judge _____

Magistrate _____

Instructions: Check local court rules to determine when this form must be filed.
This form is used to request temporary orders in your divorce or legal separation case. After a party serves a Motion and Affidavit, the other party has 14 days to file a Counter Affidavit and serve it on the party who filed the motion. **If more space is needed, add additional pages.**

MOTION AND AFFIDAVIT OR COUNTER AFFIDAVIT
FOR TEMPORARY ORDERS
WITHOUT ORAL HEARING

Check one box below to show whether you are filing a (1) Motion and Affidavit or (2) Counter Affidavit.

☐ **(1) Motion and Affidavit**

(Print Your Name) _____ files this Motion and Affidavit under Rule 75(N) of the Ohio Rules of Civil Procedure to request the temporary orders checked here.

Check only those that apply.

_____	Residential parenting rights (custody)
_____	Parenting time (visitation)
_____	Child support
_____	Spousal support (alimony)
_____	Payment of debts and/or expenses

THE OTHER PARTY HAS 14 DAYS FROM THE DATE ON WHICH THIS MOTION IS SERVED TO FILE A COUNTER AFFIDAVIT AND SERVE IT UPON THE PARTY WHO FILED THE MOTION. (See below.)

☐ **(2) Counter Affidavit**

(Print Your Name) _____ files this Counter Affidavit in response to a Motion and Affidavit.

Supreme Court of Ohio
Uniform Domestic Relations Form – Affidavit 5
Motion and Affidavit or Counter Affidavit for Temporary Orders
Without Oral Hearing
Approved under Ohio Civil Rule 84
Effective Date: July 1, 2010

Page 1 of 4

Complete the following information, whether filing Motion and Affidavit or Counter Affidavit. Check all that apply.

1. ☐ My spouse and I are living separately.

   Date of separation is _____ .

   ☐ My spouse and I are living together.

   ☐ We have no minor children. (Skip to number 5.)

   ☐ There are minor child(ren) who are adopted or born of this marriage.
   (List children here.)

Name	Date of birth	Living with

   ☐ In addition to the above children there is/are in my household:

   _____ adult(s)

   _____ other minor and/or dependent child(ren).

2. My child(ren) attend(s) school in:

   ☐ Father's school district

   ☐ Mother's school district

   ☐ Open enrollment

   ☐ Other (Explain.) _____ .

   ☐ All children do not attend school in the same district. (Explain.)

   _____

   _____

3. ☐ I request to be named the temporary residential parent and legal custodian of the child(ren).

   (Specify child(ren) if request is not for all children.) _____

   ☐ I do not object to my spouse being named the temporary residential parent of the child(ren).

   ☐ I request the following parenting time order:

   ☐ The Court's standard parenting order (See county's local rules of court.)

   ☐ A specific parenting time order as follows:

   _____

   _____

Supreme Court of Ohio
Uniform Domestic Relations Form – Affidavit 5
Motion and Affidavit or Counter Affidavit for Temporary Orders
Without Oral Hearing
Approved under Ohio Civil Rule 84
Effective Date: July 1, 2010   Page 2 of 4

☐ I have reached an agreement regarding parenting time with my spouse as follows:

_____

_____

☐ I request that my spouse's parenting time (visitation) be supervised. (Explain--supervised parenting time order will NOT be granted if the reasons are not explained.)

_____

_____

Name of an appropriate supervisor _____

4. ☐ A court or agency has made a child support order concerning the child(ren).

Name of Court/Agency _____

Date of Order _____

SETS No. _____

5. I request the Court to order my spouse to pay:

☐ $ _____ child support per month

☐ $ _____ spousal support per month

☐ $ _____ attorney fees, expert fees, court costs

☐ The following debts and/or expenses:

_____

_____

☐ Other

_____

6. ☐ I am willing to attend mediation.

☐ I am not willing to attend mediation.

☐ I request the following court services. (See local rules of court for available services.)

_____

_____

State specific reasons why court services are required.

_____

_____

Supreme Court of Ohio
Uniform Domestic Relations Form – Affidavit 5
Motion and Affidavit or Counter Affidavit for Temporary Orders
Without Oral Hearing
Approved under Ohio Civil Rule 84
Effective Date: July 1, 2010

Page 3 of 4

OATH

(Do not sign until notary is present.)

I, (print name) _____ , swear or affirm that I have read
this document and, to the best of my knowledge and belief, the facts and information stated in this document
are true, accurate and complete. I understand that if I do not tell the truth, I may be subject to penalties for
perjury.

_____
Your Signature

Sworn before me and signed in my presence this _____ day of _____ , _____ .

_____
Notary Public
My Commission Expires:

NOTICE OF HEARING

(Check with local court for scheduling procedure.)

You are hereby given notice that this motion for temporary orders will be heard upon affidavits only, and

without oral testimony, before Judge/Magistrate _____ ,

Hearing Room _____ , at _____ a.m./p.m. on _____ , 20 _____ , at

_____ , _____ floor .

CERTIFICATE OF SERVICE

Check the boxes that apply.

I delivered a copy of my: ☐ Motion and Affidavit or ☐ Counter Affidavit

On: (Date) _____ , 20 _____

To: (Print name of other party's attorney or, if there is no attorney, print name of the party.)

_____

At: (Print address or fax number.) _____ .

By: ☐ U.S. Mail
     ☐ Fax
     ☐ Messenger
     ☐ Clerk of courts (if address is unknown)

_____
Your Signature

Supreme Court of Ohio
Uniform Domestic Relations Form – Affidavit 5
Motion and Affidavit or Counter Affidavit for Temporary Orders
Without Oral Hearing
Approved under Ohio Civil Rule 84
Effective Date: July 1, 2010

Page 4 of 4

Disclaimer

Please be aware that these forms do not include instructions or legal advice regarding your rights, responsibilities, and legal options.

To be fully informed and get answers to your questions, you should seek the advice of an attorney.

IN THE COURT OF COMMON PLEAS

_____ **Division**

_____ **COUNTY, OHIO**

_____ Name	: : Case No. _____ :
_____ Street Address	: :
_____ City, State and Zip Code	: Judge _____ :
Plaintiff	: : Magistrate _____
	:
vs.	:
	:
_____ Name	: :
_____ Street Address	: :
_____ City, State and Zip Code	: :
Defendant	:

Instructions: This form is used to request a divorce if you and your spouse do not have (a) child(ren), adult child(ren) attending high school, or child(ren) with disabilities. Check to determine if you meet the residency requirement to file in this county. A Request for Service (Uniform Domestic Relations Form 28) must be filed with this form.

COMPLAINT FOR DIVORCE WITHOUT CHILDREN

I, the Plaintiff, for this Complaint say:

1. I have been a resident of the State of Ohio for at least six months.

2. ☐ I have been a resident of _____ County for at least 90 days immediately before the filing of this Complaint; or
    ☐ The Defendant resides in _____ County where this Complaint is filed.

3. The Defendant and I were married to one another on _____ (date of marriage)
    in _____ (city or county, and state).

Supreme Court of Ohio
Uniform Domestic Relations Form – 6
COMPLAINT FOR DIVORCE WITHOUT CHILDREN
Approved under Ohio Civil Rule 84
Effective Date: 7/1/2013

Page 1 of 2

4. I state regarding child(ren) (check all that apply):

☐ The Wife is not pregnant.

☐ All children born from or adopted during this marriage or relationship are adults and not mentally or physically disabled child(ren) incapable of supporting or maintaining themselves.

5. I state the following grounds for divorce exist (check all that apply):

☐ The Defendant and I are incompatible.

☐ The Defendant and I have lived separate and apart without cohabitation and without interruption for one year.

☐ The Defendant or I had a Husband or Wife living at the time of the marriage.

☐ The Defendant has been willfully absent for one year.

☐ The Defendant is guilty of adultery.

☐ The Defendant is guilty of extreme cruelty.

☐ The Defendant is guilty of fraudulent contract.

☐ The Defendant is guilty of gross neglect of duty.

☐ The Defendant is guilty of habitual drunkenness.

☐ The Defendant was imprisoned in a state or federal correctional institution at the time the Complaint was filed.

☐ The Defendant procured a divorce outside this state by virtue of which the Defendant has been released from the obligations of the marriage, while those obligations remain binding on me.

6. The Defendant and I are owners of real estate and/or personal property.

I request that a divorce be granted from the Defendant, that the Court determine an equitable division of debts and property, and as follows that (check all that apply):

☐ The Defendant be ordered to pay me spousal support.

☐ I be restored to my prior name of: _____

☐ The Defendant be required to pay attorney fees.

☐ The Defendant be required to pay the court costs of the proceeding.

☐ The Court make the following additional orders: _____

_____

_____

_____

and that the Court grant such other and further relief as the Court may deem proper.

_____
Your Signature

_____
Telephone number at which the Court may reach you or at which messages may be left for you

Supreme Court of Ohio
Uniform Domestic Relations Form – 6
COMPLAINT FOR DIVORCE WITHOUT CHILDREN
Approved under Ohio Civil Rule 84
Effective Date: 7/1/2013

Page 2 of 2

IN THE COURT OF COMMON PLEAS

_____ **Division**

_____ **COUNTY, OHIO**

_____	:
Name	: Case No. _____
_____	:
Street Address	:
_____	: Judge _____
City, State and Zip Code	:
Plaintiff	:
	: Magistrate _____
vs.	:
	:
_____	:
Name	:
_____	:
Street Address	:
_____	:
City, State and Zip Code	:
Defendant	:

Instructions: This form is used to request a divorce if you and your spouse have (a) minor child(ren), adult child(ren) attending high school, or child(ren) with disabilities, and/or the Wife is pregnant. Check to determine if you meet the residency requirement to file in this county. A Request for Service (Uniform Domestic Relations Form 28) must be filed with this form. The Parenting Proceeding Affidavit (Uniform Domestic Relations Form - Affidavit 3) must be filed.

COMPLAINT FOR DIVORCE WITH CHILDREN

I, the Plaintiff, for this Complaint say:

1. I have been a resident of the State of Ohio for at least six months.

2. ☐ I have been a resident of _____ County for at least 90 days immediately before the filing of this Complaint; or
   ☐ The Defendant resides in _____ County where this Complaint is filed.

3. The Defendant and I were married to one another on _____ (date of marriage) in _____ (city or county, and state).

Supreme Court of Ohio
Uniform Domestic Relations Form – 7
COMPLAINT FOR DIVORCE WITH CHILDREN
Approved under Ohio Civil Rule 84
Effective Date: 7/1/2013

Page 1 of 3

4. I state regarding children (check all that apply):
☐ The Wife is not pregnant.
☐ The Wife is pregnant and the approximate due date is: _____
☐ The following child(ren) were born from or adopted during this marriage or relationship (name and date of birth of each child):

Name of Child	Date of Birth
_____	_____
_____	_____
_____	_____

☐ Husband is not the biological father of the following child(ren) who were born during the marriage (name and date of birth of each child): _____

_____

_____

5. I state the following grounds for divorce exist (check all that apply):
☐ The Defendant and I are incompatible.
☐ The Defendant and I have lived separate and apart without cohabitation and without interruption for one year.
☐ The Defendant or I had a Husband or Wife living at the time of the marriage.
☐ The Defendant has been willfully absent for one year.
☐ The Defendant is guilty of adultery.
☐ The Defendant is guilty of extreme cruelty.
☐ The Defendant is guilty of fraudulent contract.
☐ The Defendant is guilty of gross neglect of duty.
☐ The Defendant is guilty of habitual drunkenness.
☐ The Defendant was imprisoned in a state or federal correctional institution at the time the Complaint was filed.
☐ The Defendant procured a divorce outside this state by virtue of which the Defendant has been released from the obligations of the marriage, while those obligations remain binding on me.

6. The Defendant and I are owners of real estate and/or personal property.

I request that a divorce be granted from the Defendant, that the Court determine an equitable division of debts and property, and as follows that (check all that apply):
☐ The Defendant be required to pay me spousal support.
☐ The Plaintiff be named the residential parent and legal custodian of the following minor child(ren): _____

_____

☐ The Defendant be named the residential parent and legal custodian of the following

Supreme Court of Ohio
Uniform Domestic Relations Form – 7
COMPLAINT FOR DIVORCE WITH CHILDREN
Approved under Ohio Civil Rule 84
Effective Date: 7/1/2013

Page 2 of 3

child(ren): _____

☐ The non-residential parent be granted specific parenting time.

☐ The Defendant and I be granted shared parenting of the following child(ren): _____

pursuant to a Shared Parenting Plan (Uniform Domestic Relations Form 17), which I will prepare and file with the Court.

☐ The Defendant be ordered to pay child support and medical support.

☐ I be restored to my prior name of: _____

☐ The Defendant be required to pay attorney fees.

☐ The Defendant be required to pay the court costs of the proceeding.

☐ The Court make the following additional orders: _____

_____

_____

and that the Court grant such other and further relief as the Court may deem proper.

_____
Your Signature

_____
Telephone number at which the Court may reach you
or at which messages may be left for you

Supreme Court of Ohio
Uniform Domestic Relations Form – 7
COMPLAINT FOR DIVORCE WITH CHILDREN
Approved under Ohio Civil Rule 84
Effective Date: 7/1/2013

Page 3 of 3

IN THE COURT OF COMMON PLEAS

_____ **Division**

_____ **COUNTY, OHIO**

_____	:
Name	: Case No. _____
_____	:
Street Address	:
_____	: Judge _____
City, State and Zip Code	:
Plaintiff	:
	: Magistrate _____
vs.	:
	:
_____	:
Name	:
_____	:
Street Address	:
_____	:
City, State and Zip Code	:
Defendant	:

Instructions: This form is used to Counterclaim a Complaint for Divorce with or without Children. A Request for Service (Uniform Domestic Relations Form 28) must be filed with this form. The Parenting Proceeding Affidavit (Uniform Domestic Relations Form 3) must be filed, if you and your spouse have (a) minor child(ren), adult child(ren) attending high school, adult child(ren) with disabilities, and/or the Wife is pregnant.

COUNTERCLAIM FOR DIVORCE

I, the Defendant, for this Counterclaim say:

1. I have been a resident of the State of Ohio for at least six months.

2. ☐ I have been a resident of _____ County for at least 90 days immediately before the filing of this Complaint; or
   ☐ The Plaintiff resides in _____ County where this Complaint is filed.

3. The Plaintiff and I were married to one another on _____ (date of marriage) in _____ (city or county, and state).

Supreme Court of Ohio
Uniform Domestic Relations Form – 8
COUNTERCLAIM FOR DIVORCE
Approved under Ohio Civil Rule 84
Effective Date: 7/1/2013

Page 1 of 3

4. I state regarding children (check all that apply):

☐ The Wife is not pregnant.

☐ The Wife is pregnant and the approximate due date is: _____

☐ No children were born from or adopted during this marriage or relationship.

☐ The following child(ren) were born from or adopted during this marriage or relationship (name and date of birth of each child):

Name of Child	Date of Birth
_____	_____
_____	_____
_____	_____

☐ Husband is not the biological father of the following child(ren) who were born during the marriage (name and date of birth of each child): _____

_____

_____

_____

5. I state the following grounds for divorce exist (check all that apply):

☐ The Plaintiff and I are incompatible.

☐ The Plaintiff and I have lived separate and apart without cohabitation and without interruption for one year.

☐ The Plaintiff or I had a Husband or Wife living at the time of the marriage.

☐ The Plaintiff has been willfully absent for one year.

☐ The Plaintiff is guilty of adultery.

☐ The Plaintiff is guilty of extreme cruelty.

☐ The Plaintiff is guilty of fraudulent contract.

☐ The Plaintiff is guilty of gross neglect of duty.

☐ The Plaintiff is guilty of habitual drunkenness.

☐ The Plaintiff was imprisoned in a state or federal correctional institution at the time the Complaint was filed.

☐ The Plaintiff procured a divorce outside this state by virtue of which the Plaintiff has been released from the obligations of the marriage, while those obligations remain binding on me.

6. The Plaintiff and I are owners of real estate and/or personal property.

I request that a divorce be granted from the Plaintiff, that the Court determine an equitable division of debts and property, and as follows that (check all that apply):

☐ The Plaintiff be required to pay spousal support.

☐ The Plaintiff be named the residential parent and legal custodian of the following child(ren): _____

Supreme Court of Ohio
Uniform Domestic Relations Form – 8
COUNTERCLAIM FOR DIVORCE
Approved under Ohio Civil Rule 84
Effective Date: 7/1/2013

Page 2 of 3

☐ The Defendant be named the residential parent and legal custodian of the following child(ren): _____

☐ The non-residential parent be granted specific parenting time.
☐ The Plaintiff and I be granted shared parenting of the following child(ren): _____

pursuant to a Shared Parenting Plan (Uniform Domestic Relations Form 17), which I will prepare and file with the Court.

☐ The Plaintiff be ordered to pay child support and medical support.
☐ I be restored to my prior name of: _____
☐ The Plaintiff be required to pay attorney fees.
☐ The Plaintiff be required to pay the court costs of the proceeding.
☐ The Court make the following additional orders: _____

_____

_____

and that the Court grant such other and further relief as the Court may deem proper.

_____
Your Signature

_____
Telephone number at which the Court may reach you
or at which messages may be left for you

Supreme Court of Ohio
Uniform Domestic Relations Form – 8
COUNTERCLAIM FOR DIVORCE
Approved under Ohio Civil Rule 84
Effective Date: 7/1/2013

Page 3 of 3

IN THE COURT OF COMMON PLEAS

_____ **Division**

_____ **COUNTY, OHIO**

_____	:
Plaintiff	: Case No. _____
_____	:
Street Address	:
_____	: Judge _____
City, State and Zip Code	:
	:
vs.	: Magistrate _____
	:
_____	:
Defendant	:
_____	:
Street Address	:
_____	:
City, State and Zip Code	:

Instructions: This form is used in response to a filing of a Complaint for Divorce without Children. This form is used to agree with or dispute the statements made in the Complaint for Divorce without Children or a Counterclaim to a Divorce without Children.

☐ **ANSWER TO COMPLAINT FOR DIVORCE WITHOUT CHILDREN**
☐ **REPLY TO COUNTERCLAIM**

1. I, _____ (name) **ADMIT or DENY** the following allegations, as listed in my Spouse's Complaint or Counterclaim.

ADMIT	DENY	
☐	☐	My Spouse's state of residence
☐	☐	My Spouse's length of residence in state
☐	☐	My Spouse's county of residence
☐	☐	My Spouse's length of residence in county
☐	☐	My county of residence
☐	☐	The date of our marriage
☐	☐	The place of our marriage
☐	☐	My Spouse is not pregnant.
☐	☐	No children were born from or adopted during the marriage or relationship.
☐	☐	All children who were born from or adopted during the marriage or relationship are emancipated adults and not mentally or physically disabled child(ren) incapable of maintaining supporting or maintaining themselves.

Supreme Court of Ohio
Uniform Domestic Relations Form – 9
ANSWER TO COMPLAINT FOR DIVORCE WITHOUT CHILDREN
Approved under Ohio Civil Rule 84
Effective Date: 7/1/2013

Page 1 of 3

☐   ☐ My Spouse and I are owners of real estate and/or personal property.

2. I further **ADMIT or DENY** the following grounds for divorce:
   ADMIT   **DENY**
   ☐   ☐ My Spouse and I are incompatible.
   ☐   ☐ My Spouse and I have lived separate and apart without cohabitation and without interruption for one year.
   ☐   ☐ My Spouse or I had a Husband or Wife living at the time of the marriage.
   ☐   ☐ I have been willfully absent for one year.
   ☐   ☐ I am guilty of adultery.
   ☐   ☐ I am guilty of extreme cruelty.
   ☐   ☐ I am guilty of fraudulent contract.
   ☐   ☐ I am guilty of gross neglect of duty.
   ☐   ☐ I am guilty of habitual drunkenness.
   ☐   ☐ I was imprisoned in a state or federal correctional institution at the time the Complaint was filed.
   ☐   ☐ I procured a divorce outside this state by virtue of which I have been released from the obligations of the marriage, while those obligations remain binding on my Spouse.

3. Anything not specifically admitted is denied.

4. Other information about the above admissions, denials, or responses: _____
   _____
   _____

I ask that the request for a divorce be ☐ dismissed ☐ granted (select one), and I be awarded such other relief as the Court finds fair and equitable, including ordering the cost of this action be paid as the Court may determine.

_____   _____
Your Signature   Address

_____   _____
Typed or printed Name   Telephone number at which the Court may reach
                                          you or at which messages may be left for you

Supreme Court of Ohio
Uniform Domestic Relations Form – 9
ANSWER TO COMPLAINT FOR DIVORCE WITHOUT CHILDREN
Approved under Ohio Civil Rule 84
Effective Date: 7/1/2013

Page 2 of 3

CERTIFICATE OF SERVICE

I delivered a copy of my Answer to Complaint for Divorce without Children

On: (date) _____

To: (name of your Spouse's attorney or, if there is no attorney, name of your Spouse)

_____

At: (address or fax number) _____

_____

By: ☐ U.S. Mail

☐ Fax

☐ Personal delivery

☐ Other: _____

_____
Your Signature

Supreme Court of Ohio
Uniform Domestic Relations Form – 9
ANSWER TO COMPLAINT FOR DIVORCE WITHOUT CHILDREN
Approved under Ohio Civil Rule 84
Effective Date: 7/1/2013

Page 3 of 3

IN THE COURT OF COMMON PLEAS

_____ **Division**

_____ **COUNTY, OHIO**

_____	:
Plaintiff	: Case No. _____
_____	:
Street Address	:
_____	: Judge _____
City, State and Zip Code	:
	:
vs.	: Magistrate _____
	:
_____	:
Defendant	:
_____	:
Street Address	:
_____	:
City, State and Zip Code	:

> **Instructions:** This form is used in response to a filing of a Complaint for Divorce with Children. This form is used to agree with or dispute the statements made in the Complaint for Divorce with Children or a Counterclaim to a Divorce with Children.

☐ ANSWER TO COMPLAINT FOR DIVORCE WITH CHILDREN
☐ REPLY TO COUNTERCLAIM

1. I, _____ (name) **ADMIT or DENY** the following allegations, as listed in my Spouse's Complaint or Counterclaim.

ADMIT **DENY**

☐ ☐ My Spouse's state of residence

☐ ☐ My Spouse's length of residence in state

☐ ☐ My Spouse's county of residence

☐ ☐ My Spouse's length of residence in county

☐ ☐ My county of residence

☐ ☐ The date of our marriage

☐ ☐ The place of our marriage

☐ ☐ My Spouse is not pregnant.

☐ ☐ The number of children who were born from or adopted during the marriage or relationship.

☐ ☐ The names of children who were born or adopted during the marriage or relationship.

Supreme Court of Ohio
Uniform Domestic Relations Form – 10
ANSWER TO COMPLAINT FOR DIVORCE WITH CHILDREN
Approved under Ohio Civil Rule 84
Effective Date: 7/1/2013

Page 1 of 3

    ☐   ☐ The dates of birth of children who were born or adopted during the marriage or relationship.

    ☐   ☐ My Spouse and I are owners of real estate and/or personal property.

2.   I further **ADMIT or DENY** the following grounds for divorce:

ADMIT DENY

    ☐   ☐ My Spouse and I are incompatible.

    ☐   ☐ My Spouse and I have lived separate and apart without cohabitation and without interruption for one year.

    ☐   ☐ My Spouse or I had a Husband or Wife living at the time of the marriage.

    ☐   ☐ I have been willfully absent for one year.

    ☐   ☐ I am guilty of adultery.

    ☐   ☐ I am guilty of extreme cruelty.

    ☐   ☐ I am guilty of fraudulent contract.

    ☐   ☐ I am guilty of gross neglect of duty.

    ☐   ☐ I am guilty of habitual drunkenness.

    ☐   ☐ I was imprisoned in a state or federal correctional institution at the time the Complaint was filed.

    ☐   ☐ I procured a divorce outside this state by virtue of which I have been released from the obligations of the marriage, while those obligations remain binding on my Spouse.

3.   Anything not specifically admitted is denied.

4.   Other information about the above admissions, denials, or responses: _____

_____

_____

I ask that the request for a divorce be ☐ dismissed ☐ granted (select one), and I be awarded such other relief as the Court finds fair and equitable, including ordering the cost of this action be paid as the Court may determine.

_____   _____
Your Signature   Address

_____   _____
Typed or printed Name   Telephone number at which the Court may reach
                                             you or at which messages may be left for you

Supreme Court of Ohio
Uniform Domestic Relations Form – 10
ANSWER TO COMPLAINT FOR DIVORCE WITH CHILDREN
Approved under Ohio Civil Rule 84
Effective Date: 7/1/2013

Page 2 of 3

CERTIFICATE OF SERVICE

I delivered a copy of my Answer to Complaint for Divorce with Children

On: (date)   _____

To: (name of your Spouse's attorney or, if there is no attorney, name of your Spouse)

_____

At: (address or fax number)   _____

_____

By: ☐ U.S. Mail

      ☐ Fax

      ☐ Personal delivery

      ☐ Other: _____

_____
Your Signature

Supreme Court of Ohio
Uniform Domestic Relations Form – 10
ANSWER TO COMPLAINT FOR DIVORCE WITH CHILDREN
Approved under Ohio Civil Rule 84
Effective Date: 7/1/2013

Page 3 of 3

IN THE COURT OF COMMON PLEAS

_____ **Division**

_____ **COUNTY, OHIO**

_____	:	Case No. _____
Plaintiff	:	
_____	:	
Street Address	:	
_____	:	Judge _____
City, State and Zip Code	:	
	:	
vs.	:	Magistrate _____
	:	
_____	:	
Defendant	:	
_____	:	
Street Address	:	
_____	:	
City, State and Zip Code	:	

FINAL JUDGMENT FOR DIVORCE WITHOUT CHILDREN

This matter came on for final hearing on _____ before ☐ Judge ☐ Magistrate
_____ upon the Plaintiff's Complaint for Divorce without Children filed on
_____ and/or Defendant's Counterclaim filed on _____
and upon the following: _____ .

FINDINGS

Upon a review of the record, testimony, and evidence presented, the Court makes the following findings:

A. Check all that apply:

☐ The Defendant was properly served with summons, copy of the Complaint, and notice of the hearing.

☐ The Defendant's waiver of service of summons and Complaint have been filed in this case.

☐ The Defendant filed an Answer.

☐ The Defendant failed to file an Answer or plead, despite being properly served with summons, copy of the Complaint, and notice of the hearing.

☐ The Plaintiff replied to the Defendant's Counterclaim.

☐ The Plaintiff failed to reply to the Defendant's Counterclaim.

Supreme Court of Ohio
Uniform Domestic Relations Form – 11
FINAL JUDGMENT FOR DIVORCE WITHOUT CHILDREN
Approved under Ohio Civil Rule 84
Effective Date: 7/1/2013

Page 1 of 7

B. Present at the hearing were the: ☐ Plaintiff, ☐ Defendant,

☐ _____ appearing as counsel for the Plaintiff.

☐ _____ appearing as counsel for the Defendant.

C. The ☐ Plaintiff and/or ☐ Defendant was/were a resident(s) of the State of Ohio for at least six months immediately before the Complaint and/or Counterclaim was/were filed.

D. At the time the Complaint and/or Counterclaim was/were filed:

☐ The Plaintiff was a resident of this county for at least 90 days.

☐ The Defendant was a resident of this county.

☐ Other grounds for venue were: _____

E. The Plaintiff and Defendant were married to one another on _____ (date of marriage) in _____ (city or county, and state). The termination of marriage is the date of ☐ final hearing or ☐ as specified: _____

F. Check all that apply regarding children:

☐ The Wife is not now pregnant.

☐ No child(ren) were born from or adopted during the marriage or relationship.

☐ All child(ren) born from or adopted during the marriage or relationship are emancipated adults and not mentally or physically disabled child(ren) incapable of supporting or maintaining themselves.

Other findings: _____

_____

_____

_____

G. Select one:

☐ Neither the Plaintiff nor the Defendant is in the military service of the United States.

☐ The ☐ Plaintiff and/or the ☐ Defendant is in the military service of the United States and his/her service did not impact his/her ability to defend this action.

H. The ☐ Plaintiff and/or the ☐ Defendant through testimony have indicated full and complete disclosure to the other of all marital property, separate property, and any other assets, debts, income, or expenses.

☐ The Defendant has not filed a response or made an appearance.

☐ The Plaintiff has not filed a response or made an appearance.

I. The parties that appeared have no additional knowledge of any other property and debts of any kind in which either party has an interest.

Supreme Court of Ohio
Uniform Domestic Relations Form – 11
FINAL JUDGMENT FOR DIVORCE WITHOUT CHILDREN
Approved under Ohio Civil Rule 84
Effective Date: 7/1/2013

Page 2 of 7

J. The parties that appeared have had the opportunity to value and verify all marital property, separate property, and other debts.

K. This Court has jurisdiction and proper venue to determine all of the issues raised by the pleadings and motions.

L. Select one:

☐ A Magistrate's Decision was filed on: _____

☐ No objections were filed. The Court approves the terms contained in the Decision and finds the terms are fair and equitable.

☐ All objections were ruled upon by a separate entry.

☐ The parties have presented the Court with a written Separation Agreement or have read into the record a settlement of all issues, which the Court finds to be a fair and equitable division of property and debts and an appropriate resolution of all issues, knowingly and voluntarily entered into by the parties.

☐ The Court has made a fair and equitable division of property and debts and an appropriate resolution of all issues of the parties after review and consideration of all evidence presented.

☐ Other: _____

_____

_____

M. The divorce is granted on the following ground(s) (check all that apply):

☐ The Plaintiff and Defendant are incompatible.

☐ The Plaintiff and Defendant have lived separate and apart without cohabitation and without interruption for one year.

☐ The Defendant or ☐ Plaintiff had a Husband or Wife living at the time of the marriage.

☐ The Defendant or ☐ Plaintiff has been willfully absent for one year.

☐ The Defendant or ☐ Plaintiff is guilty of adultery.

☐ The Defendant or ☐ Plaintiff is guilty of extreme cruelty.

☐ The Defendant or ☐ Plaintiff is guilty of fraudulent contract.

☐ The Defendant or ☐ Plaintiff is guilty of gross neglect of duty.

☐ The Defendant or ☐ Plaintiff is guilty of habitual drunkenness.

☐ The Defendant or ☐ Plaintiff was imprisoned in a state or federal correctional institution at the time the Complaint was filed.

☐ The Defendant or ☐ Plaintiff procured a divorce outside this state by virtue of which she or he has been released from the obligations of the marriage, while those obligations remain binding on the ☐ Plaintiff or ☐ Defendant.

Supreme Court of Ohio
Uniform Domestic Relations Form – 11
FINAL JUDGMENT FOR DIVORCE WITHOUT CHILDREN
Approved under Ohio Civil Rule 84
Effective Date: 7/1/2013

Page 3 of 7

JUDGMENT

Based upon the findings set out above, it is, therefore, **ORDERED, ADJUDGED and DECREED** that:

FIRST: DIVORCE GRANTED

A divorce is granted, and both parties shall be released from the obligations of their marriage except for those obligations listed below or as set out in the attached ☐ Separation Agreement ☐ Magistrate's Decision and/or ☐ Other: _____

which is incorporated in this entry.

SECOND: PROPERTY

The parties' property shall be divided as follows:

A. The Plaintiff shall have the following items of real estate and personal property, free and clear from all claims of the Defendant, subject to any indebtedness which the Plaintiff shall pay and from which the Plaintiff shall hold the Defendant harmless: _____

_____
_____
_____

B. The Defendant shall have the following items of real estate and personal property, free and clear from all claims of the Plaintiff, subject to any indebtedness which the Defendant shall pay and from which the Defendant shall hold the Plaintiff harmless: _____

_____
_____
_____
_____
_____
_____
_____

C. The Plaintiff is awarded the following separate property: _____

_____
_____
_____
_____
_____
_____

D. The Defendant is awarded the following separate property: _____

_____
_____
_____

Supreme Court of Ohio
Uniform Domestic Relations Form – 11
FINAL JUDGMENT FOR DIVORCE WITHOUT CHILDREN
Approved under Ohio Civil Rule 84
Effective Date: 7/1/2013

Page 4 of 7

_____

_____

_____

_____

E. Other orders regarding property (specify): _____

_____

_____

_____

F. Within 30 days the parties will take all necessary steps to transfer legal title and possession of property and take appropriate actions to implement and effectuate the division of pensions and retirements.

G. Other orders regarding transfers: _____

_____

_____

_____

THIRD: DEBT

The Plaintiff and Defendant's debts shall be divided as follows.

A. The Plaintiff shall pay the following debts and shall hold the Defendant harmless from all claims:

_____

_____

_____

_____

_____

_____

B. The Defendant shall pay the following debts and shall hold the Plaintiff harmless from all claims:

_____

_____

_____

_____

_____

_____

C. Bankruptcy (select one):

☐ The Court will retain jurisdiction to enforce payment of debt obligations, in the event a party files bankruptcy. This includes, but is not limited to, the ability to determine the debt assigned is in the nature of maintenance, necessity or support and is therefore nondischargeable in bankruptcy, and/or to make a future spousal support order, regardless of the spousal support order set forth below under **FOURTH: SPOUSAL SUPPORT**.

☐ Nothing in this order shall prevent the ☐ Plaintiff and/or ☐ Defendant from being fully discharged from the debts allocated in this order in a bankruptcy proceeding except for any orders expressly for spousal support and the following debts: _____

_____

_____

_____

Neither party shall incur liabilities against the other party in the future.

FOURTH: SPOUSAL SUPPORT

A. Spousal Support Not Awarded
    ☐ Neither the Plaintiff nor Defendant shall pay spousal support to the other. The Court shall not retain jurisdiction, except as set forth above under **THIRD: DEBTS**.

B. Spousal Support Awarded
    The ☐ Plaintiff ☐ Defendant shall pay spousal support to the ☐ Plaintiff ☐ Defendant
    in the amount of $_____   per month plus 2% processing charge,
    commencing on _____ and due on the _____ day of the month.
    This spousal support shall continue ☐ indefinitely ☐ for a period of _____ .

    ☐ The Court shall not retain jurisdiction to modify spousal support.

    ☐ The Court shall retain jurisdiction to modify the ☐ amount ☐ duration of the spousal support Order.

C. Termination of Spousal Support
    This spousal support shall terminate sooner than the above stated date upon the Plaintiff's or the Defendant's death or in the event of the following (check all that apply):
    ☐ The cohabitation of the person receiving support in a relationship comparable to marriage
    ☐ The remarriage of the person receiving support.
    ☐ Other (specify): _____

    _____

D. Method of Payment of Spousal Support (select one):
    ☐ The spousal support payment shall be made directly to the ☐ Plaintiff ☐ Defendant.
    ☐ The spousal support payment, plus 2% processing charge, shall be made to the Ohio Child Support Payment Central, P. O. Box 182372, Columbus, Ohio 43218-2372, as administered through the _____ County Child Support Enforcement Agency by income withholding at his/her place of employment.

Supreme Court of Ohio
Uniform Domestic Relations Form – 11
FINAL JUDGMENT FOR DIVORCE WITHOUT CHILDREN
Approved under Ohio Civil Rule 84
Effective Date: 7/1/2013

Page 6 of 7

E. Deductibility of Spousal Support for All Tax Purposes (select one):
☐ The spousal support paid shall be deducted from income to the person paying the support and included by the person receiving the support.
☐ The spousal support paid shall be included in income of the person paying the support.

F. Other orders regarding spousal support (specify): _____
_____

G. Arrearage
☐ Any temporary spousal support arrearage will survive this judgment entry.
☐ Any temporary spousal support arrearage will not survive this judgment entry.
☐ Other: _____
_____
_____

FIFTH: NAME
☐ _____ is restored to
the prior name of: _____

SIXTH: OTHER ORDERS
_____
_____

SEVENTH: COURT COSTS
Court costs shall be (select one):
☐ Taxed to the deposit. Court costs due above the deposit shall be paid as follows:
_____
☐ Other (specify): _____
_____

EIGHTH: CLERK OF COURTS
The Clerk of Courts shall provide:
☐ a certified copy to: _____
☐ a file stamped copy to: _____

NOTICE. Pursuant to Civil Rule 58(B), the Clerk is directed to serve upon the parties a notice of the filing of this Judgment Entry and of the date of entry upon the Journal.

_____   _____
Date   JUDGE

Supreme Court of Ohio
Uniform Domestic Relations Form – 11
FINAL JUDGMENT FOR DIVORCE WITHOUT CHILDREN
Approved under Ohio Civil Rule 84
Effective Date: 7/1/2013

Page 7 of 7

IN THE COURT OF COMMON PLEAS

_____ **Division**

_____ **COUNTY, OHIO**

_____	:	
Plaintiff	:	Case No. _____
_____	:	
Street Address	:	
_____	:	Judge _____
City, State and Zip Code	:	
	:	
vs.	:	Magistrate _____
	:	
_____	:	
Defendant	:	
_____	:	
Street Address	:	
_____	:	
City, State and Zip Code	:	

FINAL JUDGMENT FOR DIVORCE WITH CHILDREN

This matter came on for final hearing on _____ before ☐ Judge ☐ Magistrate _____ upon the Plaintiff's Complaint for Divorce with Children filed on _____ and/or Defendant's Counterclaim filed on _____ and upon the following: _____ .

FINDINGS

Upon a review of the record, testimony, and evidence presented, the Court makes the following findings:

A. Check all that apply:

☐ The Defendant was properly served with summons, copy of the Complaint, and notice of the hearing.

☐ The Defendant's waiver of service of summons and Complaint have been filed in this case.

☐ The Defendant filed an Answer.

☐ The Defendant failed to file an Answer or plead, despite being properly served with summons, copy of the Complaint, and notice of the hearing.

☐ The Plaintiff replied to the Defendant's Counterclaim.

☐ The Plaintiff failed to reply to the Defendant's Counterclaim.

Supreme Court of Ohio
Uniform Domestic Relations Form – 12
FINAL JUDGMENT FOR DIVORCE WITH CHILDREN
Approved under Ohio Civil Rule 84
Effective Date: 7/1/2013

Page 1 of 16

B. Present at the hearing were the: ☐ Plaintiff, ☐ Defendant,

☐ _____ appearing as counsel for the Plaintiff.

☐ _____ appearing as counsel for the Defendant.

C. The ☐ Plaintiff and/or ☐ Defendant was/were a resident(s) of the State of Ohio for at least six months immediately before the Complaint and/or Counterclaim was/were filed.

D. At the time the Complaint and/or Counterclaim was/were filed:

☐ The Plaintiff was a resident of this county for at least 90 days.

☐ The Defendant was a resident of this county.

☐ Other grounds for venue were: _____

E. The Plaintiff and Defendant were married to one another on _____ (date of marriage) in _____ (city or county, and state). The termination of marriage is the date of ☐ final hearing or ☐ as specified: _____

F. Check all that apply regarding children:

☐ The Wife is not now pregnant.

☐ The Wife is pregnant and the approximate due date is: _____

☐ Other findings: _____

☐ The parties are parents of _____ (number) born from or adopted during the marriage or relationship. Of the children, _____ (number) is/are emancipated adult(s) and not under any disability. The following _____ (number) child(ren) is/are minor child(ren) and/or mentally or physically disabled and incapable of supporting or maintaining themselves. (name and date of birth of each child):

Name of Child	Date of Birth
_____	_____
_____	_____
_____	_____

☐ Husband is not the biological father of the following child(ren) who was/were born during the marriage (name and date of birth of each child): _____

_____

_____

_____

G. ☐ The following child(ren) from the marriage or relationship are subject to a custody or parenting order in a different Court proceeding (name of each child and the Court that has issued the custody or parenting order): _____

_____

_____

_____

Supreme Court of Ohio
Uniform Domestic Relations Form – 12
FINAL JUDGMENT FOR DIVORCE WITH CHILDREN
Approved under Ohio Civil Rule 84
Effective Date: 7/1/2013

Page 2 of 16

H. Select one:

☐ Neither the Plaintiff nor Defendant is in the military service of the United States.

☐ The ☐ Plaintiff and/or ☐ Defendant is in the military service of the United States and his/her service did not impact his/her ability to defend this action.

I. The ☐ Plaintiff and/or ☐ Defendant through testimony have indicated full and complete disclosure to the other of all marital property, separate property, and any other assets, debts, income, or expenses.

☐ The Defendant has not filed a response or made an appearance.

☐ The Plaintiff has not filed a response or made an appearance.

J. The parties that appeared have no knowledge of any other property and debts of any kind in which either party has an interest.

K. The parties that appeared have had the opportunity to value and verify all marital property, separate property, and other debts.

L. This Court has jurisdiction and proper venue to determine all of the issues raised by the pleadings and motions.

M. Select one:

☐ A Magistrate's Decision was filed on: _____

☐ No objections were filed. The Court approves the terms contained in the Decision and finds the terms are fair and equitable.

☐ All objections were ruled upon by a separate entry.

☐ The parties have presented the Court with a written Separation Agreement or have read into the record a settlement of all issues, which the Court finds to be a fair and equitable division of property and debts and an appropriate resolution of all issues, knowingly and voluntarily entered into by the parties.

☐ The Court has made a fair and equitable division of property and debts and an appropriate resolution of all issues of the parties after review and consideration of all evidence presented.

☐ Other: _____

_____

_____

N. The divorce is granted on the following ground(s) (check all that apply):

☐ The Plaintiff and Defendant are incompatible.

☐ The Plaintiff and Defendant have lived separate and apart without cohabitation and without interruption for one year.

☐ The Defendant or ☐ Plaintiff had a Husband or Wife living at the time of the marriage.

☐ The Defendant or ☐ Plaintiff has been willfully absent for one year.

☐ The Defendant or ☐ Plaintiff is guilty of adultery.

Supreme Court of Ohio
Uniform Domestic Relations Form – 12
FINAL JUDGMENT FOR DIVORCE WITH CHILDREN
Approved under Ohio Civil Rule 84
Effective Date: 7/1/2013

Page 3 of 16

☐ The Defendant or ☐ Plaintiff is guilty of extreme cruelty.

☐ The Defendant or ☐ Plaintiff is guilty of fraudulent contract.

☐ The Defendant or ☐ Plaintiff is guilty of gross neglect of duty.

☐ The Defendant or ☐ Plaintiff is guilty of habitual drunkenness.

☐ The Defendant or ☐ Plaintiff was imprisoned in a state or federal correctional institution at the time the Complaint was filed.

☐ The Defendant or ☐ Plaintiff procured a divorce outside this state by virtue of which she or he has been released from the obligations of the marriage, while those obligations remain binding on the ☐ Plaintiff or ☐ Defendant.

JUDGMENT

Based upon the findings set out above, it is, therefore, **ORDERED, ADJUDGED and DECREED** that:

FIRST: DIVORCE GRANTED

A divorce is granted, and both parties shall be released from the obligations of their marriage except for those obligations listed below or as set out in the attached ☐ Separation Agreement

☐ Shared Parenting Plan ☐ Parenting Plan ☐ Magistrate's Decision and/or

☐ Other: _____

which is incorporated in this entry.

SECOND: PROPERTY

The parties' property shall be divided as follows:

A. The Plaintiff shall have the following items of real estate and personal property, free and clear from all claims of the Defendant, subject to any indebtedness which the Plaintiff shall pay and from which the Plaintiff shall hold the Defendant harmless: _____

_____

_____

_____

_____

_____

_____

B. The Defendant shall have the following items of real estate and personal property, free and clear from all claims of the Plaintiff, subject to any indebtedness which the Defendant shall pay and from which the Defendant shall hold the Plaintiff harmless: _____

_____

_____

_____

_____

_____

_____

Supreme Court of Ohio
Uniform Domestic Relations Form – 12
FINAL JUDGMENT FOR DIVORCE WITH CHILDREN
Approved under Ohio Civil Rule 84
Effective Date: 7/1/2013

Page 4 of 16

C. The Plaintiff is awarded the following separate property: _____

_____
_____
_____
_____
_____
_____
_____

D. The Defendant is awarded the following separate property: _____

_____
_____
_____
_____
_____
_____
_____

E. Other orders regarding property (specify): _____

_____
_____
_____

F. Within 30 days the parties will take all necessary steps to transfer legal title and possession of property and take appropriate actions to implement and effectuate the division of pensions and retirements.

G. Other orders regarding transfers: _____

_____
_____
_____

THIRD: DEBT

The Plaintiff and Defendant's debts shall be divided as follows.

A. The Plaintiff shall pay the following debts and shall hold the Defendant harmless from all claims:

_____
_____
_____
_____
_____
_____
_____

Supreme Court of Ohio
Uniform Domestic Relations Form – 12
FINAL JUDGMENT FOR DIVORCE WITH CHILDREN
Approved under Ohio Civil Rule 84
Effective Date: 7/1/2013

Page 5 of 16

B. The Defendant shall pay the following debts and shall hold the Plaintiff harmless from all claims:

_____

_____

_____

_____

_____

_____

C. Bankruptcy (select one):

☐ The Court will retain jurisdiction to enforce payment of debt obligations, in the event a party files bankruptcy, including, but not limited to, the ability to determine the debt assigned is in the nature of maintenance, necessity or support and is therefore nondischargeable in bankruptcy, and/or making a future spousal support order, regardless of the spousal support order set forth below under **FOURTH: SPOUSAL SUPPORT**.

☐ Nothing in this order shall prevent the ☐ Plaintiff and/or ☐ Defendant from being fully discharged from the debts allocated in this order in a bankruptcy proceeding except for any orders expressly for spousal support and the following debts: _____

_____

_____

_____

Neither party shall incur liabilities against the other party in the future.

FOURTH: SPOUSAL SUPPORT

A. Spousal Support Not Awarded

☐ Neither the Plaintiff nor Defendant shall pay spousal support to the other. The Court shall not retain jurisdiction, except as set forth above under **THIRD: DEBTS**.

B. Spousal Support Awarded

The ☐ Plaintiff ☐ Defendant shall pay spousal support to the ☐ Plaintiff ☐ Defendant
in the amount of $_____   per month plus 2% processing charge
commencing on _____ and due on the _____ day of the month.
This spousal support shall continue ☐ indefinitely ☐ for a period of _____

☐ The Court shall not retain jurisdiction to modify spousal support.

☐ The Court shall retain jurisdiction to modify the ☐ amount ☐ duration of the spousal support order.

C. Termination of Spousal Support

This spousal support shall terminate sooner than the above stated date upon the Plaintiff's or the

Supreme Court of Ohio
Uniform Domestic Relations Form – 12
FINAL JUDGMENT FOR DIVORCE WITH CHILDREN
Approved under Ohio Civil Rule 84
Effective Date: 7/1/2013

Page 6 of 16

Defendant's death or in the event of the following (check all that apply):

☐ The cohabitation of the person receiving support in a relationship comparable to marriage.

☐ The remarriage of the person receiving support.

☐ Other (specify): _____

_____

_____

_____

D. Method of Payment of Spousal Support:

☐ The spousal support payment, plus 2% processing charge, shall be made to the Ohio Child Support Payment Central, P. O. Box 182372, Columbus, Ohio 43218-2372, as administered through the _____ County Child Support Enforcement Agency by income withholding at his/her place of employment.

E. Deductibility of Spousal Support for All Tax Purposes (select one):

☐ The spousal support paid shall be deducted from income of the person paying the support and included by the person receiving the support.

☐ The spousal support paid shall be included in income of the person paying the support.

F. Other orders regarding spousal support (specify): _____

_____

_____

_____

G. Arrearage

☐ Any temporary spousal support arrearage will survive this judgment entry.

☐ Any temporary spousal support arrearage will not survive this judgment entry.

☐ Other: _____

_____

_____

FIFTH: NAME

☐ _____ is restored to the prior name of: _____

SIXTH: ALLOCATION OF PARENTAL RIGHTS AND RESPONSIBILITIES

A. Parental rights and responsibilities shall be allocated as follows:

☐ Father shall be the residential parent and legal custodian of the following minor child(ren):

_____

_____

_____

Supreme Court of Ohio
Uniform Domestic Relations Form – 12
FINAL JUDGMENT FOR DIVORCE WITH CHILDREN
Approved under Ohio Civil Rule 84
Effective Date: 7/1/2013

Page 7 of 16

☐ Mother shall be the residential parent and legal custodian of the following minor child(ren):

_____

_____

☐ Father ☐ Mother shall have parenting time with the minor child(ren) who is/are not residing with him/her according to the attached schedule.

☐ The parents have entered into a Shared Parenting Plan or Parenting Plan which has been filed with the Court and is adopted by the Court.

B. Relocation Notice
Pursuant to section 3109.051(G) of the Revised Code:
If the residential parent intends to move to a residence other than the residence specified in the court order, the parent shall file a notice of intent to relocate with this Court. Except as provided in divisions (G)(2), (3), and (4) of section 3109.051 of the Revised Code, the Court shall send a copy of the notice to the parent who is not the residential parent. Upon receipt of the notice, the Court, on its own motion or the motion of the parent who is not the residential parent, may schedule a hearing with notice to both parents to determine whether it is in the best interests of the child(ren) to revise the parenting time schedule for the child(ren).

☐ The obligation under this notice applies to both parents in a Shared Parenting Plan.

☐ The non-residential parent shall inform the Court and other parent in writing of changes in address and telephone, including cellular telephone number, unless otherwise provided by court order.

☐ The residential parent shall inform the Court and other parent in writing of changes in address and telephone, including cellular telephone number, unless otherwise provided by court order.

The relocation notice must be filed with the Court that granted the divorce and allocated parental rights and responsibilities (print name and address of Court): _____

_____

Other orders: _____

_____

_____

C. Records Access Notice
Pursuant to sections 3109.051(H) and 3319.321(B)(5)(a) of the Revised Code:
Subject to sections 3125.16 and 3319.321(F) of the Revised Code, the parent who is not the residential parent is entitled to access to any record that is related to the child(ren), and to

Supreme Court of Ohio
Uniform Domestic Relations Form – 12
FINAL JUDGMENT FOR DIVORCE WITH CHILDREN
Approved under Ohio Civil Rule 84
Effective Date: 7/1/2013

Page 8 of 16

which the residential parent is legally provided access under the same terms and conditions as the residential parent. Any keeper of a record who knowingly fails to comply with any record access order is in contempt of court.

Restrictions or limitations:

☐ None

☐ Restrictions or limitations to non-residential parents regarding records access are as follows:

_____

_____

_____

_____

D. Day Care Access Notice

Pursuant to section 3109.051(I) of the Revised Code:

In accordance with section 5104.11 of the Revised Code, the parent who is not the residential parent is entitled to access to any day care center that is or will be attended by the child(ren) with whom parenting time is granted, to the same extent that the residential parent is granted access to the center.

Restrictions or limitations:

☐ None

☐ Restrictions or limitations to non-residential parents regarding day care access are as follows:

_____

_____

_____

_____

E. School Activities Access Notice

Pursuant to section 3109.051(J) of the Revised Code:

Subject to section 3319.321(F), the parent who is not the residential parent is entitled to access to any student activity that is related to the child(ren) and to which the residential parent is legally provided access, under the same terms and conditions as the residential parent. Any school employee or official who knowingly fails to comply with this school activities access order is in contempt of court.

Restrictions or limitations:

☐ None

☐ Restrictions or limitations to non-residential parents regarding school activities access are as follows: _____

_____

_____

Supreme Court of Ohio
Uniform Domestic Relations Form – 12
FINAL JUDGMENT FOR DIVORCE WITH CHILDREN
Approved under Ohio Civil Rule 84
Effective Date: 7/1/2013

Page 9 of 16

SEVENTH: HEALTH INSURANCE COVERAGE

As required by law, the parties have completed a Child Support Worksheet, which is attached to and incorporated in this Agreement.

Select one:

A. ☐ Health Insurance Coverage Available to at Least One Parent

1. Private health insurance coverage is accessible and reasonable in cost through a group policy, contract, or plan to: ☐ Father ☐ Mother ☐ Both parents. ☐ Father ☐ Mother ☐ Both parents shall provide private health insurance coverage for the benefit of the child(ren).

2. If both parents are ordered to provide private health insurance coverage for the benefit of the child(ren), ☐ Father's ☐ Mother's health insurance plan shall be considered the primary health insurance plan for the child(ren).

3. The parent required to provide private health insurance coverage shall provide proof of insurance to the _____ County Child Support Enforcement Agency (CSEA) and the other parent.

4. Both parents shall cooperate in the preparation of insurance forms to obtain reimbursement or payment of expenses, as applicable. A copy of medical bills must be submitted to the party holding the insurance and responsible for payment or the other parent within 30 days of receipt.

5. Should the health insurance coverage be cancelled for any reason, the parent ordered to maintain insurance shall immediately notify the other parent and take immediate steps to obtain replacement coverage. Unless the cancellation was intentional, the uncovered expenses shall be paid as provided above. If the cancellation was intentionally caused by the parent ordered to maintain insurance coverage, that parent shall be responsible for all medical expenses that would have been covered had the insurance been in effect.

B. ☐ Health Insurance Coverage Unavailable to Either Parent

1. Private health insurance coverage is **not** accessible and reasonable in cost through a group policy, contract, or plan to either parent.

2. If private health insurance coverage becomes available to either parent at reasonable cost, he/she will immediately obtain the insurance, notify the other parent and the _____ County CSEA, and submit to the other parent proof of insurance, insurance forms, and an insurance card. The CSEA shall determine whether the cost of the insurance is of sufficient amount to justify an administrative review of the amount of child support payable. In the event an administrative review is warranted, one shall be conducted.

C. Division of Uninsured Expenses

1. The cost of any uninsured medical expenses, incurred by or on the behalf of the child(ren) not paid by a health insurance plan, and exceeding $100 per child per year, including

Supreme Court of Ohio
Uniform Domestic Relations Form – 12
FINAL JUDGMENT FOR DIVORCE WITH CHILDREN
Approved under Ohio Civil Rule 84
Effective Date: 7/1/2013

Page 10 of 16

co-payments and deductibles, shall be paid by the parents as follows: _____

_____

_____

_____

The first $100 per child per year of uninsured expenses shall be paid by the Mother for the following child(ren): _____

_____

The first $100 per child per year of uninsured expenses shall be paid by the Father for the following child(ren): _____

_____

_____

Other orders regarding uninsured medical expenses: _____

_____

_____

2. The parent incurring the expenses shall provide the other parent the original or copies of all medical bills, and Explanation of Benefits (EOB), if available, within 30 days of the date on the bill or EOB, whichever is later, absent extraordinary circumstances. The other parent shall, within 30 days of receipt of the bill, reimburse the parent incurring the expenses or pay directly to the health care provider, that parent's percentage share of the bill as shown above.

D. Other Important Information about Medical Records and Expenses
1. Each party shall have access to all medical records of the child(ren) as provided by law.

2. The term "medical expense" or "medical records" shall include but not be limited to medical, dental, orthodontic, optical, surgical, hospital, major medical, psychological, psychiatric, outpatient, doctor, therapy, counseling, prosthetic, and/or all other expenses/records including preventative health care expenses/records related to the treatment of the human body and mind.

EIGHTH: CHILD SUPPORT

A completed Child Support Work Sheet is attached and incorporated in this Decree.

A. Child Support with Private Health Insurance Coverage
When private health insurance coverage is being provided for the child(ren), ☐ Father ☐ Mother, the Obligor, shall pay child support in the amount of $ _____ per child per month, for _____ (number) child(ren) for a total of $ _____ per month.

B. Child Support without Private Health Insurance Coverage
When private health insurance is **not** available for child(ren), ☐ Father ☐ Mother, the Obligor, shall pay child support in the amount of $ _____ per child per month, and $ _____ per child per month as cash medical support.

Supreme Court of Ohio
Uniform Domestic Relations Form – 12
FINAL JUDGMENT FOR DIVORCE WITH CHILDREN
Approved under Ohio Civil Rule 84
Effective Date: 7/1/2013

Page 11 of 16

The total of child support and cash medical support for _____ (number) child(ren) is $ _____ per month.

C. Child Support Payment
Child support payment (including cash medical support, if any) plus a 2% processing charge shall commence on _____ and shall be paid to the Ohio Child Support Payment Center, P. O. Box 182372, Columbus, Ohio 43218-2372, as administered through the _____ County Child Support Enforcement Agency (CSEA) by income withholding at Obligor's place of employment or from nonexempt funds on deposit at a financial institution.

D. Deviation of Child Support Amount
The child support calculated pursuant to the child support schedule $ _____ is unjust or inappropriate and is not in the best interest of the minor child(ren) for the following reason(s), as provided in R.C. 3119.22, 3119.23, and 3119.24, and shall be adjusted as follows:

_____

_____

_____

E. Duration of Child Support
The child support order will terminate upon the child's 18th birthday unless one of the following circumstances applies:
- The child is mentally or physically disabled and is incapable of supporting or maintaining himself or herself.
- The parents have agreed to continue child support beyond the date it would otherwise terminate.
- The child continuously attends a recognized and accredited high school on a full-time basis so long as the child has not, as yet, reached the age of 19 years old. (Under these circumstances, child support will end at the time the child ceases to attend a recognized and accredited high school on a full-time basis or when he or she reaches the age of 19, whichever occurs first.)

This Support Order will remain in effect during seasonal vacation periods until the order terminates.

☐ The Court finds by agreement that child support will extend beyond the time when it would otherwise end. The terms and conditions of that agreement are as follows: _____

_____

_____

☐ The Court finds the parties have (a) child(ren) who is/are mentally or physically disabled and incapable of supporting or maintaining themselves, and that child support will extend beyond the time when it would otherwise end. The name of the child and the nature of the mental or physical disability are as follows: _____

Supreme Court of Ohio
Uniform Domestic Relations Form – 12
FINAL JUDGMENT FOR DIVORCE WITH CHILDREN
Approved under Ohio Civil Rule 84
Effective Date: 7/1/2013

Page 12 of 16

F. Important Child Support Orders and Information
Obligee must immediately notify and Obligor may notify the CSEA of any reason for which the support order should terminate. A willful failure to notify the CSEA as required is contempt of court. The following are reasons for termination of the Order:
- Child's attainment of the age of majority if the child no longer attends an accredited high school on a full-time basis and the support order does not provide for the duty of support to continue past the age of majority
- Child stops attending an accredited high school on a full-time basis after attaining the age of majority
- Child's death
- Child's marriage
- Child's emancipation
- Child's enlistment in the Armed Services
- Child's deportation
- Change of legal custody of the child

All support payments must be made through the CSEA or the office of child support in the Ohio Department of Job and Family Services (Child Support Payment Central). Any payment of money not made through the CSEA will be considered a gift, unless the payment is made to discharge an obligation other than support.

All support under this Order shall be withheld or deducted from the income or assets of the Obligor pursuant to a withholding or deduction notice or appropriate order issued in accordance with Chapters 3119., 3121., 3123., and 3125. of the Revised Code or a withdrawal directive issued pursuant to sections 3123.24 to 3123.38 of the Revised Code and shall be forwarded to the Obligee in accordance with Chapters 3119., 3121., 3123., and 3125. of the Revised Code.

The Obligor and/or Obligee required under this Order to provide private health insurance coverage for the child(ren) is also required to provide the other party within 30 days after the issuance of the Order, the following:
- Information regarding the benefits, limitations, and exclusions of the health insurance coverage
- Copies of any insurance form necessary to receive reimbursement, payment, or other benefits under the coverage
- A copy of any necessary health insurance cards

The Health Plan Administrator that provides the private health insurance coverage for the child(ren) may continue making payment for medical, optical, hospital, dental, or prescription services directly to any health care provider in accordance with the applicable private health insurance policy, contract, or plan.

Supreme Court of Ohio
Uniform Domestic Relations Form – 12
FINAL JUDGMENT FOR DIVORCE WITH CHILDREN
Approved under Ohio Civil Rule 84
Effective Date: 7/1/2013

Page 13 of 16

The Obligor and/or Obligee required to provide private health insurance for the child(ren) must designate said child(ren) as dependents under any private health insurance policy, contract, or plan for which the person contracts.

The employer of the person required to provide private health insurance coverage is required to release to the other parent, any person subject to an order issued under section 3109.19 of the Revised Code, or the CSEA, upon written request, any necessary information regarding health insurance coverage, including the name and address of the health plan administrator and any policy, contract, or plan number, and the employer will otherwise comply with all orders and notices issued.

If the person required to obtain private health insurance coverage for the child(ren) subject to this Support Order obtains new employment, the agency shall comply with the requirements of section 3119.34 of the Revised Code, which may result in the issuance of a notice requiring the new employer to take whatever action is necessary to enroll the child(ren) in private health insurance coverage provided by the new employer.

Upon receipt of notice by the CSEA that private health insurance coverage is not available at a reasonable cost, cash medical support shall be paid in the amount as determined by the child support computation worksheets in section 3119.022 or 3119.023 of the Revised Code, as applicable. The CSEA may change the financial obligations of the parties to pay child support in accordance with the terms of the court or administrative order and cash medical support without a hearing or additional notice to the parties.

An Obligor that is in arrears in his/her child support obligation is subject to having any federal, state and/or local income tax refund to which the Obligor may be entitled forwarded to the CSEA for payment toward these arrears. Such refunds will continue to be forwarded to the CSEA for payment until all arrears owed are paid in full. If the Obligor is married and files a joint tax return, the Obligor's spouse may contact the CSEA about filing an "Injured Spouse" claim after the Obligor is notified by the Internal Revenue Service that his/her refund is being forwarded to the CSEA.

Pursuant to section 3121.29 of the Revised Code, the parties are notified as follows:
EACH PARTY TO THIS SUPPORT ORDER MUST NOTIFY THE CHILD SUPPORT AGENCY IN WRITING OF HIS OR HER CURRENT MAILING ADDRESS, CURRENT RESIDENCE ADDRESS, CURRENT RESIDENCE TELEPHONE NUMBER, CURRENT DRIVER'S LICENSE NUMBER AND OF ANY CHANGES IN THAT INFORMATION. EACH PARTY MUST NOTIFY THE AGENCY OF ALL CHANGES UNTIL FURTHER NOTICE FROM THE COURT. IF YOU ARE THE OBLIGOR UNDER A CHILD SUPPORT ORDER AND YOU FAIL TO MAKE THE REQUIRED NOTIFICATIONS, YOU MAY BE FINED UP TO $50.00 FOR A FIRST OFFENSE, $100.00 FOR A SECOND OFFENSE, AND $500.00 FOR EACH SUBSEQUENT OFFENSE. IF YOU ARE AN OBLIGOR OR OBLIGEE UNDER ANY SUPPORT ORDER AND YOU

Supreme Court of Ohio
Uniform Domestic Relations Form – 12
FINAL JUDGMENT FOR DIVORCE WITH CHILDREN
Approved under Ohio Civil Rule 84
Effective Date: 7/1/2013

Page 14 of 16

WILLFULLY FAIL TO MAKE THE REQUIRED NOTIFICATIONS YOU MAY BE SUBJECTED TO FINES OF UP TO $1,000.00 AND IMPRISONMENT FOR NOT MORE THAN 90 DAYS.

IF YOU ARE AN OBLIGOR AND YOU FAIL TO MAKE THE REQUIRED NOTIFICATIONS, YOU MAY NOT RECEIVE NOTICE OF THE FOLLOWING ENFORCEMENT ACTIONS AGAINST YOU: IMPOSITION OF LIENS AGAINST YOUR PROPERTY; LOSS OF YOUR PROFESSIONAL OR OCCUPATIONAL LICENSE, DRIVER'S LICENSE, OR RECREATIONAL LICENSE; WITHHOLDING FROM YOUR INCOME; ACCESS RESTRICTIONS AND DEDUCTIONS FROM YOUR ACCOUNTS IN FINANCIAL INSTITUTIONS; AND ANY OTHER ACTION PERMITTED BY LAW TO OBTAIN MONEY FROM YOU AND TO SATISFY YOUR SUPPORT OBLIGATION.

G.   Payment shall be made in accordance with Chapter 3121. of the Revised Code.

H.   Arrearage
☐ Any temporary child support arrearage will survive this judgment entry.
☐ Any temporary child support arrearage will not survive this judgment entry.
☐ Other: _____
_____
_____

NINTH: TAX EXEMPTION
Income tax dependency exemptions (check all that apply):
A.   ☐ The Father shall be entitled to claim the following minor child(ren) for all tax purposes for
☐ even-numbered tax years ☐ odd-numbered tax years ☐ all eligible tax years, so long as he is substantially current in any child support he is required to pay as of December 31 of the tax year in question: _____

☐ The Mother shall be entitled to claim the following minor child(ren) for all tax purposes for
☐ even-numbered tax years ☐ odd-numbered tax years ☐ all eligible tax years, so long as she is substantially current in any child support she is required to pay as of December 31 of the tax year in question: _____

B.   ☐ Other orders regarding tax exemptions (specify): _____
_____
_____
_____

If a non-residential parent is entitled to claim the child(ren), the residential parent is required to execute and deliver Internal Revenue Service Form 8332, or its successor, together with any other required forms as set out in section 152 of the Internal Revenue Code, as amended, on or before February 15th of the year following the tax year in question, to allow the non-residential parent to

Supreme Court of Ohio
Uniform Domestic Relations Form – 12
FINAL JUDGMENT FOR DIVORCE WITH CHILDREN
Approved under Ohio Civil Rule 84
Effective Date: 7/1/2013

Page 15 of 16

claim the minor child(ren).

TENTH: OTHER ORDERS

_____

_____

ELEVENTH: COURT COSTS

Court costs shall be (select one):

☐ Taxed to the deposit. Court costs due above the deposit shall be paid as follows: _____

_____

☐ Other (specify): _____

_____

TWELFTH: CLERK OF COURTS

The Clerk of Courts shall provide:

☐ a certified copy to: _____

☐ a file stamped copy to: _____

NOTICE. Pursuant to Civil Rule 58(B), the Clerk is directed to serve upon the parties a notice of the filing of this Judgment Entry and of the date of entry upon the Journal.

_____   _____
Date   JUDGE

Supreme Court of Ohio
Uniform Domestic Relations Form – 12
FINAL JUDGMENT FOR DIVORCE WITH CHILDREN
Approved under Ohio Civil Rule 84
Effective Date: 7/1/2013

Page 16 of 16

IN THE COURT OF COMMON PLEAS

_____ **Division**

_____ **COUNTY, OHIO**

_____ :
Name   :   Case No. _____
                                  :
_____ :
Street Address   :
                                  :
_____ :   Judge _____
City, State and Zip Code   :
                        Plaintiff :
vs.   :   Magistrate _____
                                  :
_____ :
Name   :
                                  :
_____ :
Street Address   :
                                  :
_____ :
City, State and Zip Code   :
                        Defendant :

JUDGMENT ENTRY CONVERTING INTEREST IN REAL ESTATE

Pursuant to the Judgment Entry filed on _____ , the marriage of the parties, _____
and _____ , was terminated.

Pursuant to the Judgment Entry, it is ORDERED that _____ is divested of all
rights, title, and interest in the real estate as set forth in the legal description, including deed reference and parcel
number attached.

It is further ORDERED that _____ is vested with all rights, title, and interest of the
real estate attached. The Auditor and Recorder of _____ County are ORDERED to accept this
Entry as transferral of such interest and transfer the above real estate on its books and records. The filing of this
Entry with the Recorder and Auditor will effectuate the conveyance of the real estate interest.

Court costs shall be (select one):

☐ Taxed to the deposit. Court costs due above the deposit shall be paid as follows: _____

_____

☐ Other (specify): _____

_____
JUDGE

Supreme Court of Ohio
Uniform Domestic Relations Form – 13
JUDGMENT ENTRY CONVERTING INTEREST IN REAL ESTATE
Approved under Ohio Civil Rule 84
Effective Date: 7/1/2013

IN THE COURT OF COMMON PLEAS

_____ **Division**

_____ **COUNTY, OHIO**

_____
Name

:

: Case No. _____

:

_____
Street Address

:

:

_____
City, State and Zip Code
        Petitioner

: Judge _____

:

: Magistrate _____

and

:

:

_____
Name

:

:

_____
Street Address

:

:

_____
City, State and Zip Code
        Petitioner

:

:

Instructions: This form is used to request ending the marriage when the parties have agreed on all aspects of the termination, including the division of real estate, personal property, debts, spousal support, and, if there is/are (a) child(ren), allocation of parental rights and responsibilities (custody), parenting time (companionship and visitation) and child support. A Separation Agreement (Uniform Domestic Relations Form 16) and either a Shared Parenting Plan (Uniform Domestic Relations Form 17) or a Parenting Plan (Uniform Domestic Relations Form 18), if applicable, must be filed with this Petition.

PETITION FOR DISSOLUTION OF MARRIAGE AND
WAIVER OF SERVICE OF SUMMONS ☐ WITH CHILDREN ☐ WITHOUT CHILDREN

The Petitioners, Husband, _____ (name) and

Wife, _____ (name), say as follows:

1. The ☐ Husband ☐ Wife ☐ Both parties has/have been (a) resident(s) of the State of Ohio for at least six months.

2. The ☐ Husband ☐ Wife ☐ Both parties has/have been (a) resident(s) of _____ County for at least 90 days immediately before the filing of this Petition.

3. The Petitioners were married to one another on _____ (date of marriage) in _____ (city or county, and state).

Supreme Court of Ohio
Uniform Domestic Relations Form – 14
PETITION FOR DISSOLUTION OF MARRIAGE AND WAIVER OF SERVICE OF SUMMONS
Approved under Ohio Civil Rule 84
Effective Date: 7/1/2013

Page 1 of 3

4. Check all that apply:
   ☐ The Wife is not pregnant.
   ☐ The Wife is pregnant and the approximate due date is _____ .
   ☐ No children were born from or adopted during this marriage or relationship.
   ☐ All children born from or adopted during this marriage or relationship are adults and not
   mentally or physically disabled child(ren) incapable of supporting or maintaining themselves.
   ☐ The Petitioners are the parents of _____ (number) child(ren) born from or adopted
   during this marriage or relationship. Of the child(ren), _____ (number) is/are
   emancipated adult(s) and not under any disability. The following _____ (number) of
   child(ren) is/are minor child(ren) and/or mentally or physically disabled and incapable of
   supporting or maintaining themselves (name and date of birth of each child):

Name of Child	Date of Birth
_____	_____
_____	_____
_____	_____

   ☐ Husband is not the biological father of the following child(ren) who was/were born during
   the marriage (name and date of birth of each child): _____
   _____
   _____
   _____

5. ☐ The following child(ren) of this marriage or relationship is/are subject to a custody or parenting
   order in a different Court proceeding (name of each child and the Court that issued the custody
   or parenting order): _____
   _____
   _____

6. ☐ The Petitioners have entered into a Separation Agreement which is attached.
   If Petitioners have (a) minor child(ren) (select one):
   ☐ The Petitioners have agreed to a Parenting Plan which is attached.
   ☐ The Petitioners have agreed to a Shared Parenting Plan which is attached.

7. The Petitioners further say as follows:
   ☐ We are both over 18 years of age.
   ☐ We are not under any legal disability.
   ☐ We waive all rights to receive summons for the dissolution action through the Clerk of Courts.
   ☐ We have read this Petition and voluntarily ask this Court to dissolve the marriage.

8. ☐ The Petitioner _____ requests to be restored
   to the former name of: _____

Supreme Court of Ohio
Uniform Domestic Relations Form – 14
PETITION FOR DISSOLUTION OF MARRIAGE AND WAIVER OF SERVICE OF SUMMONS
Approved under Ohio Civil Rule 84
Effective Date: 7/1/2013

Page 2 of 3

The Petitioners request the Court for a Decree of Dissolution of their marriage pursuant to the terms of the Separation Agreement and the Shared Parenting Plan or Parenting Plan, if there is/are (a) child(ren).

_____   _____
Your Signature (Husband)   Your Signature (Wife)

_____   _____
Telephone number at which the Court may reach   Telephone number at which the Court may reach
you or at which messages may be left for you   you or at which messages may be left for you

IN THE COURT OF COMMON PLEAS

_____ **Division**

_____ **COUNTY, OHIO**

_____ :	
Petitioner :	Case No. _____
_____ :	
Street Address :	
_____ :	Judge _____
City, State and Zip Code :	
:	
and :	Magistrate _____
:	
_____ :	
Petitioner :	
_____ :	
Street Address :	
_____ :	
City, State and Zip Code :	

JUDGMENT ENTRY OF DISSOLUTION OF MARRIAGE
☐ WITH CHILDREN ☐ WITHOUT CHILDREN

This matter came on for hearing on _____ before ☐ Judge ☐ Magistrate

_____ , upon the Petition for Dissolution of Marriage filed on _____ .

Present at the hearing were the following persons: _____

_____

FINDINGS

1. At the time of the filing of the Petition, the ☐ Husband ☐ Wife ☐ Both parties was/were (a) resident(s) of the State of Ohio for at least six months.

2. The ☐ Husband ☐ Wife ☐ Both parties was/were (a) resident(s) of _____ County for at least 90 days immediately before the filing of the Petition.

3. The parties were married to one another on _____ (date of marriage) in _____ (city or county, and state).

Supreme Court of Ohio
Uniform Domestic Relations Form – 15
JUDGMENT ENTRY OF DISSOLUTION OF MARRIAGE
Approved under Ohio Civil Rule 84
Effective Date: 7/1/2013

Page 1 of 3

4. Check all that apply:

☐ The Wife is not pregnant.

☐ The Wife is pregnant and the approximate due date is: _____ .

☐ No children were born from or adopted during this marriage or relationship.

☐ All children born from or adopted during this marriage or relationship are adults and not mentally or physically disabled child(ren) incapable of supporting or maintaining themselves.

☐ The parties are parents of _____ (number) child(ren) born from or adopted during the marriage or relationship. Of the child(ren), _____ (number) is/are now emancipated adult(s) and not under any disability. The following _____ (number) child(ren) is/are minor child(ren) and/or mentally or physically disabled and incapable of supporting or maintaining themselves (name and date of birth of each child):

Name of Child	Date of Birth
_____	_____
_____	_____
_____	_____

☐ Husband is not the biological father of the following child(ren) who was/were born during the marriage (name and date of birth of each child): _____

_____

_____

5. ☐ The following child(ren) of this marriage or relationship is/are subject to a custody or parenting order in a different Court proceeding (name of each child with the Court that has issued the custody or parenting order): _____

_____

6. Petitioner _____ requests to be restored to the former name of:

_____

7. The parties personally appeared before this Court, and more than 30 and less than 90 days have elapsed after the filing of the Petition.

8. Upon examination under oath, the parties acknowledge that they have agreed on the ☐ Shared Parenting Plan or ☐ Parenting Plan for their child(ren), which they believe to be in their best interests. The Court's adoption of the Plan is in the best interests of the child(ren).

9. Upon examination under oath, the parties acknowledge that they voluntarily entered into a Separation Agreement, attached and incorporated in the Petition, ☐ as modified on _____ and the parties are satisfied with the terms of the Separation Agreement and Plan and fully understand the same. Each Petitioner desires to have the marriage dissolved, and the Separation Agreement approved by the Court.

Supreme Court of Ohio
Uniform Domestic Relations Form – 15
JUDGMENT ENTRY OF DISSOLUTION OF MARRIAGE
Approved under Ohio Civil Rule 84
Effective Date: 7/1/2013

Page 2 of 3

JUDGMENT

Based upon the findings set out above, it is, therefore, **ORDERED, ADJUDGED and DECREED** that:

FIRST: DISSOLUTION GRANTED

The dissolution of marriage is granted. The Court approves the ☐ Separation Agreement
☐ Amended Separation Agreement ☐ Shared Parenting Plan ☐ Amended Shared Parenting Plan or
☐ Parenting Plan ☐ Amended Parenting Plan as submitted and releases the parties from the obligations of
their marriage except as set out in the attached ☐ Agreement and ☐ Plan, which is incorporated in this entry.

The parties shall fulfill each and every obligation imposed by the ☐ Agreement and ☐ Plan as submitted
and modified, if applicable. The Plan is approved and this entry shall constitute a Parenting Decree
under R.C. 3109.04(D).

☐ SECOND: NAME

Petitioner _____ is restored to the

prior name of: _____

☐ THIRD: OTHER _____

_____

FOURTH: COURT COSTS

Court costs shall be (select one):

☐ Taxed to the deposit. Court costs due above the deposit shall be paid as follows: _____

_____

☐ Other (specify): _____

_____

_____
JUDGE

_____   _____
Your Signature (Husband)   Your Signature (Wife)

_____   _____
Husband's Attorney   Wife's Attorney

Supreme Court of Ohio
Uniform Domestic Relations Form – 15
JUDGMENT ENTRY OF DISSOLUTION OF MARRIAGE
Approved under Ohio Civil Rule 84
Effective Date: 7/1/2013

Page 3 of 3

IN THE COURT OF COMMON PLEAS
Division
_____ COUNTY, OHIO

_____	:	
Plaintiff/Petitioner	:	Case No. _____
_____	:	
Street Address	:	
_____	:	Judge _____
City, State and Zip Code	:	
	:	
and	:	Magistrate _____
	:	
_____	:	
Plaintiff/Petitioner	:	
_____	:	
Street Address	:	
_____	:	
City, State and Zip Code	:	

Instructions: This form is used to present an agreement to the Court regarding spousal support, the division of personal property, real estate, and debts resulting from the termination of marriage. If the parties have any minor child(ren), child(ren) with disabilities, or the Wife is pregnant, a Shared Parenting Plan (Uniform Domestic Relations Form 17) or Parenting Plan (Uniform Domestic Relations Form 18) must be attached.

SEPARATION AGREEMENT

The parties, _____ , Husband, and
_____ , Wife, state the following.

1. The parties were married to one another on _____ (date of marriage)
   in _____ (city or county, and state), and request
   that the termination of marriage be the date ☐ of final hearing or ☐ as specified: _____

2. The parties intend to live separate and apart.

3. Each party has made full and complete disclosure to the other of all marital property, separate property, and any other assets, debts, income, and expenses.

4. Neither party has knowledge of any other property and debts of any kind in which either party has an interest.

Supreme Court of Ohio
Uniform Domestic Relations Form – 16
SEPARATION AGREEMENT
Approved under Ohio Civil Rule 84
Effective Date: 7/1/2013

Page 1 of 13

5.   Each party has had the opportunity to value and verify all marital property, separate property, and debts.

6.   A party's willful failure to disclose may result in the Court awarding the other party three times the value of the property, assets, income, or expenses that were not disclosed by the other party.

7.   This Agreement addresses spousal support, property, and debt division.

8.   This written Agreement is the complete agreement of the parties.

9.   There are no other representations, agreements, statements, or prior writings that shall have any effect on this Agreement.

10.   Each party fully understands the Agreement and has knowingly and voluntarily signed the Agreement.

11.   No change to the terms of this Agreement shall be valid unless in writing and knowingly and voluntarily signed by both parties.

The parties agree as follows:

FIRST: SEPARATION
The parties shall live separate and apart. Neither party shall interfere with the activities, personal life, or privacy of the other; harass the other, nor engage in any conduct calculated to restrain, embarrass, injure, or hinder the other in any way.

SECOND: PROPERTY
Marital property as defined in R.C. 3105.171 is property owned by either or both spouses and property in which either spouse has an interest in the property. Separate property as defined in R.C. 3105.171 is real or personal property that was inherited, acquired by one spouse prior to the date of marriage, acquired after a decree of legal separation under R.C. 3107.17, excluded by a valid antenuptial agreement, compensation for personal injury, except for loss of marital earnings and compensation for expenses paid from marital assets, or any gift of property that was given to only one spouse. If separate property is involved, the owner should consider consulting an attorney. The party not receiving the separate property waives all interest in the property.

A.   Real Estate (select one):
Real estate includes lands, mortgaged properties, buildings, fixtures attached to buildings, attached structures (for example, garage, in-ground pool), condominiums, time shares, mobile homes, natural condition stakes (for example, gas, oil, mineral rights, existing soil, including trees and landscape), and inheritance rights in real estate. The property's legal description is on the deed or mortgage papers.
1.   ☐ The parties do not own any real estate.

Supreme Court of Ohio
Uniform Domestic Relations Form – 16
SEPARATION AGREEMENT
Approved under Ohio Civil Rule 84
Effective Date: 7/1/2013

Page 2 of 13

2. Marital Real Estate
   ☐ The parties owned real estate in one or both of their names and agree to award it as follows. A legal description of the property must be attached. (Attach a copy of the property's deed or mortgage papers.)

Location of Property	Awarded to
_____	_____
_____	_____
_____	_____

3. ☐ Each party shall pay and hold the other harmless from any debt owing on real estate he/she receives unless otherwise stated in this Agreement.

4. ☐ Other debt payment arrangements, including refinancing: _____
   _____
   _____
   _____

If the real estate is not in the name of the party to whom it is awarded, the parties shall make arrangements to transfer the property to the proper party as soon as possible.

B. Titled Vehicles (select one):
Titled vehicles include boats, trailers, automobiles, motorcycles, trucks, mobile homes, golf carts, motor scooters, sport utility vehicles (SUV), recreational vehicles (RV), all purpose vehicles (APV). Provide vehicle model, make, year, and serial number for all titled vehicle(s) that will be transferred.

1. ☐ The parties do not own any titled vehicle(s) in either party's name.

2. ☐ The titled vehicle(s) has/have already been divided or transferred, including all rights, title and interest in the vehicle(s) and is/are in the possession of the proper party. The parties are satisfied with the division.

3. ☐ The parties own titled vehicle(s) which has/have not been divided or transferred.
   Husband shall receive the following vehicle(s), free and clear of any claims from the Wife:
   _____
   _____
   _____

   and Wife shall receive the following vehicle(s), free and clear of any claims of the Husband:
   _____
   _____
   _____

4. Each party shall pay for and hold the other harmless from any debt owing on the titled vehicle(s) he/she receives unless otherwise stated in this Agreement.

Supreme Court of Ohio
Uniform Domestic Relations Form – 16
SEPARATION AGREEMENT
Approved under Ohio Civil Rule 84
Effective Date: 7/1/2013

Page 3 of 13

5. Other debt payment arrangements regarding titled vehicle(s): _____

_____

_____

_____

If the vehicle's title is not in the name of the party to whom the vehicle is awarded, the current title holder shall transfer that title to the proper party as soon as the title is available for transfer. If title cannot be transferred immediately to the party to whom the vehicle is awarded, the party holding the title shall make the following arrangements to obtain and pay for license plates, registration, and insurance: _____

_____

_____

_____

C. Household Goods and Personal Property (select one):

Household goods and personal property include appliances, tools, air conditioner window units, doghouses, lawn mowers, riding lawn mowers, above ground pools, safety deposit boxes, jewelry, furniture, refrigerators, silverware, collections, china, and books.

1. ☐ The household goods and personal property are already divided and in the possession of the proper party. The parties are satisfied with the division.

2. ☐ The parties have household goods and personal property which have not been divided. Husband shall have the following: _____

_____

_____

_____

and Wife shall have the following: _____

_____

_____

_____

3. Delivery or pick-up of household goods and personal property shall be as follows: _____

_____

_____

_____

4. Each party shall pay for and hold the other harmless from any debt owing on the household goods and personal property he/she receives unless otherwise stated in this Agreement.

5. Other debt arrangements regarding household goods and personal property: _____

_____

Supreme Court of Ohio
Uniform Domestic Relations Form – 16
SEPARATION AGREEMENT
Approved under Ohio Civil Rule 84
Effective Date: 7/1/2013

Page 4 of 13

_____
_____
_____

The parties shall make arrangements to transfer possession of the household goods and personal property to the proper party as soon as possible.

D.   Financial Accounts (select one):
Financial accounts include checking, savings, certificates of deposit, money market accounts, medical or health savings accounts, education or college saving plans (for example, 529 Plan) and trusts.

1.   ☐ The parties do not have any financial accounts.

2.   ☐ The parties have financial accounts and agree the accounts are already divided and in the name of the proper party. The parties are satisfied with the division.

3.   ☐ The parties have financial accounts which are not divided.
     Husband shall receive the following:

Institution	**Current Name(s) on Account**	**Type of Account**
		☐ checking ☐ saving
		☐ other: _____
_____	_____	☐ checking ☐ saving
		☐ other: _____
_____	_____	☐ checking ☐ saving
		☐ other: _____
_____	_____	

and Wife shall receive the following:

Institution	**Current Name(s) on Account**	**Type of Account**
		☐ checking ☐ saving
		☐ other: _____
_____	_____	☐ checking ☐ saving
		☐ other: _____
_____	_____	☐ checking ☐ saving
		☐ other: _____
_____	_____	

4.   Each party shall pay for and hold the other harmless from any debt owing on the financial accounts he/she receives unless otherwise stated in this Agreement.

5.   Other arrangements regarding financial accounts: _____
_____

The parties shall make arrangements to transfer the financial accounts to the proper party as soon as possible.

E. Stocks, Bonds, Securities, and Mutual Funds (select one):

1. ☐ The parties do not have any stocks, bonds, securities, or mutual funds.

2. ☐ One or both parties has/have stocks, bonds, securities, or mutual funds which are already divided and in the name of the proper party. The parties are satisfied with the division.

3. ☐ One or both parties has/have stocks, bonds, securities, or mutual funds which are not divided. Husband shall receive the following:

Institution	Current Name(s) on Account	Number of Shares

and Wife shall receive the following:

Institution	Current Name(s) on Account	Number of Shares

4. Each party shall pay for and hold the other harmless from any debt owing on the stocks, bonds, securities, or mutual funds he/she receives unless otherwise stated in this Agreement.

5. Other arrangements regarding the stocks, bonds, securities, or mutual funds:

_____

_____

_____

The parties shall make arrangements to sell or transfer the stocks, bonds, securities, or mutual funds to the proper party as soon as possible.

F. Business Interests (select one):

1. ☐ The parties do not have any business interests.

2. ☐ One or both parties has/have business interests and which are already divided and in the name of the proper party. The parties are satisfied with the division.

Supreme Court of Ohio
Uniform Domestic Relations Form – 16
SEPARATION AGREEMENT
Approved under Ohio Civil Rule 84
Effective Date: 7/1/2013

Page 6 of 13

3. ☐ One or both parties has/have business interests which have not been divided.
   Husband shall receive the following:

Name of Business	Ownership Interest
_____	_____
_____	_____
_____	_____

   and Wife shall receive the following:

Name of Business	Ownership Interest
_____	_____
_____	_____
_____	_____
_____	_____

4. Each party shall pay for and hold the other harmless from any debt owing on the business interests he/she receives unless otherwise stated in this Agreement.

5. Other arrangements regarding business interests: _____

   _____

   _____

   _____

The parties shall make arrangements to transfer the business interests to the proper party as soon as possible.

G. Pension, Profit Sharing, IRA, 401(k), and Other Retirement Plans (select one):

1. ☐ The parties do not have any pension, profit sharing, IRA, 401(k), or other retirement plans.

2. ☐ The pension(s), profit sharing, IRA, 401(k), or other retirement plans are already divided and in the proper party's name. The parties are satisfied with the division.

3. ☐ The parties have pension(s), profit sharing, IRA, 401(k), or other retirement plans which have not been divided.
   Husband shall receive the following:

Company	Name(s) on Plan	Amount/Share
_____	_____	_____
_____	_____	_____
_____	_____	_____
_____	_____	_____

Supreme Court of Ohio
Uniform Domestic Relations Form – 16
SEPARATION AGREEMENT
Approved under Ohio Civil Rule 84
Effective Date: 7/1/2013

Page 7 of 13

and Wife shall receive the following:

Company	Name(s) on Plan	Amount/Share
_____	_____	_____
_____	_____	_____
_____	_____	_____
_____	_____	_____

4. Each party shall pay for and hold the other harmless from any debt owing on the pension(s), profit sharing, IRA, 401(k), or other retirement plans he/she receives unless otherwise stated in this Agreement.

5. Other arrangements regarding pension(s), profit sharing, IRA, 401(k), or other retirement plans:

_____

_____

_____

The parties shall make arrangements to transfer interest in the pension(s), profit sharing, IRA, 401(k), or other retirement plans to the proper party as soon as possible.

A Qualified Domestic Relations Order (QDRO) or Division of Property Order (DOPO) may be necessary to divide some of these assets. If so, the QDRO and DOPO will be prepared by:

_____

and submitted to the Court within 90 days after the final hearing. Expenses of preparation shall be paid as follows: _____

_____

_____

The Court retains jurisdiction to interpret and enforce the terms of the documents of transfer.

H. Life Insurance Policies (select one):
1. ☐ The parties do not have any life insurance policy(ies) with a cash value.

2. ☐ The parties have life insurance policy(ies) and agree the cash value of all life insurance policy(ies) has/have already been divided. The parties are satisfied with the division.

3. ☐ The parties' life insurance policy(ies) has/have not been divided.
   Husband shall receive the following policy(ies), free and clear of any claims of the Wife: _____

_____

_____

_____

Supreme Court of Ohio
Uniform Domestic Relations Form – 16
SEPARATION AGREEMENT
Approved under Ohio Civil Rule 84
Effective Date: 7/1/2013

Page 8 of 13

and Wife shall receive the following policy(ies), free and clear of any claims of the Husband:

_____

_____

_____

4. Each party shall pay for and hold the other harmless from any debt owing on the life insurance policy(ies) he/she receives unless otherwise stated in this Agreement.

5. Other arrangements regarding life insurance policy(ies): _____

_____

_____

_____

The parties shall make arrangements to transfer interest in the life insurance policy(ies) to the proper party as soon as possible.

I. Other Property (select one):

1. ☐ The parties do not have any other property.

2. ☐ The property shall be awarded as follows:

Description of Property	To Be Kept By		
_____	☐ Husband ☐ Wife ☐ Other	_____
_____	☐ Husband ☐ Wife ☐ Other	_____
_____	☐ Husband ☐ Wife ☐ Other	_____
_____	☐ Husband ☐ Wife ☐ Other	_____

3. Each party shall pay for and hold the other harmless from any debt owing on the property he/she receives unless otherwise stated in this Agreement.

4. Other arrangements regarding the property above: _____

_____

_____

_____

The parties shall make arrangements to transfer interest in the property listed above to the proper party as soon as possible.

THIRD: DEBTS (select one):

☐ The parties do not have any debts.

☐ Each party shall pay all debts incurred by him or her individually and in their individual name and shall hold the other party harmless for these debts.

Supreme Court of Ohio
Uniform Domestic Relations Form – 16
SEPARATION AGREEMENT
Approved under Ohio Civil Rule 84
Effective Date: 7/1/2013

Page 9 of 13

☐ The parties have the following debts and have agreed to the payment of all debts owed, and agree to hold the other party harmless on those debts, as follows:

Creditor	Purpose of Debt	Balance	Who Will Pay	
_____	_____	_____	☐ Husband	☐ Wife
_____	_____	_____	☐ Husband	☐ Wife
_____	_____	_____	☐ Husband	☐ Wife
_____	_____	_____	☐ Husband	☐ Wife

Bankruptcy (select one):

☐ The Court will retain jurisdiction to enforce payment of debt obligations, in the event a party files bankruptcy, including, but not limited to, the ability to determine the debt assigned is in the nature of maintenance, necessity or support and is therefore nondischargeable in bankruptcy, and/or making a future spousal support order, regardless of the spousal support order set forth below under **FOURTH: SPOUSAL SUPPORT.**

☐ Nothing in this order shall prevent the ☐ Plaintiff and ☐ Defendant from being fully discharged from the debts allocated in this order in a bankruptcy proceeding except for any orders expressly for spousal support and the following debts: _____

_____

_____

_____

Neither party shall incur liabilities against the other party in the future and each shall pay any debt incurred by him or her individually after the date of this agreement.

FOURTH: SPOUSAL SUPPORT

A.   Spousal Support Not Awarded

☐ Neither the Husband nor Wife shall pay spousal support to the other. The Court shall not retain jurisdiction to modify spousal support, except as set forth above under **THIRD: DEBT.**

B.   Spousal Support Awarded

The ☐ Husband ☐ Wife shall pay spousal support to the ☐ Husband ☐ Wife
in the amount of $ _____ per month plus 2% processing charge
for a total of $ _____ per month, commencing on _____ and
due on the _____ day of the month. This spousal support shall continue
☐ indefinitely ☐ for a period of _____ .

C.   Method of Payment of Spousal Support (select one):

☐ If there are no child(ren), the spousal support payment shall be made directly to
the ☐ Plaintiff ☐ Defendant.

☐ The spousal support payment, plus 2% processing charge, shall be made to the Ohio Child Support Payment Central, P. O. Box 182372, Columbus, Ohio 43218-2372, as administered through

Supreme Court of Ohio
Uniform Domestic Relations Form – 16
SEPARATION AGREEMENT
Approved under Ohio Civil Rule 84
Effective Date: 7/1/2013

Page 10 of 13

the _____ County Child Support Enforcement Agency by income withholding at his/her place of employment.

☐ The Court shall not retain jurisdiction to modify spousal support.

☐ The Court shall retain jurisdiction to modify the ☐ amount ☐ duration of the spousal support Order.

D. Termination of Spousal Support
This spousal support shall terminate sooner than the above stated date upon the Plaintiff's or the Defendant's death or in the event of the following (check all that apply):
☐ The cohabitation of the person receiving support in a relationship comparable to marriage.
☐ The remarriage of the person receiving support.
☐ Other (specify): _____

_____

_____

_____

E. Deductibility of Spousal Support for All Tax Purposes (select one):
☐ The spousal support paid shall be deducted from income to the person paying the support and included in income by the person receiving the support.
☐ The spousal support paid shall be included in income of the person paying the support.

F. Other orders regarding spousal support (specify): _____

_____

G. Arrearage
☐ Any temporary spousal support arrearage will survive this judgment entry.
☐ Any temporary spousal support arrearage will not survive this judgment entry.
☐ Other: _____

FIFTH: NAME
☐ _____ shall be restored to
the prior name of: _____

SIXTH: ALLOCATION OF PARENTAL RIGHTS AND RESPONSIBILITIES, PARENTING TIME, CHILD SUPPORT AND HEALTH CARE
☐ The parties do not have child(ren) subject to the jurisdiction of the Court.
☐ The parties have minor child(ren) subject to the jurisdiction of the Court, and
a ☐ Parenting Plan or ☐ Shared Parenting Plan is attached.

Supreme Court of Ohio
Uniform Domestic Relations Form – 16
SEPARATION AGREEMENT
Approved under Ohio Civil Rule 84
Effective Date: 7/1/2013

Page 11 of 13

SEVENTH: OTHER

The parties agree to the following additional matters: _____

_____

_____

EIGHTH: NON-USE OF OTHER'S CREDIT

From now on, neither party shall incur any debt or obligation upon the credit of the other or in their joint names. If a party incurs such a debt or obligation that party shall repay, indemnify, and hold the other harmless as to any such debt or obligation. All joint credit card accounts shall be immediately cancelled, and the cards shall be immediately destroyed.

NINTH: INCORPORATION INTO DECREE/EFFECTIVENESS OF AGREEMENT

If one or both of the parties institute or have instituted proceedings for dissolution, divorce, or separation, this Agreement shall be presented to the Court with the request that it be adjudicated to be fair, just, and proper, and incorporated into the decree of the Court.

TENTH: PERFORMANCE OF NECESSARY ACTS

Upon execution and approval of this Agreement by the Court, each party shall deliver to the other party, or permit the other party to take possession of all items of property to which each is entitled under the terms of this Agreement, and shall make all periodic payments required under the terms of this Agreement.

Upon failure of either party to execute and deliver any deed, conveyance, title, certificate or other document or instrument to the other party, an order of the Court incorporating this Agreement shall constitute and operate as a properly executed document, and the County Auditor, County Recorder, Clerk of Courts and/or all other public and private officials shall be authorized and directed to accept a properly certified copy of a court order incorporating this Agreement, a properly certified copy of the Agreement or an order of the Court in lieu of the document regularly required for the conveyance or transfer.

ELEVENTH: SEVERABILITY

If any provision of this Agreement is held to be invalid or unenforceable, all other provisions shall continue in full force and effect.

TWELFTH: APPLICABLE LAW

All of the provisions of this Agreement shall be construed and enforced in accordance with the laws of the State of Ohio.

THIRTEENTH: MUTUAL RELEASE

Except as otherwise provided, the parties do release and forever discharge each other from any and all actions, suits, debts, claims, demands, and obligations whatsoever, both in law and in equity, which either of them ever had, now has, or may have or assert against the other upon or by reason of any matter or cause to the date of the execution of this Agreement.

Supreme Court of Ohio
Uniform Domestic Relations Form – 16
SEPARATION AGREEMENT
Approved under Ohio Civil Rule 84
Effective Date: 7/1/2013

Page 12 of 13

Each party waives all rights of inheritance and the right to share in the estate of the other, and waives all rights which would otherwise be available as a surviving spouse, except payments or rights included in this Agreement.

_____   _____
Your Signature (Husband)   Your Signature (Wife)

_____   _____
Date   Date

IN THE COURT OF COMMON PLEAS

_____ **Division**

_____ **COUNTY, OHIO**

IN THE MATTER OF:

_____

A Minor

_____ :	
Plaintiff/Petitioner :	Case No. _____
_____ :	
Street Address :	
_____ :	Judge _____
City, State and Zip Code :	
vs./and :	Magistrate _____
_____ :	
:	
Defendant/Petitioner :	
_____ :	
Street Address :	
_____ :	
City, State and Zip Code :	
:	

> Instructions: The Parenting Time Schedule must be attached to this Plan. Parents are urged to consult the Planning for Parenting Time Guide: Ohio's Guide for Parents Living Apart available at http://www.supremecourt.ohio.gov/Publications/JCS/parentingGuide.pdf.

SHARED PARENTING PLAN

We, the parents, _____ , "Father", and _____ ,"Mother",

have _____ (number) child(ren) born from or adopted during the marriage or relationship.

Of the child(ren), _____ (number) is/are emancipated adult(s) and not under any disability,

and the following _____ (number) child(ren) are minor child(ren) and/or mentally or physically

disabled child(ren) incapable of supporting or maintaining themselves (name and date of birth of each

child): _____

_____

_____

The parents agree to the care, parenting, and control of their child(ren) as provided in this
Shared Parenting Plan.

Supreme Court of Ohio
Uniform Domestic Relations Form – 17
SHARED PARENTING PLAN
Approved under Ohio Civil Rule 84 and Ohio Juvenile Rule 46
Effective Date: 7/1/2013

Page 1 of 14

FIRST: PARENTS' RIGHTS

The parents shall have:

A. The right to participate in major decisions concerning the child(ren)'s health, social situation, morals, welfare, education, and economic environment.

B. The right to reasonable telephone contact with the child(ren) when they are with the other parent.

C. The right to participate in the selection of doctors, psychologists, psychiatrists, hospitals, and other health care providers for the child(ren).

D. The right to authorize medical, surgical, hospital, dental, institutional, psychological and psychiatric care for the child(ren) and obtain a second opinion regarding medical conditions or treatment.

E. The right to be notified in case of an injury to or illness of the child(ren).

F. The right to be present with the child(ren) at medical, dental and other health-related examinations and treatments, including, but not limited to psychological and psychiatric care.

G. The right to inspect and receive the child(ren)'s medical and dental records and the right to consult with any treating physician, dentist and/or other health care provider, including but not limited to psychologists and psychiatrists.

H. The right to consult with school officials concerning the child(ren)'s welfare and educational status, and the right to inspect and receive the child(ren)'s student records to the extent permitted by law.

I. The right to receive copies of all school reports, calendars of school events, notices of parent-teacher conferences, and school programs.

J. The right to attend and participate in parent-teacher conferences, school trips, school programs, and other school activities in which parents are invited to participate.

K. The right to attend and participate with the child(ren) in athletic programs and other extracurricular activities.

L. The right to receive notice of the other parent's intention to relocate.

SECOND: ALLOCATION OF PARENTAL RIGHTS AND RESPONSIBILITIES

A. General Responsibilities

Each parent shall take all measures necessary to foster respect and affection between the child(ren) and the other parent. Neither parent shall do anything that may estrange the child(ren) from the other parent, or impair the child(ren)'s high regard for the other parent.

B. Medical Responsibilities

A parent shall notify the other parent promptly if a child experiences a serious injury, has a serious or chronic illness, or receives treatment in an emergency room or hospital. A parent shall notify the other parent of the emergency, the child's status, locale, and any other pertinent information as soon as practical, but in any event within 24 hours.

The parents shall consult with each other about the child(ren)'s medical care needs and each shall immediately notify the other parent about all major non-emergency medical decisions before authorizing a course of treatment. Parents have a right to know the necessity for treatment, proposed cost, and proposed payment schedule. Each parent may also secure an independent evaluation at his/her expense to determine the necessity for treatment. If the parties cannot agree regarding a course of treatment, the ☐ Father's ☐ Mother's (select one) decision shall control. The parents shall provide the other with the names and telephone numbers of all health care providers for the child(ren).

C. Both parents have shared parenting of the child(ren) as specified in this Plan. Each parent, regardless of where an individual child is residing at a particular point in time, as specified in this Plan, is the "residential parent", "the residential parent and legal custodian", or the "custodial parent" of that child.

D. Parenting Time Schedule
Unless otherwise agreed, the parents shall have parenting time with the child(ren) according to the attached Parenting Time Schedule, which shows the times that the child(ren) shall be with each parent on weekdays, weekends, holidays, and vacation times.

(The Parenting Time Schedule must be attached to this Plan.)

E. School Designation
Father shall be designated as the residential parent for school attendance and enrollment purposes of the following child(ren): _____

_____

Mother shall be designated as the residential parent for school attendance and enrollment purposes of the following child(ren): _____

_____

In the event that a change in schools is being considered, after consultation with the other parent:
☐ Father is authorized to change school placement of the following child(ren): _____

_____

☐ Mother is authorized to change school placement of the following child(ren): _____

_____

☐ Without a written agreement or court order, neither parent is authorized to change school placement of the following child(ren): _____

_____

_____

Supreme Court of Ohio
Uniform Domestic Relations Form – 17
SHARED PARENTING PLAN
Approved under Ohio Civil Rule 84 and Ohio Juvenile Rule 46
Effective Date: 7/1/2013

Page 3 of 14

F. Other orders: _____

_____

_____

_____

G. Public Benefits
Father shall be designated as the residential parent for receipt of public benefits purposes of the following child(ren): _____

_____

Mother shall be designated as the residential parent for receipt of public benefits purposes of the following child(ren): _____

_____

H. This designation of a particular parent as the residential parent for the purposes of determining the school attendance and enrollment of the child(ren) or the receipt of public benefits of the child(ren) does not affect the designation of each parent as the "residential parent," "residential parent and legal custodian," or the "custodial parent of the child(ren)".

I. Transportation (select one):
☐ Each parent shall be responsible for providing transportation for the child(ren) at the beginning of his/her parenting period. Each parent shall be responsible for providing transportation for the child(ren) to and from school and activities during his/her parenting period.

☐ We agree to the following arrangements for providing transportation for our child(ren) at the beginning, during, or end of a parenting period: _____

_____

_____

J. Current Address and Telephone Number
Father's current home address and telephone number, including cellular telephone number:

_____

_____

_____

Mother's current home address and telephone number, including cellular telephone number:

_____

_____

_____

_____

_____

K. Relocation Notice

Pursuant to section 3109.051(G) of the Revised Code:

If either of the residential parents intends to move to a residence other than the residence specified in the court order, the parent shall file a notice of intent to relocate with this Court. Except as provided in divisions (G)(2), (3), and (4) of section 3109.051 of the Revised Code, the Court shall send a copy of the notice to the other parent. Upon receipt of the notice, the Court, on its own motion or the motion of the nonmoving parent, may schedule a hearing with notice to both parents to determine whether it is in the best interests of the child(ren) to revise the parenting time schedule for the child(ren).

Each residential parent shall inform in writing the Court and the other parent of changes in address and telephone, including cellular telephone number, unless otherwise provided by court order.

The relocation notice must be filed with the Court granting the allocation of parental rights and responsibilities (name and address of Court): _____

_____

_____

L. Records Access Notice

Pursuant to sections 3109.051(H) and 3319.321(B)(5)(a) of the Revised Code:

Subject to sections 3125.16 and 3319.321(F) of the Revised Code, each parent is entitled to access to any record that is related to the child(ren), under the same terms and conditions as the other parent unless otherwise restricted. Any keeper of a record who knowingly fails to comply with any record order is in contempt of court.

Restrictions or limitations:

☐ None

☐ Restrictions or limitations to records access are as follows: _____

_____

_____

M. Day Care Access Notice

Pursuant to section 3109.051(I) of the Revised Code:

In accordance with section 5104.11 of the Revised Code, each parent is entitled to access to any day care center that is or will be attended by the child(ren) unless otherwise restricted.

Restrictions or limitations:

☐ None

☐ Restrictions or limitations to day care access are as follows: _____

_____

_____

Supreme Court of Ohio
Uniform Domestic Relations Form – 17
SHARED PARENTING PLAN
Approved under Ohio Civil Rule 84 and Ohio Juvenile Rule 46
Effective Date: 7/1/2013

Page 5 of 14

N. School Activities Access Notice

Pursuant to section 3109.051(J) of the Revised Code:

Subject to section 3319.321(F), each parent is entitled to access to any student activity that is related to the child(ren) and to which the residential parent is legally provided access, under the same terms and conditions as the residential parent. Any school employee or official who knowingly fails to comply with this school activities access order is in contempt of court.

Restrictions or limitations:

☐ None

☐ Restrictions or limitations to school activities access are as follows: _____

_____

_____

_____

THIRD: HEALTH INSURANCE COVERAGE.

As required by law, the parties have completed a Child Support Worksheet, which is attached to and incorporated in this Agreement.

Select one:

A.   ☐ Health Insurance Coverage Available to at Least One Parent

1. Private health insurance coverage is accessible and reasonable in cost through a group policy, contract, or plan to: ☐ Father ☐ Mother ☐ Both parents. ☐ Father ☐ Mother ☐ Both parents shall provide private health insurance coverage for the benefit of the child(ren).

2. If both parents are ordered to provide private health insurance coverage for the benefit of the child(ren), ☐ Father's ☐ Mother's health insurance plan shall be considered the primary health insurance plan for the child(ren).

3. The parent required to provide private health insurance coverage shall provide proof of insurance to the _____ County Child Support Enforcement Agency (CSEA) and the other parent.

4. Both parents shall cooperate in the preparation of insurance forms to obtain reimbursement or payment of expenses, as applicable. A copy of medical bills must be submitted to the party holding the insurance and responsible for payment or the other parent within 30 days of receipt.

5. Should the health insurance coverage be cancelled for any reason, the parent ordered to maintain insurance shall immediately notify the other parent and take immediate steps to obtain replacement coverage. Unless the cancellation was intentional, the uncovered expenses shall be paid as provided above. If the cancellation was intentionally caused by the parent ordered to maintain insurance coverage, that parent shall be responsible for all medical expenses that would have been covered had the insurance been in effect.

Supreme Court of Ohio
Uniform Domestic Relations Form – 17
SHARED PARENTING PLAN
Approved under Ohio Civil Rule 84 and Ohio Juvenile Rule 46
Effective Date: 7/1/2013

Page 6 of 14

B. ☐ Health Insurance Coverage Unavailable to Either Parent
   1. Private health insurance coverage is **not** accessible and reasonable in cost through a group policy, contract, or plan to either parent.

   2. If private health insurance coverage becomes available to either parent at reasonable cost, he/she will immediately obtain the insurance, notify the other parent and the _____ County CSEA, and submit to the other parent proof of insurance, insurance forms, and an insurance card. The CSEA shall determine whether the cost of the insurance is of sufficient amount to justify an administrative review of the amount of child support payable. In the event an administrative review is warranted, one shall be conducted.

C. Division of Uninsured Expenses
   1. The cost of any uninsured medical expenses, incurred by or on behalf of the child(ren) not paid by a health insurance plan and exceeding $100 per child per year, including co-payments and deductibles, shall be paid by the parents as follows:
      _____ % by Father _____ % by Mother.
      The first $100 per child per year shall be paid by Mother for the following child(ren): _____
      _____
      _____
      The first $100 per child per year shall be paid by Father for the following child(ren): _____
      _____
      _____

      Other orders regarding payment of uninsured medical expenses: _____
      _____
      _____

   2. The parent incurring the expenses shall provide the other parent the original or copies of all medical bills, and Explanation of Benefits (EOB), if available, within 30 days of the date on the bill or EOB, whichever is later, absent extraordinary circumstances. The other parent shall, within 30 days of receipt of the bill, reimburse the parent incurring the expenses or pay directly to the health care provider that parent's percentage share of the bill as shown above.

D. Other Important Information about Medical Records and Expenses
   1. Each party shall have access to all medical records of the child(ren) as provided by law.

   2. The term "medical expense" or "medical records" shall include but not be limited to medical, dental, orthodontic, optical, surgical, hospital, major medical, psychological, psychiatric, outpatient, doctor, therapy, counseling, prosthetic, and/or all other expenses/records including preventative health care expenses/records related to the treatment of the human body and mind.

FOURTH: CHILD SUPPORT

As required by law, the parties have completed a Child Support Worksheet, which is attached to and incorporated in this Agreement.

A. Child Support with Private Health Insurance Coverage

When private health insurance coverage is being provided for the child(ren), ☐ Father ☐ Mother, Obligor, shall pay child support in the amount of $_____ per child per month, for _____ (number) child(ren) for a total of $_____ per month.

B. Child Support without Private Health Insurance Coverage

When private health insurance coverage is **not** available for the benefit of the child(ren), ☐ Father ☐ Mother, the Obligor, shall pay child support in the amount of $_____ per child per month and $_____ per child per month as cash medical support. The total of child support and cash medical support for _____ (number) child(ren) is $_____ per month.

C. Child Support Payment

The child support payment (including cash medical support, if any) plus a 2% processing charge shall commence on _____ and shall be paid to the Ohio Child Support Payment Center, P. O. Box 182372, Columbus, Ohio 43218-2372, as administered through the _____ County Child Support Enforcement Agency (CSEA) by income withholding at Obligor's place of employment or from nonexempt funds on deposit at a financial institution.

D. Deviation of Child Support Amount

The child support amount agreed upon is different than the amount calculated on the attached Child Support Worksheet because the amount calculated on the Worksheet would be unjust or inappropriate and would not be in the best interests of the child(ren) for the following reason(s) as provided in R.C. 3119.22, 3119.23, 3119.24 and shall be adjusted as follows: _____

_____

_____

☐ Special and unusual needs of the child(ren) as follows: _____

_____

_____

☐ Extraordinary obligations for child(ren) or obligations for handicapped child(ren) who is/are not stepchild(ren) and who are not offspring from the marriage or relationship that is the basis of the immediate child support determination as follows: _____

_____

_____

☐ Other court-ordered payments as follows: _____

Supreme Court of Ohio
Uniform Domestic Relations Form – 17
SHARED PARENTING PLAN
Approved under Ohio Civil Rule 84 and Ohio Juvenile Rule 46
Effective Date: 7/1/2013

Page 8 of 14

_____
_____
_____

☐ The Obligor obtained additional employment after a child support order was issued to support a second family as follows: _____

_____
_____

☐ Extended parenting time or extraordinary costs associated with parenting time, provided that this division does not authorize and shall not be construed as authorizing any deviation from the schedule and the applicable worksheet, through the line establishing the actual annual obligation, or any escrowing, impoundment, or withholding of child support because of a denial of or interference with a right of parenting time granted by court order as follows: _____

_____
_____

☐ The financial resources and the earning ability of the child(ren) as follows: _____

_____
_____

☐ Disparity in income between parents or households as follows: _____

_____
_____

☐ Benefits that either parent receives from remarriage or sharing living expenses with another person as follows: _____

_____
_____

☐ The amount of federal, state, and local taxes actually paid or estimated to be paid by a parent or both of the parents as follows: _____

_____
_____

☐ Significant, in-kind contributions from a parent, including, but not limited to, direct payment for lessons, sports equipment, schooling, or clothing as follows: _____

_____
_____
_____
_____

Supreme Court of Ohio
Uniform Domestic Relations Form – 17
SHARED PARENTING PLAN
Approved under Ohio Civil Rule 84 and Ohio Juvenile Rule 46
Effective Date: 7/1/2013

Page 9 of 14

☐ The relative financial resources, other assets and resources, and needs of each parent as follows: _____

_____

_____

☐ The standard of living and circumstances of each parent and the standard of living the child(ren) would have enjoyed had the marriage continued or had the parents been married as follows:

_____

_____

_____

☐ The physical and emotional condition and needs of the child(ren) as follows: _____

_____

_____

☐ The need and capacity of the child(ren) for an education and the educational opportunities that would have been available to the child(ren) had the circumstances requiring a court order for support not arisen as follows: _____

_____

_____

☐ The responsibility of each parent for the support of others as follows: _____

_____

_____

☐ Any other relevant factor: _____

_____

_____

E. Duration of Child Support.
The child support order will terminate upon the child's 18th birthday unless one of the following circumstances applies:

- The child is mentally or physically disabled and incapable of supporting or maintaining himself or herself.
- The parents have agreed to continue child support beyond the date it would otherwise terminate, as set out below.
- The child continuously attends a recognized and accredited high school on a full-time basis so long as the child has not as yet reached the age of 19 years old. (Under these circumstances, child support will end at the time the child ceases to attend a recognized and accredited high school on a full-time basis or when he or she reaches the age of 19, whichever occurs first.)

This Support Order will remain in effect during seasonal vacation periods until the order terminates. The parents agree that child support will extend beyond the time when it would otherwise end. The terms and conditions of that agreement are as follows: _____

_____
_____
_____

The parents have (a) child(ren) who is/are mentally or physically disabled and incapable of supporting or maintaining themselves. The name of the child(ren) and the nature of the mental or physical disability are as follows: _____

_____
_____
_____

F. Important Child Support Orders and Information

Obligee must immediately notify and Obligor may notify the CSEA of any reason for which the support order should terminate. A willful failure to notify the CSEA as required is contempt of court. The following are reasons for termination of the Order:

- Child's attainment of the age of majority if the child no longer attends an accredited high school on a full-time basis and the support order does not provide for the duty of support to continue past the age of majority
- Child stops attending an accredited high school on a full-time basis after attaining the age of majority
- Child's death
- Child's marriage
- Child's emancipation
- Child's enlistment in the Armed Services
- Child's deportation
- Change of legal custody of the child

All support payments must be made through the CSEA or the office of child support in the Ohio Department of Job and Family Services (Child Support Payment Central). Any payment of money not made through the CSEA will be presumed to be a gift, unless the payment is made to discharge an obligation other than support.

All support under this Order shall be withheld or deducted from the income or assets of the Obligor pursuant to a withholding or deduction notice or appropriate order issued in accordance with Chapters 3119., 3121., 3123., and 3125. of the Revised Code or a withdrawal directive issued pursuant to sections 3123.24 to 3123.38 of the Revised Code and shall be forwarded to the Obligee in accordance with Chapters 3119., 3121., 3123., and 3125. of the Revised Code.

The Obligor and/or Obligee required under this Order to provide private health insurance coverage

Supreme Court of Ohio
Uniform Domestic Relations Form – 17
SHARED PARENTING PLAN
Approved under Ohio Civil Rule 84 and Ohio Juvenile Rule 46
Effective Date: 7/1/2013

Page 11 of 14

for the child(ren) is also required to provide the other party within 30 days after the issuance of the Order, the following:

- Information regarding the benefits, limitations, and exclusions of the health insurance coverage
- Copies of any insurance form necessary to receive reimbursement, payment, or other benefits under the coverage
- A copy of any necessary health insurance cards

The Health Plan Administrator that provides the private health insurance coverage for the child(ren) may continue making payment for medical, optical, hospital, dental, or prescription services directly to any health care provider in accordance with the applicable private health insurance policy, contract, or plan.

The Obligor and/or Obligee required to provide private health insurance for the child(ren) must designate said child(ren) as dependents under any private health insurance policy, contract, or plan for which the person contracts.

The employer of the person required to provide private health insurance coverage is required to release to the other parent, any person subject to an order issued under section 3109.19 of the Revised Code, or the CSEA, upon written request, any necessary information regarding health insurance coverage, including the name and address of the health plan administrator and any policy, contract, or plan number, and the employer will otherwise comply with all orders and notices issued.

If the person required to obtain private health insurance coverage for the child(ren) subject to this Support Order obtains new employment, the agency shall comply with the requirements of section 3119.34 of the Revised Code, which may result in the issuance of a notice requiring the new employer to take whatever action is necessary to enroll the child(ren) in private health insurance coverage provided by the new employer.

Upon receipt of notice by the CSEA that private health insurance coverage is not available at a reasonable cost, cash medical support shall be paid in the amount as determined by the child support computation worksheets in section 3119.022 or 3119.023 of the Revised Code, as applicable. The CSEA may change the financial obligations of the parties to pay child support in accordance with the terms of the court or administrative order and cash medical support without a hearing or additional notice to the parties.

An Obligor that is in arrears in his/her child support obligation is subject to having any federal, state and/or local income tax refund to which the Obligor may be entitled forwarded to the CSEA for payment toward these arrears. Such refunds will continue to be forwarded to the CSEA for payment until all arrears owed are paid in full. If the Obligor is married and files a joint tax return, the Obligor's spouse may contact the CSEA about filing an "Injured Spouse" claim after the Obligor is notified by the Internal Revenue Service that his/her refund is being forwarded to the CSEA.

Pursuant to section 3121.29 of the Revised Code, the parties are notified as follows:

EACH PARTY TO THIS SUPPORT ORDER MUST NOTIFY THE CHILD SUPPORT AGENCY IN WRITING OF HIS OR HER CURRENT MAILING ADDRESS, CURRENT RESIDENCE ADDRESS, CURRENT RESIDENCE TELEPHONE NUMBER, CURRENT DRIVER'S LICENSE NUMBER AND OF ANY CHANGES IN THAT INFORMATION. EACH PARTY MUST NOTIFY THE AGENCY OF ALL CHANGES UNTIL FURTHER NOTICE FROM THE COURT. IF YOU ARE THE OBLIGOR UNDER A CHILD SUPPORT ORDER AND YOU FAIL TO MAKE THE REQUIRED NOTIFICATIONS, YOU MAY BE FINED UP TO $50.00 FOR A FIRST OFFENSE, $100.00 FOR A SECOND OFFENSE, AND $500.00 FOR EACH SUBSEQUENT OFFENSE. IF YOU ARE AN OBLIGOR OR OBLIGEE UNDER ANY SUPPORT ORDER AND YOU WILLFULLY FAIL TO MAKE THE REQUIRED NOTIFICATIONS YOU MAY BE SUBJECTED TO FINES OF UP TO $1,000.00 AND IMPRISONMENT FOR NOT MORE THAN 90 DAYS.

IF YOU ARE AN OBLIGOR AND YOU FAIL TO MAKE THE REQUIRED NOTIFICATIONS, YOU MAY NOT RECEIVE NOTICE OF THE FOLLOWING ENFORCEMENT ACTIONS AGAINST YOU: IMPOSITION OF LIENS AGAINST YOUR PROPERTY; LOSS OF YOUR PROFESSIONAL OR OCCUPATIONAL LICENSE, DRIVER'S LICENSE, OR RECREATIONAL LICENSE; WITHHOLDING FROM YOUR INCOME; ACCESS RESTRICTIONS AND DEDUCTIONS FROM YOUR ACCOUNTS IN FINANCIAL INSTITUTIONS; AND ANY OTHER ACTION PERMITTED BY LAW TO OBTAIN MONEY FROM YOU AND TO SATISFY YOUR SUPPORT OBLIGATION.

G. Payment shall be made in accordance with Chapter 3121. of the Revised Code.

H. Arrearage
☐ Any temporary child support arrearage will survive this judgment entry.
☐ Any temporary child support arrearage will not survive this judgment entry.
☐ Other: _____

_____
_____
_____

FIFTH: TAX EXEMPTIONS

Income tax dependency exemptions (check all that apply):

A. ☐ The Father shall be entitled to claim the following minor child(ren) for all tax purposes for
☐ even-numbered tax years ☐ odd-numbered tax years ☐ all eligible tax years, so long as he is substantially current in any child support he is required to pay as of December 31 of the tax year in question:

☐ The Mother shall be entitled to claim the following minor child(ren) for all tax purposes for
☐ even-numbered tax years ☐ odd-numbered tax years ☐ all eligible tax years, so long as she is substantially current in any child support she is required to pay as of December 31 of the tax year

in question: _____

B.   ☐ Other orders regarding tax exemptions (specify): _____

_____

If a non-residential parent is entitled to claim the child(ren), the residential parent is required to execute and deliver Internal Revenue Service Form 8332, or its successor, together with any other required forms as set out in section 152 of the Internal Revenue Code, as amended, on or before February 15th of the year following the tax year in question, to allow the non-residential parent to claim the child(ren).

SIXTH: MODIFICATION
This Shared Parenting Plan may be modified by agreement of the parties or by the Court.

SEVENTH: OTHER

_____
_____
_____
_____
_____

Upon approval by the Court, this Shared Parenting Plan shall be incorporated in the Judgment Entry.

_____   _____
Your Signature (Father)   Your Signature (Mother)

_____   _____
Date   Date

IN THE COURT OF COMMON PLEAS

_____ **Division**

_____ **COUNTY, OHIO**

IN THE MATTER OF:

_____

A Minor

_____
Plaintiff/Petitioner

_____
Street Address

_____
City, State and Zip Code

vs./and

_____
Defendant/Petitioner

_____
Street Address

_____
City, State and Zip Code

:
:
: Case No. _____
:
:
:
: Judge _____
:
:
: Magistrate _____
:
:
:
:
:
:

Instructions: The Parenting Time Schedule must be attached to this Plan. Parents are urged to consult the Planning for Parenting Time Guide: Ohio's Guide for Parents Living Apart available at http://www.supremecourt.ohio.gov/Publications/JCS/parentingGuide.pdf.

PARENTING PLAN

We, the parents, _____ , "Father", and _____ ,"Mother",

have _____ (number) child(ren) born from or adopted during the marriage or relationship.

Of the child(ren), _____ (number) is/are emancipated adult(s) and not under any disability, and

the following _____ (number) child(ren) is/are minor child(ren) and/or mentally or physically disabled

child(ren) incapable of supporting or maintaining themselves (name and date of birth of each child):

_____

_____

_____

The parents agree to the care, parenting, and control of their child(ren) as provided in this Parenting Plan.

Supreme Court of Ohio
Uniform Domestic Relations Form – 18
PARENTING PLAN
Approved under Ohio Civil Rule 84 and Ohio Juvenile Rule 46
Effective Date: 7/1/2013

Page 1 of 12

FIRST: PARENTS' RIGHTS

We, the parents, shall have, unless limited:

A. The right to reasonable telephone contact with the child(ren) when they are with the other parent.

B. The right to be notified in case of an injury to or illness of the minor child(ren).

C. The right to inspect and receive the minor child(ren)'s medical and dental records and the right to consult with any treating physician, dentist and/or other health care provider, including but not limited to psychologists and psychiatrists.

D. The right to consult with school officials concerning the minor child(ren)'s welfare and educational status, and the right to inspect and receive the child(ren)'s student records to the extent permitted by law.

E. The right to receive copies of all school reports, calendars of school events, notices of parent-teacher conferences, and school programs.

F. The right to attend and participate in parent-teacher conferences, school trips, school programs, and other school activities in which parents are invited to participate.

G. The right to attend and participate with the child(ren) in athletic programs and other extracurricular activities.

SECOND: ALLOCATION OF PARENTAL RIGHTS AND RESPONSIBILITIES

A. General Responsibilities

Each parent shall take all measures necessary to foster respect and affection between the child(ren) and the other parent. Neither parent shall do anything that may estrange the child(ren) from the other parent, or impair the child(ren)'s high regard for the other parent.

B. Medical Responsibilities

The parents shall notify the other parent promptly if a child experiences a serious injury, has a serious or chronic illness, or receives treatment in an emergency room or hospital. The notification shall include the emergency, the child's status, locale, and any other pertinent information as soon as practical, but in any event within 24 hours.

The parents shall consult with each other about the minor child(ren)'s medical care needs and the residential parent shall immediately notify the other parent about all major non- emergency medical decisions before authorizing a course of treatment. Parents have a right to know the necessity for treatment, proposed cost, and proposed payment schedule. Each parent may also secure an independent evaluation at his/her expense to determine the necessity for treatment. If the parties cannot agree regarding a course of treatment, the residential parent's decision shall control. The parents shall provide the other with the names and telephone numbers of all health care providers for the child(ren).

C. Residential Parent and Legal Custodian

☐ Father shall be the residential parent and legal custodian of the following child(ren):

_____

_____

_____

_____

☐ Mother shall be the residential parent and legal custodian of the following child(ren):

_____

_____

_____

D. Parenting Time Schedule
Unless otherwise agreed, the parents shall have parenting time with the child(ren) according to the attached Parenting Time Schedule that shows the times that the child(ren) shall be with each parent on weekdays, weekends, holidays, and vacation times.

(The Parenting Time Schedule must be attached to this Plan.)

E. Transportation (select one):
☐ Each parent shall be responsible for providing transportation for the child(ren) at the beginning of his/her parenting period. Each parent shall be responsible for providing transportation for the child(ren) to and from school and activities during his/her parenting period.

☐ We agree to the following arrangements for providing transportation for our child(ren) at the beginning, during, or end of a parenting period: _____

_____

_____

F. Current Address and Telephone Number
Father's current home address and telephone number, including cellular telephone number:

_____

_____

_____

Mother's current home address and telephone number, including cellular telephone number:

_____

_____

_____

G. Relocation Notice
Pursuant to section 3109.051(G) of the Revised Code:
If the residential parent intends to move to a residence other than the residence specified in the court order, the parent shall file a notice of intent to relocate with this Court. Except as provided in divisions (G)(2), (3), and (4) of section 3109.051 of the Revised Code, the Court shall send a copy of the notice to the parent who is not the residential parent. Upon receipt of the notice, the Court, on its own motion or the motion of the parent who is not the residential parent, may schedule a hearing

Supreme Court of Ohio
Uniform Domestic Relations Form – 18
PARENTING PLAN
Approved under Ohio Civil Rule 84 and Ohio Juvenile Rule 46
Effective Date: 7/1/2013

Page 3 of 12

with notice to both parents to determine whether it is in the best interests of the child(ren) to revise the parenting time schedule for the child(ren).

☐ The non-residential parent shall inform in writing the Court and the other parent of changes in address and telephone, including cellular telephone number, unless otherwise provided by court order.

The relocation notice must be filed with the Court granting the allocation of parental rights and responsibilities (name and address of the Court): _____

_____

_____

H. Records Access Notice
Pursuant to sections 3109.051(H) and 3319.321(B)(5)(a) of the Revised Code:
Subject to sections 3125.16 and 3319.321(F) of the Revised Code, the parent who is not the residential parent is entitled to access to any record that is related to the child(ren), and to which the residential parent is legally provided access under the same terms and conditions as the residential parent. Any keeper of a record who knowingly fails to comply with any record access order is in contempt of court.

Restrictions or limitations:
☐ None
☐ Restrictions or limitations to non-residential parents regarding records access are as follows:

_____

_____

I. Day Care Access Notice
Pursuant to section 3109.051(I) of the Revised Code:
In accordance with section 5104.11 of the Revised Code, the parent who is not the residential parent is entitled to access to any day care center that is or will be attended by the child(ren) with whom parenting time is granted, to the same extent that the residential parent is granted access to the center.

Restrictions or limitations:
☐ None
☐ Restrictions or limitations to non-residential parents regarding day care access are as follows:

_____

_____

J. School Activities Access Notice
Pursuant to section 3109.051(J) of the Revised Code:
Subject to section 3319.321(F), the parent who is not the residential parent is entitled to access

to any student activity that is related to the child(ren) and to which the residential parent is legally provided access, under the same terms and conditions as the residential parent. Any school employee or official who knowingly fails to comply with this school activities access order is in contempt of court.

Restrictions or limitations:

☐ None

☐ Restrictions or limitations to non-residential parents regarding school activities access are as follows: _____

_____

_____

THIRD: HEALTH INSURANCE COVERAGE

As required by law, the parties have completed a Child Support Worksheet, which is attached to and incorporated in this Agreement.

Select one:

A.   ☐ Health Insurance Coverage Available to at Least One Parent

    1.   Private health insurance coverage is accessible and reasonable in cost through a group policy, contract, or plan to: ☐ Father ☐ Mother ☐ Both parents. ☐ Father ☐ Mother ☐ Both parents shall provide private health insurance coverage for the benefit of the child(ren).

    2.   If both parents are ordered to provide private health insurance coverage for the benefit of the child(ren), ☐ Father's ☐ Mother's health insurance plan shall be considered the primary health insurance plan for the child(ren).

    3.   The parent required to provide private health insurance coverage shall provide proof of insurance to the _____ County Child Support Enforcement Agency (CSEA) and the other parent.

    4.   Both parents shall cooperate in the preparation of insurance forms to obtain reimbursement or payment of expenses, as applicable. A copy of medical bills must be submitted to the party holding the insurance and responsible for payment or the other parent within 30 days of receipt.

    5.   Should the health insurance coverage be cancelled for any reason, the parent ordered to maintain insurance shall immediately notify the other parent and take immediate steps to obtain replacement coverage. Unless the cancellation was intentional, the uncovered expenses shall be paid as provided above. If the cancellation was intentionally caused by the parent ordered to maintain insurance coverage, that parent shall be responsible for all medical expenses that would have been covered had the insurance been in effect.

B.   ☐ Health Insurance Coverage Unavailable to Either Parent

    1.   Private health insurance coverage is **not** accessible and reasonable in cost through a group

Supreme Court of Ohio
Uniform Domestic Relations Form – 18
PARENTING PLAN
Approved under Ohio Civil Rule 84 and Ohio Juvenile Rule 46
Effective Date: 7/1/2013

Page 5 of 12

policy, contract, or plan to either parent.

2. If private health insurance coverage becomes available to either parent at reasonable cost, he/she will immediately obtain the insurance, notify the other parent and the _____ County CSEA, and submit to the other parent proof of insurance, insurance forms, and an insurance card. The CSEA shall determine whether the cost of the insurance is of sufficient amount to justify an administrative review of the amount of child support payable. In the event an administrative review is warranted, one shall be conducted.

C. Division of Uninsured Expenses
1. The cost of any uninsured medical expenses, incurred by or on the behalf of the child(ren) not paid by a health insurance plan, and exceeding $100 per child per year, including co-payments and deductibles, shall be paid by the parents as follows:
_____ % by Father _____ % by Mother.
The first $100 per child per year of uninsured expenses shall be paid by the residential parent.

Other orders regarding payment of uninsured medical expenses: _____
_____
_____
_____

2. The parent incurring the expenses shall provide the other parent the original or copies of all medical bills, and Explanation of Benefits (EOB), if available, within 30 days of the date on the bill or EOB, whichever is later, absent extraordinary circumstances. The other parent shall, within 30 days of receipt of the bill, reimburse the parent incurring the expenses or pay directly to the health care provider that parent's percentage share of the bill as shown above.

D. Other Important Information about Medical Records and Expenses
1. Each party shall have access to all medical records of the child(ren) as provided by law.

2. The term "medical expense" or "medical records" shall include but not be limited to medical, dental, orthodontic, optical, surgical, hospital, major medical, psychological, psychiatric, outpatient, doctor, therapy, counseling, prosthetic, and/or all other expenses/records including preventative health care expenses/records related to the treatment of the human body and mind.

FOURTH: CHILD SUPPORT
As required by law, the parties have completed a Child Support Worksheet, which is attached to and incorporated in this Agreement.
A. Child Support with Private Health Insurance Coverage
When private health insurance coverage is being provided for the child(ren), ☐ Father ☐ Mother, Obligor, shall pay child support in the amount of $_____ per child per month, for _____ (number) of child(ren) for a total $_____ per month.

Supreme Court of Ohio
Uniform Domestic Relations Form – 18
PARENTING PLAN
Approved under Ohio Civil Rule 84 and Ohio Juvenile Rule 46
Effective Date: 7/1/2013

Page 6 of 12

B. Child Support without Private Health Insurance Coverage

When private health insurance coverage is **not** available for the child(ren), ☐ Father ☐ Mother, the Obligor, shall pay child support in the amount of $_____ per child per month and $_____ per child per month as cash medical support. The total child support and cash medical support for _____ (number) of child(ren) is $_____ per month.

C. Child Support Payment

Child support payment (including cash medical support, if any) plus a 2% processing charge shall commence on _____ and shall be paid to the Ohio Child Support Payment Center, P. O. Box 182372,Columbus, Ohio 43218-2372, as administered through the _____ County Child Support Enforcement Agency (CSEA) by income withholding at Obligor's place of employment or from nonexempt funds on deposit at a financial institution.

D. Deviation of Child Support Amount

The child support amount agreed upon is different than the amount calculated on the attached Child Support Worksheet, because the amount calculated on the Worksheet would be unjust or inappropriate and would not be in the best interests of the child(ren) for the following reason(s) as provided in R.C. 3119.22, 3119.23, and 3119.24 and shall be adjusted as follows: _____

_____

_____

☐ Special and unusual needs of the child(ren) as follows: _____

_____

_____

☐ Extraordinary obligations for minor child(ren) or obligations for handicapped child(ren) who is/are not stepchild(ren) and who are not offspring from the marriage or relationship that is the basis of the immediate child support determination as follows: _____

_____

_____

☐ Other court-ordered payments as follows: _____

_____

_____

☐ The Obligor obtained additional employment after a child support order was issued to support a second family as follows: _____

_____

_____

Supreme Court of Ohio
Uniform Domestic Relations Form – 18
PARENTING PLAN
Approved under Ohio Civil Rule 84 and Ohio Juvenile Rule 46
Effective Date: 7/1/2013

Page 7 of 12

☐ Extended parenting time or extraordinary costs associated with parenting time, provided that this division does not authorize and shall not be construed as authorizing any deviation from the schedule and the applicable worksheet, through the line establishing the actual annual obligation, or any escrowing, impoundment, or withholding of child support because of a denial of or interference with a right of parenting time granted by court order as follows: _____

_____

☐ The financial resources and the earning ability of the child(ren) as follows: _____

_____

☐ Disparity in income between parents or households as follows: _____

_____

☐ Benefits that either parent receives from remarriage or sharing living expenses with another person as follows: _____

_____

☐ The amount of federal, state, and local taxes actually paid or estimated to be paid by a parent or both of the parents as follows: _____

_____

☐ Significant, in-kind contributions from a parent, including, but not limited to, direct payment for lessons, sports equipment, schooling, or clothing as follows: _____

_____

☐ The relative financial resources, other assets and resources, and needs of each parent as follows: _____

_____

☐ The standard of living and circumstances of each parent and the standard of living the child(ren) would have enjoyed had the marriage continued or had the parents been married as follows: _____

_____

☐ The physical and emotional condition and needs of the child(ren) as follows: _____

_____

☐ The need and capacity of the child(ren) for an education and the educational opportunities that would have been available to the child(ren) had the circumstances requiring a court order for support not arisen as follows: _____

_____

_____

Supreme Court of Ohio
Uniform Domestic Relations Form – 18
PARENTING PLAN
Approved under Ohio Civil Rule 84 and Ohio Juvenile Rule 46
Effective Date: 7/1/2013

Page 8 of 12

☐ The responsibility of each parent for the support of others as follows: _____

_____

_____

☐ Any other relevant factor: _____

_____

_____

E. Duration of Child Support.
The child support order will terminate upon the child's 18th birthday unless one of the following circumstances applies:

- The child is mentally or physically disabled and incapable of supporting or maintaining himself or herself.
- The parents have agreed to continue child support beyond the date it would otherwise terminate as set out below.
- The child continuously attends a recognized and accredited high school on a full-time basis so long as the child has not, as yet, reached the age of 19 years old. (Under these circumstances, child support will end at the time the child ceases to attend a recognized and accredited high school on a full-time basis or when he or she reaches the age of 19, whichever occurs first.)

This Support Order will remain in effect during seasonal vacation periods until the order terminates.

The parents agree that child support will extend beyond when it would otherwise end. The terms and conditions of that agreement are as follows: _____

_____

_____

_____

The parents have (a) child(ren) who is/are mentally or physically disabled and incapable of supporting or maintaining themselves. The name of the child and the nature of the mental or physical disability are as follows: _____

_____

_____

F. Important Child Support Orders and Information.
Obligee must immediately notify and Obligor may notify the CSEA of any reason for which the support order should terminate. A willful failure to notify the CSEA as required is contempt of court. The following are reasons for termination of the Order:

- Child's attainment of the age of majority if the child no longer attends an accredited high school on a full-time basis and the support order does not provide for the duty of support to continue past the age of majority
- Child stops attending an accredited high school on a full-time basis after attaining the age of majority

Supreme Court of Ohio
Uniform Domestic Relations Form – 18
PARENTING PLAN
Approved under Ohio Civil Rule 84 and Ohio Juvenile Rule 46
Effective Date: 7/1/2013

Page 9 of 12

- Child's death
- Child's marriage
- Child's emancipation
- Child's enlistment in the Armed Services
- Child's deportation
- Change of legal custody of the child

All support payments must be made through the CSEA or the office of child support in the Ohio Department of Job and Family Services (Child Support Payment Central). Any payment of money not made through the CSEA will be presumed to be a gift, unless the payment is made to discharge an obligation other than support.

All support under this Order shall be withheld or deducted from the income or assets of the Obligor pursuant to a withholding or deduction notice or appropriate order issued in accordance with Chapters 3119., 3121., 3123., and 3125. of the Revised Code or a withdrawal directive issued pursuant to sections 3123.24 to 3123.38 of the Revised Code and shall be forwarded to the Obligee in accordance with Chapters 3119., 3121., 3123., and 3125. of the Revised Code.

The Obligor and/or Obligee required under this Order to provide private health insurance coverage for the child(ren) is also required to provide the other party within 30 days after the issuance of the Order, the following:
- Information regarding the benefits, limitations, and exclusions of the health insurance coverage
- Copies of any insurance form necessary to receive reimbursement, payment, or other benefits under the coverage
- A copy of any necessary health insurance cards

The Health Plan Administrator that provides the private health insurance coverage for the child(ren) may continue making payment for medical, optical, hospital, dental, or prescription services directly to any health care provider in accordance with the applicable private health insurance policy, contract, or plan.

The Obligor and/or Obligee required to provide private health insurance for the child(ren) must designate said child(ren) as dependents under any private health insurance policy, contract, or plan for which the person contracts.

The employer of the person required to provide private health insurance coverage is required to release to the other parent, any person subject to an order issued under section 3109.19 of the Revised Code, or the CSEA, upon written request, any necessary information regarding health insurance coverage, including the name and address of the health plan administrator and any policy, contract, or plan number, and the employer will otherwise comply with all orders and notices issued.

If the person required to obtain private health insurance coverage for the child(ren) subject to this

Support Order obtains new employment, the agency shall comply with the requirements of section 3119.34 of the Revised Code, which may result in the issuance of a notice requiring the new employer to take whatever action is necessary to enroll the child(ren) in private health insurance coverage provided by the new employer.

Upon receipt of notice by the CSEA that private health insurance coverage is not available at a reasonable cost, cash medical support shall be paid in the amount as determined by the child support computation worksheets in section 3119.022 or 3119.023 of the Revised Code, as applicable. The CSEA may change the financial obligations of the parties to pay child support in accordance with the terms of the court or administrative order and cash medical support without a hearing or additional notice to the parties.

An Obligor that is in arrears in his/her child support obligation is subject to having any federal, state and/or local income tax refund to which the Obligor may be entitled forwarded to the CSEA for payment toward these arrears. Such refunds will continue to be forwarded to the CSEA for payment until all arrears owed are paid in full. If the Obligor is married and files a joint tax return, the Obligor's spouse may contact the CSEA about filing an "Injured Spouse" claim after the Obligor is notified by the Internal Revenue Service that his/her refund is being forwarded to the CSEA.

Pursuant to section 3121.29 of the Revised Code, the parties are notified as follows:
EACH PARTY TO THIS SUPPORT ORDER MUST NOTIFY THE CHILD SUPPORT AGENCY IN WRITING OF HIS OR HER CURRENT MAILING ADDRESS, CURRENT RESIDENCE ADDRESS, CURRENT RESIDENCE TELEPHONE NUMBER, CURRENT DRIVER'S LICENSE NUMBER AND OF ANY CHANGES IN THAT INFORMATION. EACH PARTY MUST NOTIFY THE AGENCY OF ALL CHANGES UNTIL FURTHER NOTICE FROM THE COURT. IF YOU ARE THE OBLIGOR UNDER A CHILD SUPPORT ORDER AND YOU FAIL TO MAKE THE REQUIRED NOTIFICATIONS, YOU MAY BE FINED UP TO $50.00 FOR A FIRST OFFENSE, $100.00 FOR A SECOND OFFENSE, AND $500.00 FOR EACH SUBSEQUENT OFFENSE. IF YOU ARE AN OBLIGOR OR OBLIGEE UNDER ANY SUPPORT ORDER AND YOU WILLFULLY FAIL TO MAKE THE REQUIRED NOTIFICATIONS YOU MAY BE SUBJECTED TO FINES OF UP TO $1,000.00 AND IMPRISONMENT FOR NOT MORE THAN 90 DAYS.

IF YOU ARE AN OBLIGOR AND YOU FAIL TO MAKE THE REQUIRED NOTIFICATIONS, YOU MAY NOT RECEIVE NOTICE OF THE FOLLOWING ENFORCEMENT ACTIONS AGAINST YOU: IMPOSITION OF LIENS AGAINST YOUR PROPERTY; LOSS OF YOUR PROFESSIONAL OR OCCUPATIONAL LICENSE, DRIVER'S LICENSE, OR RECREATIONAL LICENSE; WITHHOLDING FROM YOUR INCOME; ACCESS RESTRICTIONS AND DEDUCTIONS FROM YOUR ACCOUNTS IN FINANCIAL INSTITUTIONS; AND ANY OTHER ACTION PERMITTED BY LAW TO OBTAIN MONEY FROM YOU AND TO SATISFY YOUR SUPPORT OBLIGATION.

G.   Payment shall be made in accordance with Chapter 3121. of the Revised Code.

H. Arrearage
- ☐ Any temporary child support arrearage will survive this judgment entry.
- ☐ Any temporary child support arrearage will not survive this judgment entry.
- ☐ Other: _____

FIFTH: TAX EXEMPTIONS

Income tax dependency exemptions (check all that apply):

A. ☐ The Father shall be entitled to claim the following minor child(ren) for all tax purposes for ☐ even-numbered tax years ☐ odd-numbered tax years ☐ all eligible tax years, so long as he is substantially current in any child support he is required to pay as of December 31 of the tax year in question: _____

☐ The Mother shall be entitled to claim the following minor child(ren) for all tax purposes for ☐ even-numbered tax years ☐ odd-numbered tax years ☐ all eligible tax years, so long as she is substantially current in any child support she is required to pay as of December 31 of the tax year in question: _____

B. ☐ Other orders regarding tax exemptions (specify): _____

If a non-residential parent is entitled to claim the child(ren), the residential parent is required to execute and deliver Internal Revenue Service Form 8332, or its successor, together with any other required forms as set out in section 152 of the Internal Revenue Code, as amended, on or before February 15th of the year following the tax year in question, to allow the non-residential parent to claim the minor child(ren).

SIXTH: MODIFICATION

This Parenting Plan may be modified by agreement of the parties or by the Court.

SEVENTH: OTHER

_____
_____

Upon approval by the Court, this Parenting Plan shall be incorporated in the Judgment Entry.

_____   _____
Your Signature (Father)   Your Signature (Mother)

_____   _____
Date   Date

IN THE COURT OF COMMON PLEAS

_____ **Division**

_____ **COUNTY, OHIO**

IN THE MATTER OF:

_____
A Minor

_____ :
Plaintiff/Petitioner

                             :   Case No. _____

_____ :
Street Address

                             :

_____ :   Judge _____
City, State and Zip Code   :

                             :

vs./and   :   Magistrate _____

_____ :
Defendant/Petitioner

                             :

_____ :
Street Address

_____ :
City, State and Zip Code

PARENTING JUDGMENT ENTRY

This case came before the Court on _____ for an Order allocating parental rights and responsibilities for the care of the following child(ren) (name and date of birth of each child):

Name of Child	**Date of Birth**
_____	_____
_____	_____
_____	_____

according to the ☐ Parenting Plan or ☐ Shared Parenting Plan attached.

The Court approves the Plan and incorporates it into this Judgment Entry.

A copy of this Judgment Entry shall be provided to the Child Support Enforcement Agency.

This Judgment Entry is effective on _____ .

_____   _____
Date   JUDGE

_____   _____
Your Signature (Father)   Your Signature (Mother)

_____   _____
Attorney for Father   Attorney for Mother

Supreme Court of Ohio
Uniform Domestic Relations Form – 19
Uniform Juvenile Form - 1
PARENTING JUDGMENT ENTRY
Approved under Ohio Civil Rule 84 and Ohio Juvenile Rule 46
Effective Date: 7/1/2013

IN THE COURT OF COMMON PLEAS

_____ **Division**

_____ **COUNTY, OHIO**

IN THE MATTER OF:

_____

A Minor

_____	:
Plaintiff	: Case No. _____
_____	:
Street Address	:
_____	: Judge _____
City, State and Zip Code	:
	:
	: Magistrate _____
vs.	:
	:
	:
_____	:
Defendant	:
_____	:
Street Address	:
_____	:
City, State and Zip Code	:

Instructions: This form is used to be legally recognized as the parent of the child, be named as the residential parent, or obtain visitation with the child(ren). The Parenting Proceeding Affidavit (Uniform Domestic Relations Form - Affidavit 3) and the Affidavit of Income and Expenses (Uniform Domestic Relations Form - Affidavit 1) must be filed with this Complaint.

COMPLAINT FOR PARENTAGE,
ALLOCATION OF PARENTAL RIGHTS AND RESPONSIBILITIES (CUSTODY), AND
PARENTING TIME (COMPANIONSHIP AND VISITATION)

1. I, _____ (name), am the Plaintiff and biological
    ☐ Father ☐ Mother (select one) of the following child(ren):

Name of Child	Date of Birth
_____	_____
_____	_____
_____	_____

2. Defendant, _____ is the biological ☐ Father ☐ Mother (select one)
    of the child(ren).

3. The child(ren) has/have resided in _____ County, Ohio since _____
    (date residence established) as set out in the Parenting Proceeding Affidavit (Uniform Domestic

Supreme Court of Ohio
Uniform Domestic Relations Form – 20
Uniform Juvenile Form – 2
COMPLAINT FOR PARENTAGE, ALLOCATION OF PARENTAL RIGHTS AND RESPONSIBILITIES
AND PARENTING TIME
Approved under Ohio Civil Rule 84 and Ohio Juvenile Rule 46
Effective Date: 7/1/2013

Page 1 of 2

Relations Form - Affidavit 3).

4. The father-child relationship ☐ has ☐ has not (select one) been established. If it has been established, a copy of the order establishing the father-child relationship is attached. A copy of the child(ren)'s birth certificate is also attached.

5. ☐ No court has issued an order about the following child(ren):

    _____

    _____

    _____

    ☐ The following Court has issued an order about the following child(ren):

    _____

    _____

6. I request that the Court (check all that apply):
    ☐ Name _____ (Father's name) as the
    Father of the child(ren) _____
    _____ (child(ren)'s name).
    ☐ Correct the child(ren)'s birth certificate to indicate the child(ren)'s father.
    ☐ Order genetic testing and determine the father of the child(ren).
    ☐ Name the ☐ Plaintiff ☐ Defendant (select one) as the residential parent and legal custodian of the child(ren).
    ☐ Grant reasonable parenting time (visitation) to the ☐ Mother ☐ Father (select one).
    ☐ Change the child(ren)'s name to _____
    ☐ Adopt the proposed Shared Parenting Plan for the child(ren) which is attached.
    ☐ Order the appropriate amount of child support for the child(ren), allocate the income tax dependency exemption for the child(ren), and determine who should provide health insurance coverage for the child(ren).
    ☐ Other (specify): _____

    _____

    _____

    _____

    _____
    Your Signature

    _____
    Telephone number at which the Court may reach you
    or at which messages may be left for you

Supreme Court of Ohio
Uniform Domestic Relations Form – 20
Uniform Juvenile Form – 2
COMPLAINT FOR PARENTAGE, ALLOCATION OF PARENTAL RIGHTS AND RESPONSIBILITIES
AND PARENTING TIME
Approved under Ohio Civil Rule 84 and Ohio Juvenile Rule 46
Effective Date: 7/1/2013   Page 2 of 2

IN THE COURT OF COMMON PLEAS

_____ **Division**

_____ **COUNTY, OHIO**

IN THE MATTER OF:

_____

A Minor

_____
Name

_____
Street Address

_____
City, State and Zip Code

Plaintiff/Petitioner

vs.

_____
Name

_____
Street Address

_____
City, State and Zip Code

Defendant/Petitioner

:
:
:
:
:
:
:
:
:
:
:
:
:
:
:
:
:
:

Case No. _____

Judge _____

Magistrate _____

Instructions: This form is used to request the enforcement of a court order and hold the other party in contempt for violating the court order. A Request for Service (Uniform Domestic Relations Form 28) and a proposed Show Cause Order, Notice and Instructions to the Clerk (Uniform Domestic Relations Form 22) must be filed with this Motion. Check local court procedures.

MOTION FOR CONTEMPT AND AFFIDAVIT

I, _____ (name), request an order for

_____ (other party's name) to appear and show cause

why he/she should not be held in contempt for violating a court order and a finding of contempt for violating the court order regarding the following (check all that apply):

1. ☐ Interference with parenting time or other parenting orders filed on _____ (date).

2. ☐ Failure to pay child support, as required by the order filed on _____ (date)
   and the total arrearage owed is $ _____
   (Bring to the hearing an up-to-date printout from the County Child Support Enforcement Agency showing the amount of the child support owed to you.)

3. ☐ Failure to pay spousal support, as required by the order filed on _____ (date)

Supreme Court of Ohio
Uniform Domestic Relations Form – 21
Uniform Juvenile Form – 3
MOTION FOR CONTEMPT AND AFFIDAVIT
Approved under Ohio Civil Rule 84 and Ohio Juvenile Rule 46
Effective Date: 7/1/2013

and the total arrearage owed is $ _____

(Bring to the hearing an up-to-date printout from the County Child Support Enforcement Agency or other independent proof showing the amount owed to you.)

4. ☐ Payment or reimbursement of health care expenses incurred for the minor child(ren). Attach an Explanation of Health Care Bills (Uniform Domestic Relations Form 26) and bring to the hearing the following documents:

    a. Copies of each bill for which you seek reimbursement;

    b. Proof of payment by you. Proof of payment may include a receipt for payment signed by the health care provider, a copy of a cancelled check, or a copy of a credit card statement verifying the amount paid; and

    c. Explanation of Benefits forms showing payment made by the health insurance carrier.

5. ☐ Failure to comply with the Court's orders of _____ (date) regarding (check all that apply):

    ☐ Transfer of real estate, as follows: _____

    ☐ Payment of debt, as follows: _____

    ☐ Refinance of debt, as follows: _____

    ☐ Distribution of personal property, as follows: _____

    ☐ Other (specify): _____

6. Costs and any other relief as necessary and proper are also requested.

_____
Your Signature

_____
Telephone number at which the Court may reach you or at which messages may be left for you

OATH
(Do not sign until Notary is present.)

I, _____ (name), swear or affirm that I have read this document and, to the best of my knowledge and belief, the facts and information stated in this document are true, accurate and complete. I understand that if I do not tell the truth, I may be subject to penalties for perjury.

_____
Your Signature

Sworn before me and signed in my presence this _____ day of _____ , _____ .

_____
Notary Public
My Commission Expires: _____

Supreme Court of Ohio
Uniform Domestic Relations Form – 21
Uniform Juvenile Form – 3
MOTION FOR CONTEMPT AND AFFIDAVIT
Approved under Ohio Civil Rule 84 and Ohio Juvenile Rule 46
Effective Date: 7/1/2013

Page 2 of 2

IN THE COURT OF COMMON PLEAS

_____ **Division**

_____ **COUNTY, OHIO**

IN THE MATTER OF:

_____
A Minor

_____ Name	: : Case No. _____
_____ Street Address	: :
_____ City, State and Zip Code	: Judge _____ :
Plaintiff/Petitioner	: : Magistrate _____
	:
vs./and	: :
	:
_____ Name	: :
	:
_____ Street Address	: :
_____ City, State and Zip Code	:
Defendant/Petitioner	:

Instructions: This form is used to bring the other party to Court to defend his/her failure to follow the court order. A Motion for Contempt and Affidavit (Uniform Domestic Relations Form 21) must be filed with this order.

SHOW CAUSE ORDER, NOTICE AND INSTRUCTIONS TO THE CLERK

TO: _____   TO: _____
　　　　PLAINTIFF/PETITIONER　　　　　　　　　DEFENDANT/PETITIONER

You are hereby ORDERED to appear and show cause why you should not be held in contempt for failure to obey the court order as described in the Motion you are now receiving.

Supreme Court of Ohio
Uniform Domestic Relations Form – 22
Uniform Juvenile Form – 4
SHOW CAUSE ORDER, NOTICE AND INSTRUCTIONS TO THE CLERK
Approved under Ohio Civil Rule 84 and Ohio Juvenile Rule 46
Effective Date: 7/1/2013

COURT
(The Court will complete this part.)

You are ORDERED to appear in the _____ County Common Pleas Court

_____ Division, in Courtroom _____ located at _____

_____

on _____ at _____ o'clock and show cause why you

should not be held in contempt of this Court.

NOTICE

1. Failure to appear as ordered may result in the issuance of a bench warrant for an immediate arrest.

2. Failure to appear may result in an immediate income withholding or deduction.

3. You have the right to be represented by an attorney.

4. If you cannot afford an attorney, you must apply for a public defender or appointed counsel, as appropriate, within three business days after receipt of this show cause order.

5. A continuance may not be granted to obtain counsel if you have made no good faith effort to secure one.

6. If found guilty, you may be sentenced as follows:
   a. First offense – a fine of not more than $250.00 and/or a definite term of imprisonment of not more than thirty days in jail or both.
   b. Second offense – a fine of not more than $500.00 and/or a definite term of imprisonment of not more than sixty days in jail or both.
   c. Third offense – a fine of not more than $1,000.00 and/or a definite term of imprisonment of not more than ninety days in jail or both.

7. The court may grant you limited driving privileges under 4510.021 of the Revised Code if your driver's license was suspended based on a notice issued by a child support enforcement agency because you are in default under a child support order or you have failed to comply with a subpoena or warrant issued by a court or agency with respect to a proceeding to enforce a child support order. You must request limited driving privileges and your request must be accompanied by a recent copy of your driver's abstract driving record from the registrar of motor vehicles.

_____
JUDGE/MAGISTRATE

Supreme Court of Ohio
Uniform Domestic Relations Form – 22
Uniform Juvenile Form – 4
SHOW CAUSE ORDER, NOTICE AND INSTRUCTIONS TO THE CLERK
Approved under Ohio Civil Rule 84 and Ohio Juvenile Rule 46
Effective Date: 7/1/2013

INSTRUCTIONS TO THE CLERK

You are directed to serve this Order along with the Motion for Contempt and Affidavit to the
☐ Defendant/Petitioner or ☐ Plaintiff/Petitioner by:

    ☐ Certified Mail, Return Receipt Requested

    ☐ Issuance to Sheriff of _____ County, Ohio for ☐ Personal or ☐ Residence service

    ☐ Other (specify) _____

_____
Your Signature

Supreme Court of Ohio
Uniform Domestic Relations Form – 22
Uniform Juvenile Form – 4
SHOW CAUSE ORDER, NOTICE AND INSTRUCTIONS TO THE CLERK
Approved under Ohio Civil Rule 84 and Ohio Juvenile Rule 46
Effective Date: 7/1/2013

IN THE COURT OF COMMON PLEAS

_____ **Division**

_____ **COUNTY, OHIO**

IN THE MATTER OF:

_____
A Minor

_____
Name

   :

_____
Street Address

   :   Case No. _____

   :

_____
City, State and Zip Code

   :   Judge _____

   Plaintiff/Petitioner   :

   :   Magistrate _____

vs./and   :

   :

_____
Name

   :

   :

_____
Street Address

   :

   :

_____
City, State and Zip Code

   :

   Defendant/Petitioner   :

Instructions: This form is used to request a change in the parenting time (visitation) order. A Request for Service (Uniform Domestic Relations Form 28) and a Parenting Proceeding Affidavit (Uniform Domestic Relations Form – Affidavit 3) must be filed with this Motion.

MOTION FOR CHANGE OF PARENTING TIME (COMPANIONSHIP AND VISITATION) AND MEMORANDUM IN SUPPORT

1. I, _____ (name), request this Court change the existing parenting time (companionship and visitation) Order filed on this date _____ (date filed) regarding the following minor child(ren):

Name of Child	Date of Birth
_____	_____
_____	_____
_____	_____

Supreme Court of Ohio
Uniform Domestic Relations Form – 23
Uniform Juvenile Form – 5
MOTION FOR CHANGE OF PARENTING TIME (VISITATION) AND MEMORANDUM IN SUPPORT
Approved under Ohio Civil Rule 84 and Ohio Juvenile Rule 46
Effective Date: 7/1/2013

Page 1 of 2

2. Select one:

☐ _____ (name) is currently designated the residential parent and/or legal custodian of the child(ren).

☐ The parties now have a Shared Parenting Plan.

3. I request that the Court change the parenting time (companionship and visitation) Order because:

_____

_____

_____

4. I request that the Court change the existing parenting time (companionship and visitation) Order in the following way: _____

_____

_____

_____

5. I believe that the changes I am requesting are in the child(ren)'s best interests.

_____
Your Signature

_____
Telephone number at which the Court may reach you or at which messages may be left for you

Supreme Court of Ohio
Uniform Domestic Relations Form – 23
Uniform Juvenile Form – 5
MOTION FOR CHANGE OF PARENTING TIME (VISITATION) AND MEMORANDUM IN SUPPORT
Approved under Ohio Civil Rule 84 and Ohio Juvenile Rule 46
Effective Date: 7/1/2013

Page 2 of 2

IN THE COURT OF COMMON PLEAS

_____ **Division**

_____ **COUNTY, OHIO**

IN THE MATTER OF:

_____
A Minor

_____
Name   :

_____   :   Case No. _____
Street Address   :

_____   :   Judge _____
City, State and Zip Code   :

Plaintiff/Petitioner   :

:   Magistrate _____

:

vs.   :

:

:

_____   :
Name   :

_____   :
Street Address   :

_____   :
City, State and Zip Code   :

Defendant/Petitioner   :

Instructions: This form is used to request a change in a shared parenting plan or a change in the designation of the sole residential parent and legal custodian. A Request for Service (Uniform Domestic Relations Form 28) and a Parenting Proceeding Affidavit (Uniform Domestic Relations Form – Affidavit 3) must be filed with this Motion.

MOTION FOR CHANGE OF PARENTAL RIGHTS AND RESPONSIBILITIES (CUSTODY) AND MEMORANDUM IN SUPPORT

1. I, _____ (name), request this Court change the allocation of parental rights and responsibilities (custody) Order filed on this date _____ (filed date) regarding the following minor child(ren): _____

Name of Child	Date of Birth
_____	_____
_____	_____
_____	_____

Supreme Court of Ohio
Uniform Domestic Relations Form – 24
Uniform Juvenile Form – 6
MOTION FOR CHANGE OF PARENTAL RIGHTS AND RESPONSIBILITIES (CUSTODY)
AND MEMORANDUM IN SUPPORT
Approved under Ohio Civil Rule 84 and Ohio Juvenile Rule 46
Effective Date: 7/1/2013

2. Select one:

☐ _____ (name) is currently designated as the residential parent and/or legal custodian of the children and resides in the _____ School District.

☐ The parents now have a Shared Parenting Plan.

3. The circumstances have changed since the Court issued the existing order. The change in circumstances and any other reason for the requested change are as follows:

_____
_____
_____

4. I request that the Court change the existing order in the following way:

_____
_____
_____

5. I believe that the changes I am requesting are in the child(ren)'s best interests.

_____
Your Signature

_____
Telephone number at which the Court may reach you or at which messages may be left for you

Supreme Court of Ohio
Uniform Domestic Relations Form – 24
Uniform Juvenile Form – 6
MOTION FOR CHANGE OF PARENTAL RIGHTS AND RESPONSIBILITIES (CUSTODY)
AND MEMORANDUM IN SUPPORT
Approved under Ohio Civil Rule 84 and Ohio Juvenile Rule 46
Effective Date: 7/1/2013   Page 2 of 2

IN THE COURT OF COMMON PLEAS

_____ **Division**

_____ **COUNTY, OHIO**

IN THE MATTER OF:

_____
A Minor

_____   :
Name   :   Case No. _____
_____   :
Street Address   :
_____   :   Judge _____
City, State and Zip Code   :
                   Plaintiff/Petitioner   :
                                                            :   Magistrate _____
                                                            :
                                                            :
vs.   :
                                                            :
                                                            :
_____   :
Name   :
_____   :
Street Address   :
_____   :
City, State and Zip Code   :
                   Defendant/Petitioner   :

Instructions: This form is used to request a change in the child support or child support-related matters. A Request for Service (Uniform Domestic Relations Form 28) and an Affidavit of Income and Expenses (Uniform Domestic Relations Form–Affidavit 1) must be filed with this Motion.

MOTION FOR CHANGE OF CHILD SUPPORT, MEDICAL SUPPORT, TAX EXEMPTION, OR OTHER CHILD-RELATED EXPENSES AND MEMORANDUM IN SUPPORT

I, _____ (name), request this Court change my obligation to provide support or my right to receive support for the minor child(ren) as follows (check all that apply):

1. ☐ The amount of child support to be paid each month. The change I want the Court to order is:

_____

_____

Supreme Court of Ohio
Uniform Domestic Relations Form – 25
Uniform Juvenile Form – 7
MOTION FOR CHANGE OF CHILD SUPPORT, MEDICAL SUPPORT, TAX EXEMPTION,
OR OTHER CHILD-RELATED EXPENSES AND MEMORANDUM IN SUPPORT
Approved under Ohio Civil Rule 84 and Ohio Juvenile Rule 46
Effective Date: 7/1/2013

Page 1 of 2

2. ☐ The person responsible for providing health insurance for the child(ren). The change I want the Court to order is: _____

_____

_____

3. ☐ The amount of non-insured health care expenses of the minor child(ren) that I have to pay. The change I want the Court to order is: _____

_____

_____

4. ☐ The person who can claim the child(ren) as tax dependents. The change I want the Court to order is: _____

_____

_____

5. ☐ Other child-related expenses. The change I want the Court to order is: _____

_____

_____

6. The circumstances have changed since the Court issued the existing order. The change in circumstances and any other reason for the requested change are as follows: _____

_____

_____

_____

7. I believe that the requested changes are in the child(ren)'s best interests.

_____
Your Signature

_____
Telephone number at which the Court may reach you
or at which messages may be left for you

Supreme Court of Ohio
Uniform Domestic Relations Form – 25
Uniform Juvenile Form – 7
MOTION FOR CHANGE OF CHILD SUPPORT, MEDICAL SUPPORT, TAX EXEMPTION,
OR OTHER CHILD-RELATED EXPENSES AND MEMORANDUM IN SUPPORT
Approved under Ohio Civil Rule 84 and Ohio Juvenile Rule 46
Effective Date: 7/1/2013   Page 2 of 2

Name of Child: _____

Case No. _____

EXPLANATION OF HEALTH CARE BILLS

Date of Treatment	Name of Service Provider (e.g., Doctor, Dentist, Therapist, Hospital) & Services Provided	Total Bill	Date Bill Sent to Other Party	Amount Insurance Paid	Amount You Paid	Amount Paid by Other Party	Amount of Unpaid Bill	Amount Due from Other Party

Total Amount of Claim $ _____

_____   _____
Your Signature   Date

Supreme Court of Ohio
Uniform Domestic Relations Form – 26
Uniform Juvenile Form – 8
EXPLANATION OF HEALTH CARE BILLS
Approved under Ohio Civil Rule 84 and Ohio Juvenile Rule 46
Effective Date: 7/1/2013

IN THE COURT OF COMMON PLEAS

_____ Division

_____ COUNTY, OHIO

IN THE MATTER OF:

_____

A Minor

_____	:	
Plaintiff/Petitioner	:	Case No. _____
_____	:	
Street Address	:	
_____	:	Judge _____
City, State and Zip	:	
vs.	:	Magistrate _____
	:	
_____	:	
Defendant/Respondent/Petitioner	:	
_____	:	
Street Address	:	
_____	:	
City, State and Zip Code	:	
	:	

WAIVER OF SERVICE OF SUMMONS

I, _____ (name), acknowledge that I am the ☐ Petitioner ☐ Plaintiff
☐ Defendant ☐ Respondent (select one) and that I have received a copy of the following documents filed or to be filed by the other party:

☐ Complaint for Parentage
☐ Complaint ☐ Motion (select one) for Allocation of Parental Rights and Responsibilities (Custody)
☐ Complaint ☐ Motion (select one) for Parenting Time (Companionship and Visitation)
☐ Complaint ☐ Motion (select one) for Establishment or Change of Child Support
☐ Journal Entry and Findings of Fact Supporting Child Support Deviation
☐ Health Insurance Affidavit
☐ Complaint for Divorce with Children
☐ Complaint for Divorce without Children
☐ Separation Agreement
☐ Shared Parenting Plan
☐ Parenting Plan
☐ Petition for Dissolution
☐ Agreed Judgment Entry, Magistrate's Decision, Order, and/or Magistrate's Order
☐ Affidavit of Income and Expenses

Supreme Court of Ohio
Uniform Domestic Relations Form – 27
Uniform Juvenile Form – 9
WAIVER OF SERVICE OF SUMMONS
Approved under Ohio Civil Rule 84 and Ohio Juvenile Rule 46
Effective Date: 7/1/2013

Page 1 of 2

☐ Affidavit of Property
☐ Parenting Proceeding Affidavit
☐ Motion for Contempt and Affidavit
☐ Motion and Affidavit or Counter Affidavit for Temporary Orders with Oral Hearing
☐ Other (specify): _____

I waive service of summons of said document by the Clerk of Court.

_____
Date

_____
Your Signature

_____
Telephone number at which the Court may reach you
or at which messages may be left for you

Supreme Court of Ohio
Uniform Domestic Relations Form – 27
Uniform Juvenile Form – 9
WAIVER OF SERVICE OF SUMMONS
Approved under Ohio Civil Rule 84 and Ohio Juvenile Rule 46
Effective Date: 7/1/2013

Page 2 of 2

IN THE COURT OF COMMON PLEAS

_____ **Division**

_____ **COUNTY, OHIO**

IN THE MATTER OF:

_____

A Minor

_____
Name

Case No. _____

_____
Street Address

Judge _____

_____
City, State and Zip Code

          Plaintiff/Petitioner

Magistrate _____

vs./and

_____
Name

_____
Street Address

_____
City, State and Zip Code

          Defendant/Petitioner

Instructions: This form is used when you want to request documents to be served on the other party. You must indicate the requested method of service by marking the appropriate box.

REQUEST FOR SERVICE

TO THE CLERK OF COURT:

Please serve the following documents on the following parties as I have indicated below:

_____

_____

☐ Defendant/Petitioner at the address shown above.
    ☐ Certified Mail, Return Receipt Requested
    ☐ Issuance to Sheriff of _____ County, Ohio for ☐ Personal or ☐ Residence service
    ☐ Other (specify) _____

Supreme Court of Ohio
Uniform Domestic Relations Form – 28
Uniform Juvenile Form – 10
REQUEST FOR SERVICE
Approved under Ohio Civil Rule 84 and Ohio Juvenile Rule 46
Effective Date: 7/1/2013

Page 1 of 2

☐ Plaintiff/Petitioner at the address shown above.
    ☐ Certified Mail, Return Receipt Requested
    ☐ Issuance to Sheriff of _____ County, Ohio for ☐ Personal or ☐ Residence service
    ☐ Other (specify) _____

☐ _____ County Child Support Enforcement Agency (provide address below):

_____

    ☐ Certified Mail, Return Receipt Requested
    ☐ Issuance to Sheriff of _____ County, Ohio for ☐ Personal or ☐ Residence service
    ☐ Other (specify) _____

☐ Other (address): _____
    ☐ Certified Mail, Return Receipt Requested
    ☐ Issuance to Sheriff of _____ County, Ohio for ☐ Personal or ☐ Residence service
    ☐ Other (specify) _____

SPECIAL INSTRUCTIONS TO SHERIFF:

_____
_____
_____

_____
Your Signature

Supreme Court of Ohio
Uniform Domestic Relations Form – 28
Uniform Juvenile Form – 10
REQUEST FOR SERVICE
Approved under Ohio Civil Rule 84 and Ohio Juvenile Rule 46
Effective Date: 7/1/2013

Page 2 of 2

COURT OF COMMON PLEAS
_____ COUNTY, OHIO

_____
Plaintiff/Petitioner 1

v./and

_____
Defendant/Petitioner 2

Case No. _____

Judge _____

Magistrate _____

Instructions: Check local court rules to determine when this form must be filed.
This affidavit is used to disclose health insurance coverage that is available for children. It is also used to determine child support. It must be filed if there are minor children of the relationship. **If more space is needed, add additional pages.**

HEALTH INSURANCE AFFIDAVIT

Affidavit of _____
(Print Your Name)

	_____ **Your Name**	_____ **Spouse's Name**
Are your child(ren) currently enrolled in a low-income government-assisted health care program (Healthy Start/Medicaid)?	☐ Yes ☐ No	☐ Yes ☐ No
Are you enrolled in an individual (non-group or COBRA) health insurance plan?	☐ Yes ☐ No	☐ Yes ☐ No
Are you enrolled in a health insurance plan through a group (employer or other organization)?	☐ Yes ☐ No	☐ Yes ☐ No
If you are not enrolled, do you have health insurance available through a group (employer or other organization)?	☐ Yes ☐ No	☐ Yes ☐ No
Does the available insurance cover primary care services within 30 miles of the child(ren)'s home?	☐ Yes ☐ No	☐ Yes ☐ No

Supreme Court of Ohio
Uniform Domestic Relations Form – Affidavit 4
Health Insurance Affidavit
Approved under Ohio Civil Rule 84
Amended: March 15, 2016

Page 1 of 2

	_____ **Your Name**	_____ **Spouse's Name**

Under the available insurance, what would be the annual premium for a plan covering you and the child(ren) of this relationship (not including a spouse)?

$ _____ $ _____

Under the available insurance, what would be the annual premium for a plan covering you alone (not including children or spouse)?

$ _____ $ _____

If you are enrolled in a health insurance plan through a group (employer or other organization) or individual insurance plan, which of the following people is/are covered:

Yourself?   ☐ Yes ☐ No   ☐ Yes ☐ No

Your spouse?   ☐ Yes ☐ No   ☐ Yes ☐ No

Minor child(ren) of this
relationship?   ☐ Yes ☐ No   ☐ Yes ☐ No
                             Number _____   Number _____

Other individuals?   ☐ Yes ☐ No   ☐ Yes ☐ No
                             Number _____   Number _____

Name of group (employer or organization) that provides health insurance

_____   _____

Address

_____   _____

_____   _____

Phone number

_____   _____

OATH

(Do not sign until notary is present.)

I, (print name) _____ , swear or affirm that I have read this document and, to the best of my knowledge and belief, the facts and information stated in this document are true, accurate, and complete. I understand that if I do not tell the truth, I may be subject to penalties for perjury.

_____
Your Signature

Sworn before me and signed in my presence this _____ day of _____ , _____ .

_____
Notary Public
My Commission Expires:

_____

Supreme Court of Ohio
Uniform Domestic Relations Form – Affidavit 4
Health Insurance Affidavit
Approved under Ohio Civil Rule 84
Amended: March 15, 2016

Page 2 of 2

COURT OF COMMON PLEAS

_____ COUNTY, OHIO

_____
Plaintiff

v.

_____
Defendant

Case No. _____

Judge _____

Magistrate _____

Instructions: Check local court rules to determine when this form must be filed.
This form is used to request temporary orders in your divorce or legal separation case. After a party serves a Motion and Affidavit, the other party has 14 days to file a Counter Affidavit and serve it on the party who filed the motion. **If more space is needed, add additional pages.**

☐ MOTION AND AFFIDAVIT OR ☐ COUNTER AFFIDAVIT
FOR TEMPORARY ORDERS
WITHOUT ORAL HEARING

Check one box below to show whether you are filing a (1) Motion and Affidavit or (2) Counter Affidavit.

☐ **(1) Motion and Affidavit**

(Print Your Name) _____ files this Motion and Affidavit under Rule 75(N) of the Ohio Rules of Civil Procedure to request the temporary orders checked here.

Check only those that apply.

_____	Residential parenting rights (custody)
_____	Parenting time (visitation)
_____	Child support
_____	Spousal support (alimony)
_____	Payment of debts and/or expenses

THE OTHER PARTY HAS 14 DAYS FROM THE DATE ON WHICH THIS MOTION IS SERVED TO FILE A COUNTER AFFIDAVIT AND SERVE IT UPON THE PARTY WHO FILED THE MOTION. (See below.)

☐ **(2) Counter Affidavit**

(Print Your Name) _____ files this Counter Affidavit in response to a Motion and Affidavit.

Supreme Court of Ohio
Uniform Domestic Relations Form – Affidavit 5
Motion and Affidavit or Counter Affidavit for Temporary Orders
Without Oral Hearing
Approved under Ohio Civil Rule 84
Amended: March 15, 2016

Page 1 of 4

Complete the following information, whether filing Motion and Affidavit or Counter Affidavit. Check all that apply.

1. ☐ My spouse and I are living separately.

   Date of separation is _____ .

   ☐ My spouse and I are living together.

   ☐ We have no minor children. (Skip to number 5.)

   ☐ There are minor child(ren) who are adopted or born of this marriage. (List children here.)

Name	Date of birth	Living with
_____	_____	_____
_____	_____	_____
_____	_____	_____
_____	_____	_____

   ☐ In addition to the above children there is/are in my household:

   _____ adult(s)

   _____ other minor and/or dependent child(ren).

2. My child(ren) attend(s) school in:

   ☐ My school district

   ☐ The other parent's school district

   ☐ Open enrollment

   ☐ Other (Explain.) _____ .

   ☐ All children do not attend school in the same district. (Explain.)

   _____

3. ☐ I request to be named the temporary residential parent and legal custodian of the child(ren).

   (Specify child(ren) if request is not for all children.) _____

   ☐ I do not object to my spouse being named the temporary residential parent of the child(ren).

   ☐ I request the following parenting time order:

   ☐ The Court's standard parenting order (See county's local rules of court.)

   ☐ A specific parenting time order as follows:

   _____

   _____

Supreme Court of Ohio
Uniform Domestic Relations Form – Affidavit 5
Motion and Affidavit or Counter Affidavit for Temporary Orders
Without Oral Hearing
Approved under Ohio Civil Rule 84
Amended: March 15, 2016

Page 2 of 4

☐ I have reached an agreement regarding parenting time with my spouse as follows:

_____

_____

☐ I request that my spouse's parenting time (visitation) be supervised. (Explain--supervised parenting time order will NOT be granted if the reasons are not explained.)

_____

_____

Name of an appropriate supervisor _____

4. ☐ A court or agency has made a child support order concerning the child(ren).

Name of Court/Agency _____

Date of Order _____

SETS No. _____

5. I request the Court to order my spouse to pay:

☐ $ _____ child support per month

☐ $ _____ spousal support per month

☐ $ _____ attorney fees, expert fees, court costs

☐ The following debts and/or expenses:

_____

_____

☐ Other

_____

6. ☐ I am willing to attend mediation.

☐ I am not willing to attend mediation.

☐ I request the following court services. (See local rules of court for available services.)

_____

_____

State specific reasons why court services are required.

_____

_____

Supreme Court of Ohio
Uniform Domestic Relations Form – Affidavit 5
Motion and Affidavit or Counter Affidavit for Temporary Orders
Without Oral Hearing
Approved under Ohio Civil Rule 84
Amended: March 15, 2016

Page 3 of 4

OATH

(Do not sign until notary is present.)

I, (print name) _____ , swear or affirm that I have read this document and, to the best of my knowledge and belief, the facts and information stated in this document are true, accurate, and complete. I understand that if I do not tell the truth, I may be subject to penalties for perjury.

_____
Your Signature

Sworn before me and signed in my presence this _____ day of _____ , _____ .

_____
Notary Public
My Commission Expires:

NOTICE OF HEARING
(Check with local court for scheduling procedure.)

You are hereby given notice that this motion for temporary orders will be heard upon affidavits only, and

without oral testimony, before Judge/Magistrate _____ ,

Hearing Room _____ , at _____ a.m./p.m. on _____ , 20 _____ , at

_____ , _____ floor .

CERTIFICATE OF SERVICE

Check the boxes that apply.

I delivered a copy of my: ☐ Motion and Affidavit or ☐ Counter Affidavit

On: (Date) _____ , 20 _____

To: (Print name of other party's attorney or, if there is no attorney, print name of the party.)

_____

At: (Print address or fax number.) _____ .

_____

By: ☐ U.S. Mail

☐ Fax

☐ Messenger

☐ Clerk of courts (if address is unknown)

_____
Your Signature

Supreme Court of Ohio
Uniform Domestic Relations Form – Affidavit 5
Motion and Affidavit or Counter Affidavit for Temporary Orders
Without Oral Hearing
Approved under Ohio Civil Rule 84
Amended: March 15, 2016

Page 4 of 4

Disclaimer

Please be aware that these forms do not include instructions or legal advice regarding your rights, responsibilities, and legal options.

To be fully informed and get answers to your questions, you should seek the advice of an attorney.

IN THE COURT OF COMMON PLEAS

_____ **Division**

_____ **COUNTY, OHIO**

_____ Name	Case No. _____
_____ Street Address	
_____ City, State and Zip Code	Judge _____
Plaintiff	
	Magistrate _____
vs.	
_____ Name	
_____ Street Address	
_____ City, State and Zip Code	
Defendant	

> **Instructions:** This form is used to request a divorce if you and your spouse do not have (a) child(ren), adult child(ren) attending high school, or child(ren) with disabilities. Check to determine if you meet the residency requirement to file in this county. A Request for Service (Uniform Domestic Relations Form 28) must be filed with this form.

COMPLAINT FOR DIVORCE WITHOUT CHILDREN

I, the Plaintiff, for this Complaint say:

1. I have been a resident of the State of Ohio for at least six months.

2. ☐ I have been a resident of _____ County for at least 90 days immediately before the filing of this Complaint; or
   ☐ The Defendant resides in _____ County where this Complaint is filed.

3. The Defendant and I were married to one another on _____ (date of marriage) in _____ (city or county, and state).

Supreme Court of Ohio
Uniform Domestic Relations Form – 6
COMPLAINT FOR DIVORCE WITHOUT CHILDREN
Approved under Ohio Civil Rule 84
Amended: March 15, 2016

Page 1 of 3

4. I state regarding child(ren) (check all that apply):

☐ There is/are no child(ren) expected from this marriage or relationship.
☐ There is/are child(ren) expected from this marriage or relationship and the approximate due date is:

_____.

☐ There is/are no child(ren) from this marriage or relationship.
☐ The parties are parents of _____ (number) child(ren) from the marriage or relationship. Of the child(ren), _____ (number) is/are emancipated adult(s) and not under a disability. The following _____(number) child(ren) is/are minor child(ren) and/or mentally or physically disabled and incapable of supporting or maintaining themselves (name and date of birth of each child):

Name of Child	Date of Birth
_____	_____
_____	_____
_____	_____

5. I state the following grounds for divorce exist (check all that apply):

☐ The Defendant and I are incompatible.
☐ The Defendant and I have lived separate and apart without cohabitation and without interruption for one year.
☐ The Defendant or I had a Spouse living at the time of the marriage.
☐ The Defendant has been willfully absent for one year.
☐ The Defendant is guilty of adultery.
☐ The Defendant is guilty of extreme cruelty.
☐ The Defendant is guilty of fraudulent contract.
☐ The Defendant is guilty of gross neglect of duty.
☐ The Defendant is guilty of habitual drunkenness.
☐ The Defendant was imprisoned in a state or federal correctional institution at the time the Complaint was filed.
☐ The Defendant procured a divorce outside this state by virtue of which the Defendant has been released from the obligations of the marriage, while those obligations remain binding on me.

6. The Defendant and I are owners of real estate and/or personal property.

I request that a divorce be granted from the Defendant, that the Court determine an equitable division of debts and property, and as follows that (check all that apply):

☐ The Defendant be ordered to pay me spousal support.
☐ I be restored to my prior name of: _____
☐ The Defendant be required to pay attorney fees.
☐ The Defendant be required to pay the court costs of the proceeding.
☐ The Court make the following additional orders: _____

_____
_____

_____

_____

and that the Court grant such other and further relief as the Court may deem proper.

_____
Your Signature

_____
Telephone number at which the Court may reach you
or at which messages may be left for you

Supreme Court of Ohio
Uniform Domestic Relations Form – 6
COMPLAINT FOR DIVORCE WITHOUT CHILDREN
Approved under Ohio Civil Rule 84
Amended: March 15, 2016

Page 3 of 3

IN THE COURT OF COMMON PLEAS

_____ **Division**

_____ **COUNTY, OHIO**

_____	:
Name	: Case No. _____
_____	:
Street Address	:
_____	: Judge _____
City, State and Zip Code	:
Plaintiff	:
	: Magistrate _____
vs.	:
	:
_____	:
Name	:
_____	:
Street Address	:
_____	:
City, State and Zip Code	:
Defendant	:

> **Instructions:** This form is used to request a divorce if you and your spouse have (a) minor child(ren), adult child(ren) attending high school, or child(ren) with disabilities, and/or you or the Spouse are/is pregnant. Check to determine if you meet the residency requirement to file in this county. A Request for Service (Uniform Domestic Relations Form 28) must be filed with this form. The Parenting Proceeding Affidavit (Uniform Domestic Relations Form - Affidavit 3) must be filed.

COMPLAINT FOR DIVORCE WITH CHILDREN

I, the Plaintiff, for this Complaint say:

1. I have been a resident of the State of Ohio for at least six months.

2. ☐ I have been a resident of _____ County for at least 90 days immediately before the filing of this Complaint; or
   ☐ The Defendant resides in _____ County where this Complaint is filed.

3. The Defendant and I were married to one another on _____ (date of marriage) in _____ (city or county, and state).

Supreme Court of Ohio
Uniform Domestic Relations Form – 7
COMPLAINT FOR DIVORCE WITH CHILDREN
Approved under Ohio Civil Rule 84
Amended: March 15, 2016

Page 1 of 3

4. I state regarding child(ren) (check all that apply):

☐ There is/are no child(ren) expected from this marriage or relationship.

☐ There is/are child(ren) expected from this marriage or relationship and the approximate due date is: _____.

☐ There is/are no child(ren) from this marriage or relationship.

☐ The parties are parents of _____ (number) child(ren) from this marriage or relationship. Of the child(ren), _____ (number) is/are emancipated adult(s) and not under a disability. The following _____ (number) child(ren) is/are minor child(ren) and/or mentally or physically disabled and incapable of supporting or maintaining themselves (name and date of birth of each child):

Name of Child	Date of Birth
_____	_____
_____	_____
_____	_____

☐ I am not the parent of the following child(ren) (name and date of birth of each child):
_____
_____

☐ The Spouse is not the parent of the following child(ren) (name and date of birth of each child):
_____
_____

5. I state the following grounds for divorce exist (check all that apply):

☐ The Defendant and I are incompatible.

☐ The Defendant and I have lived separate and apart without cohabitation and without interruption for one year.

☐ The Defendant or I had a Spouse living at the time of the marriage.

☐ The Defendant has been willfully absent for one year.

☐ The Defendant is guilty of adultery.

☐ The Defendant is guilty of extreme cruelty.

☐ The Defendant is guilty of fraudulent contract.

☐ The Defendant is guilty of gross neglect of duty.

☐ The Defendant is guilty of habitual drunkenness.

☐ The Defendant was imprisoned in a state or federal correctional institution at the time the Complaint was filed.

☐ The Defendant procured a divorce outside this state by virtue of which the Defendant has been released from the obligations of the marriage, while those obligations remain binding on me.

6. The Defendant and I are owners of real estate and/or personal property.

I request that a divorce be granted from the Defendant, that the Court determine an equitable division of debts and property, and as follows that (check all that apply):

Supreme Court of Ohio
Uniform Domestic Relations Form – 7
COMPLAINT FOR DIVORCE WITH CHILDREN
Approved under Ohio Civil Rule 84
Amended: March 15, 2016

Page 2 of 3

☐ The Defendant be required to pay me spousal support.

☐ The Plaintiff be named the residential parent and legal custodian of the following minor child(ren): _____

_____

☐ The Defendant be named the residential parent and legal custodian of the following child(ren): _____

_____

☐ The non-residential parent be granted specific parenting time.

☐ The Defendant and I be granted shared parenting of the following child(ren):

_____

_____

pursuant to a Shared Parenting Plan (Uniform Domestic Relations Form 17), which I will prepare and file with the Court.

☐ The Defendant be ordered to pay child support and medical support.

☐ I be restored to my prior name of: _____

☐ The Defendant be required to pay attorney fees.

☐ The Defendant be required to pay the court costs of the proceeding.

☐ The Court make the following additional orders: _____

_____

_____

_____

and that the Court grant such other and further relief as the Court may deem proper.

_____
Your Signature

_____
Telephone number at which the Court may reach you or at which messages may be left for you

IN THE COURT OF COMMON PLEAS

_____ **Division**

_____ **COUNTY, OHIO**

_____
Name

_____
Street Address

_____
City, State and Zip Code

                         Plaintiff

vs.

_____
Name

_____
Street Address

_____
City, State and Zip Code

                       Defendant

:
:
: Case No. _____
:
:
: Judge _____
:
:
: Magistrate _____
:
:
:
:
:
:
:
:
:

Instructions: This form is used to Counterclaim a Complaint for Divorce with or without Children. A Request for Service (Uniform Domestic Relations Form 28) must be filed with this form. The Parenting Proceeding Affidavit (Uniform Domestic Relations Form 3) must be filed, if you and your spouse have (a) minor child(ren), adult child(ren) attending high school, adult child(ren) with disabilities, and/or you or the Spouse are/is pregnant.

COUNTERCLAIM FOR DIVORCE

I, the Defendant, for this Counterclaim say:

1. I have been a resident of the State of Ohio for at least six months.

2. ☐ I have been a resident of _____ County for at least 90 days immediately before the filing of this Complaint; or
   ☐ The Plaintiff resides in _____ County where this Complaint is filed.

3. The Plaintiff and I were married to one another on _____ (date of marriage) in _____ (city or county, and state).

Supreme Court of Ohio
Uniform Domestic Relations Form – 8
COUNTERCLAIM FOR DIVORCE
Approved under Ohio Civil Rule 84
Amended: March 15, 2016

Page 1 of 3

4. I state regarding child(ren) (check all that apply):

☐ There is/are no children expected from this marriage or relationship.

☐ There is/are child(ren) expected from this marriage or relationship and the approximate due date is: _____.

☐ There is/are no child(ren) from this marriage or relationship.

☐ The parties are parents of _____(number) child(ren) from this marriage or relationship. Of the child(ren), _____(number) is/are emancipated adult(s) and not under a disability. The following _____(number) child(ren) is/are minor child(ren) and/or mentally or physically disabled and incapable of supporting or maintain themselves (name and date of birth of each child):

Name of Child	Date of Birth
_____	_____
_____	_____
_____	_____

☐ I am not the parent of the following child(ren) (name and date of birth of each child):

_____

_____

_____

☐ The Spouse is not the parent of the following child(ren) (name and date of birth of each child):

_____

_____

_____

5.

☐ The Plaintiff and I are incompatible.

☐ The Plaintiff and I have lived separate and apart without cohabitation and without interruption for one year.

☐ The Plaintiff or I had a Spouse living at the time of the marriage.

☐ The Plaintiff has been willfully absent for one year.

☐ The Plaintiff is guilty of adultery.

☐ The Plaintiff is guilty of extreme cruelty.

☐ The Plaintiff is guilty of fraudulent contract.

☐ The Plaintiff is guilty of gross neglect of duty.

☐ The Plaintiff is guilty of habitual drunkenness.

☐ The Plaintiff was imprisoned in a state or federal correctional institution at the time the Complaint was filed.

☐ The Plaintiff procured a divorce outside this state by virtue of which the Plaintiff has been released from the obligations of the marriage, while those obligations remain binding on me.

6. The Plaintiff and I are owners of real estate and/or personal property.

I request that a divorce be granted from the Plaintiff, that the Court determine an equitable division of debts and property, and as follows that (check all that apply):

☐ The Plaintiff be required to pay spousal support.

☐ The Plaintiff be named the residential parent and legal custodian of the following child(ren): _____

☐ The Defendant be named the residential parent and legal custodian of the following child(ren): _____

☐ The non-residential parent be granted specific parenting time.

☐ The Plaintiff and I be granted shared parenting of the following child(ren): _____

_____

_____

pursuant to a Shared Parenting Plan (Uniform Domestic Relations Form 17), which I will prepare and file with the Court.

☐ The Plaintiff be ordered to pay child support and medical support.

☐ I be restored to my prior name of: _____

☐ The Plaintiff be required to pay attorney fees.

☐ The Plaintiff be required to pay the court costs of the proceeding.

☐ The Court make the following additional orders: _____

_____

_____

_____

and that the Court grant such other and further relief as the Court may deem proper.

_____
Your Signature

_____
Telephone number at which the Court may reach you
or at which messages may be left for you

Supreme Court of Ohio
Uniform Domestic Relations Form – 8
COUNTERCLAIM FOR DIVORCE
Approved under Ohio Civil Rule 84
Amended: March 15, 2016

Page 3 of 3

IN THE COURT OF COMMON PLEAS

_____ **Division**

_____ **COUNTY, OHIO**

_____	:
Plaintiff	: Case No. _____
_____	:
Street Address	:
_____	: Judge _____
City, State and Zip Code	:
	:
vs.	: Magistrate _____
	:
_____	:
Defendant	:
_____	:
Street Address	:
_____	:
City, State and Zip Code	:

Instructions: This form is used in response to a filing of a Complaint for Divorce without Children. This form is used to agree with or dispute the statements made in the Complaint for Divorce without Children or a Counterclaim to a Divorce without Children.

☐ ANSWER TO COMPLAINT FOR DIVORCE WITHOUT CHILDREN
☐ REPLY TO COUNTERCLAIM

1. I, _____ (name) **ADMIT or DENY** the following allegations, as listed in my Spouse's Complaint or Counterclaim.

ADMIT	DENY	
☐	☐	My Spouse's state of residence.
☐	☐	My Spouse's length of residence in state.
☐	☐	My Spouse's county of residence.
☐	☐	My Spouse's length of residence in county.
☐	☐	My county of residence.
☐	☐	The date of our marriage.
☐	☐	The place of our marriage.
☐	☐	I am not pregnant.
☐	☐	My Spouse is not pregnant.
☐	☐	There are no children from the marriage or relationship.
☐	☐	All children from the marriage or relationship are emancipated adults and not mentally

Supreme Court of Ohio
Uniform Domestic Relations Form – 9
ANSWER TO COMPLAINT FOR DIVORCE WITHOUT CHILDREN
Approved under Ohio Civil Rule 84
Amended: March 15, 2016

Page 1 of 3

or physically disabled child(ren) incapable of maintaining supporting or maintaining themselves.

☐   ☐ My Spouse and I are owners of real estate and/or personal property.

2.   I further **ADMIT or DENY** the following grounds for divorce:

ADMIT   **DENY**

☐   ☐ My Spouse and I are incompatible.

☐   ☐ My Spouse and I have lived separate and apart without cohabitation and without interruption for one year.

☐   ☐ My Spouse or I had a Spouse living at the time of the marriage.

☐   ☐ I have been willfully absent for one year.

☐   ☐ I am guilty of adultery.

☐   ☐ I am guilty of extreme cruelty.

☐   ☐ I am guilty of fraudulent contract.

☐   ☐ I am guilty of gross neglect of duty.

☐   ☐ I am guilty of habitual drunkenness.

☐   ☐ I was imprisoned in a state or federal correctional institution at the time the Complaint was filed.

☐   ☐ I procured a divorce outside this state by virtue of which I have been released from the obligations of the marriage, while those obligations remain binding on my Spouse.

3.   Anything not specifically admitted is denied.

4.   Other information about the above admissions, denials, or responses: _____

_____

_____

I ask that the request for a divorce be ☐ dismissed ☐ granted (select one), and I be awarded such other relief as the Court finds fair and equitable, including ordering the cost of this action be paid as the Court may determine.

_____   _____
Your Signature   Address

_____   _____
Typed or printed Name   Telephone number at which the Court may reach you or at which messages may be left for you

CERTIFICATE OF SERVICE

I delivered a copy of my Answer to Complaint for Divorce without Children

On: (date) _____

To: (name of your Spouse's attorney or, if there is no attorney, name of your Spouse)

_____

At: (address or fax number) _____

_____

By: ☐ U.S. Mail

☐ Fax

☐ Personal delivery

☐ Other: _____

_____
Your Signature

Supreme Court of Ohio
Uniform Domestic Relations Form – 9
ANSWER TO COMPLAINT FOR DIVORCE WITHOUT CHILDREN
Approved under Ohio Civil Rule 84
Amended: March 15, 2016

Page 3 of 3

IN THE COURT OF COMMON PLEAS

_____ **Division**

_____ **COUNTY, OHIO**

_____ Plaintiff	Case No. _____
_____ Street Address	
_____ City, State and Zip Code	Judge _____
vs.	Magistrate _____
_____ Defendant	
_____ Street Address	
_____ City, State and Zip Code	

Instructions: This form is used in response to a filing of a Complaint for Divorce with Children. This form is used to agree with or dispute the statements made in the Complaint for Divorce with Children or a Counterclaim to a Divorce with Children.

☐ **ANSWER TO COMPLAINT FOR DIVORCE WITH CHILDREN**
☐ **REPLY TO COUNTERCLAIM**

1. I, _____ (name) **ADMIT or DENY** the following allegations, as listed in my Spouse's Complaint or Counterclaim.

ADMIT	DENY	
☐	☐	My Spouse's state of residence.
☐	☐	My Spouse's length of residence in state.
☐	☐	My Spouse's county of residence.
☐	☐	My Spouse's length of residence in county.
☐	☐	My county of residence.
☐	☐	The date of our marriage.
☐	☐	The place of our marriage.
☐	☐	I am not pregnant.
☐	☐	My Spouse is not pregnant.
☐	☐	The number of children from the marriage or relationship.
☐	☐	The names of children from the marriage or relationship.

Supreme Court of Ohio
Uniform Domestic Relations Form – 10
ANSWER TO COMPLAINT FOR DIVORCE WITH CHILDREN
Approved under Ohio Civil Rule 84
Amended: March 15, 2016

Page 1 of 3

☐   ☐ The dates of birth of children from the marriage or relationship.

☐   ☐ My Spouse and I are owners of real estate and/or personal property.

2. I further **ADMIT or DENY** the following grounds for divorce:

   ADMIT   **DENY**

☐   ☐ My Spouse and I are incompatible.

☐   ☐ My Spouse and I have lived separate and apart without cohabitation and without interruption for one year.

☐   ☐ My Spouse or I had a Spouse living at the time of the marriage.

☐   ☐ I have been willfully absent for one year.

☐   ☐ I am guilty of adultery.

☐   ☐ I am guilty of extreme cruelty.

☐   ☐ I am guilty of fraudulent contract.

☐   ☐ I am guilty of gross neglect of duty.

☐   ☐ I am guilty of habitual drunkenness.

☐   ☐ I was imprisoned in a state or federal correctional institution at the time the Complaint was filed.

☐   ☐ I procured a divorce outside this state by virtue of which I have been released from the obligations of the marriage, while those obligations remain binding on my Spouse.

3. Anything not specifically admitted is denied.

4. Other information about the above admissions, denials, or responses: _____

_____

_____

I ask that the request for a divorce be ☐ dismissed ☐ granted (select one), and I be awarded such other relief as the Court finds fair and equitable, including ordering the cost of this action be paid as the Court may determine.

_____   _____
Your Signature   Address

_____   _____
Typed or printed Name   Telephone number at which the Court may reach you or at which messages may be left for you

CERTIFICATE OF SERVICE

I delivered a copy of my Answer to Complaint for Divorce with Children

On: (date) _____

To: (name of your Spouse's attorney or, if there is no attorney, name of your Spouse)

_____

At: (address or fax number) _____

_____

By: ☐ U.S. Mail

☐ Fax

☐ Personal delivery

☐ Other: _____

_____
Your Signature

Supreme Court of Ohio
Uniform Domestic Relations Form – 10
ANSWER TO COMPLAINT FOR DIVORCE WITH CHILDREN
Approved under Ohio Civil Rule 84
Amended: March 15, 2016

Page 3 of 3

IN THE COURT OF COMMON PLEAS

_____ **Division**

_____ **COUNTY, OHIO**

_____	:
Plaintiff	: Case No. _____
_____	:
Street Address	:
_____	: Judge _____
City, State and Zip Code	:
	:
vs.	: Magistrate _____
	:
_____	:
Defendant	:
	:
_____	:
Street Address	:
	:
_____	:
City, State and Zip Code	:

FINAL JUDGMENT FOR DIVORCE WITHOUT CHILDREN

This matter came on for final hearing on _____ before ☐ Judge ☐ Magistrate _____ upon the Plaintiff's Complaint for Divorce without Children filed on _____ and/or Defendant's Counterclaim filed on _____ and upon the following: _____ .

FINDINGS

Upon a review of the record, testimony, and evidence presented, the Court makes the following findings:

A. Check all that apply:

☐ The Defendant was properly served with summons, copy of the Complaint, and notice of the hearing.

☐ The Defendant's waiver of service of summons and Complaint have been filed in this case.

☐ The Defendant filed an Answer.

☐ The Defendant failed to file an Answer or plead, despite being properly served with summons, copy of the Complaint, and notice of the hearing.

☐ The Plaintiff replied to the Defendant's Counterclaim.

☐ The Plaintiff failed to reply to the Defendant's Counterclaim.

Supreme Court of Ohio
Uniform Domestic Relations Form – 11
FINAL JUDGMENT FOR DIVORCE WITHOUT CHILDREN
Approved under Ohio Civil Rule 84
Amended: March 15, 2016

B. Present at the hearing were the: ☐ Plaintiff, ☐ Defendant,

    ☐ _____ appearing as counsel for the Plaintiff.

    ☐ _____ appearing as counsel for the Defendant.

C. The ☐ Plaintiff and/or ☐ Defendant was/were a resident(s) of the State of Ohio for at least six months immediately before the Complaint and/or Counterclaim was/were filed.

D. At the time the Complaint and/or Counterclaim was/were filed:

    ☐ The Plaintiff was a resident of this county for at least 90 days.

    ☐ The Defendant was a resident of this county.

    ☐ Other grounds for venue were: _____

E. The Plaintiff and Defendant were married to one another on _____ (date of marriage) in _____ (city or county, and state). The termination of marriage is the date of ☐ final hearing or ☐ as specified: _____

F. Check all that apply regarding child(ren):

    ☐ There is/are no child(ren) expected from this marriage or relationship.

    ☐ There is/are child(ren) expected from this marriage or relationship and the approximate due date is:_____.

    ☐ There is/are no child(ren) from this marriage or relationship.

    ☐ The parties are parents of _____ (number) child(ren) from the marriage or relationship. Of the child(ren),_____ (number) is/are emancipated adult(s) and not under a disability. The following _____ (number) child(ren) is/are minor child(ren) and/or mentally or physically disabled and incapable of supporting or maintaining themselves (name and date of birth of each child):

Name of Child	Date of Birth
_____	_____
_____	_____
_____	_____

G. Select one:

    ☐ Neither the Plaintiff nor the Defendant is in the military service of the United States.

    ☐ The ☐ Plaintiff and/or the ☐ Defendant is in the military service of the United States and the service did not impact the ability to defend this action.

H. The ☐ Plaintiff and/or the ☐ Defendant through testimony have indicated full and complete disclosure to the other of all marital property, separate property, and any other assets, debts, income, or expenses.

    ☐ The Defendant has not filed a response or made an appearance.

    ☐ The Plaintiff has not filed a response or made an appearance.

I. The parties that appeared have no additional knowledge of any other property and debts of any

Supreme Court of Ohio
Uniform Domestic Relations Form – 11
FINAL JUDGMENT FOR DIVORCE WITHOUT CHILDREN
Approved under Ohio Civil Rule 84
Amended: March 15, 2016

Page 2 of 7

kind in which either party has an interest.

J. The parties that appeared have had the opportunity to value and verify all marital property, separate property, and other debts.

K. This Court has jurisdiction and proper venue to determine all of the issues raised by the pleadings and motions.

L. Select one:

☐ A Magistrate's Decision was filed on: _____

☐ No objections were filed. The Court approves the terms contained in the Decision and finds the terms are fair and equitable.

☐ All objections were ruled upon by a separate entry.

☐ The parties have presented the Court with a written Separation Agreement or have read into the record a settlement of all issues, which the Court finds to be a fair and equitable division of property and debts and an appropriate resolution of all issues, knowingly and voluntarily entered into by the parties.

☐ The Court has made a fair and equitable division of property and debts and an appropriate resolution of all issues of the parties after review and consideration of all evidence presented.

☐ Other: _____

_____

_____

M. The divorce is granted on the following ground(s) (check all that apply):

☐ The Plaintiff and Defendant are incompatible.

☐ The Plaintiff and Defendant have lived separate and apart without cohabitation and without interruption for one year.

☐ The Defendant or ☐ Plaintiff had a Spouse living at the time of the marriage.

☐ The Defendant or ☐ Plaintiff has been willfully absent for one year.

☐ The Defendant or ☐ Plaintiff is guilty of adultery.

☐ The Defendant or ☐ Plaintiff is guilty of extreme cruelty.

☐ The Defendant or ☐ Plaintiff is guilty of fraudulent contract.

☐ The Defendant or ☐ Plaintiff is guilty of gross neglect of duty.

☐ The Defendant or ☐ Plaintiff is guilty of habitual drunkenness.

☐ The Defendant or ☐ Plaintiff was imprisoned in a state or federal correctional institution at the time the Complaint was filed.

☐ The Defendant or ☐ Plaintiff procured a divorce outside this state by virtue of which she or he has been released from the obligations of the marriage, while those obligations remain binding on the ☐ Plaintiff or ☐ Defendant.

Supreme Court of Ohio
Uniform Domestic Relations Form – 11
FINAL JUDGMENT FOR DIVORCE WITHOUT CHILDREN
Approved under Ohio Civil Rule 84
Amended: March 15, 2016

Page 3 of 7

JUDGMENT

Based upon the findings set out above, it is, therefore, **ORDERED, ADJUDGED and DECREED** that:

FIRST: DIVORCE GRANTED

A divorce is granted, and both parties shall be released from the obligations of their marriage except for those obligations listed below or as set out in the attached ☐ Separation Agreement ☐ Magistrate's Decision and/or ☐ Other: _____ , which is incorporated in this entry.

SECOND: PROPERTY

The parties' property shall be divided as follows:

A. The Plaintiff shall have the following items of real estate and personal property, free and clear from all claims of the Defendant, subject to any indebtedness which the Plaintiff shall pay and from which the Plaintiff shall hold the Defendant harmless: _____

_____

_____

_____

B. The Defendant shall have the following items of real estate and personal property, free and clear from all claims of the Plaintiff, subject to any indebtedness which the Defendant shall pay and from which the Defendant shall hold the Plaintiff harmless: _____

_____

_____

_____

_____

_____

_____

C. The Plaintiff is awarded the following separate property: _____

_____

_____

_____

_____

_____

_____

D. The Defendant is awarded the following separate property: _____

_____

_____

_____

Supreme Court of Ohio
Uniform Domestic Relations Form – 11
FINAL JUDGMENT FOR DIVORCE WITHOUT CHILDREN
Approved under Ohio Civil Rule 84
Amended: March 15, 2016

Page 4 of 7

_____

_____

_____

_____

E.   Other orders regarding property (specify): _____

_____

_____

_____

F.   Within 30 days the parties will take all necessary steps to transfer legal title and possession of property and take appropriate actions to implement and effectuate the division of pensions and retirements.

G.   Other orders regarding transfers: _____

_____

_____

_____

THIRD: DEBT

The Plaintiff and Defendant's debts shall be divided as follows.

A.   The Plaintiff shall pay the following debts and shall hold the Defendant harmless from all claims:

_____

_____

_____

_____

_____

_____

B.   The Defendant shall pay the following debts and shall hold the Plaintiff harmless from all claims:

_____

_____

_____

_____

_____

_____

C.   Bankruptcy (select one):

☐ The Court will retain jurisdiction to enforce payment of debt obligations, in the event a party files bankruptcy. This includes, but is not limited to, the ability to determine the debt assigned is in the nature of maintenance, necessity or support and is therefore nondischargeable in bankruptcy, and/or to make a future spousal support order, regardless of the spousal support order set forth below under **FOURTH: SPOUSAL SUPPORT**.

☐ Nothing in this order shall prevent the ☐ Plaintiff and/or ☐ Defendant from being fully discharged from the debts allocated in this order in a bankruptcy proceeding except for any orders expressly for spousal support and the following debts: _____

_____

_____

_____

Neither party shall incur liabilities against the other party in the future.

FOURTH: SPOUSAL SUPPORT

A. Spousal Support Not Awarded

☐ Neither the Plaintiff nor Defendant shall pay spousal support to the other. The Court shall not retain jurisdiction, except as set forth above under **THIRD: DEBTS**.

B. Spousal Support Awarded

The ☐ Plaintiff ☐ Defendant shall pay spousal support to the ☐ Plaintiff ☐ Defendant in the amount of $_____ per month plus 2% processing charge, commencing on _____ and due on the _____ day of the month. This spousal support shall continue ☐ indefinitely ☐ for a period of _____ .

☐ The Court shall not retain jurisdiction to modify spousal support.

☐ The Court shall retain jurisdiction to modify the ☐ amount ☐ duration of the spousal support Order.

C. Termination of Spousal Support

This spousal support shall terminate sooner than the above stated date upon the Plaintiff's or the Defendant's death or in the event of the following (check all that apply):

☐ The cohabitation of the person receiving support in a relationship comparable to marriage

☐ The remarriage of the person receiving support.

☐ Other (specify): _____

_____

D. Method of Payment of Spousal Support (select one):

☐ The spousal support payment shall be made directly to the ☐ Plaintiff ☐ Defendant.

☐ The spousal support payment, plus 2% processing charge, shall be made to the Ohio Child Support Payment Central, P. O. Box 182372, Columbus, Ohio 43218-2372, as administered through the _____ County Child Support Enforcement Agency by income withholding at the party's place of employment.

Supreme Court of Ohio
Uniform Domestic Relations Form – 11
FINAL JUDGMENT FOR DIVORCE WITHOUT CHILDREN
Approved under Ohio Civil Rule 84
Amended: March 15, 2016

Page 6 of 7

E. Deductibility of Spousal Support for All Tax Purposes (select one):
☐ The spousal support paid shall be deducted from income to the person paying the support and included by the person receiving the support.
☐ The spousal support paid shall be included in income of the person paying the support.

F. Other orders regarding spousal support (specify): _____
_____

G. Arrearage
☐ Any temporary spousal support arrearage will survive this judgment entry.
☐ Any temporary spousal support arrearage will not survive this judgment entry.
☐ Other: _____
_____
_____

FIFTH: NAME

☐ _____ is restored to
the prior name of: _____

SIXTH: OTHER ORDERS

_____
_____

SEVENTH: COURT COSTS

Court costs shall be (select one):

☐ Taxed to the deposit. Court costs due above the deposit shall be paid as follows:
_____

☐ Other (specify): _____
_____

EIGHTH: CLERK OF COURTS

The Clerk of Courts shall provide:

☐ a certified copy to: _____

☐ a file stamped copy to: _____

NOTICE. Pursuant to Civil Rule 58(B), the Clerk is directed to serve upon the parties a notice of the filing of this Judgment Entry and of the date of entry upon the Journal.

_____   _____
Date   JUDGE

IN THE COURT OF COMMON PLEAS

_____ **Division**

_____ **COUNTY, OHIO**

_____	:	Case No. _____
Plaintiff	:	
_____	:	
Street Address	:	
_____	:	Judge _____
City, State and Zip Code	:	
	:	
vs.	:	Magistrate _____
	:	
_____	:	
Defendant	:	
_____	:	
Street Address	:	
_____	:	
City, State and Zip Code	:	

FINAL JUDGMENT FOR DIVORCE WITH CHILDREN

This matter came on for final hearing on _____ before ☐ Judge ☐ Magistrate
_____ upon the Plaintiff's Complaint for Divorce with Children filed on
_____ and/or Defendant's Counterclaim filed on _____
and upon the following: _____ .

FINDINGS

Upon a review of the record, testimony, and evidence presented, the Court makes the following findings:

A. Check all that apply:

☐ The Defendant was properly served with summons, copy of the Complaint, and notice of the hearing.

☐ The Defendant's waiver of service of summons and Complaint have been filed in this case.

☐ The Defendant filed an Answer.

☐ The Defendant failed to file an Answer or plead, despite being properly served with summons, copy of the Complaint, and notice of the hearing.

☐ The Plaintiff replied to the Defendant's Counterclaim.

☐ The Plaintiff failed to reply to the Defendant's Counterclaim.

Supreme Court of Ohio
Uniform Domestic Relations Form – 12
FINAL JUDGMENT FOR DIVORCE WITH CHILDREN
Approved under Ohio Civil Rule 84
Amended: March 15, 2016

Page 1 of 16

B. Present at the hearing were the: ☐ Plaintiff, ☐ Defendant,

☐ _____ appearing as counsel for the Plaintiff.

☐ _____ appearing as counsel for the Defendant.

C. The ☐ Plaintiff and/or ☐ Defendant was/were a resident(s) of the State of Ohio for at least six months immediately before the Complaint and/or Counterclaim was/were filed.

D. At the time the Complaint and/or Counterclaim was/were filed:

☐ The Plaintiff was a resident of this county for at least 90 days.

☐ The Defendant was a resident of this county.

☐ Other grounds for venue were: _____

E. The Plaintiff and Defendant were married to one another on _____ (date of marriage) in _____ (city or county, and state). The termination of marriage is the date of ☐ final hearing or ☐ as specified: _____

F. Check all that apply regarding child(ren):

☐ There is/are no child(ren) expected from this marriage or relationship.

☐ There is/are child(ren) expected from this marriage or relationship and the approximate due date is:_____.

☐ There is/are no child(ren) from this marriage or relationship.

☐ The parties are parents of _____ (number) child(ren) from the marriage or relationship. Of the child(ren), _____(number) is/are emancipated adult(s) and not under any disability. The following _____(number) child(ren) is/are minor child(ren) and/or mentally or physically disabled and incapable of supporting or maintaining themselves (name and date of birth of each child):

Name of Child	Date of Birth
_____	_____
_____	_____
_____	_____

☐ Plaintiff is not the parent of the following child(ren) who was/were born during the marriage (name and date of birth of each child):

_____

_____

☐ Defendant is not the parent of the following child(ren) who was/were born during the marriage (name and date of birth of each child):

_____

_____

G. ☐ The following child(ren) from the marriage or relationship are subject to a custody or parenting order in a different Court proceeding (name of each child and the Court that has issued the custody or parenting order): _____

_____

Supreme Court of Ohio
Uniform Domestic Relations Form – 12
FINAL JUDGMENT FOR DIVORCE WITH CHILDREN
Approved under Ohio Civil Rule 84
Amended: March 15, 2016

Page 2 of 16

H. Select one:

☐ Neither the Plaintiff nor Defendant is in the military service of the United States.

☐ The ☐ Plaintiff and/or ☐ Defendant is in the military service of the United States and the service did not impact the ability to defend this action.

I. The ☐ Plaintiff and/or ☐ Defendant through testimony have indicated full and complete disclosure to the other of all marital property, separate property, and any other assets, debts, income, or expenses.

☐ The Defendant has not filed a response or made an appearance.

☐ The Plaintiff has not filed a response or made an appearance.

J. The parties that appeared have no knowledge of any other property and debts of any kind in which either party has an interest.

K. The parties that appeared have had the opportunity to value and verify all marital property, separate property, and other debts.

L. This Court has jurisdiction and proper venue to determine all of the issues raised by the pleadings and motions.

M. Select one:

☐ A Magistrate's Decision was filed on: _____

☐ No objections were filed. The Court approves the terms contained in the Decision and finds the terms are fair and equitable.

☐ All objections were ruled upon by a separate entry.

☐ The parties have presented the Court with a written Separation Agreement or have read into the record a settlement of all issues, which the Court finds to be a fair and equitable division of property and debts and an appropriate resolution of all issues, knowingly and voluntarily entered into by the parties.

☐ The Court has made a fair and equitable division of property and debts and an appropriate resolution of all issues of the parties after review and consideration of all evidence presented.

☐ Other: _____

_____

_____

N. The divorce is granted on the following ground(s) (check all that apply):

☐ The Plaintiff and Defendant are incompatible.

☐ The Plaintiff and Defendant have lived separate and apart without cohabitation and without interruption for one year.

☐ The Defendant or ☐ Plaintiff had a Spouse living at the time of the marriage.

Supreme Court of Ohio
Uniform Domestic Relations Form – 12
FINAL JUDGMENT FOR DIVORCE WITH CHILDREN
Approved under Ohio Civil Rule 84
Amended: March 15, 2016

Page 3 of 16

☐ The Defendant or ☐ Plaintiff has been willfully absent for one year.

☐ The Defendant or ☐ Plaintiff is guilty of adultery.

☐ The Defendant or ☐ Plaintiff is guilty of extreme cruelty.

☐ The Defendant or ☐ Plaintiff is guilty of fraudulent contract.

☐ The Defendant or ☐ Plaintiff is guilty of gross neglect of duty.

☐ The Defendant or ☐ Plaintiff is guilty of habitual drunkenness.

☐ The Defendant or ☐ Plaintiff was imprisoned in a state or federal correctional institution at the time the Complaint was filed.

☐ The Defendant or ☐ Plaintiff procured a divorce outside this state by virtue of which she or he has been released from the obligations of the marriage, while those obligations remain binding on the ☐ Plaintiff or ☐ Defendant.

JUDGMENT

Based upon the findings set out above, it is, therefore, **ORDERED, ADJUDGED, and DECREED** that:

FIRST: DIVORCE GRANTED

A divorce is granted, and both parties shall be released from the obligations of their marriage except for those obligations listed below or as set out in the attached ☐ Separation Agreement

☐ Shared Parenting Plan ☐ Parenting Plan ☐ Magistrate's Decision and/or

☐ Other: _____

which is incorporated in this entry.

SECOND: PROPERTY

The parties' property shall be divided as follows:

A. The Plaintiff shall have the following items of real estate and personal property, free and clear from all claims of the Defendant, subject to any indebtedness which the Plaintiff shall pay and from which the Plaintiff shall hold the Defendant harmless: _____

_____

_____

_____

_____

_____

_____

B. The Defendant shall have the following items of real estate and personal property, free and clear from all claims of the Plaintiff, subject to any indebtedness which the Defendant shall pay and from which the Defendant shall hold the Plaintiff harmless: _____

_____

_____

_____

_____

Supreme Court of Ohio
Uniform Domestic Relations Form – 12
FINAL JUDGMENT FOR DIVORCE WITH CHILDREN
Approved under Ohio Civil Rule 84
Amended: March 15, 2016

Page 4 of 16

_____
_____

C.   The Plaintiff is awarded the following separate property: _____
_____
_____
_____
_____
_____
_____
_____

D.   The Defendant is awarded the following separate property: _____
_____
_____
_____
_____
_____
_____
_____

E.   Other orders regarding property (specify): _____
_____
_____
_____

F.   Within 30 days the parties will take all necessary steps to transfer legal title and possession of property and take appropriate actions to implement and effectuate the division of pensions and retirements.

G.   Other orders regarding transfers: _____
_____
_____
_____

THIRD: DEBT

The Plaintiff and Defendant's debts shall be divided as follows.

A.   The Plaintiff shall pay the following debts and shall hold the Defendant harmless from all claims:
_____
_____
_____
_____
_____
_____

Supreme Court of Ohio
Uniform Domestic Relations Form – 12
FINAL JUDGMENT FOR DIVORCE WITH CHILDREN
Approved under Ohio Civil Rule 84
Amended: March 15, 2016

Page 5 of 16

_____
_____

B. The Defendant shall pay the following debts and shall hold the Plaintiff harmless from all claims:

_____
_____
_____
_____
_____
_____

C. Bankruptcy (select one):

☐ The Court will retain jurisdiction to enforce payment of debt obligations, in the event a party files bankruptcy, including, but not limited to, the ability to determine the debt assigned is in the nature of maintenance, necessity or support and is therefore nondischargeable in bankruptcy, and/or making a future spousal support order, regardless of the spousal support order set forth below under **FOURTH: SPOUSAL SUPPORT**.

☐ Nothing in this order shall prevent the ☐ Plaintiff and/or ☐ Defendant from being fully discharged from the debts allocated in this order in a bankruptcy proceeding except for any orders expressly for spousal support and the following debts: _____

_____
_____
_____

Neither party shall incur liabilities against the other party in the future.

FOURTH: SPOUSAL SUPPORT

A. Spousal Support Not Awarded

☐ Neither the Plaintiff nor Defendant shall pay spousal support to the other. The Court shall not retain jurisdiction, except as set forth above under **THIRD: DEBTS**.

B. Spousal Support Awarded

The ☐ Plaintiff ☐ Defendant shall pay spousal support to the ☐ Plaintiff ☐ Defendant in the amount of $_____   per month plus 2% processing charge commencing on _____ and due on the _____ day of the month. This spousal support shall continue ☐ indefinitely ☐ for a period of _____

☐ The Court shall not retain jurisdiction to modify spousal support.

☐ The Court shall retain jurisdiction to modify the ☐ amount ☐ duration of the spousal support order.

Supreme Court of Ohio
Uniform Domestic Relations Form – 12
FINAL JUDGMENT FOR DIVORCE WITH CHILDREN
Approved under Ohio Civil Rule 84
Amended: March 15, 2016

Page 6 of 16

C. Termination of Spousal Support

This spousal support shall terminate sooner than the above stated date upon the Plaintiff's or the Defendant's death or in the event of the following (check all that apply):

☐ The cohabitation of the person receiving support in a relationship comparable to marriage.

☐ The remarriage of the person receiving support.

☐ Other (specify): _____

_____

_____

_____

D. Method of Payment of Spousal Support:

☐ The spousal support payment, plus 2% processing charge, shall be made to the Ohio Child Support Payment Central, P. O. Box 182372, Columbus, Ohio 43218-2372, as administered through the _____ County Child Support Enforcement Agency by income withholding at the party's place of employment.

E. Deductibility of Spousal Support for All Tax Purposes (select one):

☐ The spousal support paid shall be deducted from income of the person paying the support and included by the person receiving the support.

☐ The spousal support paid shall be included in income of the person paying the support.

F. Other orders regarding spousal support (specify): _____

_____

_____

_____

G. Arrearage

☐ Any temporary spousal support arrearage will survive this judgment entry.

☐ Any temporary spousal support arrearage will not survive this judgment entry.

☐ Other: _____

_____

_____

FIFTH: NAME

☐ _____ is restored to

the prior name of: _____

SIXTH: ALLOCATION OF PARENTAL RIGHTS AND RESPONSIBILITIES

A. Parental rights and responsibilities shall be allocated as follows:

☐ Plaintiff shall be the residential parent and legal custodian of the following minor child(ren):

_____

_____

Supreme Court of Ohio
Uniform Domestic Relations Form – 12
FINAL JUDGMENT FOR DIVORCE WITH CHILDREN
Approved under Ohio Civil Rule 84
Amended: March 15, 2016

Page 7 of 16

_____

_____

_____

☐ Defendant shall be the residential parent and legal custodian of the following minor child(ren):

_____

_____

_____

☐ Plaintiff ☐ Defendant shall have parenting time with the minor child(ren) who is/are not residing with him/her according to the attached schedule.

☐ The parents have entered into a Shared Parenting Plan or Parenting Plan which has been filed with the Court and is adopted by the Court.

B.   Relocation Notice
Pursuant to section 3109.051(G) of the Revised Code:
If the residential parent intends to move to a residence other than the residence specified in the court order, the parent shall file a notice of intent to relocate with this Court. Except as provided in divisions (G)(2), (3), and (4) of section 3109.051 of the Revised Code, the Court shall send a copy of the notice to the parent who is not the residential parent. Upon receipt of the notice, the Court, on its own motion or the motion of the parent who is not the residential parent, may schedule a hearing with notice to both parents to determine whether it is in the best interests of the child(ren) to revise the parenting time schedule for the child(ren).

☐ The obligation under this notice applies to both parents in a Shared Parenting Plan.

☐ The non-residential parent shall inform the Court and other parent in writing of changes in address and telephone, including cellular telephone number, unless otherwise provided by court order.

☐ The residential parent shall inform the Court and other parent in writing of changes in address and telephone, including cellular telephone number, unless otherwise provided by court order.

The relocation notice must be filed with the Court that granted the divorce and allocated parental rights and responsibilities (print name and address of Court): _____

_____

Other orders: _____

_____

_____

C.   Records Access Notice
Pursuant to sections 3109.051(H) and 3319.321(B)(5)(a) of the Revised Code:

Subject to sections 3125.16 and 3319.321(F) of the Revised Code, the parent who is not the residential parent is entitled to access to any record that is related to the child(ren), and to which the residential parent is legally provided access under the same terms and conditions as the residential parent. Any keeper of a record who knowingly fails to comply with any record access order is in contempt of court.

Restrictions or limitations:

☐ None

☐ Restrictions or limitations to non-residential parents regarding records access are as follows:

_____

_____

_____

_____

D. Day Care Access Notice

Pursuant to section 3109.051(I) of the Revised Code:

In accordance with section 5104.11 of the Revised Code, the parent who is not the residential parent is entitled to access to any day care center that is or will be attended by the child(ren) with whom parenting time is granted, to the same extent that the residential parent is granted access to the center.

Restrictions or limitations:

☐ None

☐ Restrictions or limitations to non-residential parents regarding day care access are as follows:

_____

_____

_____

_____

E. School Activities Access Notice

Pursuant to section 3109.051(J) of the Revised Code:

Subject to section 3319.321(F), the parent who is not the residential parent is entitled to access to any student activity that is related to the child(ren) and to which the residential parent is legally provided access, under the same terms and conditions as the residential parent. Any school employee or official who knowingly fails to comply with this school activities access order is in contempt of court.

Restrictions or limitations:

☐ None

☐ Restrictions or limitations to non-residential parents regarding school activities access are as follows: _____

_____

Supreme Court of Ohio
Uniform Domestic Relations Form – 12
FINAL JUDGMENT FOR DIVORCE WITH CHILDREN
Approved under Ohio Civil Rule 84
Amended: March 15, 2016

Page 9 of 16

_____

_____

SEVENTH: HEALTH INSURANCE COVERAGE

As required by law, the parties have completed a Child Support Worksheet, which is attached to and incorporated in this Agreement.

Select one:

A. ☐ Health Insurance Coverage Available to at Least One Parent

1. Private health insurance coverage is accessible and reasonable in cost through a group policy, contract, or plan to: ☐ Plaintiff ☐ Defendant ☐ Both parents. ☐ Plaintiff ☐ Defendant ☐ Both parents shall provide private health insurance coverage for the benefit of the child(ren).

2. If both parents are ordered to provide private health insurance coverage for the benefit of the child(ren), ☐ Plaintiff's ☐ Defendant's health insurance plan shall be considered the primary health insurance plan for the child(ren).

3. The parent required to provide private health insurance coverage shall provide proof of insurance to the _____ County Child Support Enforcement Agency (CSEA) and the other parent.

4. Both parents shall cooperate in the preparation of insurance forms to obtain reimbursement or payment of expenses, as applicable. A copy of medical bills must be submitted to the party holding the insurance and responsible for payment or the other parent within 30 days of receipt.

5. Should the health insurance coverage be cancelled for any reason, the parent ordered to maintain insurance shall immediately notify the other parent and take immediate steps to obtain replacement coverage. Unless the cancellation was intentional, the uncovered expenses shall be paid as provided above. If the cancellation was intentionally caused by the parent ordered to maintain insurance coverage, that parent shall be responsible for all medical expenses that would have been covered had the insurance been in effect.

B. ☐ Health Insurance Coverage Unavailable to Either Parent

1. Private health insurance coverage is **not** accessible and reasonable in cost through a group policy, contract, or plan to either parent.

2. If private health insurance coverage becomes available to either parent at reasonable cost, the party will immediately obtain the insurance, notify the other parent and the_____ County CSEA, and submit to the other parent proof of insurance, insurance forms, and an insurance card. The CSEA shall determine whether the cost of the insurance is of sufficient amount to justify an administrative review of the amount of child support payable. In the event an administrative review is warranted, one shall be conducted.

C. Division of Uninsured Expenses

1. The cost of any uninsured medical expenses, incurred by or on the behalf of the child(ren)

not paid by a health insurance plan, and exceeding $100 per child per year, including co-payments and deductibles, shall be paid by the parents as follows: _____

_____

_____

_____

The first $100 per child per year of uninsured expenses shall be paid by the Plaintiff for the following child(ren): _____

_____

The first $100 per child per year of uninsured expenses shall be paid by the Defendant for the following child(ren): _____

_____

_____

Other orders regarding uninsured medical expenses: _____

_____

_____

2. The parent incurring the expenses shall provide the other parent the original or copies of all medical bills, and Explanation of Benefits (EOB), if available, within 30 days of the date on the bill or EOB, whichever is later, absent extraordinary circumstances. The other parent shall, within 30 days of receipt of the bill, reimburse the parent incurring the expenses or pay directly to the health care provider, that parent's percentage share of the bill as shown above.

D. Other Important Information about Medical Records and Expenses
1. Each party shall have access to all medical records of the child(ren) as provided by law.

2. The term "medical expense" or "medical records" shall include but not be limited to medical, dental, orthodontic, optical, surgical, hospital, major medical, psychological, psychiatric, outpatient, doctor, therapy, counseling, prosthetic, and/or all other expenses/records including preventative health care expenses/records related to the treatment of the human body and mind.

EIGHTH: CHILD SUPPORT
A completed Child Support Work Sheet is attached and incorporated in this Decree.
A. Child Support with Private Health Insurance Coverage
When private health insurance coverage is being provided for the child(ren), ☐ Plaintiff ☐ Defendant, the Obligor, shall pay child support in the amount of $_____ per child per month, for _____ (number) child(ren) for a total of $_____ per month.

B. Child Support without Private Health Insurance Coverage
When private health insurance is **not** available for child(ren), ☐ Plaintiff ☐ Defendant, the Obligor, shall pay child support in the amount of $_____ per

Supreme Court of Ohio
Uniform Domestic Relations Form – 12
FINAL JUDGMENT FOR DIVORCE WITH CHILDREN
Approved under Ohio Civil Rule 84
Amended: March 15, 2016

Page 11 of 16

child per month, and $ _____ per child per month as cash medical support.
The total of child support and cash medical support for _____ (number) child(ren)
is $ _____ per month.

C. Child Support Payment

Child support payment (including cash medical support, if any) plus a 2% processing charge
shall commence on _____ and shall be paid to the Ohio Child Support Payment
Center, P. O. Box 182372, Columbus, Ohio 43218-2372, as administered through the
_____ County Child Support Enforcement Agency (CSEA) by income withholding at
Obligor's place of employment or from nonexempt funds on deposit at a financial institution.

D. Deviation of Child Support Amount

The child support calculated pursuant to the child support schedule $ _____ is unjust
or inappropriate and is not in the best interest of the minor child(ren) for the following reason(s),
as provided in R.C. 3119.22, 3119.23, and 3119.24, and shall be adjusted as follows:

_____

_____

_____

E. Duration of Child Support

The child support order will terminate upon the child's 18th birthday unless one of the following
circumstances applies:
- The child is mentally or physically disabled and is incapable of supporting or maintaining
  himself or herself.
- The parents have agreed to continue child support beyond the date it would otherwise
  terminate.
- The child continuously attends a recognized and accredited high school on a full-time basis so
  long as the child has not, as yet, reached the age of 19 years old. (Under these circumstances,
  child support will end at the time the child ceases to attend a recognized and accredited high
  school on a full-time basis or when he or she reaches the age of 19, whichever occurs first.)

This Support Order will remain in effect during seasonal vacation periods until the order
terminates.

☐ The Court finds by agreement that child support will extend beyond the time when it would
otherwise end. The terms and conditions of that agreement are as follows: _____

_____

_____

☐ The Court finds the parties have (a) child(ren) who is/are mentally or physically disabled and
incapable of supporting or maintaining themselves, and that child support will extend beyond
the time when it would otherwise end. The name of the child and the nature of the mental or

physical disability are as follows: _____

_____

_____

F. Important Child Support Orders and Information

Obligee must immediately notify and Obligor may notify the CSEA of any reason for which the support order should terminate. A willful failure to notify the CSEA as required is contempt of court. The following are reasons for termination of the Order:

- Child's attainment of the age of majority if the child no longer attends an accredited high school on a full-time basis and the support order does not provide for the duty of support to continue past the age of majority
- Child stops attending an accredited high school on a full-time basis after attaining the age of majority
- Child's death
- Child's marriage
- Child's emancipation
- Child's enlistment in the Armed Services
- Child's deportation
- Change of legal custody of the child

All support payments must be made through the CSEA or the office of child support in the Ohio Department of Job and Family Services (Child Support Payment Central). Any payment of money not made through the CSEA will be considered a gift, unless the payment is made to discharge an obligation other than support.

All support under this Order shall be withheld or deducted from the income or assets of the Obligor pursuant to a withholding or deduction notice or appropriate order issued in accordance with Chapters 3119., 3121., 3123., and 3125. of the Revised Code or a withdrawal directive issued pursuant to sections 3123.24 to 3123.38 of the Revised Code and shall be forwarded to the Obligee in accordance with Chapters 3119., 3121., 3123., and 3125. of the Revised Code.

The Obligor and/or Obligee required under this Order to provide private health insurance coverage for the child(ren) is also required to provide the other party within 30 days after the issuance of the Order, the following:

- Information regarding the benefits, limitations, and exclusions of the health insurance coverage
- Copies of any insurance form necessary to receive reimbursement, payment, or other benefits under the coverage
- A copy of any necessary health insurance cards

The Health Plan Administrator that provides the private health insurance coverage for the child(ren) may continue making payment for medical, optical, hospital, dental, or prescription services directly to any health care provider in accordance with the applicable private health

Supreme Court of Ohio
Uniform Domestic Relations Form – 12
FINAL JUDGMENT FOR DIVORCE WITH CHILDREN
Approved under Ohio Civil Rule 84
Amended: March 15, 2016

Page 13 of 16

insurance policy, contract, or plan.

The Obligor and/or Obligee required to provide private health insurance for the child(ren) must designate said child(ren) as dependents under any private health insurance policy, contract, or plan for which the person contracts.

The employer of the person required to provide private health insurance coverage is required to release to the other parent, any person subject to an order issued under section 3109.19 of the Revised Code, or the CSEA, upon written request, any necessary information regarding health insurance coverage, including the name and address of the health plan administrator and any policy, contract, or plan number, and the employer will otherwise comply with all orders and notices issued.

If the person required to obtain private health insurance coverage for the child(ren) subject to this Support Order obtains new employment, the agency shall comply with the requirements of section 3119.34 of the Revised Code, which may result in the issuance of a notice requiring the new employer to take whatever action is necessary to enroll the child(ren) in private health insurance coverage provided by the new employer.

Upon receipt of notice by the CSEA that private health insurance coverage is not available at a reasonable cost, cash medical support shall be paid in the amount as determined by the child support computation worksheets in section 3119.022 or 3119.023 of the Revised Code, as applicable. The CSEA may change the financial obligations of the parties to pay child support in accordance with the terms of the court or administrative order and cash medical support without a hearing or additional notice to the parties.

An Obligor that is in arrears in the Obligor's child support obligation is subject to having any federal, state and/or local income tax refund to which the Obligor may be entitled forwarded to the CSEA for payment toward these arrears. Such refunds will continue to be forwarded to the CSEA for payment until all arrears owed are paid in full. If the Obligor is married and files a joint tax return, the Obligor's spouse may contact the CSEA about filing an "Injured Spouse" claim after the Obligor is notified by the Internal Revenue Service that the Obligor's refund is being forwarded to the CSEA.

Pursuant to section 3121.29 of the Revised Code, the parties are notified as follows:
EACH PARTY TO THIS SUPPORT ORDER MUST NOTIFY THE CHILD SUPPORT AGENCY IN WRITING OF HIS OR HER CURRENT MAILING ADDRESS, CURRENT RESIDENCE ADDRESS, CURRENT RESIDENCE TELEPHONE NUMBER, CURRENT DRIVER'S LICENSE NUMBER AND OF ANY CHANGES IN THAT INFORMATION. EACH PARTY MUST NOTIFY THE AGENCY OF ALL CHANGES UNTIL FURTHER NOTICE FROM THE COURT. IF YOU ARE THE OBLIGOR UNDER A CHILD SUPPORT ORDER AND YOU FAIL TO MAKE THE REQUIRED NOTIFICATIONS, YOU MAY BE FINED UP TO $50.00 FOR A FIRST OFFENSE,

$100.00 FOR A SECOND OFFENSE, AND $500.00 FOR EACH SUBSEQUENT OFFENSE. IF YOU ARE AN OBLIGOR OR OBLIGEE UNDER ANY SUPPORT ORDER AND YOU WILLFULLY FAIL TO MAKE THE REQUIRED NOTIFICATIONS YOU MAY BE SUBJECTED TO FINES OF UP TO $1,000.00 AND IMPRISONMENT FOR NOT MORE THAN 90 DAYS.

IF YOU ARE AN OBLIGOR AND YOU FAIL TO MAKE THE REQUIRED NOTIFICATIONS, YOU MAY NOT RECEIVE NOTICE OF THE FOLLOWING ENFORCEMENT ACTIONS AGAINST YOU: IMPOSITION OF LIENS AGAINST YOUR PROPERTY; LOSS OF YOUR PROFESSIONAL OR OCCUPATIONAL LICENSE, DRIVER'S LICENSE, OR RECREATIONAL LICENSE; WITHHOLDING FROM YOUR INCOME; ACCESS RESTRICTIONS AND DEDUCTIONS FROM YOUR ACCOUNTS IN FINANCIAL INSTITUTIONS; AND ANY OTHER ACTION PERMITTED BY LAW TO OBTAIN MONEY FROM YOU AND TO SATISFY YOUR SUPPORT OBLIGATION.

G.   Payment shall be made in accordance with Chapter 3121. of the Revised Code.

H.   Arrearage
☐ Any temporary child support arrearage will survive this judgment entry.
☐ Any temporary child support arrearage will not survive this judgment entry.
☐ Other: _____

_____
_____
_____

NINTH: TAX EXEMPTION
Income tax dependency exemptions (check all that apply):

A.   ☐ The Plaintiff shall be entitled to claim the following minor child(ren) for all tax purposes
for ☐ even-numbered tax years ☐ odd-numbered tax years ☐ all eligible tax years, so long
as the Plaintiff is substantially current in any child support the Plaintiff is required to pay as of
December 31 of the tax year in question: _____

☐ The Defendant shall be entitled to claim the following minor child(ren) for all tax purposes
for ☐ even-numbered tax years ☐ odd-numbered tax years ☐ all eligible tax years, so long
as the Defendant is substantially current in any child support the Defendant is required to pay
as of December 31 of the tax year in question: _____

B.   ☐ Other orders regarding tax exemptions (specify): _____

_____
_____
_____

If a non-residential parent is entitled to claim the child(ren), the residential parent is required to
execute and deliver Internal Revenue Service Form 8332, or its successor, together with any other

Supreme Court of Ohio
Uniform Domestic Relations Form – 12
FINAL JUDGMENT FOR DIVORCE WITH CHILDREN
Approved under Ohio Civil Rule 84
Amended: March 15, 2016

Page 15 of 16

required forms as set out in section 152 of the Internal Revenue Code, as amended, on or before February 15th of the year following the tax year in question, to allow the non-residential parent to claim the minor child(ren).

TENTH: OTHER ORDERS

_____

_____

ELEVENTH: COURT COSTS

Court costs shall be (select one):

☐ Taxed to the deposit. Court costs due above the deposit shall be paid as follows: _____

_____

☐ Other (specify): _____

_____

TWELFTH: CLERK OF COURTS

The Clerk of Courts shall provide:

☐ a certified copy to: _____

☐ a file stamped copy to: _____

NOTICE. Pursuant to Civil Rule 58(B), the Clerk is directed to serve upon the parties a notice of the filing of this Judgment Entry and of the date of entry upon the Journal.

_____   _____
Date   JUDGE

IN THE COURT OF COMMON PLEAS

_____ **Division**

_____ **COUNTY, OHIO**

_____ Name	: : Case No. _____ :
_____ Street Address	: :
_____ City, State and Zip Code	: Judge _____ : :
Plaintiff	:
vs.	: Magistrate _____ :
_____ Name	: : :
_____ Street Address	: :
_____ City, State and Zip Code	: :
Defendant	:

JUDGMENT ENTRY CONVERTING INTEREST IN REAL ESTATE

Pursuant to the Judgment Entry filed on _____ , the marriage of the parties, _____ and _____ , was terminated.

Pursuant to the Judgment Entry, it is ORDERED that _____ is divested of all rights, title, and interest in the real estate as set forth in the legal description, including deed reference and parcel number attached.

It is further ORDERED that _____ is vested with all rights, title, and interest of the real estate attached. The Auditor and Recorder of _____ County are ORDERED to accept this Entry as transferral of such interest and transfer the above real estate on its books and records. The filing of this Entry with the Recorder and Auditor will effectuate the conveyance of the real estate interest.

Court costs shall be (select one):

☐ Taxed to the deposit. Court costs due above the deposit shall be paid as follows: _____

_____

☐ Other (specify): _____

_____
               JUDGE

Supreme Court of Ohio
Uniform Domestic Relations Form – 13
JUDGMENT ENTRY CONVERTING INTEREST IN REAL ESTATE
Approved under Ohio Civil Rule 84
Effective Date: 7/1/2013

Page 1 of 1

IN THE COURT OF COMMON PLEAS

_____ **Division**

_____ **COUNTY, OHIO**

_____	:	
Name	:	Case No. _____
_____	:	
Street Address	:	
_____	:	Judge _____
City, State and Zip Code	:	
Petitioner 1	:	
	:	Magistrate _____
and	:	
	:	
_____	:	
Name	:	
_____	:	
Street Address	:	
_____	:	
City, State and Zip Code	:	
Petitioner 2	:	

> **Instructions:** This form is used to request ending the marriage when the parties have agreed on all aspects of the termination, including the division of real estate, personal property, debts, spousal support, and, if there is/are (a) child(ren), allocation of parental rights and responsibilities (custody), parenting time (companionship and visitation) and child support. A Separation Agreement (Uniform Domestic Relations Form 16) and either a Shared Parenting Plan (Uniform Domestic Relations Form 17) or a Parenting Plan (Uniform Domestic Relations Form 18), if applicable, must be filed with this Petition.

PETITION FOR DISSOLUTION OF MARRIAGE AND
WAIVER OF SERVICE OF SUMMONS ☐ WITH CHILDREN ☐ WITHOUT CHILDREN

The Petitioners, _____ (my name) and

_____ (spouse's name), say as follows:

1. ☐ _____(my name) ☐ _____(spouse's name)
   ☐ Both parties has/have been (a) resident(s) of the State of Ohio for at least six months.

2. ☐ _____(my name) ☐ _____(spouse's name)
   ☐ Both parties has/have been (a) resident(s) of _____ County for at least 90 days immediately before the filing of this Petition.

3. The Petitioners were married to one another on _____ (date of marriage) in

Supreme Court of Ohio
Uniform Domestic Relations Form – 14
PETITION FOR DISSOLUTION OF MARRIAGE AND WAIVER OF SERVICE OF SUMMONS
Approved under Ohio Civil Rule 84
Amended: March 15, 2016

Page 1 of 3

_____ (city or county, and state).

4. Check all that apply:

☐ There is/are no child(ren) expected from this marriage or relationship.

☐ There is/are child(ren) expected from this marriage or relationship and the approximate due date is:_____.

☐ There is/are no child(ren) from this marriage or relationship.

☐ The Petitioners are parents of _____ (number) child(ren) from this marriage or relationship. Of the child(ren), _____ (number) is/are emancipated adult(s) and not under any disability. The following _____ (number) of child(ren) is/are minor child(ren)and/or mentally or physically disabled and incapable of supporting or maintaining themselves (name and date of birth of each child):

Name of Child	Date of Birth
_____	_____
_____	_____
_____	_____

☐ I am not the parent of the following child(ren) who was/were born during the marriage (name and date of birth of each child):

_____

☐ My Spouse is not the parent of the following child(ren) who was/were born during the marriage (name and date of birth of each child):

_____

_____

5. ☐ The following child(ren) of this marriage or relationship is/are subject to a custody or parenting order in a different Court proceeding (name of each child and the Court that issued the custody or parenting order): _____

_____

_____

6. ☐ The Petitioners have entered into a Separation Agreement which is attached.

If Petitioners have (a) minor child(ren) (select one):

☐ The Petitioners have agreed to a Parenting Plan which is attached.

☐ The Petitioners have agreed to a Shared Parenting Plan which is attached.

7. The Petitioners further say as follows:

☐ We are both over 18 years of age.

☐ We are not under any legal disability.

Supreme Court of Ohio
Uniform Domestic Relations Form – 14
PETITION FOR DISSOLUTION OF MARRIAGE AND WAIVER OF SERVICE OF
SUMMONS
Approved under Ohio Civil Rule 84
Amended: March 15, 2016
Page 2 of 3

☐ We waive all rights to receive summons for the dissolution action through the Clerk of Courts.

☐ We have read this Petition and voluntarily ask this Court to dissolve the marriage.

8. ☐ The Petitioner _____ requests to be restored
to the former name of: _____

The Petitioners request the Court for a Decree of Dissolution of their marriage pursuant to the terms of the Separation Agreement and the Shared Parenting Plan or Parenting Plan, if there is/are (a) child(ren).

_____   _____
My Signature   My Spouse's Signature

_____   _____
Telephone number at which the Court may reach   Telephone number at which the Court may reach
you or at which messages may be left for you   you or at which messages may be left for you

Supreme Court of Ohio
Uniform Domestic Relations Form – 14
PETITION FOR DISSOLUTION OF MARRIAGE AND WAIVER OF SERVICE OF
SUMMONS
Approved under Ohio Civil Rule 84
Amended: March 15, 2016   Page 3 of 3

IN THE COURT OF COMMON PLEAS

_____ **Division**

_____ **COUNTY, OHIO**

_____	:
Petitioner 1	: Case No. _____
_____	:
Street Address	:
_____	: Judge _____
City, State and Zip Code	:
	:
and	: Magistrate _____
	:
_____	:
Petitioner 2	:
_____	:
Street Address	:
_____	:
City, State and Zip Code	:

JUDGMENT ENTRY OF DISSOLUTION OF MARRIAGE
☐ WITH CHILDREN ☐ WITHOUT CHILDREN

This matter came on for hearing on _____ before ☐ Judge ☐ Magistrate
_____ , upon the Petition for Dissolution of Marriage filed on _____ .
Present at the hearing were the following persons: _____

_____

FINDINGS

1. At the time of the filing of the Petition, ☐ _____ (my name)
    ☐ _____ (my Spouse's name)
    ☐ Both parties was/were a) resident(s) of the State of Ohio for at least six months.

2. ☐ _____ (my name)
    ☐ _____ (my Spouse's name)
    ☐ Both parties was/were (a) resident(s) of _____ County for at least 90 days immediately
    before the filing of the Petition.

3. The parties were married to one another on _____ (date of marriage) in
    _____ (city or county, and state).

Supreme Court of Ohio
Uniform Domestic Relations Form – 15
JUDGMENT ENTRY OF DISSOLUTION OF MARRIAGE
Approved under Ohio Civil Rule 84
Amended: March 15, 2016

4. Check all that apply regarding child(ren):

☐ There is/are no child(ren) expected from this marriage or relationship.
☐ There is/are child(ren) expected from this marriage or relationship and the approximate due date is: _____.

☐ There is/are no child(ren) from this marriage or relationship.
☐ The parties are parents of _____ (number) child(ren) from the marriage or relationship. Of the child(ren), _____ (number) is/are now emancipated adult(s) and not under any disability. The following _____ (number) child(ren) is/are minor child(ren) and/or mentally or physically disabled and incapable of supporting or maintaining themselves (name and date of birth of each child):

Name of Child	Date of Birth
_____	_____
_____	_____
_____	_____

☐ _____(other parent's name) is not the parent of the following child(ren) who was/were born during the marriage (name and date of birth of each child):

_____

_____

☐ _____(other parent's name) is not the parent of the following child(ren) who was/were born during the marriage (name and date of birth of each child):

_____

_____

5. ☐ The following child(ren) of this marriage or relationship is/are subject to a custody or parenting order in a different Court proceeding (name of each child with the Court that has issued the custody or parenting order): _____

_____

6. Petitioner _____ requests to be restored to the former name of:

_____

7. The parties personally appeared before this Court, and more than 30 and less than 90 days have elapsed after the filing of the Petition.

8. Upon examination under oath, the parties acknowledge that they have agreed on the ☐ Shared Parenting Plan or ☐ Parenting Plan for their child(ren), which they believe to be in their best interests. The Court's adoption of the Plan is in the best interests of the child(ren).

9. Upon examination under oath, the parties acknowledge that they voluntarily entered into a Separation Agreement, attached and incorporated in the Petition, ☐ as modified on _____ and the parties are satisfied with the terms of the Separation Agreement and Plan and fully understand the same. Each

Petitioner desires to have the marriage dissolved, and the Separation Agreement approved by the Court.

JUDGMENT

Based upon the findings set out above, it is, therefore, **ORDERED, ADJUDGED, and DECREED** that:

FIRST: DISSOLUTION GRANTED

The dissolution of marriage is granted. The Court approves the ☐ Separation Agreement
☐ Amended Separation Agreement ☐ Shared Parenting Plan ☐ Amended Shared Parenting Plan or
☐ Parenting Plan ☐ Amended Parenting Plan as submitted and releases the parties from the obligations of
their marriage except as set out in the attached ☐ Agreement and ☐ Plan, which is incorporated in this entry.

The parties shall fulfill each and every obligation imposed by the ☐ Agreement and ☐ Plan as submitted
and modified, if applicable. The Plan is approved and this entry shall constitute a Parenting Decree
under R.C. 3109.04(D).

☐ SECOND: NAME

Petitioner _____ is restored to the
prior name of: _____

☐ THIRD: OTHER _____

_____

FOURTH: COURT COSTS

Court costs shall be (select one):

☐ Taxed to the deposit. Court costs due above the deposit shall be paid as follows: _____

_____

☐ Other (specify): _____

_____

_____
JUDGE

_____   _____
My Signature _____ (Name)   Your Signature _____ (Spouse's Name)

_____   _____
Attorney   Attorney

Supreme Court of Ohio
Uniform Domestic Relations Form – 15
JUDGMENT ENTRY OF DISSOLUTION OF MARRIAGE
Approved under Ohio Civil Rule 84
Amended: March 15, 2016

Page 3 of 3

IN THE COURT OF COMMON PLEAS

_____ **Division**

_____ **COUNTY, OHIO**

_____	:
Plaintiff/Petitioner 1	: Case No. _____
_____	:
Street Address	:
_____	: Judge _____
City, State and Zip Code	:
	:
and	: Magistrate _____
	:
_____	:
Plaintiff/Petitioner 2	:
_____	:
Street Address	:
_____	:
City, State and Zip Code	:

Instructions: This form is used to present an agreement to the Court regarding spousal support, the division of personal property, real estate, and debts resulting from the termination of marriage. If the parties have any minor child(ren), child(ren) with disabilities, or you or the Spouse are/is pregnant, a Shared Parenting Plan (Uniform Domestic Relations Form 17) or Parenting Plan (Uniform Domestic Relations Form 18) must be attached.

SEPARATION AGREEMENT

The parties, _____ , (name), and

_____ , (Spouse's name), state the following.

1. The parties were married to one another on _____ (date of marriage)
   in _____ (city or county, and state), and request
   that the termination of marriage be the date ☐ of final hearing or ☐ as specified: _____

2. The parties intend to live separate and apart.

3. Each party has made full and complete disclosure to the other of all marital property, separate property, and any other assets, debts, income, and expenses.

4. Neither party has knowledge of any other property and debts of any kind in which either party has an interest.

Supreme Court of Ohio
Uniform Domestic Relations Form – 16
SEPARATION AGREEMENT
Approved under Ohio Civil Rule 84
Amended: March 15, 2016

5. Each party has had the opportunity to value and verify all marital property, separate property, and debts.

6. A party's willful failure to disclose may result in the Court awarding the other party three times the value of the property, assets, income, or expenses that were not disclosed by the other party.

7. This Agreement addresses spousal support, property, and debt division.

8. This written Agreement is the complete agreement of the parties.

9. There are no other representations, agreements, statements, or prior writings that shall have any effect on this Agreement.

10. Each party fully understands the Agreement and has knowingly and voluntarily signed the Agreement.

11. No change to the terms of this Agreement shall be valid unless in writing and knowingly and voluntarily signed by both parties.

The parties agree as follows:

FIRST: SEPARATION

The parties shall live separate and apart. Neither party shall interfere with the activities, personal life, or privacy of the other; harass the other, nor engage in any conduct calculated to restrain, embarrass, injure, or hinder the other in any way.

SECOND: PROPERTY

Marital property as defined in R.C. 3105.171 is property owned by either or both spouses and property in which either spouse has an interest in the property. Separate property as defined in R.C. 3105.171 is real or personal property that was inherited, acquired by one spouse prior to the date of marriage, acquired after a decree of legal separation under R.C. 3107.17, excluded by a valid antenuptial agreement, compensation for personal injury, except for loss of marital earnings and compensation for expenses paid from marital assets, or any gift of property that was given to only one spouse. If separate property is involved, the owner should consider consulting an attorney. The party not receiving the separate property waives all interest in the property.

A. Real Estate (select one):

Real estate includes lands, mortgaged properties, buildings, fixtures attached to buildings, attached structures (for example, garage, in-ground pool), condominiums, time shares, mobile homes, natural condition stakes (for example, gas, oil, mineral rights, existing soil, including trees and landscape), and inheritance rights in real estate. The property's legal description is on the deed or mortgage papers.

1. ☐ The parties do not own any real estate.

Supreme Court of Ohio
Uniform Domestic Relations Form – 16
SEPARATION AGREEMENT
Approved under Ohio Civil Rule 84
Amended: March 15, 2016

Page 2 of 13

2. Marital Real Estate

☐ The parties owned real estate in one or both of their names and agree to award it as follows. A legal description of the property must be attached. (Attach a copy of the property's deed or mortgage papers.)

Location of Property	Awarded to
_____	_____
_____	_____
_____	_____

3. ☐ Each party shall pay and hold the other harmless from any debt owing on real estate the party receives unless otherwise stated in this Agreement.

4. ☐ Other debt payment arrangements, including refinancing: _____
_____
_____
_____

If the real estate is not in the name of the party to whom it is awarded, the parties shall make arrangements to transfer the property to the proper party as soon as possible.

B. Titled Vehicles (select one):

Titled vehicles include boats, trailers, automobiles, motorcycles, trucks, mobile homes, golf carts, motor scooters, sport utility vehicles (SUV), recreational vehicles (RV), all purpose vehicles (APV). Provide vehicle model, make, year, and serial number for all titled vehicle(s) that will be transferred.

1. ☐ The parties do not own any titled vehicle(s) in either party's name.

2. ☐ The titled vehicle(s) has/have already been divided or transferred, including all rights, title and interest in the vehicle(s) and is/are in the possession of the proper party. The parties are satisfied with the division.

3. ☐ The parties own titled vehicle(s) which has/have not been divided or transferred.
_____(name) shall receive the following vehicle(s), free and clear of any claims from the _____ (Spouse's name):_____
_____
_____
_____
and _____ (Spouse's name) shall receive the following vehicle(s), free and clear of any claims of the _____ (name):_____
_____
_____
_____

Supreme Court of Ohio
Uniform Domestic Relations Form – 16
SEPARATION AGREEMENT
Approved under Ohio Civil Rule 84
Amended: March 15, 2016

Page 3 of 13

4. Each party shall pay for and hold the other harmless from any debt owing on the titled vehicle(s) The party receives unless otherwise stated in this Agreement.

5. Other debt payment arrangements regarding titled vehicle(s): _____
_____
_____
_____

If the vehicle's title is not in the name of the party to whom the vehicle is awarded, the current title holder shall transfer that title to the proper party as soon as the title is available for transfer. If title cannot be transferred immediately to the party to whom the vehicle is awarded, the party holding the title shall make the following arrangements to obtain and pay for license plates, registration, and insurance: _____
_____
_____
_____

C. Household Goods and Personal Property (select one):
Household goods and personal property include appliances, tools, air conditioner window units, doghouses, lawn mowers, riding lawn mowers, above ground pools, safety deposit boxes, jewelry, furniture, refrigerators, silverware, collections, china, and books.

1. ☐ The household goods and personal property are already divided and in the possession of the proper party. The parties are satisfied with the division.

2. ☐ The parties have household goods and personal property which have not been divided. _____ (name) shall have the following: _____
_____
_____
_____

and _____Spouse's name) shall have the following: _____
_____
_____
_____

3. Delivery or pick-up of household goods and personal property shall be as follows: _____
_____
_____
_____

4. Each party shall pay for and hold the other harmless from any debt owing on the household goods and personal property the party receives unless otherwise stated in this Agreement.

Supreme Court of Ohio
Uniform Domestic Relations Form – 16
SEPARATION AGREEMENT
Approved under Ohio Civil Rule 84
Amended: March 15, 2016

Page 4 of 13

5. Other debt arrangements regarding household goods and personal property: _____
_____
_____
_____

The parties shall make arrangements to transfer possession of the household goods and personal property to the proper party as soon as possible.

D. Financial Accounts (select one):
Financial accounts include checking, savings, certificates of deposit, money market accounts, medical or health savings accounts, education or college saving plans (for example, 529 Plan) and trusts.

1. ☐ The parties do not have any financial accounts.

2. ☐ The parties have financial accounts and agree the accounts are already divided and in the name of the proper party. The parties are satisfied with the division.

3. ☐ The parties have financial accounts which are not divided.
_____ (name) shall receive the following:

Institution	Current Name(s) on Account	Type of Account
_____	_____	☐ checking ☐ saving ☐ other: _____
_____	_____	☐ checking ☐ saving ☐ other: _____
_____	_____	☐ checking ☐ saving ☐ other: _____

and _____ (Spouse's name) shall receive the following:

Institution	Current Name(s) on Account	Type of Account
_____	_____	☐ checking ☐ saving ☐ other: _____
_____	_____	☐ checking ☐ saving ☐ other: _____
_____	_____	☐ checking ☐ saving ☐ other: _____

4. Each party shall pay for and hold the other harmless from any debt owing on the financial accounts the party receives unless otherwise stated in this Agreement.

5. Other arrangements regarding financial accounts: _____
_____
_____

The parties shall make arrangements to transfer the financial accounts to the proper party as soon as possible.

E. Stocks, Bonds, Securities, and Mutual Funds (select one):

1. ☐ The parties do not have any stocks, bonds, securities, or mutual funds.

2. ☐ One or both parties has/have stocks, bonds, securities, or mutual funds which are already divided and in the name of the proper party. The parties are satisfied with the division.

3. ☐ One or both parties has/have stocks, bonds, securities, or mutual funds which are not divided.
   _____(name) shall receive the following:

Institution	Current Name(s) on Account	Number of Shares
_____	_____	_____
_____	_____	_____
_____	_____	_____
_____	_____	_____

and _____ (Spouse's name) shall receive the following:

Institution	Current Name(s) on Account	Number of Shares
_____	_____	_____
_____	_____	_____
_____	_____	_____
_____	_____	_____

4. Each party shall pay for and hold the other harmless from any debt owing on the stocks, bonds, securities, or mutual funds the party receives unless otherwise stated in this Agreement.

5. Other arrangements regarding the stocks, bonds, securities, or mutual funds:
   _____
   _____
   _____

The parties shall make arrangements to sell or transfer the stocks, bonds, securities, or mutual funds to the proper party as soon as possible.

F. Business Interests (select one):

1. ☐ The parties do not have any business interests.

2. ☐ One or both parties has/have business interests and which are already divided and in the name of the proper party. The parties are satisfied with the division.

Supreme Court of Ohio
Uniform Domestic Relations Form – 16
SEPARATION AGREEMENT
Approved under Ohio Civil Rule 84
Amended: March 15, 2016

Page 6 of 13

3. ☐ One or both parties has/have business interests which have not been divided.

_____ (name) shall receive the following:

Name of Business	**Ownership Interest**
_____	_____
_____	_____
_____	_____

and _____ (Spouse's name) shall receive the following:

Name of Business	**Ownership Interest**
_____	_____
_____	_____
_____	_____
_____	_____

4. Each party shall pay for and hold the other harmless from any debt owing on the business interests the party receives unless otherwise stated in this Agreement.

5. Other arrangements regarding business interests: _____
_____
_____
_____

The parties shall make arrangements to transfer the business interests to the proper party as soon as possible.

G. Pension, Profit Sharing, IRA, 401(k), and Other Retirement Plans (select one):

1. ☐ The parties do not have any pension, profit sharing, IRA, 401(k), or other retirement plans.

2. ☐ The pension(s), profit sharing, IRA, 401(k), or other retirement plans are already divided and in the proper party's name. The parties are satisfied with the division.

3. ☐ The parties have pension(s), profit sharing, IRA, 401(k), or other retirement plans which have not been divided.

_____ (name) shall receive the following:

Company	**Name(s) on Plan**	**Amount/Share**
_____	_____	_____
_____	_____	_____
_____	_____	_____
_____	_____	_____

Supreme Court of Ohio
Uniform Domestic Relations Form – 16
SEPARATION AGREEMENT
Approved under Ohio Civil Rule 84
Amended: March 15, 2016

Page 7 of 13

and _____ (Spouse's name) shall receive the following:

Company	Name(s) on Plan	Amount/Share
_____	_____	_____
_____	_____	_____
_____	_____	_____
_____	_____	_____

4. Each party shall pay for and hold the other harmless from any debt owing on the pension(s), profit sharing, IRA, 401(k), or other retirement plans received unless otherwise stated in this Agreement.

5. Other arrangements regarding pension(s), profit sharing, IRA, 401(k), or other retirement plans:

_____

_____

_____

The parties shall make arrangements to transfer interest in the pension(s), profit sharing, IRA, 401(k), or other retirement plans to the proper party as soon as possible.

A Qualified Domestic Relations Order (QDRO) or Division of Property Order (DOPO) may be necessary to divide some of these assets. If so, the QDRO and DOPO will be prepared by:

_____

and submitted to the Court within 90 days after the final hearing. Expenses of preparation shall be paid as follows: _____

_____

_____

The Court retains jurisdiction to interpret and enforce the terms of the documents of transfer.

H. Life Insurance Policies (select one):

1. ☐ The parties do not have any life insurance policy(ies) with a cash value.

2. ☐ The parties have life insurance policy(ies) and agree the cash value of all life insurance policy(ies) has/have already been divided. The parties are satisfied with the division.

3. ☐ The parties' life insurance policy(ies) has/have not been divided.
    _____ (name) shall receive the following policy(ies), free and clear of any claims of the _____ (Spouse's name):

_____

_____

_____

Supreme Court of Ohio
Uniform Domestic Relations Form – 16
SEPARATION AGREEMENT
Approved under Ohio Civil Rule 84
Amended: March 15, 2016

Page 8 of 13

and _____ (Spouse's name) shall receive the following
policy(ies), free and clear of any claims of the _____ (name):

_____

_____

_____

4. Each party shall pay for and hold the other harmless from any debt owing on the life insurance
    policy(ies) the party receives unless otherwise stated in this Agreement.

5. Other arrangements regarding life insurance policy(ies): _____

_____

_____

_____

**The parties shall make arrangements to transfer interest in the life insurance policy(ies) to the
proper party as soon as possible.**

I. Other Property (select one):

1. ☐ The parties do not have any other property.

2. ☐ The property shall be awarded as follows:

Description of Property		**To Be Kept By**
	☐	_____
		(name)
	☐	_____
		(Spouse's name)
	☐	_____
		(Other)
_____	☐	_____
		(name)
	☐	_____
		(Spouse's name)
	☐	_____
		(Other)
_____	☐	_____
		(name)
	☐	_____
		(Spouse's name)
	☐	_____
		(Other)
_____	☐	_____
		(name)
	☐	_____
		(Spouse's name)
	☐	_____
		(Other)

3. Each party shall pay for and hold the other harmless from any debt owing on the property the party
    receives unless otherwise stated in this Agreement.

4. Other arrangements regarding the property above: _____
_____
_____
_____

The parties shall make arrangements to transfer interest in the property listed above to the proper party as soon as possible.

THIRD: DEBTS (select one):

☐ The parties do not have any debts.

☐ Each party shall pay all debts incurred by him or her individually and in their individual name and shall hold the other party harmless for these debts.

☐ The parties have the following debts and have agreed to the payment of all debts owed, and agree to hold the other party harmless on those debts, as follows:

Creditor	Purpose of Debt	Balance	Who Will Pay
			☐ _____ (name)
			☐ _____ (Spouse's name)
_____	_____	_____	
			☐ _____ (name)
			☐ _____ (Spouse's name)
_____	_____	_____	
			☐ _____ (name)
			☐ _____ (Spouse's name)
_____	_____	_____	
			☐ _____ (name)
			☐ _____ (Spouse's name)
_____	_____	_____	

Bankruptcy (select one):

☐ The Court will retain jurisdiction to enforce payment of debt obligations, in the event a party files bankruptcy, including, but not limited to, the ability to determine the debt assigned is in the nature of maintenance, necessity or support and is therefore nondischargeable in bankruptcy, and/or making a future spousal support order, regardless of the spousal support order set forth below under **FOURTH: SPOUSAL SUPPORT**.

☐ Nothing in this order shall prevent the ☐ Plaintiff and ☐ Defendant from being fully discharged from the debts allocated in this order in a bankruptcy proceeding except for any orders expressly for

Supreme Court of Ohio
Uniform Domestic Relations Form – 16
SEPARATION AGREEMENT
Approved under Ohio Civil Rule 84
Amended: March 15, 2016

Page 10 of 13

spousal support and the following debts: _____

_____

_____

_____

Neither party shall incur liabilities against the other party in the future and each shall pay any debt incurred by him or her individually after the date of this agreement.

FOURTH: SPOUSAL SUPPORT

A. Spousal Support Not Awarded
    ☐ Neither _____ (name) nor
    _____ (Spouse's name) shall pay spousal support to the other. The Court shall not retain jurisdiction to modify spousal support, except as set forth above under **THIRD: DEBT**.

B. Spousal Support Awarded
    ☐ _____ (name) ☐ _____
    (Spouse's name) shall pay spousal support to _____
    (Spouse's name) in the amount of $ _____ per month plus 2%
    processing charge for a total of $ _____ per month, commencing on
    _____ and due on the _____ day of the month. This spousal support
    shall continue ☐ indefinitely ☐ for a period of _____.

C. Method of Payment of Spousal Support (select one):
    ☐ If there are no child(ren), the spousal support payment shall be made directly to the
    ☐ _____ (name)
    ☐ _____ (Spouse's name).
    ☐ The spousal support payment, plus 2% processing charge, shall be made to the Ohio Child
    Support Payment Central, P. O. Box 182372, Columbus, Ohio 43218-2372, as administered through
    the _____ County Child Support Enforcement Agency by income withholding
    at the spouse's place of employment.

    ☐ The Court shall not retain jurisdiction to modify spousal support.

    ☐ The Court shall retain jurisdiction to modify the ☐ amount ☐ duration of the spousal support
    Order.

D. Termination of Spousal Support
    This spousal support shall terminate sooner than the above stated date upon the Plaintiff's or the
    Defendant's death or in the event of the following (check all that apply):
    ☐ The cohabitation of the person receiving support in a relationship comparable to marriage.
    ☐ The remarriage of the person receiving support.
    ☐ Other (specify): _____

_____

_____

E. Deductibility of Spousal Support for All Tax Purposes (select one):

☐ The spousal support paid shall be deducted from income to the person paying the support and included in income by the person receiving the support.

☐ The spousal support paid shall be included in income of the person paying the support.

F. Other orders regarding spousal support (specify): _____

_____

G. Arrearage

☐ Any temporary spousal support arrearage will survive this judgment entry.

☐ Any temporary spousal support arrearage will not survive this judgment entry.

☐ Other: _____

FIFTH: NAME

☐ _____ shall be restored to

the prior name of: _____

SIXTH: ALLOCATION OF PARENTAL RIGHTS AND RESPONSIBILITIES, PARENTING TIME, CHILD SUPPORT AND HEALTH CARE

☐ The parties do not have child(ren) subject to the jurisdiction of the Court.

☐ The parties have minor child(ren) subject to the jurisdiction of the Court, and a ☐ Parenting Plan or ☐ Shared Parenting Plan is attached.

SEVENTH: OTHER

The parties agree to the following additional matters: _____

_____

_____

EIGHTH: NON-USE OF OTHER'S CREDIT

From now on, neither party shall incur any debt or obligation upon the credit of the other or in their joint names. If a party incurs such a debt or obligation that party shall repay, indemnify, and hold the other harmless as to any such debt or obligation. All joint credit card accounts shall be immediately cancelled, and the cards shall be immediately destroyed.

NINTH: INCORPORATION INTO DECREE/EFFECTIVENESS OF AGREEMENT

If one or both of the parties institute or have instituted proceedings for dissolution, divorce, or separation, this Agreement shall be presented to the Court with the request that it be adjudicated to be fair, just, and proper, and incorporated into the decree of the Court.

Supreme Court of Ohio
Uniform Domestic Relations Form – 16
SEPARATION AGREEMENT
Approved under Ohio Civil Rule 84
Amended: March 15, 2016

Page 12 of 13

TENTH: PERFORMANCE OF NECESSARY ACTS

Upon execution and approval of this Agreement by the Court, each party shall deliver to the other party, or permit the other party to take possession of all items of property to which each is entitled under the terms of this Agreement, and shall make all periodic payments required under the terms of this Agreement.

Upon failure of either party to execute and deliver any deed, conveyance, title, certificate or other document or instrument to the other party, an order of the Court incorporating this Agreement shall constitute and operate as a properly executed document, and the County Auditor, County Recorder, Clerk of Courts and/or all other public and private officials shall be authorized and directed to accept a properly certified copy of a court order incorporating this Agreement, a properly certified copy of the Agreement or an order of the Court in lieu of the document regularly required for the conveyance or transfer.

ELEVENTH: SEVERABILITY

If any provision of this Agreement is held to be invalid or unenforceable, all other provisions shall continue in full force and effect.

TWELFTH: APPLICABLE LAW

All of the provisions of this Agreement shall be construed and enforced in accordance with the laws of the State of Ohio.

THIRTEENTH: MUTUAL RELEASE

Except as otherwise provided, the parties do release and forever discharge each other from any and all actions, suits, debts, claims, demands, and obligations whatsoever, both in law and in equity, which either of them ever had, now has, or may have or assert against the other upon or by reason of any matter or cause to the date of the execution of this Agreement.

Each party waives all rights of inheritance and the right to share in the estate of the other, and waives all rights which would otherwise be available as a surviving spouse, except payments or rights included in this Agreement.

_____	_____
My Signature	Spouse's Signature
_____	_____
Date	Date

IN THE COURT OF COMMON PLEAS

_____ **Division**

_____ **COUNTY, OHIO**

IN THE MATTER OF:

_____
A Minor

_____ :
Plaintiff/Petitioner 1   :   Case No. _____
                              :
_____ :
Street Address   :
                              :
_____ :   Judge _____
City, State and Zip Code   :
                              :
vs./and   :   Magistrate _____
                              :
                              :
_____ :
Defendant/Petitioner 2   :
                              :
_____ :
Street Address   :
                              :
_____ :
City, State and Zip Code   :
                              :

Instructions: The Parenting Time Schedule must be attached to this Plan. Parents are urged to consult the Planning for Parenting Time Guide: Ohio's Guide for Parents Living Apart available at http://www.supremecourt.ohio.gov/Publications/JCS/parentingGuide.pdf.

SHARED PARENTING PLAN

We, the parents, _____, "(name) Plaintiff/Petitioner 1",
and_____,"(name) Defendant/Petitioner 2", have
_____ (number) child(ren) from the marriage or relationship. Of the child(ren), _____
(number) is/are emancipated adult(s) and not under any disability, and the following_____
(number) child(ren) are minor child(ren) and/or mentally or physically disabled child(ren) incapable of
supporting or maintaining themselves (name and date of birth of each child):

_____

_____

_____

The parents agree to the care, parenting, and control of their child(ren) as provided in this
Shared Parenting Plan.

Supreme Court of Ohio
Uniform Domestic Relations Form – 17
SHARED PARENTING PLAN
Approved under Ohio Civil Rule 84 and Ohio Juvenile Rule 46
Amended: March 15, 2016

FIRST: PARENTS' RIGHTS

The parents shall have:

A.   The right to participate in major decisions concerning the child(ren)'s health, social situation, morals, welfare, education, and economic environment.

B.   The right to reasonable telephone contact with the child(ren) when they are with the other parent.

C.   The right to participate in the selection of doctors, psychologists, psychiatrists, hospitals, and other health care providers for the child(ren).

D.   The right to authorize medical, surgical, hospital, dental, institutional, psychological and psychiatric care for the child(ren) and obtain a second opinion regarding medical conditions or treatment.

E.   The right to be notified in case of an injury to or illness of the child(ren).

F.   The right to be present with the child(ren) at medical, dental and other health-related examinations and treatments, including, but not limited to psychological and psychiatric care.

G.   The right to inspect and receive the child(ren)'s medical and dental records and the right to consult with any treating physician, dentist and/or other health care provider, including but not limited to psychologists and psychiatrists.

H.   The right to consult with school officials concerning the child(ren)'s welfare and educational status, and the right to inspect and receive the child(ren)'s student records to the extent permitted by law.

I.   The right to receive copies of all school reports, calendars of school events, notices of parent-teacher conferences, and school programs.

J.   The right to attend and participate in parent-teacher conferences, school trips, school programs, and other school activities in which parents are invited to participate.

K.   The right to attend and participate with the child(ren) in athletic programs and other extracurricular activities.

L.   The right to receive notice of the other parent's intention to relocate.

SECOND: ALLOCATION OF PARENTAL RIGHTS AND RESPONSIBILITIES

A.   General Responsibilities

Each parent shall take all measures necessary to foster respect and affection between the child(ren) and the other parent. Neither parent shall do anything that may estrange the child(ren) from the other parent, or impair the child(ren)'s high regard for the other parent.

B.   Medical Responsibilities

A parent shall notify the other parent promptly if a child experiences a serious injury, has a serious or chronic illness, or receives treatment in an emergency room or hospital. A parent shall notify the other parent of the emergency, the child's status, locale, and any other pertinent information as soon as practical, but in any event within 24 hours.

The parents shall consult with each other about the child(ren)'s medical care needs and each shall immediately notify the other parent about all major non-emergency medical decisions before authorizing a course of treatment. Parents have a right to know the necessity for treatment, proposed cost, and proposed payment schedule. Each parent may also secure an independent evaluation at the parent's expense to determine the necessity for treatment. If the parties cannot agree regarding a course of treatment, the ☐ Plaintiff's/Petitioner 1's ☐ Defendant's/Petitioner 2's (select one) decision shall control. The parents shall provide the other with the names and telephone numbers of all health care providers for the child(ren).

C. Both parents have shared parenting of the child(ren) as specified in this Plan. Each parent, regardless of where an individual child is residing at a particular point in time, as specified in this Plan, is the "residential parent", "the residential parent and legal custodian", or the "custodial parent" of that child.

D. Parenting Time Schedule
Unless otherwise agreed, the parents shall have parenting time with the child(ren) according to the attached Parenting Time Schedule, which shows the times that the child(ren) shall be with each parent on weekdays, weekends, holidays, and vacation times.

(The Parenting Time Schedule must be attached to this Plan.)

E. School Designation
Plaintiff/Petitioner 1 shall be designated as the residential parent for school attendance and enrollment purposes of the following child(ren): _____

_____

Defendant/Petitioner 2 shall be designated as the residential parent for school attendance and enrollment purposes of the following child(ren): _____

_____

In the event that a change in schools is being considered, after consultation with the other parent:
☐ Plaintiff/Petitioner 1 is authorized to change school placement of the following child(ren):

_____

_____

☐ Defendant/Petitioner 2 is authorized to change school placement of the following child(ren):

_____

_____

☐ Without a written agreement or court order, neither parent is authorized to change school placement of the following child(ren): _____

_____

_____

F. Other orders: _____
_____
_____
_____

G. Public Benefits
Plaintiff/Petitioner 1 shall be designated as the residential parent for receipt of public benefits purposes of the following child(ren): _____
_____

Defendant/Petitioner 2 shall be designated as the residential parent for receipt of public benefits purposes of the following child(ren): _____

H. This designation of a particular parent as the residential parent for the purposes of determining the school attendance and enrollment of the child(ren) or the receipt of public benefits of the child(ren) does not affect the designation of each parent as the "residential parent," "residential parent and legal custodian," or the "custodial parent of the child(ren)".

I. Transportation (select one):
☐ Each parent shall be responsible for providing transportation for the child(ren) at the beginning of the parent's parenting period. Each parent shall be responsible for providing transportation for the child(ren) to and from school and activities during the parent's parenting period.

☐ We agree to the following arrangements for providing transportation for our child(ren) at the beginning, during, or end of a parenting period: _____
_____
_____

J. Current Address and Telephone Number
Plaintiff's/Petitioner 1's current home address and telephone number, including cellular telephone number:
_____
_____
_____

Defendant's/Petitioner 2's current home address and telephone number, including cellular telephone number:
_____
_____
_____
_____

K. Relocation Notice
    Pursuant to section 3109.051(G) of the Revised Code:
    If either of the residential parents intends to move to a residence other than the residence specified in the court order, the parent shall file a notice of intent to relocate with this Court. Except as provided in divisions (G)(2), (3), and (4) of section 3109.051 of the Revised Code, the Court shall send a copy of the notice to the other parent. Upon receipt of the notice, the Court, on its own motion or the motion of the nonmoving parent, may schedule a hearing with notice to both parents to determine whether it is in the best interests of the child(ren) to revise the parenting time schedule for the child(ren).

    Each residential parent shall inform in writing the Court and the other parent of changes in address and telephone, including cellular telephone number, unless otherwise provided by court order.

    The relocation notice must be filed with the Court granting the allocation of parental rights and responsibilities (name and address of Court): _____

    _____

    _____

L. Records Access Notice
    Pursuant to sections 3109.051(H) and 3319.321(B)(5)(a) of the Revised Code:
    Subject to sections 3125.16 and 3319.321(F) of the Revised Code, each parent is entitled to access to any record that is related to the child(ren), under the same terms and conditions as the other parent unless otherwise restricted. Any keeper of a record who knowingly fails to comply with any record order is in contempt of court.

    Restrictions or limitations:
    ☐ None
    ☐ Restrictions or limitations to records access are as follows: _____

    _____

    _____

M. Day Care Access Notice
    Pursuant to section 3109.051(I) of the Revised Code:
    In accordance with section 5104.11 of the Revised Code, each parent is entitled to access to any day care center that is or will be attended by the child(ren) unless otherwise restricted.

    Restrictions or limitations:
    ☐ None
    ☐ Restrictions or limitations to day care access are as follows: _____

    _____

    _____

N.   School Activities Access Notice
Pursuant to section 3109.051(J) of the Revised Code:
Subject to section 3319.321(F), each parent is entitled to access to any student activity that is related to the child(ren) and to which the residential parent is legally provided access, under the same terms and conditions as the residential parent. Any school employee or official who knowingly fails to comply with this school activities access order is in contempt of court.

Restrictions or limitations:
☐ None
☐ Restrictions or limitations to school activities access are as follows: _____

_____

_____

_____

THIRD: HEALTH INSURANCE COVERAGE.

As required by law, the parties have completed a Child Support Worksheet, which is attached to and incorporated in this Agreement.
Select one:

A.   ☐ Health Insurance Coverage Available to at Least One Parent

1.   Private health insurance coverage is accessible and reasonable in cost through a group policy, contract, or plan to: ☐ Plaintiff's/Petitioner 1's ☐ Defendant's/Petitioner 2's ☐ Both parents. ☐ Plaintiff's/Petitioner 1's ☐ Defendant's/Petitioner 2's ☐ Both parents shall provide private health insurance coverage for the benefit of the child(ren).

2.   If both parents are ordered to provide private health insurance coverage for the benefit of the child(ren), ☐ Plaintiff's/Petitioner 1's ☐ Defendant's/Petitioner 2's health insurance plan shall be considered the primary health insurance plan for the child(ren).

3.   The parent required to provide private health insurance coverage shall provide proof of insurance to the _____ County Child Support Enforcement Agency (CSEA) and the other parent.

4.   Both parents shall cooperate in the preparation of insurance forms to obtain reimbursement or payment of expenses, as applicable. A copy of medical bills must be submitted to the party holding the insurance and responsible for payment or the other parent within 30 days of receipt.

5.   Should the health insurance coverage be cancelled for any reason, the parent ordered to maintain insurance shall immediately notify the other parent and take immediate steps to obtain replacement coverage. Unless the cancellation was intentional, the uncovered expenses shall be paid as provided above. If the cancellation was intentionally caused by the parent ordered to maintain insurance coverage, that parent shall be responsible for all medical expenses that would have been covered had the insurance been in effect.

B. ☐ Health Insurance Coverage Unavailable to Either Parent
   1. Private health insurance coverage is **not** accessible and reasonable in cost through a group policy, contract, or plan to either parent.

   2. If private health insurance coverage becomes available to either parent at reasonable cost, The parent will immediately obtain the insurance, notify the other parent and the _____ County CSEA, and submit to the other parent proof of insurance, insurance forms, and an insurance card. The CSEA shall determine whether the cost of the insurance is of sufficient amount to justify an administrative review of the amount of child support payable. In the event an administrative review is warranted, one shall be conducted.

C. Division of Uninsured Expenses
   1. The cost of any uninsured medical expenses, incurred by or on behalf of the child(ren) not paid by a health insurance plan and exceeding $100 per child per year, including co-payments and deductibles, shall be paid by the parents as follows:
      _____ % by Plaintiff/Petitioner 1   _____ % by Defendant/Petitioner 2.
      The first $100 per child per year shall be paid by Defendant/Petitioner 2 for the following child(ren):

      _____
      _____

      The first $100 per child per year shall be paid by Plaintiff/Petitioner 1 for the following child(ren):

      _____
      _____

      Other orders regarding payment of uninsured medical expenses: _____

      _____
      _____

   2. The parent incurring the expenses shall provide the other parent the original or copies of all medical bills, and Explanation of Benefits (EOB), if available, within 30 days of the date on the bill or EOB, whichever is later, absent extraordinary circumstances. The other parent shall, within 30 days of receipt of the bill, reimburse the parent incurring the expenses or pay directly to the health care provider that parent's percentage share of the bill as shown above.

D. Other Important Information about Medical Records and Expenses
   1. Each party shall have access to all medical records of the child(ren) as provided by law.

   2. The term "medical expense" or "medical records" shall include but not be limited to medical, dental, orthodontic, optical, surgical, hospital, major medical, psychological, psychiatric, outpatient, doctor, therapy, counseling, prosthetic, and/or all other expenses/records including preventative health care expenses/records related to the treatment of the human body and mind.

FOURTH: CHILD SUPPORT

As required by law, the parties have completed a Child Support Worksheet, which is attached to and incorporated in this Agreement.

A. Child Support with Private Health Insurance Coverage

When private health insurance coverage is being provided for the child(ren), ☐ Plaintiff/Petitioner 1 ☐ Defendant/Petitioner 2, Obligor, shall pay child support in the amount of $_____ per child per month, for _____ (number) child(ren) for a total of $_____ per month.

B. Child Support without Private Health Insurance Coverage

When private health insurance coverage is **not** available for the benefit of the child(ren), ☐ Plaintiff/Petitioner 1 ☐ Defendant/Petitioner 2, the Obligor, shall pay child support in the amount of $_____ per child per month and $_____ per child per month as cash medical support. The total of child support and cash medical support for _____ (number) child(ren) is $_____ per month.

C. Child Support Payment

The child support payment (including cash medical support, if any) plus a 2% processing charge shall commence on _____ and shall be paid to the Ohio Child Support Payment Center, P. O. Box 182372, Columbus, Ohio 43218-2372, as administered through the _____ County Child Support Enforcement Agency (CSEA) by income withholding at Obligor's place of employment or from nonexempt funds on deposit at a financial institution.

D. Deviation of Child Support Amount

The child support amount agreed upon is different than the amount calculated on the attached Child Support Worksheet because the amount calculated on the Worksheet would be unjust or inappropriate and would not be in the best interests of the child(ren) for the following reason(s) as provided in R.C. 3119.22, 3119.23, 3119.24 and shall be adjusted as follows: _____

_____

_____

☐ Special and unusual needs of the child(ren) as follows: _____

_____

_____

☐ Extraordinary obligations for child(ren) or obligations for handicapped child(ren) who is/are not stepchild(ren) and who are not children from the marriage or relationship that is the basis of the immediate child support determination as follows: _____

_____

_____

☐ Other court-ordered payments as follows: _____

_____

_____

☐ The Obligor obtained additional employment after a child support order was issued to support a second family as follows: _____

_____

_____

☐ Extended parenting time or extraordinary costs associated with parenting time, provided that this division does not authorize and shall not be construed as authorizing any deviation from the schedule and the applicable worksheet, through the line establishing the actual annual obligation, or any escrowing, impoundment, or withholding of child support because of a denial of or interference with a right of parenting time granted by court order as follows: _____

_____

_____

☐ The financial resources and the earning ability of the child(ren) as follows: _____

_____

_____

☐ Disparity in income between parents or households as follows: _____

_____

_____

☐ Benefits that either parent receives from remarriage or sharing living expenses with another person as follows: _____

_____

_____

☐ The amount of federal, state, and local taxes actually paid or estimated to be paid by a parent or both of the parents as follows: _____

_____

_____

☐ Significant, in-kind contributions from a parent, including, but not limited to, direct payment for lessons, sports equipment, schooling, or clothing as follows: _____

_____

_____

_____

_____

☐ The relative financial resources, other assets and resources, and needs of each parent as follows: _____

_____

_____

☐ The standard of living and circumstances of each parent and the standard of living the child(ren) would have enjoyed had the marriage continued or had the parents been married as follows:

_____

_____

_____

☐ The physical and emotional condition and needs of the child(ren) as follows: _____

_____

_____

☐ The need and capacity of the child(ren) for an education and the educational opportunities that would have been available to the child(ren) had the circumstances requiring a court order for support not arisen as follows: _____

_____

_____

☐ The responsibility of each parent for the support of others as follows: _____

_____

_____

☐ Any other relevant factor: _____

_____

_____

E. Duration of Child Support.
The child support order will terminate upon the child's 18th birthday unless one of the following circumstances applies:
- The child is mentally or physically disabled and incapable of supporting or maintaining himself or herself.
- The parents have agreed to continue child support beyond the date it would otherwise terminate, as set out below.
- The child continuously attends a recognized and accredited high school on a full-time basis so long as the child has not as yet reached the age of 19 years old. (Under these circumstances, child support will end at the time the child ceases to attend a recognized and accredited high school on a full-time basis or when he or she reaches the age of 19, whichever occurs first.)

This Support Order will remain in effect during seasonal vacation periods until the order terminates.

The parents agree that child support will extend beyond the time when it would otherwise end. The terms and conditions of that agreement are as follows: _____

_____
_____
_____

The parents have (a) child(ren) who is/are mentally or physically disabled and incapable of supporting or maintaining themselves. The name of the child(ren) and the nature of the mental or physical disability are as follows: _____

_____
_____
_____

F.   Important Child Support Orders and Information
Obligee must immediately notify and Obligor may notify the CSEA of any reason for which the support order should terminate. A willful failure to notify the CSEA as required is contempt of court. The following are reasons for termination of the Order:
- Child's attainment of the age of majority if the child no longer attends an accredited high school on a full-time basis and the support order does not provide for the duty of support to continue past the age of majority
- Child stops attending an accredited high school on a full-time basis after attaining the age of majority
- Child's death
- Child's marriage
- Child's emancipation
- Child's enlistment in the Armed Services
- Child's deportation
- Change of legal custody of the child

All support payments must be made through the CSEA or the office of child support in the Ohio Department of Job and Family Services (Child Support Payment Central). Any payment of money not made through the CSEA will be presumed to be a gift, unless the payment is made to discharge an obligation other than support.

All support under this Order shall be withheld or deducted from the income or assets of the Obligor pursuant to a withholding or deduction notice or appropriate order issued in accordance with Chapters 3119., 3121., 3123., and 3125. of the Revised Code or a withdrawal directive issued pursuant to sections 3123.24 to 3123.38 of the Revised Code and shall be forwarded to the Obligee in accordance with Chapters 3119., 3121., 3123., and 3125. of the Revised Code.

The Obligor and/or Obligee required under this Order to provide private health insurance coverage for the child(ren) is also required to provide the other party within 30 days after the issuance of the

Order, the following:

- Information regarding the benefits, limitations, and exclusions of the health insurance coverage
- Copies of any insurance form necessary to receive reimbursement, payment, or other benefits under the coverage
- A copy of any necessary health insurance cards

The Health Plan Administrator that provides the private health insurance coverage for the child(ren) may continue making payment for medical, optical, hospital, dental, or prescription services directly to any health care provider in accordance with the applicable private health insurance policy, contract, or plan.

The Obligor and/or Obligee required to provide private health insurance for the child(ren) must designate said child(ren) as dependents under any private health insurance policy, contract, or plan for which the person contracts.

The employer of the person required to provide private health insurance coverage is required to release to the other parent, any person subject to an order issued under section 3109.19 of the Revised Code, or the CSEA, upon written request, any necessary information regarding health insurance coverage, including the name and address of the health plan administrator and any policy, contract, or plan number, and the employer will otherwise comply with all orders and notices issued.

If the person required to obtain private health insurance coverage for the child(ren) subject to this Support Order obtains new employment, the agency shall comply with the requirements of section 3119.34 of the Revised Code, which may result in the issuance of a notice requiring the new employer to take whatever action is necessary to enroll the child(ren) in private health insurance coverage provided by the new employer.

Upon receipt of notice by the CSEA that private health insurance coverage is not available at a reasonable cost, cash medical support shall be paid in the amount as determined by the child support computation worksheets in section 3119.022 or 3119.023 of the Revised Code, as applicable. The CSEA may change the financial obligations of the parties to pay child support in accordance with the terms of the court or administrative order and cash medical support without a hearing or additional notice to the parties.

An Obligor that is in arrears in the Obligor's child support obligation is subject to having any federal, state and/or local income tax refund to which the Obligor may be entitled forwarded to the CSEA for payment toward these arrears. Such refunds will continue to be forwarded to the CSEA for payment until all arrears owed are paid in full. If the Obligor is married and files a joint tax return, the Obligor's spouse may contact the CSEA about filing an "Injured Spouse" claim after the Obligor is notified by the Internal Revenue Service that the Obligor's refund is being forwarded to the CSEA.

Pursuant to section 3121.29 of the Revised Code, the parties are notified as follows:

EACH PARTY TO THIS SUPPORT ORDER MUST NOTIFY THE CHILD SUPPORT AGENCY IN WRITING OF HIS OR HER CURRENT MAILING ADDRESS, CURRENT RESIDENCE ADDRESS, CURRENT RESIDENCE TELEPHONE NUMBER, CURRENT DRIVER'S LICENSE NUMBER AND OF ANY CHANGES IN THAT INFORMATION. EACH PARTY MUST NOTIFY THE AGENCY OF ALL CHANGES UNTIL FURTHER NOTICE FROM THE COURT. IF YOU ARE THE OBLIGOR UNDER A CHILD SUPPORT ORDER AND YOU FAIL TO MAKE THE REQUIRED NOTIFICATIONS, YOU MAY BE FINED UP TO $50.00 FOR A FIRST OFFENSE, $100.00 FOR A SECOND OFFENSE, AND $500.00 FOR EACH SUBSEQUENT OFFENSE. IF YOU ARE AN OBLIGOR OR OBLIGEE UNDER ANY SUPPORT ORDER AND YOU WILLFULLY FAIL TO MAKE THE REQUIRED NOTIFICATIONS YOU MAY BE SUBJECTED TO FINES OF UP TO $1,000.00 AND IMPRISONMENT FOR NOT MORE THAN 90 DAYS.

IF YOU ARE AN OBLIGOR AND YOU FAIL TO MAKE THE REQUIRED NOTIFICATIONS, YOU MAY NOT RECEIVE NOTICE OF THE FOLLOWING ENFORCEMENT ACTIONS AGAINST YOU: IMPOSITION OF LIENS AGAINST YOUR PROPERTY; LOSS OF YOUR PROFESSIONAL OR OCCUPATIONAL LICENSE, DRIVER'S LICENSE, OR RECREATIONAL LICENSE; WITHHOLDING FROM YOUR INCOME; ACCESS RESTRICTIONS AND DEDUCTIONS FROM YOUR ACCOUNTS IN FINANCIAL INSTITUTIONS; AND ANY OTHER ACTION PERMITTED BY LAW TO OBTAIN MONEY FROM YOU AND TO SATISFY YOUR SUPPORT OBLIGATION.

G. Payment shall be made in accordance with Chapter 3121. of the Revised Code.

H. Arrearage
☐ Any temporary child support arrearage will survive this judgment entry.
☐ Any temporary child support arrearage will not survive this judgment entry.
☐ Other: _____

_____
_____
_____

FIFTH: TAX EXEMPTIONS

Income tax dependency exemptions (check all that apply):

A. ☐ The Plaintiff/Petitioner 1 shall be entitled to claim the following minor child(ren) for all tax purposes for ☐ even-numbered tax years ☐ odd-numbered tax years ☐ all eligible tax years, so long as Plaintiff is substantially current in any child support Plaintiff is required to pay as of December 31 of the tax year in question: _____

☐ The Defendant/Petitioner 2 shall be entitled to claim the following minor child(ren) for all tax purposes for ☐ even-numbered tax years ☐ odd-numbered tax years ☐ all eligible tax years, so long as Defendant is substantially current in any child support Defendant is required to pay as of December 31 of the tax year in question: _____

B.   ☐ Other orders regarding tax exemptions (specify): _____

_____

If a non-residential parent is entitled to claim the child(ren), the residential parent is required to execute and deliver Internal Revenue Service Form 8332, or its successor, together with any other required forms as set out in section 152 of the Internal Revenue Code, as amended, on or before February 15th of the year following the tax year in question, to allow the non-residential parent to claim the child(ren).

SIXTH: MODIFICATION

This Shared Parenting Plan may be modified by agreement of the parties or by the Court.

SEVENTH: OTHER

_____

_____

_____

_____

_____

Upon approval by the Court, this Shared Parenting Plan shall be incorporated in the Judgment Entry.

_____   _____
Your Signature (Plaintiff/Petitioner 1)   Your Signature (Defendant/Petitioner 2)

_____   _____
Date   Date

Supreme Court of Ohio
Uniform Domestic Relations Form – 17
SHARED PARENTING PLAN
Approved under Ohio Civil Rule 84 and Ohio Juvenile Rule 46
Amended: March 15, 2016   Page 14 of 14

IN THE COURT OF COMMON PLEAS

_____ **Division**

_____ **COUNTY, OHIO**

IN THE MATTER OF:

_____
A Minor

_____   :
Plaintiff/Petitioner 1   :   Case No. _____
                                :
_____   :
Street Address   :
                                :
_____   :   Judge _____
City, State and Zip Code   :
                                :
vs./and   :   Magistrate _____
                                :
_____   :
Defendant/Petitioner 2   :
                                :
_____   :
Street Address   :
                                :
_____   :
City, State and Zip Code   :

Instructions: The Parenting Time Schedule must be attached to this Plan. Parents are urged to consult the Planning for Parenting Time Guide: Ohio's Guide for Parents Living Apart available at http://www.supremecourt.ohio.gov/Publications/JCS/parentingGuide.pdf.

PARENTING PLAN

We, the parents, _____, " (name) Plaintiff/Petitioner 1", and
_____," (other parent's name) Defendant/Petitioner 2", have
_____ (number) child(ren) from the marriage or relationship. Of the child(ren), _____
(number) is/are emancipated adult(s) and not under any disability, and the following _____
(number) child(ren) are minor child(ren) and/or mentally or physically disabled child(ren) incapable of
supporting or maintaining themselves (name and date of birth of each child):

_____

_____

_____

The parents agree to the care, parenting, and control of their child(ren) as provided in this Parenting Plan.

Supreme Court of Ohio
Uniform Domestic Relations Form – 18
PARENTING PLAN
Approved under Ohio Civil Rule 84 and Ohio Juvenile Rule 46
Amended: March 15, 2016

Page 1 of 12

FIRST: PARENTS' RIGHTS

We, the parents, shall have, unless limited:

A. The right to reasonable telephone contact with the child(ren) when they are with the other parent.

B. The right to be notified in case of an injury to or illness of the minor child(ren).

C. The right to inspect and receive the minor child(ren)'s medical and dental records and the right to consult with any treating physician, dentist and/or other health care provider, including but not limited to psychologists and psychiatrists.

D. The right to consult with school officials concerning the minor child(ren)'s welfare and educational status, and the right to inspect and receive the child(ren)'s student records to the extent permitted by law.

E. The right to receive copies of all school reports, calendars of school events, notices of parent-teacher conferences, and school programs.

F. The right to attend and participate in parent-teacher conferences, school trips, school programs, and other school activities in which parents are invited to participate.

G. The right to attend and participate with the child(ren) in athletic programs and other extracurricular activities.

SECOND: ALLOCATION OF PARENTAL RIGHTS AND RESPONSIBILITIES

A. General Responsibilities

Each parent shall take all measures necessary to foster respect and affection between the child(ren) and the other parent. Neither parent shall do anything that may estrange the child(ren) from the other parent, or impair the child(ren)'s high regard for the other parent.

B. Medical Responsibilities

The parents shall notify the other parent promptly if a child experiences a serious injury, has a serious or chronic illness, or receives treatment in an emergency room or hospital. The notification shall include the emergency, the child's status, locale, and any other pertinent information as soon as practical, but in any event within 24 hours.

The parents shall consult with each other about the minor child(ren)'s medical care needs and the residential parent shall immediately notify the other parent about all major non- emergency medical decisions before authorizing a course of treatment. Parents have a right to know the necessity for treatment, proposed cost, and proposed payment schedule. Each parent may also secure an independent evaluation at the parent's expense to determine the necessity for treatment. If the parties cannot agree regarding a course of treatment, the residential parent's decision shall control. The parents shall provide the other with the names and telephone numbers of all health care providers for the child(ren).

C. Residential Parent and Legal Custodian

☐ Plaintiff/Petitioner 1 shall be the residential parent and legal custodian of the following child(ren):

_____

_____

_____

_____

☐ Defendant/Petitioner 2 shall be the residential parent and legal custodian of the following child(ren):

_____

_____

_____

D. Parenting Time Schedule
Unless otherwise agreed, the parents shall have parenting time with the child(ren) according to the attached Parenting Time Schedule that shows the times that the child(ren) shall be with each parent on weekdays, weekends, holidays, and vacation times.

(The Parenting Time Schedule must be attached to this Plan.)

E. Transportation (select one):
☐ Each parent shall be responsible for providing transportation for the child(ren) at the beginning of the parent's parenting period. Each parent shall be responsible for providing transportation for the child(ren) to and from school and activities during the parent's parenting period.

☐ We agree to the following arrangements for providing transportation for our child(ren) at the beginning, during, or end of a parenting period: _____

_____

_____

F. Current Address and Telephone Number
Plaintiff's/Petitioner 1's current home address and telephone number, including cellular telephone number:

_____

_____

_____

Defendant's/Petitioner 2's current home address and telephone number, including cellular telephone number:

_____

_____

_____

G. Relocation Notice
Pursuant to section 3109.051(G) of the Revised Code:
If the residential parent intends to move to a residence other than the residence specified in the court order, the parent shall file a notice of intent to relocate with this Court. Except as provided in divisions (G)(2), (3), and (4) of section 3109.051 of the Revised Code, the Court shall send a copy of the notice to the parent who is not the residential parent. Upon receipt of the notice, the Court, on

its own motion or the motion of the parent who is not the residential parent, may schedule a hearing with notice to both parents to determine whether it is in the best interests of the child(ren) to revise the parenting time schedule for the child(ren).

☐ The non-residential parent shall inform in writing the Court and the other parent of changes in address and telephone, including cellular telephone number, unless otherwise provided by court order.

The relocation notice must be filed with the Court granting the allocation of parental rights and responsibilities (name and address of the Court): _____

_____

_____

H. Records Access Notice
    Pursuant to sections 3109.051(H) and 3319.321(B)(5)(a) of the Revised Code:
    Subject to sections 3125.16 and 3319.321(F) of the Revised Code, the parent who is not the residential parent is entitled to access to any record that is related to the child(ren), and to which the residential parent is legally provided access under the same terms and conditions as the residential parent. Any keeper of a record who knowingly fails to comply with any record access order is in contempt of court.

    Restrictions or limitations:
    ☐ None
    ☐ Restrictions or limitations to non-residential parents regarding records access are as follows:

    _____

    _____

I. Day Care Access Notice
    Pursuant to section 3109.051(I) of the Revised Code:
    In accordance with section 5104.11 of the Revised Code, the parent who is not the residential parent is entitled to access to any day care center that is or will be attended by the child(ren) with whom parenting time is granted, to the same extent that the residential parent is granted access to the center.

    Restrictions or limitations:
    ☐ None
    ☐ Restrictions or limitations to non-residential parents regarding day care access are as follows:

    _____

    _____

J. School Activities Access Notice
    Pursuant to section 3109.051(J) of the Revised Code:

Subject to section 3319.321(F), the parent who is not the residential parent is entitled to access to any student activity that is related to the child(ren) and to which the residential parent is legally provided access, under the same terms and conditions as the residential parent. Any school employee or official who knowingly fails to comply with this school activities access order is in contempt of court.

Restrictions or limitations:

☐ None

☐ Restrictions or limitations to non-residential parents regarding school activities access are as follows: _____

_____

_____

THIRD: HEALTH INSURANCE COVERAGE

As required by law, the parties have completed a Child Support Worksheet, which is attached to and incorporated in this Agreement.

Select one:

A.   ☐ Health Insurance Coverage Available to at Least One Parent

    1.   Private health insurance coverage is accessible and reasonable in cost through a group policy, contract, or plan to: ☐ Plaintiff/Petitioner 1 ☐ Defendant/Petitioner 2 ☐ Both parents. ☐ Plaintiff/Petitioner 1 ☐ Defendant/Petitioner 2 ☐ Both parents shall provide private health insurance coverage for the benefit of the child(ren).

    2.   If both parents are ordered to provide private health insurance coverage for the benefit of the child(ren), ☐ Plaintiff's/Petitioner 1's ☐ Defendant's/Petitioner 2's health insurance plan shall be considered the primary health insurance plan for the child(ren).

    3.   The parent required to provide private health insurance coverage shall provide proof of insurance to the _____ County Child Support Enforcement Agency (CSEA) and the other parent.

    4.   Both parents shall cooperate in the preparation of insurance forms to obtain reimbursement or payment of expenses, as applicable. A copy of medical bills must be submitted to the party holding the insurance and responsible for payment or the other parent within 30 days of receipt.

    5.   Should the health insurance coverage be cancelled for any reason, the parent ordered to maintain insurance shall immediately notify the other parent and take immediate steps to obtain replacement coverage. Unless the cancellation was intentional, the uncovered expenses shall be paid as provided above. If the cancellation was intentionally caused by the parent ordered to maintain insurance coverage, that parent shall be responsible for all medical expenses that would have been covered had the insurance been in effect.

Supreme Court of Ohio
Uniform Domestic Relations Form – 18
PARENTING PLAN
Approved under Ohio Civil Rule 84 and Ohio Juvenile Rule 46
Amended: March 15, 2016   Page 5 of 12

B. ☐ Health Insurance Coverage Unavailable to Either Parent
    1. Private health insurance coverage is **not** accessible and reasonable in cost through a group policy, contract, or plan to either parent.

    2. If private health insurance coverage becomes available to either parent at reasonable cost, the parent will immediately obtain the insurance, notify the other parent and the _____ County CSEA, and submit to the other parent proof of insurance, insurance forms, and an insurance card. The CSEA shall determine whether the cost of the insurance is of sufficient amount to justify an administrative review of the amount of child support payable. In the event an administrative review is warranted, one shall be conducted.

C. Division of Uninsured Expenses
    1. The cost of any uninsured medical expenses, incurred by or on the behalf of the child(ren) not paid by a health insurance plan, and exceeding $100 per child per year, including co-payments and deductibles, shall be paid by the parents as follows:
    _____ % by Plaintiff/Petitioner 1 _____ % by Defendant/Petitioner 2.
    The first $100 per child per year of uninsured expenses shall be paid by the residential parent.

    Other orders regarding payment of uninsured medical expenses: _____
    _____
    _____
    _____

    2. The parent incurring the expenses shall provide the other parent the original or copies of all medical bills, and Explanation of Benefits (EOB), if available, within 30 days of the date on the bill or EOB, whichever is later, absent extraordinary circumstances. The other parent shall, within 30 days of receipt of the bill, reimburse the parent incurring the expenses or pay directly to the health care provider that parent's percentage share of the bill as shown above.

D. Other Important Information about Medical Records and Expenses
    1. Each party shall have access to all medical records of the child(ren) as provided by law.

    2. The term "medical expense" or "medical records" shall include but not be limited to medical, dental, orthodontic, optical, surgical, hospital, major medical, psychological, psychiatric, outpatient, doctor, therapy, counseling, prosthetic, and/or all other expenses/records including preventative health care expenses/records related to the treatment of the human body and mind.

FOURTH: CHILD SUPPORT

As required by law, the parties have completed a Child Support Worksheet, which is attached to and incorporated in this Agreement.

A. Child Support with Private Health Insurance Coverage
When private health insurance coverage is being provided for the child(ren), ☐ Plaintiff/Petitioner 1 ☐ Defendant/Petitioner 2, the Obligor, shall pay child support in the amount of $ _____ per child per month, for _____ (number) of child(ren) for a total $ _____ per month.

B. Child Support without Private Health Insurance Coverage
When private health insurance coverage is **not** available for the child(ren), ☐ Plaintiff/Petitioner 1 ☐ Defendant/Petitioner 2, the Obligor, shall pay child support in the amount of $_____ per child per month and $_____ per child per month as cash medical support. The total child support and cash medical support for _____(number) of child(ren) is $ _____ per month.

C. Child Support Payment
Child support payment (including cash medical support, if any) plus a 2% processing charge shall commence on _____ and shall be paid to the Ohio Child Support Payment Center, P. O. Box 182372,Columbus, Ohio 43218-2372, as administered through the _____ County Child Support Enforcement Agency (CSEA) by income withholding at Obligor's place of employment or from nonexempt funds on deposit at a financial institution.

D. Deviation of Child Support Amount
The child support amount agreed upon is different than the amount calculated on the attached Child Support Worksheet, because the amount calculated on the Worksheet would be unjust or inappropriate and would not be in the best interests of the child(ren) for the following reason(s) as provided in R.C. 3119.22, 3119.23, and 3119.24 and shall be adjusted as follows: _____

_____

_____

☐ Special and unusual needs of the child(ren) as follows: _____

_____

_____

☐ Extraordinary obligations for minor child(ren) or obligations for handicapped child(ren) who is/are not stepchild(ren) and who are not offspring from the marriage or relationship that is the basis of the immediate child support determination as follows: _____

_____

_____

☐ Other court-ordered payments as follows: _____

_____

_____

☐ The Obligor obtained additional employment after a child support order was issued to support a second family as follows: _____

_____
_____

☐ Extended parenting time or extraordinary costs associated with parenting time, provided that this division does not authorize and shall not be construed as authorizing any deviation from the schedule and the applicable worksheet, through the line establishing the actual annual obligation, or any escrowing, impoundment, or withholding of child support because of a denial of or interference with a right of parenting time granted by court order as follows: _____
_____

☐ The financial resources and the earning ability of the child(ren) as follows: _____
_____

☐ Disparity in income between parents or households as follows: _____
_____

☐ Benefits that either parent receives from remarriage or sharing living expenses with another person as follows: _____
_____

☐ The amount of federal, state, and local taxes actually paid or estimated to be paid by a parent or both of the parents as follows: _____
_____

☐ Significant, in-kind contributions from a parent, including, but not limited to, direct payment for lessons, sports equipment, schooling, or clothing as follows: _____
_____

☐ The relative financial resources, other assets and resources, and needs of each parent as follows: _____
_____

☐ The standard of living and circumstances of each parent and the standard of living the child(ren) would have enjoyed had the marriage continued or had the parents been married as follows: _____
_____

☐ The physical and emotional condition and needs of the child(ren) as follows: _____
_____

☐ The need and capacity of the child(ren) for an education and the educational opportunities that would have been available to the child(ren) had the circumstances requiring a court order for support not arisen as follows: _____

_____

☐ The responsibility of each parent for the support of others as follows: _____

_____

☐ Any other relevant factor: _____

_____

E. Duration of Child Support.

The child support order will terminate upon the child's 18th birthday unless one of the following circumstances applies:
- The child is mentally or physically disabled and incapable of supporting or maintaining himself or herself.
- The parents have agreed to continue child support beyond the date it would otherwise terminate as set out below.
- The child continuously attends a recognized and accredited high school on a full-time basis so long as the child has not, as yet, reached the age of 19 years old. (Under these circumstances, child support will end at the time the child ceases to attend a recognized and accredited high school on a full-time basis or when he or she reaches the age of 19, whichever occurs first.)

This Support Order will remain in effect during seasonal vacation periods until the order terminates.

The parents agree that child support will extend beyond when it would otherwise end. The terms and conditions of that agreement are as follows: _____

_____

_____

_____

The parents have (a) child(ren) who is/are mentally or physically disabled and incapable of supporting or maintaining themselves. The name of the child and the nature of the mental or physical disability are as follows: _____

_____

_____

F. Important Child Support Orders and Information.

Obligee must immediately notify and Obligor may notify the CSEA of any reason for which the support order should terminate. A willful failure to notify the CSEA as required is contempt of court. The following are reasons for termination of the Order:
- Child's attainment of the age of majority if the child no longer attends an accredited high school on a full-time basis and the support order does not provide for the duty of support to continue past the age of majority

- Child stops attending an accredited high school on a full-time basis after attaining the age of majority
- Child's death
- Child's marriage
- Child's emancipation
- Child's enlistment in the Armed Services
- Child's deportation
- Change of legal custody of the child

All support payments must be made through the CSEA or the office of child support in the Ohio Department of Job and Family Services (Child Support Payment Central). Any payment of money not made through the CSEA will be presumed to be a gift, unless the payment is made to discharge an obligation other than support.

All support under this Order shall be withheld or deducted from the income or assets of the Obligor pursuant to a withholding or deduction notice or appropriate order issued in accordance with Chapters 3119., 3121., 3123., and 3125. of the Revised Code or a withdrawal directive issued pursuant to sections 3123.24 to 3123.38 of the Revised Code and shall be forwarded to the Obligee in accordance with Chapters 3119., 3121., 3123., and 3125. of the Revised Code.

The Obligor and/or Obligee required under this Order to provide private health insurance coverage for the child(ren) is also required to provide the other party within 30 days after the issuance of the Order, the following:
- Information regarding the benefits, limitations, and exclusions of the health insurance coverage
- Copies of any insurance form necessary to receive reimbursement, payment, or other benefits under the coverage
- A copy of any necessary health insurance cards

The Health Plan Administrator that provides the private health insurance coverage for the child(ren) may continue making payment for medical, optical, hospital, dental, or prescription services directly to any health care provider in accordance with the applicable private health insurance policy, contract, or plan.

The Obligor and/or Obligee required to provide private health insurance for the child(ren) must designate said child(ren) as dependents under any private health insurance policy, contract, or plan for which the person contracts.

The employer of the person required to provide private health insurance coverage is required to release to the other parent, any person subject to an order issued under section 3109.19 of the Revised Code, or the CSEA, upon written request, any necessary information regarding health insurance coverage, including the name and address of the health plan administrator and any policy, contract, or plan number, and the employer will otherwise comply with all orders and notices issued.

If the person required to obtain private health insurance coverage for the child(ren) subject to this Support Order obtains new employment, the agency shall comply with the requirements of section 3119.34 of the Revised Code, which may result in the issuance of a notice requiring the new employer to take whatever action is necessary to enroll the child(ren) in private health insurance coverage provided by the new employer.

Upon receipt of notice by the CSEA that private health insurance coverage is not available at a reasonable cost, cash medical support shall be paid in the amount as determined by the child support computation worksheets in section 3119.022 or 3119.023 of the Revised Code, as applicable. The CSEA may change the financial obligations of the parties to pay child support in accordance with the terms of the court or administrative order and cash medical support without a hearing or additional notice to the parties.

An Obligor that is in arrears in the Obligor's child support obligation is subject to having any federal, state and/or local income tax refund to which the Obligor may be entitled forwarded to the CSEA for payment toward these arrears. Such refunds will continue to be forwarded to the CSEA for payment until all arrears owed are paid in full. If the Obligor is married and files a joint tax return, the Obligor's spouse may contact the CSEA about filing an "Injured Spouse" claim after the Obligor is notified by the Internal Revenue Service that the Obligor's refund is being forwarded to the CSEA.

Pursuant to section 3121.29 of the Revised Code, the parties are notified as follows:
EACH PARTY TO THIS SUPPORT ORDER MUST NOTIFY THE CHILD SUPPORT AGENCY IN WRITING OF HIS OR HER CURRENT MAILING ADDRESS, CURRENT RESIDENCE ADDRESS, CURRENT RESIDENCE TELEPHONE NUMBER, CURRENT DRIVER'S LICENSE NUMBER AND OF ANY CHANGES IN THAT INFORMATION. EACH PARTY MUST NOTIFY THE AGENCY OF ALL CHANGES UNTIL FURTHER NOTICE FROM THE COURT. IF YOU ARE THE OBLIGOR UNDER A CHILD SUPPORT ORDER AND YOU FAIL TO MAKE THE REQUIRED NOTIFICATIONS, YOU MAY BE FINED UP TO $50.00 FOR A FIRST OFFENSE, $100.00 FOR A SECOND OFFENSE, AND $500.00 FOR EACH SUBSEQUENT OFFENSE. IF YOU ARE AN OBLIGOR OR OBLIGEE UNDER ANY SUPPORT ORDER AND YOU WILLFULLY FAIL TO MAKE THE REQUIRED NOTIFICATIONS YOU MAY BE SUBJECTED TO FINES OF UP TO $1,000.00 AND IMPRISONMENT FOR NOT MORE THAN 90 DAYS.

IF YOU ARE AN OBLIGOR AND YOU FAIL TO MAKE THE REQUIRED NOTIFICATIONS, YOU MAY NOT RECEIVE NOTICE OF THE FOLLOWING ENFORCEMENT ACTIONS AGAINST YOU: IMPOSITION OF LIENS AGAINST YOUR PROPERTY; LOSS OF YOUR PROFESSIONAL OR OCCUPATIONAL LICENSE, DRIVER'S LICENSE, OR RECREATIONAL LICENSE; WITHHOLDING FROM YOUR INCOME; ACCESS RESTRICTIONS AND DEDUCTIONS FROM YOUR ACCOUNTS IN FINANCIAL INSTITUTIONS; AND ANY OTHER ACTION PERMITTED BY LAW TO OBTAIN MONEY FROM YOU AND TO SATISFY YOUR SUPPORT OBLIGATION.

G. Payment shall be made in accordance with Chapter 3121. of the Revised Code.
H. Arrearage

☐ Any temporary child support arrearage will survive this judgment entry.

☐ Any temporary child support arrearage will not survive this judgment entry.

☐ Other: _____

FIFTH: TAX EXEMPTIONS

Income tax dependency exemptions (check all that apply):

A. ☐ The Plaintiff/Petitioner 1 shall be entitled to claim the following minor child(ren) for all tax purposes for ☐ even-numbered tax years ☐ odd-numbered tax years ☐ all eligible tax years, so long as Plaintiff/Petitioner 1 is substantially current in any child support Plaintiff/Petitioner 1 is required to pay as of December 31 of the tax year in question:_____

☐ The Defendant/Petitioner 2 shall be entitled to claim the following minor child(ren) for all tax purposes for ☐ even-numbered tax years ☐ odd-numbered tax years ☐ all eligible tax years, so long as Defendant/Petitioner 2 is substantially current in any child support Defendant/Petitioner 2 is required to pay as of December 31 of the tax year in question:_____

B. ☐ Other orders regarding tax exemptions (specify): _____

If a non-residential parent is entitled to claim the child(ren), the residential parent is required to execute and deliver Internal Revenue Service Form 8332, or its successor, together with any other required forms as set out in section 152 of the Internal Revenue Code, as amended, on or before February 15th of the year following the tax year in question, to allow the non-residential parent to claim the minor child(ren).

SIXTH: MODIFICATION

This Parenting Plan may be modified by agreement of the parties or by the Court.

SEVENTH: OTHER

_____
_____

Upon approval by the Court, this Parenting Plan shall be incorporated in the Judgment Entry.

_____	_____
Signature (Plaintiff/Petitioner 1)	Signature (Defendant/Petitioner 2)
_____	_____
Date	Date

IN THE COURT OF COMMON PLEAS

_____ **Division**

_____ **COUNTY, OHIO**

IN THE MATTER OF:

_____
A Minor

_____
Plaintiff/Petitioner 1

_____
Street Address

_____
City, State and Zip Code

vs./and

_____
Defendant/Petitioner 2

_____
Street Address

_____
City, State and Zip Code

: Case No. _____

:

: Judge _____

:

:

: Magistrate _____

:

:

:

:

PARENTING JUDGMENT ENTRY

This case came before the Court on _____ for an Order allocating parental rights and responsibilities for the care of the following child(ren) (name and date of birth of each child):

Name of Child	Date of Birth
_____	_____
_____	_____
_____	_____

according to the ☐ Parenting Plan or ☐ Shared Parenting Plan attached.

The Court approves the Plan and incorporates it into this Judgment Entry.

A copy of this Judgment Entry shall be provided to the Child Support Enforcement Agency.

This Judgment Entry is effective on _____ .

_____
Date

_____
JUDGE

_____
Signature (Plaintiff/Petitioner 1)

_____
Signature (Defendant/Petitioner 2)

_____
Attorney for Plaintiff/Petitioner 1

_____
Attorney for Defendant/Petitioner 2

Supreme Court of Ohio
Uniform Domestic Relations Form – 19
Uniform Juvenile Form - 1
PARENTING JUDGMENT ENTRY
Approved under Ohio Civil Rule 84 and Ohio Juvenile Rule 46
Amended: March 15, 2016

Page 1 of 1

IN THE COURT OF COMMON PLEAS

_____ **Division**

_____ **COUNTY, OHIO**

IN THE MATTER OF:

_____

A Minor

_____

Plaintiff

_____

Street Address

_____

City, State and Zip Code

vs.

_____

Defendant

_____

Street Address

_____

City, State and Zip Code

:
:   Case No. _____
:
:
:   Judge _____
:
:
:   Magistrate _____
:
:
:
:
:
:
:
:

Instructions: This form is used to be legally recognized as the parent of the child, be named as the residential parent, or obtain visitation with the child(ren). The Parenting Proceeding Affidavit (Uniform Domestic Relations Form - Affidavit 3) and the Affidavit of Income and Expenses (Uniform Domestic Relations Form - Affidavit 1) must be filed with this Complaint.

COMPLAINT FOR PARENTAGE,
ALLOCATION OF PARENTAL RIGHTS AND RESPONSIBILITIES (CUSTODY), AND
PARENTING TIME (COMPANIONSHIP AND VISITATION)

1. I, _____ (name), am the Plaintiff and parent of
    the following child(ren):

Name of Child	Date of Birth
_____	_____
_____	_____
_____	_____

2. Defendant, _____ is the parent of the child(ren).

3. The child(ren) has/have resided in _____ County, Ohio since _____
    (date residence established) as set out in the Parenting Proceeding Affidavit (Uniform Domestic
    Relations Form - Affidavit 3).

Supreme Court of Ohio
Uniform Domestic Relations Form – 20
Uniform Juvenile Form – 2
COMPLAINT FOR PARENTAGE, ALLOCATION OF PARENTAL RIGHTS AND RESPONSIBILITIES
AND PARENTING TIME
Approved under Ohio Civil Rule 84 and Ohio Juvenile Rule 46
Amended: March 15, 2016   Page 1 of 2

4. The parent-child relationship ☐ has ☐ has not (select one) been established. If it has been established, a copy of the order establishing the parent-child relationship is attached. A copy of the child(ren)'s birth certificate is also attached.

5. ☐ No court has issued an order about the following child(ren):

_____
_____
_____

☐ The following Court has issued an order about the following child(ren):

_____
_____
_____

6. I request that the Court (check all that apply):
    ☐ Name _____ (parent's name) as the
    parent of the child(ren) _____
    _____ (child(ren)'s name).
    ☐ Correct the child(ren)'s birth certificate to indicate the child(ren)'s parent.
    ☐ Order genetic testing and determine the father of the child(ren).
    ☐ Name the ☐ Plaintiff ☐ Defendant (select one) as the residential parent and legal custodian of the child(ren).
    ☐ Grant reasonable parenting time (visitation) to the parent.
    ☐ Change the child(ren)'s name to _____
    ☐ Adopt the proposed Shared Parenting Plan for the child(ren) which is attached.
    ☐ Order the appropriate amount of child support for the child(ren), allocate the income tax dependency exemption for the child(ren), and determine who should provide health insurance coverage for the child(ren).
    ☐ Other (specify): _____
    _____
    _____
    _____

_____
Your Signature

_____
Telephone number at which the Court may reach you
or at which messages may be left for you

Supreme Court of Ohio
Uniform Domestic Relations Form – 20
Uniform Juvenile Form – 2
COMPLAINT FOR PARENTAGE, ALLOCATION OF PARENTAL RIGHTS AND RESPONSIBILITIES AND PARENTING TIME
Approved under Ohio Civil Rule 84 and Ohio Juvenile Rule 46
Amended: March 15, 2016   Page 2 of 2

IN THE COURT OF COMMON PLEAS

_____ **Division**

_____ **COUNTY, OHIO**

IN THE MATTER OF:

_____
A Minor

_____
Name   :

:

_____ :   Case No. _____
Street Address   :

:

_____ :
City, State and Zip Code   :   Judge _____

              Plaintiff/Petitioner   :

vs.   :   Magistrate _____

:

_____ :
Name   :

:

_____ :
Street Address   :

:

_____
City, State and Zip Code   :

             Defendant/Petitioner

Instructions: This form is used to request the enforcement of a court order and hold the other party in contempt for violating the court order. A Request for Service (Uniform Domestic Relations Form 28) and a proposed Show Cause Order, Notice and Instructions to the Clerk (Uniform Domestic Relations Form 22) must be filed with this Motion. Check local court procedures.

MOTION FOR CONTEMPT AND AFFIDAVIT

I, _____ (name), request an order for

_____ (other party's name) to appear and show cause

why he/she should not be held in contempt for violating a court order and a finding of contempt for violating the court order regarding the following (check all that apply):

1. ☐ Interference with parenting time or other parenting orders filed on _____ (date).

2. ☐ Failure to pay child support, as required by the order filed on _____ (date)
   and the total arrearage owed is $_____
   (Bring to the hearing an up-to-date printout from the County Child Support Enforcement Agency showing the amount of the child support owed to you.)

3. ☐ Failure to pay spousal support, as required by the order filed on _____ (date)

Supreme Court of Ohio
Uniform Domestic Relations Form – 21
Uniform Juvenile Form – 3
MOTION FOR CONTEMPT AND AFFIDAVIT
Approved under Ohio Civil Rule 84 and Ohio Juvenile Rule 46
Effective Date: 7/1/2013

Page 1 of 2

and the total arrearage owed is $ _____

(Bring to the hearing an up-to-date printout from the County Child Support Enforcement Agency or other independent proof showing the amount owed to you.)

4. ☐ Payment or reimbursement of health care expenses incurred for the minor child(ren). Attach an Explanation of Health Care Bills (Uniform Domestic Relations Form 26) and bring to the hearing the following documents:
    a. Copies of each bill for which you seek reimbursement;
    b. Proof of payment by you. Proof of payment may include a receipt for payment signed by the health care provider, a copy of a cancelled check, or a copy of a credit card statement verifying the amount paid; and
    c. Explanation of Benefits forms showing payment made by the health insurance carrier.

5. ☐ Failure to comply with the Court's orders of _____ (date) regarding (check all that apply):
    ☐ Transfer of real estate, as follows: _____
    ☐ Payment of debt, as follows: _____
    ☐ Refinance of debt, as follows: _____
    ☐ Distribution of personal property, as follows: _____
    ☐ Other (specify): _____

6. Costs and any other relief as necessary and proper are also requested.

_____
Your Signature

_____
Telephone number at which the Court may reach you or at which messages may be left for you

OATH
(Do not sign until Notary is present.)

I, _____ (name), swear or affirm that I have read this document and, to the best of my knowledge and belief, the facts and information stated in this document are true, accurate and complete. I understand that if I do not tell the truth, I may be subject to penalties for perjury.

_____
Your Signature

Sworn before me and signed in my presence this _____ day of _____ , _____ .

_____
Notary Public
My Commission Expires: _____

Supreme Court of Ohio
Uniform Domestic Relations Form – 21
Uniform Juvenile Form – 3
MOTION FOR CONTEMPT AND AFFIDAVIT
Approved under Ohio Civil Rule 84 and Ohio Juvenile Rule 46
Effective Date: 7/1/2013

Page 2 of 2

IN THE COURT OF COMMON PLEAS

_____ **Division**

_____ **COUNTY, OHIO**

IN THE MATTER OF:

_____

A Minor

_____   :
Name   :   Case No. _____
                             :
_____   :
Street Address   :
                             :   Judge _____
_____   :
City, State and Zip Code :
              Plaintiff/Petitioner :
                             :   Magistrate _____
                             :
vs./and   :
                             :
                             :
_____   :
Name   :
                             :
_____   :
Street Address   :
                             :
_____   :
City, State and Zip Code :
              Defendant/Petitioner :

Instructions: This form is used to bring the other party to Court to defend his/her failure to follow the court order. A Motion for Contempt and Affidavit (Uniform Domestic Relations Form 21) must be filed with this order.

SHOW CAUSE ORDER, NOTICE AND INSTRUCTIONS TO THE CLERK

TO: _____   TO: _____
         PLAINTIFF/PETITIONER   DEFENDANT/PETITIONER

You are hereby ORDERED to appear and show cause why you should not be held in contempt for failure to obey the court order as described in the Motion you are now receiving.

Supreme Court of Ohio
Uniform Domestic Relations Form – 22
Uniform Juvenile Form – 4
SHOW CAUSE ORDER, NOTICE AND INSTRUCTIONS TO THE CLERK
Approved under Ohio Civil Rule 84 and Ohio Juvenile Rule 46
Effective Date: 7/1/2013

COURT
(The Court will complete this part.)

You are ORDERED to appear in the _____ County Common Pleas Court
_____ Division, in Courtroom _____ located at _____
_____
on _____ at _____ o'clock and show cause why you
should not be held in contempt of this Court.

NOTICE

1. Failure to appear as ordered may result in the issuance of a bench warrant for an immediate arrest.

2. Failure to appear may result in an immediate income withholding or deduction.

3. You have the right to be represented by an attorney.

4. If you cannot afford an attorney, you must apply for a public defender or appointed counsel, as appropriate, within three business days after receipt of this show cause order.

5. A continuance may not be granted to obtain counsel if you have made no good faith effort to secure one.

6. If found guilty, you may be sentenced as follows:
   a. First offense – a fine of not more than $250.00 and/or a definite term of imprisonment of not more than thirty days in jail or both.
   b. Second offense – a fine of not more than $500.00 and/or a definite term of imprisonment of not more than sixty days in jail or both.
   c. Third offense – a fine of not more than $1,000.00 and/or a definite term of imprisonment of not more than ninety days in jail or both.

7. The court may grant you limited driving privileges under 4510.021 of the Revised Code if your driver's license was suspended based on a notice issued by a child support enforcement agency because you are in default under a child support order or you have failed to comply with a subpoena or warrant issued by a court or agency with respect to a proceeding to enforce a child support order. You must request limited driving privileges and your request must be accompanied by a recent copy of your driver's abstract driving record from the registrar of motor vehicles.

_____
JUDGE/MAGISTRATE

Supreme Court of Ohio
Uniform Domestic Relations Form – 22
Uniform Juvenile Form – 4
SHOW CAUSE ORDER, NOTICE AND INSTRUCTIONS TO THE CLERK
Approved under Ohio Civil Rule 84 and Ohio Juvenile Rule 46
Effective Date: 7/1/2013

Page 2 of 3

INSTRUCTIONS TO THE CLERK

You are directed to serve this Order along with the Motion for Contempt and Affidavit to the

☐ Defendant/Petitioner or ☐ Plaintiff/Petitioner by:

    ☐ Certified Mail, Return Receipt Requested

    ☐ Issuance to Sheriff of _____ County, Ohio for ☐ Personal or ☐ Residence service

    ☐ Other (specify) _____

_____
Your Signature

Supreme Court of Ohio
Uniform Domestic Relations Form – 22
Uniform Juvenile Form – 4
SHOW CAUSE ORDER, NOTICE AND INSTRUCTIONS TO THE CLERK
Approved under Ohio Civil Rule 84 and Ohio Juvenile Rule 46
Effective Date: 7/1/2013

IN THE COURT OF COMMON PLEAS

_____ **Division**

_____ **COUNTY, OHIO**

IN THE MATTER OF:

_____

A Minor

_____
Name   :
: Case No. _____
_____   :
Street Address   :
: Judge _____
_____   :
City, State and Zip Code   :
            Plaintiff/Petitioner   :
: Magistrate _____
vs./and   :
:
_____   :
Name   :
:
_____   :
Street Address   :
:
_____   :
City, State and Zip Code   :
            Defendant/Petitioner   :

Instructions: This form is used to request a change in the parenting time (visitation) order. A Request for Service (Uniform Domestic Relations Form 28) and a Parenting Proceeding Affidavit (Uniform Domestic Relations Form – Affidavit 3) must be filed with this Motion.

MOTION FOR CHANGE OF PARENTING TIME (COMPANIONSHIP AND VISITATION) AND MEMORANDUM IN SUPPORT

1. I, _____ (name), request this Court change the existing
   parenting time (companionship and visitation) Order filed on this date _____ (date filed)
   regarding the following minor child(ren):

   Name of Child   **Date of Birth**

   _____   _____

   _____   _____

   _____   _____

Supreme Court of Ohio
Uniform Domestic Relations Form – 23
Uniform Juvenile Form – 5
MOTION FOR CHANGE OF PARENTING TIME (VISITATION) AND MEMORANDUM IN SUPPORT
Approved under Ohio Civil Rule 84 and Ohio Juvenile Rule 46
Effective Date: 7/1/2013

Page 1 of 2

2. Select one:

☐ _____ (name) is currently designated the residential parent and/or legal custodian of the child(ren).

☐ The parties now have a Shared Parenting Plan.

3. I request that the Court change the parenting time (companionship and visitation) Order because:

_____
_____
_____

4. I request that the Court change the existing parenting time (companionship and visitation) Order in the following way: _____

_____
_____
_____

5. I believe that the changes I am requesting are in the child(ren)'s best interests.

_____
Your Signature

_____
Telephone number at which the Court may reach you
or at which messages may be left for you

Supreme Court of Ohio
Uniform Domestic Relations Form – 23
Uniform Juvenile Form – 5
MOTION FOR CHANGE OF PARENTING TIME (VISITATION) AND MEMORANDUM IN SUPPORT
Approved under Ohio Civil Rule 84 and Ohio Juvenile Rule 46
Effective Date: 7/1/2013   Page 2 of 2

IN THE COURT OF COMMON PLEAS
_____ **Division**
_____ **COUNTY, OHIO**

IN THE MATTER OF:

_____
A Minor

_____ :
Name : Case No. _____
_____ :
Street Address :
_____ : Judge _____
City, State and Zip Code :
Plaintiff/Petitioner :
: Magistrate _____
:
vs. :
:
:
_____ :
Name :
_____ :
Street Address :
_____ :
City, State and Zip Code :
Defendant/Petitioner :

Instructions: This form is used to request a change in a shared parenting plan or a change in the designation of the sole residential parent and legal custodian. A Request for Service (Uniform Domestic Relations Form 28) and a Parenting Proceeding Affidavit (Uniform Domestic Relations Form – Affidavit 3) must be filed with this Motion.

MOTION FOR CHANGE OF PARENTAL RIGHTS AND RESPONSIBILITIES (CUSTODY) AND MEMORANDUM IN SUPPORT

1. I, _____ (name), request this Court change the allocation of parental rights and responsibilities (custody) Order filed on this date _____ (filed date) regarding the following minor child(ren): _____

Name of Child	Date of Birth
_____	_____
_____	_____
_____	_____

Supreme Court of Ohio
Uniform Domestic Relations Form – 24
Uniform Juvenile Form – 6
MOTION FOR CHANGE OF PARENTAL RIGHTS AND RESPONSIBILITIES (CUSTODY)
AND MEMORANDUM IN SUPPORT
Approved under Ohio Civil Rule 84 and Ohio Juvenile Rule 46
Effective Date: 7/1/2013

2. Select one:

☐ _____ (name) is currently designated as the residential parent and/or legal custodian of the children and resides in the _____ School District.

☐ The parents now have a Shared Parenting Plan.

3. The circumstances have changed since the Court issued the existing order. The change in circumstances and any other reason for the requested change are as follows:

_____

_____

_____

4. I request that the Court change the existing order in the following way:

_____

_____

_____

5. I believe that the changes I am requesting are in the child(ren)'s best interests.

_____
Your Signature

_____
Telephone number at which the Court may reach you
or at which messages may be left for you

Supreme Court of Ohio
Uniform Domestic Relations Form – 24
Uniform Juvenile Form – 6
MOTION FOR CHANGE OF PARENTAL RIGHTS AND RESPONSIBILITIES (CUSTODY)
AND MEMORANDUM IN SUPPORT
Approved under Ohio Civil Rule 84 and Ohio Juvenile Rule 46
Effective Date: 7/1/2013   Page 2 of 2

IN THE COURT OF COMMON PLEAS

_____ **Division**

_____ **COUNTY, OHIO**

IN THE MATTER OF:

_____
A Minor

_____ Name	:
	:
_____ Street Address	:
	:
_____ City, State and Zip Code	:
Plaintiff/Petitioner	:
	:
	:
vs.	:
	:
	:
_____ Name	:
	:
_____ Street Address	:
	:
_____ City, State and Zip Code	:
Defendant/Petitioner	:

Case No. _____

Judge _____

Magistrate _____

Instructions: This form is used to request a change in the child support or child support-related matters. A Request for Service (Uniform Domestic Relations Form 28) and an Affidavit of Income and Expenses (Uniform Domestic Relations Form–Affidavit 1) must be filed with this Motion.

MOTION FOR CHANGE OF CHILD SUPPORT, MEDICAL SUPPORT, TAX EXEMPTION, OR OTHER CHILD-RELATED EXPENSES AND MEMORANDUM IN SUPPORT

I, _____ (name), request this Court change my obligation to provide support or my right to receive support for the minor child(ren) as follows (check all that apply):

1. ☐ The amount of child support to be paid each month. The change I want the Court to order is:

_____

_____

Supreme Court of Ohio
Uniform Domestic Relations Form – 25
Uniform Juvenile Form – 7
MOTION FOR CHANGE OF CHILD SUPPORT, MEDICAL SUPPORT, TAX EXEMPTION,
OR OTHER CHILD-RELATED EXPENSES AND MEMORANDUM IN SUPPORT
Approved under Ohio Civil Rule 84 and Ohio Juvenile Rule 46
Effective Date: 7/1/2013

Page 1 of 2

2. ☐ The person responsible for providing health insurance for the child(ren). The change I want the Court to order is: _____

_____

_____

3. ☐ The amount of non-insured health care expenses of the minor child(ren) that I have to pay. The change I want the Court to order is: _____

_____

_____

4. ☐ The person who can claim the child(ren) as tax dependents. The change I want the Court to order is: _____

_____

_____

5. ☐ Other child-related expenses. The change I want the Court to order is: _____

_____

_____

6. The circumstances have changed since the Court issued the existing order. The change in circumstances and any other reason for the requested change are as follows: _____

_____

_____

_____

7. I believe that the requested changes are in the child(ren)'s best interests.

_____
Your Signature

_____
Telephone number at which the Court may reach you
or at which messages may be left for you

Supreme Court of Ohio
Uniform Domestic Relations Form – 25
Uniform Juvenile Form – 7
MOTION FOR CHANGE OF CHILD SUPPORT, MEDICAL SUPPORT, TAX EXEMPTION,
OR OTHER CHILD-RELATED EXPENSES AND MEMORANDUM IN SUPPORT
Approved under Ohio Civil Rule 84 and Ohio Juvenile Rule 46
Effective Date: 7/1/2013   Page 2 of 2

Name of Child: _____ Case No. _____

Instructions: This form is used when you are claiming the other party has not paid health care bills. **Use a separate form for each child.** A Motion for Contempt and Affidavit (Uniform Domestic Relations Form 21) and a Show Cause Order, Notice and Instructions to the Clerk (Uniform Domestic Relations Form 22) must be filed. You must bring copies of health care bills, Explanation of Benefits forms, and proof of payment to the hearing. Be prepared to indicate the amount owed to you, service providers, collection agencies, or other entities. **If more space is needed, add additional pages.**

EXPLANATION OF HEALTH CARE BILLS

Date of Treatment	Name of Service Provider (e.g., Doctor, Dentist, Therapist, Hospital) & Services Provided	Total Bill	Date Bill Sent to Other Party	Amount Insurance Paid	Amount You Paid	Amount Paid by Other Party	Amount of Unpaid Bill	Amount Due from Other Party

Total Amount of Claim $ _____

_____   _____
Your Signature   Date

Supreme Court of Ohio
Uniform Domestic Relations Form – 26
Uniform Juvenile Form – 8
EXPLANATION OF HEALTH CARE BILLS
Approved under Ohio Civil Rule 84 and Ohio Juvenile Rule 46
Effective Date: 7/1/2013

IN THE COURT OF COMMON PLEAS

_____ Division

_____ COUNTY, OHIO

IN THE MATTER OF:

_____

A Minor

_____ Plaintiff/Petitioner	: : Case No. _____ :
_____ Street Address	: :
_____ City, State and Zip	: Judge _____ :
vs.	: Magistrate _____ :
_____ Defendant/Respondent/Petitioner	: :
_____ Street Address	: :
_____ City, State and Zip Code	: :

WAIVER OF SERVICE OF SUMMONS

I, _____ (name), acknowledge that I am the ☐ Petitioner ☐ Plaintiff
☐ Defendant ☐ Respondent (select one) and that I have received a copy of the following documents filed or
to be filed by the other party:

☐ Complaint for Parentage

☐ Complaint ☐ Motion (select one) for Allocation of Parental Rights and Responsibilities (Custody)

☐ Complaint ☐ Motion (select one) for Parenting Time (Companionship and Visitation)

☐ Complaint ☐ Motion (select one) for Establishment or Change of Child Support

☐ Journal Entry and Findings of Fact Supporting Child Support Deviation

☐ Health Insurance Affidavit

☐ Complaint for Divorce with Children

☐ Complaint for Divorce without Children

☐ Separation Agreement

☐ Shared Parenting Plan

☐ Parenting Plan

☐ Petition for Dissolution

☐ Agreed Judgment Entry, Magistrate's Decision, Order, and/or Magistrate's Order

☐ Affidavit of Income and Expenses

Supreme Court of Ohio
Uniform Domestic Relations Form – 27
Uniform Juvenile Form – 9
WAIVER OF SERVICE OF SUMMONS
Approved under Ohio Civil Rule 84 and Ohio Juvenile Rule 46
Effective Date: 7/1/2013

Page 1 of 2

☐ Affidavit of Property
☐ Parenting Proceeding Affidavit
☐ Motion for Contempt and Affidavit
☐ Motion and Affidavit or Counter Affidavit for Temporary Orders with Oral Hearing
☐ Other (specify): _____

I waive service of summons of said document by the Clerk of Court.

_____   _____
Date   Your Signature

                                            _____
                                            Telephone number at which the Court may reach you
                                            or at which messages may be left for you

Supreme Court of Ohio
Uniform Domestic Relations Form – 27
Uniform Juvenile Form – 9
WAIVER OF SERVICE OF SUMMONS
Approved under Ohio Civil Rule 84 and Ohio Juvenile Rule 46
Effective Date: 7/1/2013

Page 2 of 2

IN THE COURT OF COMMON PLEAS

_____ **Division**

_____ **COUNTY, OHIO**

IN THE MATTER OF:

_____
A Minor

_____	:
Name	: Case No. _____
	:
_____	:
Street Address	: Judge _____
_____	:
City, State and Zip Code	:
Plaintiff/Petitioner	: Magistrate _____
	:
vs./and	:
	:
_____	:
Name	:
_____	:
Street Address	:
_____	:
City, State and Zip Code	:
Defendant/Petitioner	:

Instructions: This form is used when you want to request documents to be served on the other party. You must indicate the requested method of service by marking the appropriate box.

REQUEST FOR SERVICE

TO THE CLERK OF COURT:

Please serve the following documents on the following parties as I have indicated below:

_____

_____

☐ Defendant/Petitioner at the address shown above.

    ☐ Certified Mail, Return Receipt Requested

    ☐ Issuance to Sheriff of _____ County, Ohio for ☐ Personal or ☐ Residence service

    ☐ Other (specify) _____

Supreme Court of Ohio
Uniform Domestic Relations Form – 28
Uniform Juvenile Form – 10
REQUEST FOR SERVICE
Approved under Ohio Civil Rule 84 and Ohio Juvenile Rule 46
Effective Date: 7/1/2013

Page 1 of 2

☐ Plaintiff/Petitioner at the address shown above.
    ☐ Certified Mail, Return Receipt Requested
    ☐ Issuance to Sheriff of _____ County, Ohio for ☐ Personal or ☐ Residence service
    ☐ Other (specify) _____

☐ _____ County Child Support Enforcement Agency (provide address below):

_____

    ☐ Certified Mail, Return Receipt Requested
    ☐ Issuance to Sheriff of _____ County, Ohio for ☐ Personal or ☐ Residence service
    ☐ Other (specify) _____

☐ Other (address): _____
    ☐ Certified Mail, Return Receipt Requested
    ☐ Issuance to Sheriff of _____ County, Ohio for ☐ Personal or ☐ Residence service
    ☐ Other (specify) _____

SPECIAL INSTRUCTIONS TO SHERIFF:

_____
_____
_____

_____
Your Signature

Supreme Court of Ohio
Uniform Domestic Relations Form – 28
Uniform Juvenile Form – 10
REQUEST FOR SERVICE
Approved under Ohio Civil Rule 84 and Ohio Juvenile Rule 46
Effective Date: 7/1/2013